TO: Sa...

Live for the moment,
and NEVER give up!
May God Bless You,
Carol Ann Batt

Your illness does NOT
define you. Your strength
and courage does. ♡

I know this transformation
is painful, but your not
falling apart; you'll just falling
into something different, with
a NEW capacity to be BEAUTIFUL!
♡

Don't let fear
hold you back.

The Zachary NF and Cancer Research Fund webpage :

www.zacharynfresearchfund.com

Zac Bartz was one of the most courageous young people I ever met. I met Zac in 2006 when he was four years old. I had just started my assignment at St. Bridget of Sweden Catholic Church in Lindstrom, Minnesota and Zac's family were members of the parish. Zac was struggling with multiple brain tumors and yet, he was the most joy filled person in the parish. He would greet everyone at Sunday Mass, even going up and down the aisle shaking hands. He was energetic and cheerful but many times he was weakened by his condition and he would have to lie down on the front pew to rest during Mass. I was honored to walk with Zac and his family through many of the hospital stays and the multiple surgeries. Zac never complained or ask, "why me?" but faced each challenge with courage and a deep faith that Jesus was with him through it all. Zac taught me more about acceptance of the struggles of this life than I could ever teach him. In this world, Zac brought more joy and witness of strength and courage in adversity than I have ever seen. The story of Zac's journey is a testimony and example that the Lord is with us always to give us strength to endure whatever comes to us in this life. Thanks Zac, for showing me true courage and faith.

-Father Al Backmann

"Zac is a one of a kind kid. He is an inspiration and an incredible example for others to learn from. In reading his courageous battle with brain cancer it is empowering and eye-opening to witness how far one can go when you have the support of family and friends and a strong faith to sustain you."

Kevin James

Zac has an unquenchable love of life, laughter and fun. Although he is a regular kid, he is mature beyond his years and can talk to anyone. He immediately befriended me and my lab staff members and became a part of our research team in spirit. And we love being part of Team Zac! He inspires us to continue the hard work of making a difference in the lives of cancer patients - and pursuing the ultimate dream of curing each and every one.

-David Largaespada, Ph.D.
Department of Pediatrics
Department of Genetics, Cell Biology and Development
Masonic Cancer Center
University of Minnesota

During my twenty some year career as a pediatric oncologist, I have known and loved countless children who, along with there parents, fought awful diseases with great courage and fortitude. A few, for various reasons from academic to spiritual, left lasting impressions. One, however, changed my career. His name was Zac and I first met him at the community children's hospital when he was just a little guy. He had a condition called neurofibromatosis (NF1) and was discovered to have an optic glioma. It was my responsibility to educate the family regarding neurofibromatosis and what it meant. It was also up to me to help them manage his optic glioma. When I left to lead then brain tumor program at the University of Minnesota, the family followed me there. It was discovered that Zac developed a new tumor, an anaplastic astrocytoma. This started a whole new journey – treating a cancerous tumor with a poor prognosis. It also started an association between Zac, his family and my scientific partner, Dr. David Largaespada. Zac was soon on a first name basis with the PhDs in Dr. Largaespada's lab and was a frequent visitor as they developed new models of NF1 in order to better understand the natural history of the disease and approaches to treatment of NF1-associated tumors. Zac was an inspiration to everyone in the lab – he put a face on their research and gave them a feeling that what they discovered could make a real difference for this person.

Because of Zac's complex condition others will benefit from our discoveries regarding targeted therapy that will make a huge difference in the NF community. Zac lived big, helping us to move our field forward benefiting many people today and in the years to come

-Dr.Christopher Moertel:
Medical Director, Pediatric neuro-oncology and neurofibromatosis programs
Co-medical Director, Journey Clinic

An Inspirational Story of Zachary David Bartz

the believer

(The Boy Who Never Gave Up)

Carol Ann Bartz

WESTBOW
PRESS®
A DIVISION OF THOMAS NELSON
& ZONDERVAN

This book is a work of non-fiction. Unless otherwise noted, the author and the publisher make no explicit guarantees as to the accuracy of the information contained in this book and in some cases, names of people and places have been altered to protect their privacy.

WestBow Press books may be ordered through booksellers or by contacting:

WestBow Press
A Division of Thomas Nelson & Zondervan
1663 Liberty Drive
Bloomington, IN 47403
www.westbowpress.com
1 (866) 928-1240

Front Cover and "Zac receiving the Jake Parenteau award" Images by Kirsten Thompson EyeCandyCreativePhotography.com

ISBN: 978-1-5127-1668-9 (sc)
ISBN: 978-1-5127-1669-6 (hc)
ISBN: 978-1-5127-1667-2 (e)

Library of Congress Control Number: 2015917176

Print information available on the last page.

WestBow Press rev. date: 10/30/2015

CONTENTS

Foreword by Shannon. ix

Preface xi

CHAPTER 1   two jesuses 1

CHAPTER 2   the perfect tree 5

CHAPTER 3   café au lait spots 10

CHAPTER 4   just the beginning. 23

CHAPTER 5   growing glioma 27

CHAPTER 6   chemotherapy 31

CHAPTER 7   becoming routine 38

CHAPTER 8   ups and downs. 44

CHAPTER 9   craniotomy. 53

CHAPTER 10   round three 60

CHAPTER 11   gone, but not "gone". .65

CHAPTER 12   a new diagnosis 73

CHAPTER 13   "no penalties!" 83

CHAPTER 14   "how much will a miracle cost?" 91

CHAPTER 15   good news. 96

CHAPTER 16   deadly miscommunication 105

CHAPTER 17   "i will never give up!" 116

CHAPTER 18   on a mission 133

CHAPTER 19   metastasizing. 141

CHAPTER 20   leaving home 152

CHAPTER 21   the jake parenteau award 160

CHAPTER 22   a big difference 166

CHAPTER 23   home to reality 173

CHAPTER 24   going nowhere fast 178

CHAPTER 25   storming heaven 184

CHAPTER 26   "nothing worth having comes easy" 188

CHAPTER 27   my best day ever!. 194

CHAPTER 28   baby steps 201

CHAPTER 29   no harm done. 207

CHAPTER 30   zac's pack 214

CHAPTER 31   zacstrong! 221

CHAPTER 32   barely hanging on 225

CHAPTER 33   no more chemo 236

CHAPTER 34   that cold november day. 241

CHAPTER 35   wake up call 253

CHAPTER 36   the ultimate decision 260

CHAPTER 37   going home. 268

CHAPTER 38   one last goodbye 273

CHAPTER 39   in proud victory. 277

Afterword. 281

The Gifts That Zac Gave 285

Dedication 288

Acknowledgements. 289

FOREWORD BY SHANNON

There came a time when I asked God for more purpose in my life. As a radio personality, I loved to dish about pop culture, interview artists and give away prizes but there was something missing. I wanted to help people through the media but I was not sure how to do it. I prayed about it. I asked God to give me a chance to help others, particularly children, though the radio career I loved so much. Weeks later, I got a call from a Program Director in Minneapolis telling me that there was a job opening on the KS95 Morning Show. He proceeded to tell me that a big part of what they do is help sick and injured children though their annual KS95 for Kids Radiothon. He asked me if helping kids is something that I was passionate about. Just think about that for a moment...I received a job offer from a legendary radio station that helps children on a grand scale and I never even applied for the job!

It was through KS95 for Kids that I got the privilege of meeting my buddy Zac Bartz and his inspiring family. From the first moment I met Zac, I knew I was talking to someone special. He was battling Neurofibromatosis and cancerous tumors on a daily basis since he was two years old, but he always asked how everyone else was doing. He loved people, he loved his family and above all else he loved God. He had incredible faith when most adults, let alone children, would have felt abandoned.

It became my job to tell Zac's story on the air in an effort to raise money for our children's hospital and research foundation in the Twin Cities. What started out as a job, very quickly turned into my privilege. I knew I wanted to do more than just share Zac's message of hope; I wanted to spend time with my friend. We would play Yatzee at the hospital when I got off work. We would dunk french fries into chocolate milkshakes that we smuggled into his hospital room. We would play the video game version of "Let's Make a Deal" and "Draw Something" on our phones. We were telling Cancer to go away for a little while.

During one of our talks Zac told me the story of when he and his Dad went hunting and how he "got his first bear". He would dream about being strong again so he could go on another hunting trip with his Dad or go see his Vikings play football. These are typical topics for an 11 year old boy in Minnesota, but somehow these conversations had a certain *knowing* about them...we both knew he wasn't getting stronger but he never gave up.

On a rare day or two Zac seemed frustrated by the limitations of his body but he never complained. While he wanted to be well enough to go play with his friends, Zac knew down deep that would have to wait because his life plan was bigger than ridding his four-wheeler or playing hockey with his friends. God called on him to teach others about love, faith and finding happiness even in the darkest of times. Zac answered that call diligently every single day. I saw him pray for others when he was the one who was sick. I heard him tell jokes when he was the one who was sad. I watched him thank hospital visitors for taking the time to see him, when really we should have been thanking him for showing us what strength looks like.

I will never forget the time when after years of treatment, the doctors told Zac to go home. They told him to do something fun and let his body rest. During that time he invited my family to his house for a visit. He had a list of things for me to accomplish and let's just say they were "out of my wheelhouse". I'm a born and raised Jersey Girl who knows more about getting her nails done than nature...a difference that Zac found very amusing. Within a span of an afternoon, Zac had me do the following while laughing uncontrollably:

I held a live chicken from his chicken coop, rode a 4-wheeler, ate the bear he shot on his big hunting trip, in addition to deer, and goose meat. Finally, another first...Zac had me shoot a gun for the first time under his close supervision. I shot a bull's eye my first go around and Zac celebrated more than I did! Zac was everyone's biggest fan.

There are so many more stories that I could tell you about Zac like when he came to our KS95 Radiothon at Mall of America and told his story on the air. Every single phone in the phone bank lit up as he talked to our listeners. Every single one. I told him to turn around and see all the operators on the phone and when he did he looked shocked. He started crying and said, "I did that? They are calling because of me? I'm so proud! We can help so many other kids now!" Zac wasn't thinking about his cure, he wanted to help all of the other kids.

Someone once asked me if I was afraid to get too close to my buddy Zac. While it was heartbreaking to watch his body get weaker, I also watched his spirit get stronger. There was more than a figurative light around him, there was a literal one.

Knowing Zac Bartz was more than a gift, it was a prayer answered. I'm so humbled that his beautiful family let me into their world. I made a promise to Zac. I promised him that I would do my best to help "the other kids" and I would tell his story at our Radiothon to light up his phone bank one more time. A month later during the annual Radiothon, as promised and as if on cue, Zac lit up every phone in the phone bank one more time.

Zac's mission on earth was more than the hockey, hunting and family time he held so dear...it was to heal hearts and spread his bright light. If you met Zac Bartz, then you know what I know...that there ARE angels on earth.

Always Zac Strong,

Shannon Holly
KS95 Minneapolis

PREFACE

When I was in the hospital with Zac for one of his chemo weeks and writing Zac's story, I mulled over the title of the book. I pretty much thought I knew what I wanted to call it, but something or someone nagged at me to ask Zac. When I asked him, "What would you call your story? What would you want people to know about you?"

Zac looked up from the game he was playing on his iPod and stared straight ahead. He had to only think for two seconds before answering – "The Believer."

Immediately I was excited at the wisdom and insight of Zac's sudden revelation – *That was IT!!!*

And so my book - Zac's story - was named.

My hope for you in reading about Zac's journey is that you will come to know him through my honest depiction of the life he was given, the trying challenges he faced and his perseverance in which he fought, to get the most out of life with the strength he found in God, his family and a loving community that empowered him to be the overcomer that he was.

My wish for you is that through "knowing" Zac you will come to understand what is most important in life for "you" and to learn from him how to live it through faith, hope, love, compassion, friendship and a NEVER GIVE UP attitude. *How does that old saying go? - "Nothing in life worth having comes easy."* Fight for what you want and make a difference the ZacStrong way.

CHAPTER I

two jesuses

I was downstairs dressing for a run. My husband Nathan had just come home from his weekend reserve commitment and I needed a break from the chaos of the day.

Twelve kids, including my three, were outside playing in the melting snow from a late snowfall. The kids were dressed in their light jackets and puddle boots, having a blast playing without freezing for once.

Our houses are spaced rather far apart on a road where no one has less than an acre for their yard. The next-door neighbors have a horseshoe shaped pond in their backyard that they had dug out for runoff from the melting winter snows and heavy rains.

Nathan and I preached over and over to our kids to "Never go over to the pond by yourself, only with an adult." They never did-until that day.

Without anyone knowing, my four-year-old son Zachary and his little friend, Oscar, wandered over there. I was just putting on my running tights when the phone rang.

Nathan yelled downstairs to me, "Mikes on the phone. I have no idea what's going on, so you talk to him."

"Hello?"

"I was just looking out of my back window and I saw some kid pull themselves out the pond," Mike said calmly.

"What?!"

"Yeah, I heard all of the kids in your yard so I yelled out the slider door for them to go over to your house."

"I just came downstairs to grab my running clothes for a sec," I explained out of embarrassment for neglect. "What happened?! Who was it?!"

Mike said he couldn't tell. I hung up the phone.

Nathan looked out the kitchen window as he was shoving a mouthful of leftover meatloaf in. "Zac just pulled himself out of Mike's pond!"

My heart sank. I came running up the stairs, two at a time, to look out the sliding glass door. A soaking wet Zachary was trudging across the yard toward the open garage door.

I couldn't help myself and I yelled at Zac out of fear. "What were you doing by the pond?! You know you're not supposed to go over by the pond!"

I started pulling off Zac's soaking wet clothes, thinking I could have actually lost him today to drowning and no one would have ever known! I couldn't believe what just happened!

Zachary looked at me and calmly said, "We wanted to see how deep the water was with a big stick." He wasn't scared or crying, just shivering.

This pond, it was built with the sides dropping straight down, like a swimming pool's edge. The pond was overflowing because of the melting snow-and there had been a lot of it! Mike's backyard was flooded, making it impossible to see where the actual edge of the pond was.

"You know you're not supposed to go over by Mike's pond. You never have before - why did you today?" I asked wanting to reverse time. I didn't wait for Zac's answer. I continue to ask more questions. "Well, how did you get out? Did Oscar help you? Do you have your boots?" I quickly looked down and answered the last question. His boots were still on! Zac didn't even get free of his boot! They would have been like anchors once filled with water - especially to a little boy who doesn't know how to swim.

Zac looked at me and began to answer my questions.

"Oscar got scared and ran away."

I was devastated knowing Zac was left there in the pond all on his own to fend for himself. He probably was so scared!

"So how did you get out?" I repeated.

Zac cocked his head back as if trying to keep his head from going under the water. He moved his hands in front of himself as if doing the doggie paddle while kicking one leg quickly, back and forth, "No-I went like this... And like this..."he said as he continued his demonstration.

I watched in horror, imagining his struggle in the freezing cold water. "How did you get out?" I repeat myself wanting to understand.

Zachary simply stated, "Two Jesuses helped me."

"What?" I blankly asked.

"Two Jesuses helped me," Zachary repeated without skipping a beat.

I didn't quite know what to say, but I felt a sense of sudden relief and comfort come over me. "Well, what did they look like?"

Without hesitation, Zac said as he touched the left side of his chest and then right side, "White here and white here. White fins and white wings."

I was intrigued. I wanted to know more. "Well, what did they do?"

Again without hesitation, he said, "One push and one pull," Zachary showed as he demonstrated the motion of someone putting their hands together, palm size outward, and pushing someone up on their butt. He pulsed his hands four times. Then he quickly mimicked grabbing onto someone's hands in a tug-of-war fashion and pulled three times.

I was shocked! Tears welled up and I started to cry as I sat back on my knees. I looked at Zachary's sweet face and sternly warned, "Don't you EVER go by the pond again! Don't EVER go over there without an adult." I grabbed Zachary, pulling him close and wrapped my arms around him.

"I don't know what I would ever do if I lost you. I love you so much - that's why mommy yelled at you. You really scared me. I just want you to be safe."

This was real. All of it! I was still in shock. I felt like a horrible parent, but so lucky at the same time! I prayed every single day that, *'When I can't watch over my children, that God would, and He would guide them and protect them from all things evil and harmful.'*

God heard me and He sent two of his angels dressed in white to save my son that day.

I knew Zachary wasn't making any of his story up. Strange thing is, as much as I believed in angels, I never talked about them with Zac. We talked a lot about Jesus, but not angels. I guess I thought he wouldn't understand.

When I brought Zac into the house, I noticed "the" bruise on his right leg. The bruise was a perfectly shaped cross about 3 inches long. I had spotted it two days earlier and was a bit amazed by such an unusual shaped bruise. I actually walked around the house looking at toys that could have made that shape had Zac fallen on one of them. Nothing. I examine furniture at his thigh level that he could have stumbled into. Nothing. The bruise was there and it was real. I knew in my heart that it meant something.

When I brought Zachary over to where Nathan was sitting at the kitchen table, having a snack, I had Zac tell him his frightening story. He didn't waver from his original version. He told it just as he told me.

"Take a look at this," I said to Nathan as I pulled Zac's sweatpants down to show him his bruise, for the first time. I didn't think to show him earlier. I thought I might be reading too much into the unusual shaped bruise, so I kept it to myself, although I did take a picture of it.

Nathan didn't say a word.

"Well, do you know what it looks like?"

Nathan bent his head down to take a closer look. "It looks like a cross to me. Did this just happen?"

"It would be a better story, but no. I actually found it two days ago," I explained.

Nathan looked at me a bit surprised. "That has to be a sign that Jesus is there for us when we can't be."

That was it. Perfectly said. Many times I have wondered where Jesus was in the life of brain tumors, sickness, fear and pain that Zachary has endured up until now. But because of his brush with death, I believed Zachary had a purpose, and his angels were there with him, even if I couldn't see them, to help make sure he would fulfill that purpose.

I truly believe we are all born with the purpose. Big or small. From the moment that Zac was saved from the pond by his "Two Jesuses" and the sign of the cross that was undeniably imprinted on his right thigh, I believed Zac was meant to be.

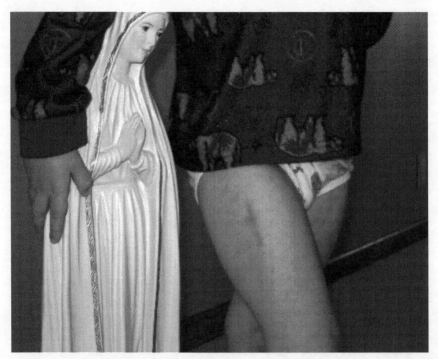

Bruised shaped cross on Zac's leg prior to falling in the pond 2007

CHAPTER 2

the perfect tree

After my second child Jessica was born I felt my life was finally coming together. I was working part-time, as a labor and delivery nurse, I had a nice size house and a big beautiful yard, two healthy kids and a hard-working, loving husband. I was feeling happy with the direction my life was finally going.

Before this time I had struggled for thirteen years with the eating disorders anorexia and bulimarexia. I had even attempted suicide twice in an effort to escape my depression and free myself from the beast that had taken over my life.

I had struggled to find out who I was and what I wanted for my life I ended up calling off my wedding, three months before the date, to a man I had known and loved for five years because I knew something wasn't right in our relationship.

I worked hard in my relationship with Nathan, who I met shortly after my breakup. I thought Nathan might be the "one," but then I wasn't sure. I didn't trust my decisions and I didn't trust myself.

I went with my gut, heart or head, I'm not sure which one (I was always confused by this statement - "go with your gut.") But I did what I thought was best for me and I married Nathan. I did love him. He was good to me and he was a wonderful involved father.

Although I still battled with body image issues, I wasn't entrenched in my eating disorder. I was happy and I was finally living. Of course everything wasn't perfect. I wanted another baby. We had discussed having four children before marriage. However, at the moment, Nathan felt stressed enough, saying, "I didn't think two would be so much work!"

With a little luck, or maybe some may call it "trickery," I got pregnant. I justified my motive because of the fact that, male or female, we all have free will. I figured if it was "meant to be," I would get pregnant, and if I didn't, I would continue working on my case for a third child.

I was so happy! I was blessed with a third child, Zachary David. I was blessed with a third child. Zachary David. He was beautiful regardless of his squished nose. He had all of his fingers and toes. He was mine.

For the most part, having three children under the age of four was manageable.

I was figuring it out. But there were some days I didn't think I could do it. God forbid, I wasn't ever going to admit Nathan was right-that having only two kids "we would have the upper hand"- and it would be easier. I knew life wasn't easy and this was life.

I told myself the recent difficulty I was having didn't really count because I was taking care of the kids all on my own. Nathan was deployed for the first time since we had children, to the Middle East in support of the war for Iraqi Freedom.

After finishing high school, Nathan went into the Navy where he was at P3 airplane mechanic. Later he transferred to the Air Force and remained in the air National Guard.

I think that was the first thing that attracted me to him-the tough, clean-cut standing up for your country kind of guy. I loved that he was a hard worker, and he was athletic and like to work out (which scored bonus points with me since I worked out almost every day) and he was mechanically inclined just like my dad. I love that! It was evident that he really cared about me which gave me my self-esteem back.

Let me tell you, it took a lot of work to get to where we were. We both struggled for a long time with the repercussions from my eating disorder. We both had our own baggage, like most people carry with them into a relationship, but ours was heavy. Eventually I was in a place I had only dreamed of.

I learned quickly to try and live one day at a time in Nathan's absence. I stayed up most nights until 2 am trying to get things done, get my workout in an end with an email to Nathan.

I didn't ask for help. I didn't want to impose. It's just the way I am. If people offered that would have been different. My father-in-law looked after the kids a couple of times so I could pick up a few shifts at the hospital, to keep my position. Other than that, it was just me.

I didn't like asking my parents because I grew up with a special-needs sister. Therese, my youngest sister, by five years, required complete care. In most ways she was like taking care of a baby-one that weighed one hundred and twenty plus pounds. I knew my mom was getting burnt out. She had been taking care of "baby" for over 25 years. Barb was two years younger than me and Marie was older by two years. For the most part, we all pitched in together and helped in caring for Therese, but the majority of the care fell upon my mom being my dad, an electrician, was the sole supporter of our family and traveled out of town from time to time. As much as I wished my parents were more involved in our kid's lives, I accepted it because I knew why.

How hard it must have been for my mom and dad when they thought they had a perfectly normal baby girl, only to find out three months later that she had a heart condition. If Therese had been born today, she would be living a normal life, but back then in the seventies, the surgery wasn't successful. It changed the lives of my parents as well as who my sister could have been.

Life was the way it was and I learned to cope, one way or the other. I was beyond excited and relieved when Nathan arrived back home just in time to celebrate Zachary's first birthday. I was grateful he was safe, but I was equally thankful I wouldn't have to be a single parent anymore.

After only being home for four months, Nathan was informed that he had to go back to the Middle East for a second deployment. I couldn't believe what I was hearing!

"You just got back! You'll be gone over Christmas!" I whined.

Of course I knew it wasn't a matter of choice. So once again we prepared ourselves for another separation. The hardest thing was telling Nic, who was five and Jessica, three-and-a-half, that their daddy would be leaving again. And poor Zachary! He was just getting reacquainted with Nathan. When Nathan came back home, Zachary had no idea who this tall strange man was that wanted to hold and kiss him. Zac fussed, squirmed and reached for me whenever Nathan tried to pick him up. I felt so bad for Nathan, and sad to think he would have to re-establish his bond with his baby boy yet once again.

In break with tradition, we called a nearby tree farm in Forest Lake to see if they would allow us to cut down our Christmas tree the day before Thanksgiving instead of the day after like we usually did. Nathan was scheduled to deploy the night after Thanksgiving.

"Of course we can make an exception," the wife of the tree farm owner obliged, "What time would you like to come?"

Nathan, the kids and I bundled up that cold November morning and set out to find the perfect Christmas tree for a Christmas that, in spite of all the decorations, presents and Christmas cookies, wouldn't be complete because Nathan wouldn't be home to celebrate with us. We plan to have a mini Christmas when Nathan returned.

We marched through the snow and headed toward the balsam pines. I loved the smell of them and they were supposed to retain their needles really long. I wanted to keep the tree up until Nathan got back, hopefully by February… who was I kidding, it wouldn't matter what type of tree I got, the needles would be showering off their limbs well before then.

I began looking for the right height and width. I explained to Nic and Jessica what I was looking for as if they actually understood what I was talking about.

"It has to be thick enough so you can't see through it," I went on. "See, this one won't do," I said, peaking at them through the tree.

I ran from tree to tree for a while comparing one to the next until Nathan said from a distance, holding Zachary, "Just pick a tree!"

I scanned the price tag of one of the Balsam's in the front section. My eyes almost popped out of my head when I saw $89 written on the cream-colored tag. I looked at another, $68! We were used to cutting our own for $34.

"Any tree?" I shouted back with a smirk on my face.

"Any tree!" Nathan confirmed.

"Okay, then give me a couple more minutes." Not too much longer I claimed the victory in finding "the" tree. To be fair, I tried not to go overboard and even tempt myself with the hundred dollar trees.

We left the lot with our tree snugly tied down to the top of our vehicle and a Christmas tree stand that the tree farm claimed could support an 18-foot-tall Christmas trees with no complaints. The owner even added that churches used them for all their tall trees.

Since Nathan was deploying once again, I reminded him of the year our tree tipped over three times. One of the times I had to hold the tree up and hurrying Nicholas, who was three at the time, to run and grab the phone so I could call Julie, my neighbor, two houses down, to come help me put it back up quickly before all the spilled water would leak through to the floor to the basement below. I only had to remember all the broken ornaments I lost that year to plead my case. Nathan didn't argue. I think he remembered all too well the hassle of wrapping up the tree trunk with fish line and tacking it up just to hold up the tree in the corner of the living room.

"Wow! That's for a tree and a tree stand?!" was all Nathan uttered, when he saw the price.

Well, you said *"any"* tree, I paused, "and that was one of the cheaper trees!" I reassured.

We were off to put up our expensive, but perfect tree, using our proclaimed infallible new tree stand. For the first time ever, I was able to have our Christmas tree in the center of our vaulted ceiling which separated the living room from the dining room. Much to Nathan's surprise, the tree went up easy with only the need to drill a hole at the base of the trunk.

I was looking forward to decorating the tree, but at the same time my spirits were dampened because Nathan would not be here celebrating with the kids and me. I always tried to make Christmas as special as possible because I remembered how I felt as a kid. I grew up with so many wonderful traditions and I wanted my kids to have the same warm memories.

I knew it would be challenging to decorate the house, bake the cookies and candy, make and mail out the Christmas cards and somehow figure out how to Christmas shop for the kids without them knowing. I even began to think of how the kids would miss having their dad read to them *'The Night Before Christmas.'* Christmas is such a time for family. I loved the thought of all of us together and I knew this year the kids and I would be missing such a valuable part of our family.

I know it was hard on Nathan too. He hated being away from the kids and me. After his last deployment, he said, "I missed the kids and you so much, that it was painful." I didn't think I could do it and be separated from my children, especially at the ages they were at.

Thanksgiving was uneventful. It was nice to be with family, but it was a reminder that it was our last full day together as a family. I was thankful we had the day we had. The great food, good conversation and the kids running around with their cousins, but I was not looking forward to saying goodbye again. It was hard having that knowledge sitting in the back of my mind all day. At least we have one more night.

Once the kids were tucked in bed, Nathan and I were able to have our time together. It's crazy how much more important a husband becomes when you know they are going away. I know I shouldn't be that way but I have to admit I am guilty for taking our time together for granted. I always felt *there is tomorrow*. It's hard to make that special time when you have three kids hanging on you, needing you all day long, and then throw in being needed at work for eight hours straight. I really had to change that way of thinking.

We lay in bed dozing until 12:45 am when Nathan got up and started getting dressed.

"What are you doing? You don't have to leave for another 45 minutes," I said groggily.

"I know. I just can't sleep. I guess I'm worked up about going. I figured if I can't relax, I might as well get myself together and quit trying to prolong the inevitable." Nathan sullenly replied.

I got out of bed and followed him around the house as he finished getting ready. I just wanted to stay as close as I could before he left. I hopped on the kitchen counter to sit as he scooped up his protein powder and put it in a bag.

"So here we go again." I whispered.

"It won't be for as long as last time. I'll be home before you know it." Nathan reassured.

He leaned into me and pulled me close and kissed me. "It will be okay. I love you." And with one more passionate kiss he was gone. I watched as he drove out of the driveway and up the hill, until I couldn't see the car taillights anymore. I took a deep breath and let out a heavy sigh. I missed him already.

Nic (7), Jessica (5) and Zac (2) Awaiting Christmas! 12-9-04

CHAPTER 3

café au lait spots

I got into the routine of life being a single parent pretty quickly this time. It had only been six months since Nathan had just returned home from his first deployment to the Middle East. Nicholas, almost six, was now in kindergarten. School was a good distraction for him. He would miss his dad and their wrestling and roughhousing that was a daily occurrence with him. I wasn't sure how I could fulfill his need for his dad when I was his mother.

It was only a couple of weeks after Nathan had left and a week before Christmas when the kids and I were eating dinner and Nicholas instantly teared up and burst out crying, "I miss my daddy!"

He was so sad and his pain was so real. Through hugs and reassuring him that his daddy would be home before long, he eventually stopped crying. Soon he was back to playing with Jessica, who was only three and wrestling Zachary on the floor.

Jessica even had her moments when you knew she was also affected by her dad being gone. On one particular occasion we were just playing on her bedroom floor and she burst out, "Daddy's not ever coming home! Daddy's dead!"

I was shocked. I didn't even know she understood what that meant. She was angry, but she didn't cry. I had to quickly divert her simple mind from a complex problem and explain what her daddy was doing and reassured her he would be home sometime after Nicholas's birthday in February. It was a good thing we had Christmas to distract us until then.

A few months earlier when Zachary was 15 months old, I had noticed faint light brown spots on the inside of his thigh when I was changing his diaper. It struck me as kind of odd that I was just noticing the spots. I planned on asking Zachary's doctor about them at his check up, but unfortunately I forgot.

I let it go until he was 17-months-old and I needed to bring him in for what seemed like a cold that would not go away. I was told that it was more than likely viral and would go away on its own. As I began to dress Zachary, I saw the spots which reminded me to ask my question.

"What are these spots? Are they just birthmarks that are now just showing up?" I casually asked, waiting for the doctor to glance away from the computer screen.

She got up from her chair to examine the spots closer. I was a bit disappointed she didn't bring it up or even notice them when she examined him earlier. She lifted his leg up and then the other turning it over to see a few more spots.

"Oh, those are café-au-lait spots." The doctor nonchalantly diagnosed. "They're not birthmarks. Birthmarks, you are born with. They just don't show up months or years after you are born."

-And no more information.

"So what are they from?" I asked waiting for more of a complete answer.

"You know, I'm not sure." She spoke puzzled.

"Well, are they from a deficiency of some sort?" I wanted an answer. "Like - showing up from the inside out?"

"Yeah, I'm pretty sure that's it. I'm going to send you to a dermatologist. Hold on for a minute while I get you that information."

I was little bit disappointed as I left the doctor's office carrying Zachary on my hip. All I got was the name of the spots, but what did they mean? I didn't really know what a dermatologist would do. A cream wasn't going to make the spots go away or cure the deficiency. What did I know? I wasn't the doctor.

A couple of weeks after his appointment, I drove all around Kingdom Come to find the referred dermatology clinic. I wasn't impressed with the dermatologist. He was quick to ask questions and seemed to not really care of the answer. He moved quickly as if he had another patient to see with more important concerns.

I knew something wasn't quite right after I found the third and fourth light brown spots on the upper inside of Zachary's thigh and low back. They did look like birthmarks. I thought that they must have been very light at birth and I just didn't see them before and now they were increasing in pigmentation. Zachary had at least 12 *café-au-lait spots*. I also began to question a lump on his forehead that had not gone away since he had fallen and hit his head on my bedside table 2 months earlier. I thought back... Then again, it was only a couple of weeks ago that he turned the corner from the entryway into the kitchen and cracked his head in the same spot, on the corner. I figured he reinjured that area.

"So what are you here for?" He asked.

I told him how just two weeks earlier I had brought Zac to see the doctor for a prolonged cough and noticed the spots. "She said they were café-au-lait spots and to come see you." I waited.

Without examining him he began to interrogate me, so it felt. "What color are they? How many does he have - more than twelve, less than twelve? Are they irregular in shape? Big or small?"

I remained patient with his questions and answered every single one although I just wanted to say 'Why don't you just examine him, for cryin'-out-loud!?' As the hair stood up in that prickly way on the top of your head when you get real mad or utterly irritated, I replied, "I'm pretty sure he has twelve spots that range from small size to about 2 inches long." I demonstrated showing my thumb and pointer finger making an oblong shape. "They are all different in size and shape, but it was the larger ones, the ones on his low back and on the inside of his upper inside and underside of his thighs that made me question what this was."

"Well, let's take a look."

"*Ya think?*" I said in my head. I undressed Zachary as the dermatologist took out his tape measurer and began to count and check the length of Zachary's spots.

"These couldn't be birthmarks that are just showing up, could they?" I double verified.

"No." Was all I got back in reply.

I waited in silence until he finished with his tape measurer as I helped turned Zachary this way and that as he checked him out. I did interject as he pointed and counted spots, if he missed any. I wanted him to be accurate.

"To be classified as café-au-lait spots, you need to have twelve or more large spots."

"Which he has…" I clarified.

"I wouldn't say that. He has over twelve spots, but I wouldn't say twelve of these are large." He stated.

"*I disagree,*" I wanted to say. I saw twelve pretty big spots. He's only 18 months how big do they have to be? I waited for the conclusion.

"I'm going to have you see another doctor - an ENT. He'll be able to better help you and answer your questions." He paused, only ask where we lived and then recommended we follow up at Fairview Lakes hospital in Wyoming, Minnesota.

I took the piece of paper he handed me and with a quick "thank you," Zachary and I were out of there.

"Well, that was a waste of time, wasn't it?" I confirmed to Zachary as I kissed him on the head.

Not long after the uneventful dermatology appointment, I was able to get Zachary in with Dr. Lindquist, the same doctor who put Zachary's ear tubes in about a year earlier. I really liked him.

When he saw us sitting in his white-walled office with bright lights and shiny endotracheal equipment, he blankly asked "What are you doing here?"

He didn't say it in a way that made me feel he didn't want to treat Zachary, but one of confusion. "I just asked that question because I read Zachary's chart and his ears don't seem to be the problem," He waited for my reply.

I explained how I noticed the spots and when I took him into the clinic because of a cold that wouldn't go away, asked the doctor about them and she said they were café-au-lait spots, but didn't know what they were a result from - maybe a possible deficiency. Then she sent me to a dermatologist who said he didn't have enough "large" spots to be café-au-lait spots. "For some reason he wanted me to bring Zachary to an ENT - to you." I took a deep breath and exhaled.

"I'll tell you what." He calmly spoke.

"What?" I cautiously asked.

"We're going to stop right here. I'm not going to examine Zachary." Dr. Lindquist explained. "Not because I don't want to, but because I think you have been sent on a wild-goose-chase. I have a colleague of mine that I think can figure out what's going on, and set you in the right direction."

"Can we see her today?" I hopefully asked.

"She unfortunately isn't here today, but we can set up the appointment today."

I knew Dr. Lindquist felt bad not being able to give me any answers. He scratched his whiskers that were starting to resurface after his morning shave with his thumb and middle finger.

"Well, can you see if she can see Zachary sooner rather than later?" I paused with minor hesitation, "- like next week? I really want to know what is going on and if it is something to worry about," I added.

Dr. Lindquist adjusted his then wired rimmed glasses and stood up. "I'll make sure they call you by the end of the day with an appointment for next week." He ruffled Zachary's hair and said, "I hope everything goes smoothly for you." He looked up at me and adamantly said, "Make sure you call and ask for me if you have any problems until you get your appointment with Dr. Rebecca Jones." He firmly shook my hand and was out the door.

"Okay Zac, I guess that means we can go home now. Pretty easy appointment, huh, sweet- pea?" I said as I put his jacket on.

"Go home?" Zachary asked wanting confirmation that there was no poking or prodding.

"Yep, go home," I confirmed with yet another sigh.

I was frustrated with the waste of time driving to the appointment for Zachary, and yet a little relieved that maybe, just maybe, Dr. Lindquist was right and Dr. Rebecca Jones would put an end to this run-around appointment business and tell me what was actually the story behind these *café-au-lait spots*.

I ended up picking up a shift at work so I wouldn't lose my position at work. Nathan's dad agreed to watch the kids so I could work the evening shift. I had a few minutes where my patients were all checked on, taken care of and had everything they needed for the time being. I was glad I was working in the antepartum unit that night. I googled "café-au-lait" spots again and read more in depth to the correlation between café-au-lait spots and something called called "neurofibromatosis."

It said neurofibromatosis, otherwise referred to as "NF" (or Von Reckinghausen's Disease) was a genetic disorder. *"Oh, good,"* I thought. *"It can't be that."* Then I read down just a little further...

"One baby in every 4,000 is born with NF. It affects both sexes equally and has no particular racial, geographic or ethnic distribution.

Neurofibromatosis (NF1) is a condition characterized by changes in skin coloring (pigmentation), freckling under the arms or in the groin regions, growths on the iris of the eye (Lisch nodules) and the growth of tumors along nerves in the skin, brain and other parts of the body. The signs and symptoms of this condition vary widely among affected people.

NF2 refers to a rare form of NF with slow growing tumors on the eighth cranial nerves, bilateral acoustic neuromas, and a few skin lesions. Early signs of NF2 include progressive hearing loss, ringing in the ear, dizziness, visual impairment, weakness in an arm or leg, seizures or skin tumors. Bilateral acoustic neuromas are tumors of the nerves of both ears and occur in NF2. NF2 is much less common then NF1, and typically, symptoms are noticed between 18 and 22 years of age. Individuals with NF2 are at risk for developing other types of nervous system tumors that grow in the spinal cord or along the protective layers surrounding the brain and spinal cord. It is caused by a different gene than the one which causes NF1."

This reconfirmed to me that Zac spots were indeed café-au-lait spots. They varied in size and number, but to me he did have at least twelve large spots. They are mostly in his groin area, the underside of his butt-cheek and along his low back. *But what does this mean? Does he have NF1?* The words *'growth of tumors'* really hit me. *Tumors!? What?* It did say something about "some people with neurofibromatosis develop cancerous tumors that grow along nerves. These tumors which usually develop in adolescence or adulthood are called malignant peripheral nerve sheath tumors." It associated these to a lumpy head.

All of a sudden I recalled the lump on Zac's upper forehead, up by his hairline. I thought further as I remembered stroking Zachary's head that there were these squiggly, rope-like bumps trailing from his upper right ear region down to the middle area of his ear. *Oh no!* This is all sounding too fitting. I read on...

"People with neurofibromatosis type I also have an estimated 3 to 5 percent risk of developing other cancers, including brain tumors and cancer of blood-forming tissue (leukemia)."

"Wait a second!" I panicked. Now they are associating café-au-lait spots to neurofibromatosis to cancerous brain tumors! I was afraid to read more, but I needed answers. I needed to diagnose my baby because no one seemed to know what was going on.

I read further about Lisch nodules and "the tumors growing along the nerve leading from the eye to the brain (the optic nerve.")" These tumors, which are called optic gliomas, may lead to reduced vision or total vision loss."

The pieces were fitting all too well for NF1. I couldn't understand why Zac was falling a lot and running into corners of walls so often, until now. Does he have an optic glioma that is compromising his vision? I was really worked up now, but it said it was a genetic disorder. It was inherited. So it couldn't really be this. Nathan and I don't have neurofibromatosis. No one on either side of our family does, that I know of. I was confused.

I went to do my rounds on my patients to make sure they were doing okay and to do their fetal monitoring. I was anxious to find a doctor to run some personal questions by them.

I casually walked up to the nurse's station where some nurses and a few resident doctors were chatting. After the conversation ended, I quickly asked, "Do any of you know anything about café-au-lait spots?"

"Yeah," One resident admitted. She went on to explain what I had read about them with accuracy. "Why?"

"Well, I have a 19-month-old son who I was told has café-au-lait spots. When I asked what that meant, the family practice doctor really didn't know what they were related to it." I continued. "I asked if they were a sign of a deficiency and she said, 'Yes, I think something like that.' - Family practice!" I scuffed, out of frustration for incapable diagnosing.

"Ohhh... So what did you do?" The resident inquisitively asked with a very lingering concerned tone.

"She sent me to a dermatologist and from there and ENT," I nervously explained.

"An ENT?! Really?" She's surprisingly said raising her eyebrows. She offered no further information.

"Nobody seems to know anything. And then I read on the Internet about the spots and how they relate them to something called neurofibromatosis. Do you think that's what he might have?" I asked hoping for some direction.

"Oh, you really need to talk to your doctor."

"You can't just say, 'Ohhh... Like - if you know something. You have to tell me what you know!" My panic level started to rise again.

"All I can say is get your son in to see someone other than family practice." She encouraged. "I'm not your son's doctor and I'm not diagnosing." She added. "It's a good thing that you and your husband don't have it."

"No, I know." I said deflated. "I do have an appointment scheduled for next week. Thanks. I'm just tired of not knowing what's going on."

The week came and went and before I knew it Zachary had his appointment at Fairview Lakes Medical Center on December 15th. I wondered what would come of this appointment. I was hoping Zachary had something that was easy to fix.

I checked Zachary in and surprisingly we didn't have to wait but a couple minutes before the nurse came to walk us back to a room. She took Zachary's blood pressure and temperature. Kind of a waste of time I thought, but I kept my mouth shut and let her do her job.

"We'll need to get a weight and height," she informed.

I followed her out of the room and down the hall to where they had the scale against the wall. Zachary clung tightly to my neck with his soft squishy arms and pudgy hands. As I tried to lower him, he squeezed my waist tightly with his knees, as I held him on my hip.

"It's okay Zachary. No owies." I reassured. "We just need to see how big you are getting. Mommy will be right here."

I started to undress him down to his diaper. "Is it okay if we just get his weight while he sits on the scale instead of lying down?" I asked hopeful she would comply.

"Yes, that should be fine. We can get his height back in the room."

The weight went a little better than trying to get his height. We had to lay him on the crinkly tissue paper, hold him down and mark with the pen at his ankle and crown of his head. Zachary struggled and cried. I quickly picked him up. "Good enough." I told Zachary hoping the nurse got my message. I hoped nothing came across as being rude, but I was frustrated with the whole situation that Zachary had to go through. I just wanted him to feel safe.

"Do you have a blanket I can wrap him in? I'm sure the doctor will want to examine him." I explained not wanting to dress him only to undress him again.

"No problem," the nurse said as she grabbed a blanket from the cupboard.

After answering repetitive questions, Zachary and I sat in the white-walled room. "Not much to entertain kids," I said quietly to myself as I found a book. "Hey, look what I found." I said as I showed Zachary the book. "Mommy will read you a story."

I propped Zachary in the middle of my lap and began to read. I left the door open so someone would know we were in here. Maybe we wouldn't have to wait too long then. I needed to get home to pick Nicholas and Jessica up from the neighbors.

Before long, a woman appeared at the door. She wore the standard white doctor's coat. She looked pretty young to be a doctor, maybe 28 or 30 years old. Her hair was brown and cut in a short bob, slightly on the fluffy side and a pleasant smile.

"Hi, I'm Dr. Rebecca Jones." She introduced herself as she stretched out her hand.

I closed the book I was reading to Zachary and shook her hand. "Nice to meet you. I'm Carol Ann and this is Zachary."

Dr. Jones interacted with Zachary momentarily to get him comfortable and then she turned to me. "I've heard from Dr. Lindquist you two have gotten the runaround. I won't make you go through the whole story all over again." Dr. Jones kindly assured. I'm sure you've repeated it a time or two. So you can just fill in the missing pieces."

I could tell I already liked this doctor. She actually seemed to care about the toll this was already taking on Zachary and myself. Maybe she sensed my frustration.

"I reviewed Zachary's records and what you have noticed as a change for Zachary. I'm thinking our next step would be for me to schedule a brain MRI." Dr. Jones explained.

"Really!? An MRI?" I nervously question. "You know with Zachary's café-au-lait spots and the lumps on his head," I paused briefly, "are you thinking he has neurofibromatosis?"

Dr. Jones probably knew I had been doing my own research. She didn't look too surprised by my diagnosis. "Well, why don't we wait and see what the MRI tells us," Dr. Jones stalled.

"But isn't neurofibromatosis supposed to be genetic related?" I said trying to find any possibility as to why this wouldn't be what Zachary might have. I didn't want it to come to pass that Zachary could have an usually large head (his head was a little bit big, come to think of it) be short, scoliosis, have learning disabilities or attention deficit hyperactivity disorder, not to mention brain tumors or leukemia, all which were complications of NF1!

It all of a sudden hit me. Was Dr. Jones thinking he had a brain tumor!? "Do you suspect that Zachary has a brain tumor?" I had to ask.

"Not necessarily, but I want to rule it out." Dr. Jones cautiously said choosing her words carefully.

Zachary was scheduled for his MRI on December 22. It really was a horrible time to have one scheduled - right before Christmas. My anticipation and excitement for the Christmas tradition and festivities quickly turned to nervousness, anxiety and fear. Nathan was still deployed overseas. I hadn't told him too much as to what was going on with Zachary because I didn't want to worry him. There was nothing he could do, so I decided to wait to say anything more until after the MRI. Dr. Jones gave me her phone number to call her if the radiologist didn't give me the preliminary results by late evening.

My sister Marie picked up Nicholas and Jessica before Zac and I had to drive down to the University of Minnesota Hospital. She was going to bring them to her place to play with her four kids.

"Here's the bags. I think they should have everything they need. Their snowsuits, hats and mittens are in this bag. I'll bring down the presents tomorrow when I come to pick them up," I rambled out of nervousness.

"Don't worry about it. I've got it under control. If you forgot something, I'm sure I'll have it," she reassured placing her hand on my arm. "Take a deep breath."

"I know," I agreed. "I just can't help it. I am so nervous."

We were off in our separate directions and 50 minutes later Zachary and I were trying to find a parking place in a jammed-packed parking garage.

After checking in, we were soon greeted by a nurse who was going to prep Zachary for his MRI.

"They told you we would need to start an IV for the dye contrast, right?" The nurse asked.

"Yes," I said looking into the rooms as we walked down to the end of the hallway trying to I eye-out the situation and what to expect for Zachary.

The room was dim and small. The stretcher bed was pushed up against the larger wall not leaving much room to move in. I set my purse and coat on one of the chairs sitting against the short wall, next to the supply cart. I held Zachary close. I feared what was to come once I let him go.

After getting his weight, height and vital signs, the nurse said, "You can lie him down here on the cart. I'll take a look at what he has for veins."

"I'll warn you - he doesn't have the best looking veins," I offered from my nursing perspective. "It's okay baby. Mommy is right here." Zachary started to struggle and whine as I lowered him to the cart. I hoped the nurse was experienced at starting children's IVs. I wanted them to be quick and efficient so as to prevent Zachary from too much pain and agony. I did know that it could take a time or two to get a person's IV in, depending on if the person's viens were "skinny," if they rolled or you just plain couldn't find them. I held my breath as they placed a rubber tourniquet on Zachary's forearm.

Zachary began to fuss and pull his arm way.

You might have to hold him down," the nurse warned. I kissed Zachary on his soft pudgy cheeks as a stretched my arms over his body to hold him down. I had done this before on other kids when I worked in the ER, but not on my own, I hated it.

"Hang in there sweet pea."

The nurse waited a minute before taking off the tourniquet. "That hand won't work."

Zachary's little body relaxed a bit as he tried to sit up, thinking he was done.

"I have to look at the other arm," the nurse informed as she repositioned herself by Zachary.

Without having to have her tell me, I outstretched Zachary's arm and said, "One more time," I kissed him again hoping he didn't think I was a traitor.

"This arm is worse than the other," the nurse admitted as she replaced the tourniquet on Zachary's other arm once again. As she attempted to insert the needle, Zac let out a scream and tried to pull away. After fishing around for the vein for a few seconds, the nurse pulled the needle out. "I'm going to get another nurse to give me a hand. With two of us, it should be a little easier."

This was not starting out so well. I picked Zachary up off of the cart and held him close, thinking it would be a few minutes before the two nurses would return. I was wrong. Almost as fast as the nurse left, she returned with a second nurse.

"Hi, I'm Mary. Hey buddy, she greeted Zachary with a smile. "So, Karen, what about this one here?" Mary asked as she sneakily peaked at Zachary's arm while I held him.

The scrutinizing and examining went on and on along with three more needle sticks. Zachary was beside himself. By now he was screaming and crying continuously.

"I'm sorry Zachary. I'm so sorry Zachary," I whispered in his ears as tears rolled down my face. I felt helpless to offer him any comfort. I knew they had to get the IV in or they couldn't do the MRI. I just wanted them to stop. Finally, after the fourth attempt, Mary got the IV in. Zachary continued to cry, but the screaming at the top of his lungs had subsided. Nurse Karen gave Zachary a cuddly stuffed raccoon animal. It wasn't much of a consolation, but it was something.

I was allowed to sit in the MRI while Zachary was being scanned. Zac was under what they called "conscious sedation," which really meant he was sleeping and would be much easier to wake up compared to if he were put under a general anesthesia. My nerves took over and my heart began to race. I sat there in a plastic white patio chair. *Is this really happening? How did we get here? My 19-month-old son is lying in an MRI scanner. Dr. Jones wants to rule out a tumor. A tumor!* I was working myself up.

The clicking noise from the MRI machine turned into loud long buzzing. The earplugs I had in my ears barely block out any of the noise. I was surprised when my sister Barb came up behind me and placed a second plastic chair next to mine, at the foot of the MRI scanner.

"What are you doing here?" I asked surprised. "I told you, you didn't have to come."

"I know, but I wanted to be here for you," Barb said, as she put her arm around my shoulders and gave me a squeeze.

"I'm glad you're here. We've only been here for a little while. It's supposed to take about an hour they said.

"How has it gone so far?"

"What took the longest was getting the IV. It took them four tries before they got in! Seriously, it sounded like they were murdering him," I explained yelling loudly so she could hear me over the loud MRI noises. "I was about to do it myself," I added.

"Poor baby!" Barb sympathetically said.

It was difficult to talk because it was so loud. So we sat quietly just holding hands. Wow, what a change our relationship had taken. We started out the best of friends when we were kids. We pretended we were twins a lot. We dressed very similar, did our hair the same (mostly the Princess Leia braided side buns - we thought we looked so pretty!) We loved making up games and playing make-believe and Barbie dolls. Our relationship became very strained over our teenage years. I attributed it to competition, different dynamics and my eating disorder that I was extremely entrenched in for a good 14 years. Actually, I spent much of those 14 years with messed up relationships. Many people didn't know how to deal with me and I told myself - "I didn't need anyone. I was fine all by myself."

I did need someone. I was so glad Barbie was there. I just told her she didn't have to come because I didn't want to impose. I didn't want her, my parents or anyone else to "feel" like they had to be here. If they "wanted" to be here, then that would be completely different.

After sitting quietly, just listening to the pounding and buzzing of the MRI, tears welled up in my eyes and quickly streamed down my cheeks. I tried brushing them away with the back of my hand, but it was useless. I was filled with fear.

Barb leaned over and put her hand in the middle of my back. "What are you most afraid of?" She asked as she pulled out her earplugs.

I'm afraid of what they are going to find," I squeaked as my nose dripped.

"I thought that's what you were going to say. Why do you think they will find something?"

"Everything is adding up. From the spp--ots, to the bum-p-p-s on his h-e-a-a-d, to running into corners and falling down so much more than he-he should," I explained searching for Kleenex in my pocket that I had used when the nurses were trying to start the IV. "I just know something is wrong," I wailed.

I'm sorry, Carol. I really am!" Barb started crying too.

We sat there without earplugs the rest of the MRI and just absorbed the loud clicking, banging and buzzing. Neither of us cared. It gave me something else to focus on as the loud sounds vibrated in my ears and penetrated to the core of my heart.

It took Zac a little while to wake up from being sedated. He wasn't allowed to go until he drank some apple juice.

"Make sure he drinks an extra 24 ounces of juice or water tonight. The dye can be hard on the kidneys," Karen explained as she showed me the discharge instructions. "Also, don't let him walk around unsupervised. Because of the Propofol, Zachary's balance will be off for a couple of hours."

I was eager to take Zachary home, but he was enjoying his juice and another graham cracker. He hadn't eaten since the night before.

Once home, I got Zachary a little more to eat. Surprisingly, he wasn't too hungry. I kept myself busy packing Zachary and my stuff, to bring to the cabin (which really is now my parent's permanent residents.) Since Nathan would be away this Christmas, I thought it would be nice to stay a few days at my parents. I planned to pick Nicholas and Jessica up at my sister Marie's tomorrow and spend Christmas

Eve going to mass with my mom and dad, let the kids open up a few gifts, and have my dad read, *T'was the Night Before Christmas*.

I put Zachary to bed and I had still not heard from the radiologist. *It's 8:30 PM! I think I have waited long enough*, I rationalized. Besides that, my nerves were getting the best of me and I needed to know. I grabbed the piece paper with Dr. Rebecca Jones's number one it from out of my purse. I waited for an answer as my throat and chest tightened.

"Hello?"

"Dr. Rebecca Jones? " I questioned.

"This is her."

I knew she was off duty. I felt a little bad that I was bothering her at home, but my need to finally know far outweighed my feelings of guilt.

"Hi. Sorry to bother you. This is Carol Ann Bartz - Zachary Bartz's mom," I explained just in case she forgot who I was. "I'm calling because it's 8:30 pm and I still haven't heard from the radiologist yet. Can you tell me anything?"

I really don't have anything in front to me right now. What I could find out would be the preliminary report which may not be fully accurate until the radiologists completely reviews it," Dr. Jones explained.

"That's okay. I just need to know something. I can't wait until after Christmas to sit here anxiously worrying," I told her, hoping she would understand where I was coming from.

"I understand your concerns. I'll see if the radiologist is still there, and if he is, I'll get the preliminary report and call you back," Dr. Jones offered.

"Would you call back, as well, to let me know if he's not there, so I don't sit and wait wondering if you got in touch with him?" I know I must have sounded like a pain, but I was desperate. I have been waiting for answers for over two months!

"No problem. "I'll call you either way."

With that, Dr. Jones hung up the phone and I let out a deep breath. My heart was still pounding fast. I felt the diagnosis would be revealed soon.

I finished cleaning up the kitchen and gathered a few things more to bring to the cabin when the phone rang. My heart revved up again. My chest tightened and my hands were shaking as I picked up the phone.

"Hello?" I meekly said.

"Carol Ann? This is Rebecca Jones."

Does she have any answers or not? As much as I didn't want to know, I needed to know.

"Yes, this is her," I nervously answered.

"I spoke with the radiologist, Dr. Casey. He was actually still at the hospital. I'll just get to the point," Dr. Jones quickly said. "Zachary's scan shows that he has what they call an intracranial optic glioma involving the left optic track. There are also focal cutaneous irregularities that could represent neurofibromas, but are nonspecific in appearance. So basically, there are changes of uncertain significance in the brain that is consistent with neurofibromatosis."

My heart sank. I could feel the blood rushing out of my face. All I really heard was "intracranial", "optic glioma", and "neurofibromas." And any word with "oma" attached to the end of it made me immediately associate it to a *tumor*. *Neuro* made me think of head- brain. "So what are they saying?" I asked. "Does he have a brain tumor!?"

"Technically, yes. It is a tumor on the nerves coming from the left eye." Dr. Jones explained.

"Can it be removed? Is it the cancerous?" I frantically asked.

"From what I know, they are low grade and I don't think they can be removed because of the involvement with the eye," Dr. Jones explained.

"So can they go away on their own or what do you do to fix it?" I asked feeling stupid for how my question probably sounded.

Dr. Jones remained patient with my questions. "These tumors don't go away on their own. The good news is they tend to be slow growing, but they can also lead to blindness."

I was speechless! I couldn't believe what I was hearing! First, my 19-month-old healthy boy has a tumor, and now, there is the possibility that he could go blind! I think Dr. Jones could feel my shock at the news. She didn't wait for me to respond.

"I will have one of the radiologist call you tomorrow to give you the final report. Remember, this is just the preliminary report," Dr. Jones tried to be empathetic. "I know this must be quite a shock, but after the final report, I'll call you or have someone call you to set up for the appointments for Zachary. He most likely will need an eye doctor appointment with a pediatrician who specializes in neurofibromatosis. Can I answer any other questions for you?"

I found my voice. "I don't really know what to ask at this point. I guess I'll wait for the radiologist to call tomorrow. Thank you for your time."

I hung up the phone and all my composure that I had while I was on the phone was gone. I fell to my knees on the kitchen floor with the phone in my hand and began to sob. "No, no, no! This can't be! How can this be?" I started hyperventilating. I folded over my legs as I sat on my feet and cried and cried until I started in with my rant all over again. "God, please help him! He's just a baby! I don't want Zachary to go blind! What should I do?! What should I do? I don't know what to do!!"

I sat and cried for half an hour – maybe an hour before I pulled myself together. I never felt so alone. I didn't know what to do with this news. I didn't think I could keep this information from Nathan. I know he was so far away and he wouldn't be able to do anything about it, but somehow telling him would make me feel closer to him and not so alone. I knew if I were away, I would want to know what was going on. I knew I couldn't hide this from him. Nathan was going to call me in a day or two. I knew as soon as I heard his voice I would start crying.

My parents, my sisters and Nathan's parents were waiting for me to call them with an update. I took a deep breath and made my first call to my mom…

Zac in the backyard when it was fun and games - 2 years old tomorrow! 5-14-04

CHAPTER 4

just the beginning

Over Christmas, I tried to hide my sadness from Nicholas, Jessica and Zachary the best I could. I didn't want to spoil the fun and the excitement that Christmas held for a child. I watched with a faint smile on my face as my dad took the place of Nathan to read 'Twas the Night Before Christmas to them. It brought back sweet memories of when he would read the same story to my sister's and me, on Christmas, when we were little. Life seemed so much simpler back then. I was surprised by my sister Barb when she walked in the front door while I was playing with the kids in front of the fireplace.

"What are you doing here?!" I asked excited to see her. "I thought you were going with Quinn to his mom's for Christmas?"

"I was in Winchester with Quinn, but I felt my place was here."

I felt a bit guilty having her leave her husband to come be with me. "I'm glad you are here, but you shouldn't have left Donna's to be with me."

"There isn't any other place I'd rather be," Barb admitted. "I talked it over with Quinn and he agreed that I should come home to be with you - especially since Nathan is in the Middle East for Christmas. Besides, we did our main Christmas celebration early Christmas Eve."

I looked over at my mom and dad. "You knew about this didn't you?"

My mom just smiled softly and said, "Yep."

I couldn't help myself. The tears started in again. This was real. It was the same as when I woke up the morning after I got the news. My heart was racing and my breathing increased faster and faster as if I had just finished going for a run. My chest was tight as I quickly realized, I was awake. It wasn't a bad dream. I cried because the news of Zachary's glioma was scary enough for Barb to fly home to be with me on Christmas morning.

I was wishing I didn't have to pack up the kids and go home already. I was feeling such a sense of comfort being at my parents, but I had invited Nathan's parents over to have a mini Christmas to open some presents with them the day after Christmas. I didn't leave until after I received the phone call from Dr. Rebecca Jones.

The news hadn't changed. She repeated what the radiologist said when he called me December 23. "The findings intracranially are significant and they could affect Zachary's vision," Dr. Jones confirmed. "He does have an increased incidence in developing brain tumors, but we won't worry about that right now."

"So where do we go from here?" I cut in holding back the tears.

I spoke with Nathan sometime after I got home from my parents. I had already given him the initial bad news when he called on the 23rd. He remembered that I was taking Zachary in for a few appointments in regards to his spots. He just had no idea that the spots would have any correlation to a tumor. He was shocked to say the least. The swear words flew. I could tell hanging around his Air Force buddies was rubbing off on him. I sat and listened as I thought how difficult it must be for him to get this kind of news when he was halfway across the world.

"Any more news after talking to the doctor?" Nathan cautiously asked.

"It's pretty much the same. The radiologist just confirmed the glioma and said it could affect his vision. He said there are findings intracranial he that are significant for neurofibromas. I think he was referring to the lumps that are growing on the side of his head as well as his forehead. You know that bump we noticed a couple months ago that didn't go away because he kept falling and hitting his head there?" I explained.

"Yeah, I think I remember."

I hesitated to share the information over the phone, but decided I should. "Um, he also said Zac has an increased chance of developing brain tumors."

"Are you kidding me!" He paused momentarily. The delay was longer than the usual pause. "Are you kidding me!?"

Not only did I have to deal with Nathan being deployed, but this horrible news. I wanted to comfort him, knowing he was all alone in a foreign country with this news to process on his own. At least I was able to call my parents and sisters.

"We are not there. The doctor said gliomas are considered a low-grade cancer. I guess that's good in the scheme of things," I quickly added.

"So what do we do?" Nathan wondered.

"Well, they have Zachary scheduled for an eye doctor appointment to check how the tumor is affecting his vision. I'm guessing that's why he has been bumping into corners and falling down so often," I informed. "It's scheduled for Monday, January 5 at 7:30 am. We are supposed to see a pediatric neurologist at Gillette Children's on Wednesday and have a genetics appointment back at the U of M."

There was a long pause. I wondered if we were cut off. "Nathan?"

The phone crackled. "Yeah, I'm here. This is a lot to take in. What do you want me to do?" Nathan asked helplessly.

"There's nothing you really can do." I reassured.

"Maybe I should come home. Maybe I should just quit," Nathan said.

"No. That's not necessary. There's really nothing you can do," I said trying to talk some sense into him. "What about working towards your nice pension that you'll get once you put in your 20 years? You only have eight more years to go," I reminded him. "I can't let you throw that all away."

"I don't know if I can do this. You know when I was deployed before, when it was just you and I, it was hard, but now that I have kids, it really hurts. It really hurts!" Nathan honestly spoke.

"I'm sorry. I know this must be really hard for you. I know I couldn't do it," I admitted.

January 7, 2004, the day of Zachary's neurology appointment seemed to take forever in coming. I was eager to have my questions answered. There were so many things I didn't understand. I decided to take the advice of Dr. Jones and asked my mom, Marie and my father-in-law, Harvey to come with. I figured if there were a lot of ears, I wouldn't miss anything. I had all the questions I could think of written down and typed up. Marie, being an elementary school teacher agreed to record the information as the questions were answered.

We sat in the white-walled room, not even a picture hanging on the wall. I was a bit surprised at such a sterile appearance for being a children's hospital. When I noticed that there were no toys in the room I quickly grabbed a few that Zachary could busy himself with while we waited for the doctor.

After a few moments, an Asian doctor walked in. She looked to be in her fifties, she had short black hair and wore glasses with a white doctors coat over her black pants and black sweater.

"Good morning", she coldly said without offering her hand. "So who here is Zachary's mother?"

"That would be me. I'm Carol Ann and this is my mom, Darlene, my sister, Marie and my father-in-law, Harvey."

The doctor just stared. I wasn't sure if she was surprised by the extra people so I quickly explained their presence. "I wanted extra ears in case I would miss something."

"I see," she said as she glanced over Zac's chart. "So tell me why you are here. Who referred you to pediatric neurology?"

"Well, I was told that Zachary had neurofibromatosis. Zac's ENT doctor, Dr. Lindquist, sent us to Dr. Rebecca Jones who referred us to you." I was feeling uneasy.

The neurologist asked to examine Zachary. He was busy playing on the floor in between my feet. She checked his reflexes, counted his spots, as I pointed them out, palpated and manipulated the bumps on his head, which caused Zachary to fuss and cry. She continued on with her exam like she was in a hurry. There was no friendly child-like play with Zachary to make him comfortable. I was getting a bad vibe from her. I didn't like her, to put it bluntly.

The neurologist then tested his gross and fine motor skills. Zachary showed difficulty stacking blocks, but throwing a ball, ringing a bell and picking up items off the floor using his thumb and pointer finger seemed appropriate. I was a bit put off that she said Zachary was a - "floppy boy, clumsy," when she was discussing his big motor skills. She definitely did not have much tact. She also felt Zac's fine motor skills were affected, but less noticeable.

Zachary had at least two of the criteria needed for the diagnosis of neurofibromatosis 1 (NF1).

- Six or more café au lait spots, greater than 5 mm
- two fibromas (lumps found along the nerves, under the skin)
- underarm freckling (develops later in adolescence)
- optic glioma

He actually had three which I questioned how Zachary all of a sudden had this. The neurologist said he was born with it and that it was usually an inherited genetic disorder, but there can be a random mutation in the gene. The café-au-lait spots are usually present at birth, or generally appear by two years of age. The extent of involvement is not the same for everyone, she stressed. The severity of NF ranges from extremely mild cases in which café-au-lait spots are only evident, to more severe cases in which one or more serious complication may develop. Once again I was informed that other tumors may develop in the brain or spinal cord, but if they found something, they would not do anything because it would result in weakness and they always grow back, and grow back bigger. I was reminded that there was no way to predict who will develop serious complications. The majority of people with NF have mild forms of the disorder and lead healthy and productive lives. Zachary was somewhere in the middle.

Talk about feeling helpless! I was given all this information and basically there was nothing that they were going to do.

She said she just wanted me to be aware, but take the information with a grain of salt. "We will deal with it if it happens."

Aside from having come back later to see the neurologist to review the MRI scans, (which I was not given to bring nor was mailed to Gillette's) it seemed like an uneventful appointment. Our next appointment was to be with the geneticist, Dr. Barry. I really didn't see why it mattered how Zachary had it if they couldn't fix it. I guess it was more of a responsible thing to do, to be able to rule out if Nathan or I were carriers in case we want to have another child.

January 20, at 9:45 am, Zachary and I were back at the University of Minnesota genetics/eye clinic for our appointment with the genetics counselor, Britney. We discussed in length about gene mutations, inherited genes, gene structure, the ninety percent probability of finding the gene change on chromosome 17 and the rare cases where the test is unable to identify an abnormality at all, although the abnormality may still exist. It's surprising how much you want to understand a subject when in some shape or form it pertains to you. I could have cared less about such scientific things back in high school. I retained some of my knowledge from nursing school, but it was not nearly as in-depth as this information was.

I agreed to have Zachary's blood tested to confirm his NF diagnosis. I didn't want anyone down the line second-guessing decisions because they weren't a hundred percent sure Zachary actually had this disorder. I also thought since it was just a poke I should do this, if the knowledge they gain would aid in medical research down the road somehow. Dependent on the findings from Zachary's blood test it would determine if Nathan, myself, Nicholas or Jessica should be tested as well.

CHAPTER 5

growing glioma

Six months had passed since Zachary's last brain MRI in December. Nathan had been home from his deployment a little over four months now. After receiving the news of Zachary's neurofibromatosis and tumor, he didn't sleep for days and complained of chest tightness. He ended up going to the medical tent to see a doctor who prescribed him anxiety pills which Nathan said didn't help much, but allowed him to sleep. When some openings became available for additional soldiers to fly back home early, Nathan put his name in, without hesitation. He arrived home the end of January.

On June 10th Zachary was scheduled for a brain MRI. I was nervous for this MRI because I was afraid what Zachary would remember from his last one. It hadn't gone so well. I couldn't bear seeing him kicking and screaming and crying out in fear. I was relieved that Nathan was home and I didn't have to do this alone.

The IV start went much more smoothly than the first time. I gave the nurse the scenario of the last IV start. I was relieved when she called in the IV specialist right away with a lot of distraction and some minor kicking and crying the IV was in, with an arm board secured in place to keep the IV from moving. Zac really didn't like the nuisance of the arm board, but Nathan and I busied him with toys and books until was time for him to be put to sleep.

The anesthesiologist allowed me to hold Zachary in my arms as they injected him with the Propofol. I cradled him in my arms as I told him I loved him. "Mommy's right here, baby. You are just going to take a little nap," I reassured. As I sang *You Are My Sunshine* to Zachary, he closed his eyes and went limp. I couldn't help myself, I started to cry. It felt like he had just died in my arms.

I had to hand him over to the anesthesiologist who took Zachary into where the MRI scanner was. "I'll take very good care of him," he promised.

I turned to Nathan and buried my face in his chest. I didn't like this.

I thought the scans should be stable as I hadn't noticed any changes in Zachary's condition. Then Dr. Rebecca Jones called June 12 at 9:50 am.

"Well, the news is that there isn't any change in the fibromas under his skin on his skull. However, the optic glioma is bigger, but without an increase in brain pressure."

"It's bigger?" I asked, making sure I heard right.

"Yes, I'm sorry, it is and because of the growth, cancer could be a possibility," Dr. Jones cautioned. "The increase in size is significant and there is the possibility that the tumor could affect the right eye."

I tried to stay calm, but I was very alarmed. "So what do we do?"

"The first thing is to take Zac to see a neurologist. Dr. Gillis comes highly recommended. Then you need to see a hematologist/ oncologist for further treatment. I'm not sure, but I think that an eye doctor will recommend patching Zachary's left eye in order to make his right eye work harder, strengthening it. You will also need to see an eye doctor again for further instruction," Dr. Jones explained.

I couldn't believe my ears! I wasn't exactly sure what we were talking about. I was too afraid to ask what seeing these other doctors would entail so I thought I would save my questions for someone who would be able to tell me with certainty how they were going to treat Zachary. I like being forewarned, but at this point I needed a concrete plan.

We had a follow-up appointment with the neurologist, Dr. Ong who was more quickly available than Dr. Gillis, on June 23. I decided to put my irritations and dislikes aside for her and take the next available appointment. Nathan would be with me to make the appointment more bearable.

Dr. Ong didn't have much more to say than Dr. Rebecca Jones. I knew it was just a formality, seeing Dr. Ong to get her expert opinion, follow the treatment process of jumping through all the hoops to eventually get to the doctor who would eventually start doing something to treat Zachary. I felt most sorry for Zac because he was the one who had to be the object of attention. He was the one who had to have strangers staring at him in the face, poking and prodding him week after week.

The appointment was relatively quick once we actually got in to see Dr. Ong. The one thing that I left with, well actually two things, were that Dr. Ong said, "It is not likely that the glioma has undergone malignant degeneration." She referred Zachary to an oncologist at St. Paul Children's. She recommended Dr. Christopher Moertel, saying he "specialized in pediatric neurofibromatosis."

Six days later, I walked into St. Paul Children's a bit apprehensive. I wondered if we were actually going to get some real answers, a definite treatment plan. Immediately I felt a little more at ease once we walked through the clinic door. The waiting room was small, but it was full of toys. There were toys to entertain kids of all different ages. In a small adjoining room, there were puzzles and crafts and video games for older kids. The lighting was soft, instead of the bright intense white light, typical of most other doctor's offices and clinics that we had been in.

As I checked in, Nathan brought Zachary over to where the kitchen set was with the real looking fake food. Zachary was only able to play for a little while before a nurse called us in. He was enthralled with the new toys and didn't want to leave.

"Go ahead and bring some of the toys back that he wants to play with," the nurse insisted.

That helped, and Zachary was agreeable to leave the kitchen set behind and go through yet another unfamiliar door.

Dr. Moertel came into the small room where Nathan and I were busily playing with Zachary. He was a man of average height, medium build, wore glasses and had a full head of peppered gray hair. I guessed him to be in his forties. He had a very approachable appearance.

"Hi. I'm Chris Moertel," he greeted as he extended his hand.

Nathan and I stood shaking his hand and introduced ourselves.

"So this must be Zachary. Hey, buddy, you want to see a cool toy?" He asked pulling a light-up handheld toy.

It looked intriguing enough to Zachary that he stood up from his pile of blocks and cars and moves towards Dr. Moertel. Dr. Moertel interacted with Zachary first. It was so refreshing to see a medical professional get on your child's level and put him at ease. Just by watching him with Zachary, I already knew I liked him, but what would he have to say?

As Zachary busied himself with his new swirly light-up toy, Dr. Moertel sat back in his chair. "So what kind of questions do you have for me? I know you have seen a lot of doctors recently so I know they have given you a lot of information. I want to start with the questions you have for me."

"I do have questions I came prepared with," I admitted.

"I'll just let her ask the questions, she's the nurse," Nathan said.

"Oh, what type of nurse are you?" Dr. Moertel asked taking interest.

We detoured from my prepared questions and shared a little about ourselves, Nathan's deployment and how I began to suspect something wasn't quite right with Zachary. Dr. Moertel listened with sincere interest.

Our conversation rerouted back to our purpose for being here. "So how much of an increase in growth in the tumor is there?" I asked.

"I won't lie, it's significant. It's about doubled in size since December," Dr. Moertel honestly admitted.

"We've been given conflicting reports that this glioma isn't cancerous – to it suggests malignancy to - it's not likely. So what would you say the chance of it being cancerous is?" I concernedly asked.

Without hesitation, Dr. Moertel said, "One hundred percent, but you need to take into consideration that there is always a degree, if you will, of tumors being cancerous. Some cancers are classified in stages while others are characterized as low, medium or high grade." Dr. Moertel went on to completely explain the grading in terms of cancer. "When someone is diagnosed with NF, like Zachary, and has a diagnosis of optic glioma, we are pretty certain that it is of low grade. Gliomas are most often classified as low grade. They tend to grow slowly and someone can just live with it."

"Yes, but Zachary's glioma grew so quickly. Over at the University of Minnesota they had us wait six months for his next MRI because they said it wouldn't change much, but wanted to keep an eye on it," I continued.

"Well, that's where things get confusing," Dr. Moertel admitted. "Gliomas typically don't grow this rapidly. I honestly don't know why in Zac's case it did, but it is concerning, especially when his sight is at stake."

"What do we do now?" I asked not having a clue what the next step was. "Biopsy it?"

"No, you would risk blindness in doing that." Dr. Moertel continued to patiently answer all of my questions.

Nathan sat there taking in the conversation while handing Zachary the Teddy Grams one at a time, after making them appear like they were walking towards him.

The plan was to shrink the tumor, but not with radiation, but with chemotherapy. Surgery was not an option at this time because Zachary would inevitably go blind. We were reassured that the glioma would not spread to his right eye. The tumor was following the left optic nerve tract and by starting chemotherapy, Dr. Moertel felt his vision could be saved. With chemotherapy Zachary's peripheral vision would be restored and his pituitary gland should also function normally, which was also being invaded by the tumor. Dr. Moertel said the main plan was to "take care of the tumor." From there, Zachary would need to see an endocrinologist and an eye doctor regularly. He told me if I desired to get a second opinion it wouldn't hurt his feelings, but he admitted without boasting that Minnesota was one of the few places that was a leader in research and in treatment of neurofibromatosis. If treatment would be the same, I didn't feel I needed to fly to Chicago or out east somewhere. For the first time in a long time I finally felt a sense of hope. Dr. Moertel really seemed like he knew what he was talking about and for having only met him once, I felt comfortable in having him treat my son. I trusted him.

CHAPTER 6

chemotherapy

In preparation for the possibility of Zachary losing his hair, because of the potential effects of chemotherapy, I decided to take the kids to Rush City's community pool for a fun, care-free day. It was a very warm July day and I thought it would be fun letting them loose to ride down the waterslide and let the filling buckets dump water on their heads. It would be a normal day for all of us before the chemotherapy schedule would become part of our normal life.

I brought my camera and camcorder and filmed every bit of fun I could capture. So many shots would become precious memories that I would cherish in the years to come - so I thought... I was very careful in removing my camera from my bag, but not careful enough, I guess. I went to get my camera again to do some more videotaping of Zachary, who in May, turned two-years-old. He was splashing in the zero-depth kiddy pool. He was having the time of his life!

I stuck my hand into the bottom of my beach bag feeling around the kid's clothes. *Where is it? I know I put it in here.* I tilted the bag to its side to peak in as I moved the clothes around. Nothing. I quickly moved to look in the bag with my towel and the snacks I smuggled in. Panic began to set in. *It's not here!* I couldn't find the camera either.

"Nicholas, you and Jessica keep an eye on Zachary. I have to run to the pool manager. Someone stole our camera! I'll be right back," I promised. *No, no,no... This can't be happening!* I told myself as I ran to the pool house.

After talking to the pool manager, he explained that there had been a group of kids around that have been causing a little trouble lately. Instantly a picture in my head flashed. I remembered a group of 12 or 13-year-old kids sitting just down from us. I didn't think anything of them. They were just kids. Come to think of it, I haven't seen them in a while. I ran outside of the gates expecting to see them in the parking lot. I don't know, I guess I was hoping to see them gathered around their newly stolen merchandise or hopping on their bikes. The lot was empty of teenagers.

I went back to the manager feeling defeated and asked if he would keep an eye out for even just the camcorder cassette tape or film. I didn't care about the cameras. I just wanted the captured memories. I explained to him why it was so important to find the film. I started to cry out of frustration and anger. I filed a police report once we got home, but the cop told me the chances of finding it didn't look good.

July 26 arrived and Zachary was scheduled for an 11:15 am surgery for a port-a-cath to be placed in his chest to prevent him from the process of week after week IV, each time he received his chemotherapy treatments. It was another early wake-up call. It always took a while getting myself put together and then three kids. I was not a morning person and neither was Nathan. Nathan and I tagged teamed getting the kids ready. Surprisingly, we arrived at the hospital right at 9:45 am. Nicholas and Jessica came with us into the pre-op room. It was a nice distraction for Zachary having them present. As soon as we walked into the small confining room, Zac let out a weary depressing groan and started to cry. It was so heartbreaking to watch his disappointment. He knew at that moment it wasn't Nicholas or Jessica, but he, himself, that was going to be poked and prodded yet once again. I felt so bad for him.

All too soon it was time to go into the operating room. I was glad that I had the choice to stay with Zachary until they put him to sleep. I wanted to offer any comfort I possibly could. I wanted him to know I was right there with them. Zachary started to kick and cry when I carried him into the sterile, white room with very bright lights. I could feel he felt trapped. I felt horrible thinking he trusted me to keep him safe and yet I was betraying him. I was handing him over to a scary stranger. I had to hold him tight and whisper to him, "It will be okay. I love you. Mommy's right here. It's okay," as the small confining gas mask was slowly placed over his terrified face. A few seconds went by and Zachary went limp in my arms. There was no more screaming. He was quiet. I started to cry again.

Surgery took about an hour. Zachary woke up crying, but settled down after he realized we were there. Shortly after waking up, we left his post-op room for an x-ray to check the placement of the port-a-cath. All was good and Zachary was given the green light to be transferred to the hematology/ oncology floor.

The rest of the day, Nathan and I took turns pulling Zachary around the floor in a little red wagon. We made several stops in to the playroom, then back out for more of a ride. He was content. A few hours after recovery, Zac's doctor said it was time to begin his first chemotherapy treatment. He was given Zofran (an IV drug used to lessen or prevent the vomiting which is a common side effect of chemotherapy). The chemo followed and did not seem to affect him in the least. I was relieved. One down...

Since Zachary tolerated surgery and the chemo so well, Dr. Moertel said we could go home that same night. I was a bit surprised since one nurse said that Zachary may have to stay in the hospital for a night or two, but if Dr. Moertel thought Zachary could go home - we were out of here! I knew Zachary would like that.

The treatment plan would entail chemotherapy every Monday for about a year. We would get a break at the end of one round of chemo to allow his little body to build back up. I felt a lot better after talking to Dr. Moertel about Zachary's treatment plan. He felt that Zachary's eye doctor would be "pleasantly surprised" with the outcome the chemotherapy would have on the tumor. I felt hopeful again. I was so glad we finally had a doctor who knew what he is doing.

The following week I brought Nicholas and Jessica to Zachary's appointment until their Grandpa Harvey came to pick them up so they wouldn't have to hang around the clinic for hours. They thought the clinic was so cool! Even Nicholas asked, "When do we get to come back here?"

The room had so many toys, movies, games and a big goldfish tank with little "Nemo's" swimming around. I thought - *You wouldn't want to trade places with Zachary for all the toys in the world!*

The chemo appointments became more routine. Zachary didn't fight the weekly weight and height checks any longer, but as soon as the blood pressure cuff was put on, he began to wail. That of course set the tone for the rest of the appointment. It didn't matter that I tried to reassure him by telling him, "No owies," he still struggled and tried to leave the room. Can you really reason with a two-year-old? I saw the terror in his eyes and could feel the fear radiate from him.

I tried to make sense of why a child, who was so innocent and didn't understand, had to endure such agony. I started to wonder if it was to get people to pray. I began think people come to expect that adults are the ones that get sick and die. It didn't seem to faze the majority of the people. But if a child is severely ill and, God forbid, dies, people take notice.

August 24 was chemo treatment number five. Zachary was started on an antibiotic to help prevent infection, particularly pneumonia, which usually lands the child in the hospital. I was instructed by Zachary's doctor and his oncologist to begin atropine eye drops. I was told to put them in his "good" eye, to dilate it, forcing his left eye, the eye with the tumor to work harder. I really didn't want to cause Zachary more discomfort, but I knew we were doing this to save the sight in his left eye. It seemed so cruel, but I guess it was better than having to keep him wearing the eye patch that was first prescribed.

Surprisingly Zachary didn't fight the eyedrops. He didn't act any different than before, other than the fact that he was walking around looking like he had a concussion - freaked my sister out seeing Zachary had one large pupil and one small one!

Today started off well until the nurse decided not to double tape Zachary's port. He thought since Zachary had such a difficult time when it came to pulling off the tape he wouldn't put so much tape on it this time. I guess Jim was wrong. The port needle pulled out while we were playing with the train set on the big wooden table. We headed back to his room to have his nurse reassess him. He thought the numbing cream was still working so Jim tried to re-stick him. Zac was fighting a bit out of nervousness and in the process screamed and pulled away causing the needle to slice him across the port site, about six inches. He obviously was not numb.

The appointment took much longer since we had to reapply the lidocaine cream and wait for it to work. In the meantime we went down for Zachary's audiology appointment for baseline check since the chemo can affect hearing. We returned back upstairs to find that all of Zachary's lab levels had dropped from the previous week, but he was still holding his own. I was just instructed to keep him away from sick people. Dr. Moertel said, "There is no need for Zac or any of his family members to wear a mask." He didn't seem too worried.

Almost immediately Zachary fell asleep on the way home. Once home, I parked the car in the garage, then carried him in to finish his nap. He woke up five hours later! I was really surprised when after only being up for three hours, he was ready to go back to sleep. He woke up 13 ½ hours later!

Within the past week I began to notice Zac becoming more tired and his appetite decreasing I was thankful he was getting a break from one of his chemo meds, otherwise, I think he would be in rough shape.

Unfortunately, because of the previous week's appointments, Zac now had a phobia of people going anywhere near his port-a-cath, even me. We started out the morning with our usual routine of getting ready for his upcoming appointment. I was trying to put the numbing cream on his port site and he ran off and hid behind a chair.

"Zac, I'm not going to hurt you," I promised.

"No, no, no!" Zac cried as the tears started to run.

"Come on Zac. Let mommy do this, then we have to go bye-bye," Nathan told him as he picked him up from behind the recliner chair. He held him down so I could proceed. I know he was having flashbacks as he cried and struggled to get away.

Once we got to the clinic, Zachary went through his little door like he always had done before. They actually had a toddler sized door right next to the standard door. It is very cute and a little intriguing for the kids. He went off to play like he usually did. Height and weight checks went fine. Zac's weight was a little down, but Dr. Moertel said he'd just keep an eye on it and if he continued to lose weight he would put him on a nutritional supplement.

Zachary did better with his blood pressure check now that I started talking him through it with the help of his favorite stuffed animal, "Bear-bear." Things were still rough with Nurse Jim. Zachary didn't want him anywhere near his port, especially with how his last appointment went. No amount of reasoning was helping. Zachary started crying and screaming. I could tell Jim was getting a bit frustrated.

"Hey, hey - settle down now, buddy." Jim was a great nurse but the few times we had him, I noticed he wasn't quite as patient as some of the female nurses. A maternal thing I guess. Well, it got to the point that Jim and I had to lay Zachary down on the bed, just to get the very sticky tegaderm tape off. When it came time to insert the port needle there was more uncontrollable screaming and crying. Zac was so afraid! He kicked and fought as hard as he could.

"Zac, Zac, it's okay, it's okay," I reassured. Yet I felt like a hypocrite as I spoke those words. Here I am the most trusted person to him and I am holding him down to allow a man with the needle, to stick it in his chest. How many times can a child break your heart? Another chip felt like it came off of mine.

Jim had no other options so he lay across Zac's little body as he told me, "Hold his arm down tight so he can't move, I have to get this in."

I could only wonder if it was going to be like this every time. For my sake as well Zachary's, I really hoped it wouldn't be.

By chemo treatment number seven, Zachary cried a little less and cooperated a little more. To my surprise he even stuck out his arm for the blood pressure.

I told him, "No owiees. The nurse is just going to give your arm a nice big hug and Bear-bears too." I guess little by little was going to be how this would work.

Taking a break from one of the chemo meds called, Carboplatin, really helped. His counts recovered nicely. He was set to resume both chemo's, so I thought until Tammie, the pediatric nurse practitioner, came into check Zachary over. I pointed out a rash on his left underarm that was spreading. My first thought was impetigo, which went around the neighborhood earlier that summer and Zachary ended up with only two spots then. I started treating him with the medicine I had at home, being the nurse I was. The problem was that whenever Nathan or I would rub the medicine on or pick him up under his arms Zac would cry something horrible! Then I thought maybe it was shingles.

That was the consensus after several other people came in to take a look at Zachary's painful rash. Zachary's patience was wearing thin.

"I think it'll be better to hold both chemo meds this week," Tammie decided.

"So it's the chemo that's causing this? I don't understand when his white blood count is 6.9," I wondered.

"Well, his immune system is still being compromised even if the numbers aren't really low," Tammie explained. "I just think if we went ahead with the chemo, the shingles could spread even more," Tammie could tell I looked confused.

Tammie went on to tell me that shingles can occur in kids who have had chickenpox or the vaccine for it. It just happens that it can become active when their immune system is down or if they are under some form of stress. And Zachary was under stress.

He was more than thrilled to get done early from his appointment. He quickly found his "little door" and closed it for yet one more week.

Zachary's counts remained low for the next two appointments, so the chemotherapy was withheld and another two treatments would be added to the end of his treatment schedule. Today, we finally had the help of a child life coordinator who distracted Zachary during the accessing the port and tape removal. The tears still came as did the kicking, but with Sarah's magic bubbles it lessened his anxiety. Sarah actually gave Zachary a stuffed cloth doll the week before that had a port in it. It looked a little scary with not having a face, so I drew a happy face and colored in some hair to spruce it up a bit. Zachary didn't care for the doll or the medical accessories that he could play with and practice on the doll to help with his fears.

Zachary just pointed to the doll's port and said, "Owieeee!" He became pretty clever in figuring out that as soon as his nurse was done with all the invasive stuff or he wasn't okay with what the doctor or nurse needed to do, he would say, "Pee, pee." He pretty much knew he would be able to delay the procedure because I had a hard time calling his bluff when he was just newly potty trained.

Over the weeks I expected Zachary to lose his hair, but Dr. Moertel said, "With these two chemotherapies, carboplatin and vincristine, some kids will lose their hair and some won't. It just depends on the child."

All I noticed was hair on the back of his shirts and that his hair was thinning.

The nursing assistant who checked in Zachary even commented after weighing him and checking his height, "He still has hair!"

I felt very lucky that he was doing so well, but at the same time a bit guilty when I saw other kids there and they didn't look as good as Zachary.

Zachary continued to surprise the doctors as to how well he was tolerating everything. He hadn't developed mouth sores or problems with weakness or tripping, due to the side effects of vincristine. The vincristine often caused tightening of the ankle muscles and made it more difficult to walk without dragging the foot. Zachary did more falling before he even started on chemotherapy. He was actually improving. Aside from occasional fevers and being more whiny, he was doing pretty well.

It seemed kind of unusual for a two-year-old to beg to go to bed, but when Zac had reached my limits in the whining department, I couldn't say I minded that he wanted to take another nap. I didn't feel I could get too upset with him considering what he was going through, but I'm no saint either.

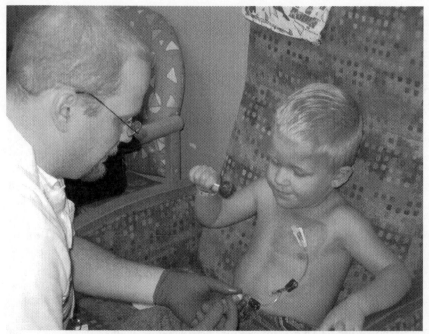

Port access before chemotherapy infusion… Zac kind of getting used to it…

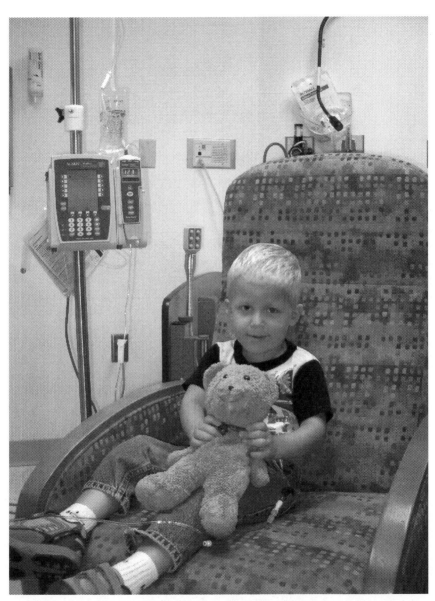

Zac and Bear-bear getting through chemo 9-27-05

CHAPTER 7

becoming routine

Three months since beginning chemotherapy, Zachary had his first MRI. His labs were all good. I didn't really expect anything less since he had been on his scheduled break from chemo to allow him to recover once again. He would start his next round after the MRI. We headed down to radiology and Zachary soon got an overwhelming sense of panic when his doctor wanted to see him. He knew something was about to happen and he didn't like it.

Zachary lay down on the floor and started to cry - "No, no, no!"

I knelt down next to him on the floor and patted his tummy, "Zac, no owiees. I promise."

If he heard me, I'm sure he thought momentarily to himself, *"Yeah where have I heard that before?"*

"Hey, Zac, the doctor is just going to give you a little medicine in your port to help you take a nap," I tried to explain. "No owies, baby." I had no clue how to explain this to him so that he would understand.

I picked him up in my arms and since nurse Jim already accessed Zac's port upstairs, the radiology doctor was able to just give Zac the medicine as I held him. Within 15 seconds, Zachary fell sleep in my arms. The whole process still did not seem any easier.

"I'll take very good care of him," the radiologist said as he took Zachary from my arms.

"I know," was all I could say. With that he turned and walked away with Zachary cradled in his arms.

Nathan sat silently in a chair in the corner. He stood up and walked toward me, "Are you okay?"

I turned into his chest and started to cry. "I just hate this."

After the hour-long MRI and then holding Zachary in my arms once the radiologist brought Zachary back to where we were waiting, he woke up 25 minutes later. He was calm for once. Everything went so much better this time. Children's Hospital really knew kids.

We headed back upstairs where Zachary was hooked up to his chemotherapy. Dr. Moertel came in to check on him.

"Do you get the MRI results today or tomorrow?" I asked.

I was so pleased when Dr. Moertel said, "Of course we'll have the results for you today."

I just recalled how long we had to wait the last two times to get any information. The waiting was torture.

"Follow me to my office. We'll look at the results on my computer."

Nathan and Dr. Moertel talked about football and hunting as he pulled up Zachary's scans on the computer screen. I held my breath as my eyes tried to read the images.

"It looks like the chemotherapy is working," Dr. Moertel said pleased. "The tumors are shrinking significantly."

"Thank God!" Nathan said letting out a deep breath that had been held for one second too long.

Dr. Moertel went on to show how the growth had receded from the hypothalamus and pituitary gland. "And see here, the tumor in the basal ganglia has also reduced in size as well. In June, the tumor was very large. It was really crowding the entire chiasm which you remember, is the space back behind the eyes were the two optic nerves cross. This whole area was full and growing outward and up... starting to affect both eyes," he said as he circled the once endangered area with his finger. "Now the tumor looks to have shrunk by about 50 to 75%. There is room in the chiasm and the optic pressure is relieved. I think we are on the right track."

"The prayers are working," I whispered as I held my folded hands over my lips. I was relieved to finally get some good news for once.

For the first time, I didn't feel any fear that Zachary would lose his sight. I knew he was doing better. He hadn't been smacking his head on corners, furniture or anything that seemed out of his peripheral line of vision. It was also encouraging when I mentioned to Dr. Moertel that I thought Zachary's fibroids on his head also seem to be getting smaller, and he didn't disagree with me. We *were* on the right track.

Weeks continued almost seeming the same. Zachary still struggled a bit with having his port accessed. He hated when Nathan would call him to come and let him put emla numbing cream on his chest in preparation for his upcoming appointment. When Zachary approached Nathan, thinking he had something fun for him and instead saw the tube of emla, Zachary quickly slapped Nathan's hands down, causing the cream to fall.

"No, daddy, no!" Zachary would cry and run off to hide behind a chair, under the table or in his room after slamming the door.

This was so un-normal for a two-year-old to have to go through, let alone even understand it. The only thing holding me together was my faith and belief that God would help us through this and help Zachary stay strong.

Occasionally Zachary threw up after having a break in the chemo cycle, once he had to resume the poisonous treatment. He fought being exhausted the best he could. Sometimes he would take three or four naps a day, but oddly all of a sudden he could get a sudden burst of energy. Sometimes Zachary would disappear and we would look for him, surprised to find him in his room and under his covers for a nap – all on his own.

I noticed more lumps on Zachary's head, in January. It seemed like I was finding new once more and more frequently. When I pointed them out to Dr. Moertel I confessed, "I'm afraid they'll keep coming and he will look like a tamer version of the Elephant Man."

"Let's take a look," Dr. Moertel said as he firmly ran his hands through Zachary's hair feeling for the fibroids. "Does this hurt, buddy?"

I cringed a bit at the amount of pressure he was exerting on Zac's lumpy skull. "They do *really* hurt him," I answered for Zachary. "I even have a difficult time pulling shirts over his head. I have to really stretch them to fit over his head without hitting the lumps. He's been bumping them more on a regular basis again and he lets out blood-curdling screams. It takes him quite a while to calm down after that."

Zachary kept trying to pull his head away from Dr. Moertel's hands. "All done? Go?" He said as he was trying to play with some blocks on the floor.

"Okay Zac. I'm all done," Dr. Moertel said as he rubbed his back.

Dr. Moertel talked about an experimental drug that was being used for fibroids, but he leaned more in the direction of seeing a plastic surgeon to see if he should have them removed now or wait. After visiting with the plastic surgeon and hearing how they cut the scalp back, creating a flap and then removing as much fibroids as possible before sewing the flap back in place, Nathan and I had our reservations. Since the doctor informed us that they are never able to remove all of the fibroids because it grows into the nerve and will eventually grow right back, Nathan and I decided if he thought it wasn't completely necessary at this time, we would wait.

Life was by no means normal for us. I knew there were so many other mothers out there who had sicker children and had other kids to care for as well. Nathan and I tried our best to treat Zachary as close to the same as Nicholas and Jessica. It was challenging at times. I knew Zachary at times didn't feel that great and the last thing he probably wanted was to eat broccoli. But Nathan felt if Zac was just running around, he was good enough to eat what the rest of us did.

I have to admit, many times I let Zachary get away with things more than I probably should. My heart ached for him with the change in life he had to endure. I just wanted for him to be happy. I knew Nathan was right to an extent, so sometimes I let things go and sometimes I fought with him for what I thought was best.

Zachary wasn't always an angel. He had his moments - especially when he was tired. Like any toddler, the more tired he was, the whiner he became and the harder it was to reason with him. He got yelled at his fair share. He even started punishing himself if he got into trouble. He would slap his own hand and run away into his room, slamming the door. I didn't quite know what to think about that. It just made me want to go even easier on him.

I sensed something different about Zachary around the age of three. I couldn't quite put my finger on it, but he even felt different from Nicholas and Jessica when I hugged him. It was something I hated to admit, but it made me question how much he was mine and how much he was God's – whatever that meant. Of course he was mine! I gave birth to him! I loved them all the same. For the time being, I just attributed it to the chemotherapy and everything he had to go through and my faith was being tested.

Nicholas and Jessica would come along to Zachary's chemo appointments from time to time, Nic not as much because he was in first grade and had school. Jessica wasn't in kindergarten until next year and I actually pulled her from preschool after only going for two months. It got to be too chaotic with coordinating Zachary's many appointments.

Both of them saw what Zachary had to go through for his appointments. They saw his crying and definitely heard his screams. Even though they would help me by trying to distract Zachary by blowing bubbles for him, getting Zachary's Bear-bear for comfort or kiss him goodbye when her Grandpa Harvey would come pick them up to go do something fun - leaving Zac behind. They could see him lying on the big white cot in his blue hospital jammies. They knew Zac had to stay for another MRI, but being five and seven years old, they didn't really understand.

I thought Jessica didn't mind spending a chunk of her day at the oncology clinic. She busied herself with all the cool toys and arts and crafts. I thought wrong. It was taking a toll on her and she was having a difficult time sharing the attention. She would ask me to draw a scarecrow for her, but then the doctor would need to examine Zachary.

"Hang on, Jessica. I have to hold Zachary still so the doctor can check him," I explained.

"Mommy, can you put the dress on the dolly for me?"

Of course the nurse would be ready to draw Zachary's blood so I would have to put her off again. "Just a minute, Jessica. I have to keep Zac still so the nurse can draw his blood. Zachary needs me right now."

A break in the action, so I thought, but then the doctor has some questions for me at the same time Jessica asked again - "Mommy, you said you would draw me a scarecrow."

I cringed at the hurt and anger in her crystal blue eyes. She really tried to be patient, but she was only five. I knew she needed me too, but what was I supposed to do?

We were out in the waiting room/ play area on a different clinic day and Jessica blurted out, "I sure wished I had to have chemo."

I was shocked! I felt like someone just punched me in the stomach. "Jessica! Don't ever say that!" I shot back.

Immediately, I realized how harsh that must have sounded to her. I was hurt she could even say anything like that. I felt I wasn't doing a good job with my other two kids. I looked at her and got down on my knees. I knew she was hurting much worse than I was.

"Jessica, I love you sooo much. I love you just as much as Zachary." I reassured. "You don't want to be sicker or have to have chemo because then you wouldn't feel good and you would have to take naps all the time and miss out on so many fun things. Zachary hates when the doctor's and nurses have to poke him with needles." I wanted to make sure Jessica knew how much I loved her and wanted her to stay healthy. "You remember when you had your tonsils out, don't you?"

"Ah-huh."

"You remember how sick you felt?" I reminded her.

"Ah-huh."

"You didn't feel like playing, did you?"

Jessica didn't have to think long. "No, I was too sick."

"Jessica, I will always, always love you and give you attention. But sometimes you and Nicholas will have to wait if Zachary needs me first," I chose my words carefully, "if he is sicker or he is hurting really bad and you aren't sick or hurt." This was hard. At that moment, six months into Zachary's treatment, I felt like we had been to the oncology clinic one too many times.

It was February 23, 2005. We had an eye doctor's appointment that I didn't have to fight Zachary to get to. It helped that there was no emla cream involved and Jessica came with as a great distraction. Dr. Moertel recommended this new eye doctor. He said she was "Experienced with NF." The best part about it was we didn't have to drive all the way to the cities to get to the clinic. I thought it would be easier on Zachary and me, for that matter, not having to deal with the longer commute. I have to say I was very disappointed. Zachary had to wait quite a while to be called in, which wasn't anything new. We had learned to keep ourselves busy. Of course we were waiting in line for the bathroom when the doctor called his name.

"Right here," I announced. "He has to go pee."

Rudely she asked, "Well, do you think you could come in here?" The lady in the white lab coat said standing by in exam room door.

I was a bit shocked. I looked at her expecting her to say, "Oh, why don't you just come in here right after he goes to the bathroom." It didn't go like that at all. I was a bit stunned and didn't quite know how to respond so being the compliant, non-confrontational person I am, I leaned down to Zachary and whispered loud enough for this rigid woman hear.

"Don't pee your pants." *For crying out loud, he's a 2 ½ year-old boy*, I thought!

"I'm the doctor that will be seeing you," she dryly said introducing herself as she sat on her rolling stool.

"This is Zachary, or Zac. And this is Jessica, the big sister. I'm Carol Ann," I cheerfully introduced hoping I could change her bad mood or whatever she was in.

She went on with her business without making any small talk with me or any comforting gestures to make Zachary feel at ease. I guess I was expecting more from a pediatric doctor.

"So, the glioma is on his right optic nerve?" The opthalmologist informed, trying to not make it sound like a statement.

"No, it's on the left." *Really? She doesn't even know?*

"Oh. So he hasn't started chemotherapy yet?" She once again informed without questioning.

"No. He's been going to treatment since July 2004," my voice rose. I wanted her to hear my irritation. I could tell she hadn't reviewed Zachary's chart beforehand.

"I'll catch up on things later," she said as she proceeded to ask me a few more questions and flashed light into Zac's eyes a couple of times, and that was it.

"Everything looks to be the same as what Dr. ummmm..."she stalled as she quickly paged through Zachary's chart looking for the last eye doctors name.

"Dr. Summers," I said in victory at beating her to the answer.

The eye doctor just peered at me as she wrote a few things down. Zachary was starting to get a little antsy and whiny.

"Sit still!" She snapped. "You're almost done."

My eyes widened. "He's getting tired. It's about the time he takes one of his naps."

I was getting angry. I wanted to put her in her place. *How dare you talk to my son that way!* I could feel the top of my head get all tingly. I couldn't believe how rude and uncaring she was. She didn't even turn on the electronic piggy that was positioned high over the door to aid in getting children to look up and focus during their eye exams, even after Zachary had asked several times. He remembered the same kind of puppy that was at the U of M clinic. Jessica even politely asked one time for her to turn it on, with no luck.

Quietly, but loud enough for the doctor to hear, I said to Zac and Jessica, "Just hang on, she will turn the piggy on in a little bit when she's done writing."

"I'll want to see Zachary in eight weeks. We won't have to dilate his eyes with that visit."

That was it? That was the extent of her examination? She looked at Zachary for about five minutes! I was not happy with her. Needless to say, we left eye clinic without even an "oink" from the piggy above the door.

As I was gathering up our coats to go, I recalled a brief conversation I had with a woman I met while we waited in the clinic. She said she was diagnosed with a pituitary tumor by Dr. Summers, a year ago and loved her care and expertise. "If you don't have confidence in your doctor, you need to find a different doctor. It's your health. It's your son's eyes." Her statement was like a foreshadowing. I definitely did not have confidence in this doctor.

CHAPTER 8

ups and downs

The weeks turned into months and Zachary continued getting fevers, rashes and struggled with vomiting on and off. I was grateful once he was prescribed Zofran, an antiemetic. It seemed to help a lot. The nausea was bad, but for Zachary, being so tired seemed to be the worst side effect of the chemotherapy. He would get so tired and so crabby that at times Nathan and I were beside ourselves. Many times Zachary would crawl into bed by 6 or 7 pm with his favorite stuffed animal that Nic and Jessica gave to him the day he was born and snuggle in and sleep without wanting to eat. Sometimes he would wake up around midnight or 2 am and eat two bowls of oatmeal and crawl back into bed. Other times he just slept.

At clinic it was a bit alarming when Zachary didn't want to play with the train set or ask to go down the slide like he always did. I knew something was up when he didn't have it in him to charm the ladies at the nurse's station. It turned into crying, pouting and kicking one clinic day and he wasn't even being poked. He was crabbier than he has ever been.

"I have never seen him act this way before," Kara the nursing assistant commented.

Jim, Zac's nurse even asked what was wrong. "Is he sick or coming down with something?"

When the extreme tiredness hit, it hit hard and fast. Eventually, he would fall asleep in my arms. My heart ached for him. I didn't understand why it had to be this way.

Early in Zachary's treatment, I was informed by a co-worker about Caringbridge as a way to communicate to family and friends when you are in a time of need to allow you to keep people updated without having to make phone calls to everyone. I quickly found it to be a source of support and encouragement as I shared my fears, frustrations and updates. It helped me feel more connected to the outside world as I journaled what was going on in mine.

One appointment in April, Zachary refused even a bite of lunch. He sat in the high-back, fake leather chair all rigid. His hands clenched. For a minute I thought maybe the port needle pulled out, but all was well. I kept looking at him waiting for something to happen.

"Do you have to throw up?" I asked.

"No."

I continued watching him. He sternly looked back and kept telling me, "No, no!"

"What is it Zac? No, no what?" I wanted to go get his nurse, but I didn't want to overreact without a justifiable reason. I hated always being on high alert with him and I didn't want to be one of "those" parents who overreacted at every cough or runny nose.

A minute or two later, Zachary's eyes closed and his head started bobbing up and down. He was so tired! That was it?!

To break the tension, Jessica stood up and stared at Zachary. "He looks just like Papa!"

I couldn't help but giggle. I saw the resemblance. My dad who was in his 60s, fell asleep a lot in his short backed wooden chair while sitting at his computer. It didn't matter if there were nine grandkids running around. He said it was because of his sleep apnea and that he never got a good night's sleep.

In spite of Zachary's illness and being crabby at times, he was a gentle, charming little boy. Everyone who met him, from the nurses, to the people in the hallways, thought he was such a sweet adorable, friendly little boy. One lady said to me, "His goodness was already ingrained in him."

I never faulted him for when he was whining or crabby. I knew it drove his dad nuts, but I soon realized it was a way of communicating when he actually couldn't speak very well because of his speech delay. He was angry that he was made to go to the doctors all the time. He was getting tired of being sick and tired. He had to know he missed out on fun because all he wanted to do was sleep or he had to go to another doctor's appointment. He was separated from his brother and sister too many times. Whining the only way he could relieve some of that pent-up stress from the torturous appointments. At times I did yell at Zachary. I felt horrible afterwards, but it was a lot of stress for me as well. Zachary didn't have a choice. He just did it because he knew he had to. I hoped one day he wouldn't blame me.

I continued to pray daily for a miracle. I wanted Zachary to have his sight be completely restored. Although he had limited vision in his left eye, he was almost considered legally blind in that eye. I wanted the optic nerve to regenerate by the hands of God. I prayed that there would be a breakthrough in gene repairing and if God wouldn't cure Zachary from the NF, He would aid the scientists and doctors. I wanted normalcy back in our lives.

Dr. Moertel referred us to another eye doctor, Dr. Evan Ballard. He was a big improvement over his partner. For starters, he is a father of seven children, he told me. I assumed he had to like kids and must have some patience for them - and he did!

Dr. Ballard had taken time to review Zachary's chart. I could tell by the questions he asked me. He seemed knowledgeable in NF and how to treat Zac. He took the time to check different aspects of Zachary sight, unlike the quick "one card" test and quick peek in his eyes that the previous eye doctor did. I loved that he used a little toy that he would press a button and make the ears standup, or the finger puppet with the blinking nose on it (that he let Zac play with after he was done with that certain test) and the barking puppy that was mantled over the door. Zac didn't even have to ask them to turn it on because he was so enthralled with all the different tricks and funny noises Dr. Ballard would use to get him to look where he wanted him to.

Dr. Ballard felt Zachary's eyesight had improved from two months ago. I couldn't help but wonder if the other eye doctor just did a rush job. It didn't matter, I trusted Dr. Ballard.

"If there were a lot of damage, Zachary's eyes wouldn't be doing what they are doing for these tests," Dr. Ballard explained. "Let's back him off a little from his atropine eye drops to two days a week instead of three. I want to keep his left eye working."

It was October 11, 2005. After 15 months of chemotherapy, Zachary was given a "chemo graduation party" with cake and presents. Jessica was excited because she got a present too. It was the most smiling I have seen from Zachary in that clinic. Dr. Moertel admitted that he was very surprised that Zachary sailed through the past fifteen months as well as he had. Kids usually landed in the hospital a few times with some sort of infection, mainly pneumonia and required IV antibiotics. I of course attributed it to the power of prayer.

So many people had been following my weekly entries on caringbridge. Prayer chains were formed and I prayed a lot myself. My faith and the support of family and friends carried me through some tough times. Zachary was a very strong-willed little three-year-old. He must have been living by my model without knowing it -"NEVER GIVE UP!"

"So the plan for Zachary is an MRI, every three months, for the first year," Dr. Moertel explained. "Remember, the tumor can continue to shrink slowly, even after chemotherapy is done."

"Is that because the chemo is still working?"

"Yes. So you will still expect Zac to feel lousy for a while," Dr. Moertel answered.

"But I was first told that his tumor would be a slow-growing tumor way back when they first found the tumor - and in six months - time it drastically increased," I informed. "Couldn't the same thing happen now that Zac is done with the chemotherapy and technically the tumor is still there?"

I knew there were no guarantees and although Zachary had a tumor, it wasn't life-threatening, but to be prepared is another thing. Dr. Moertel said, "Zac has an unusual type of tumor, so it is possible. We'll just have to keep a close eye on him."

I was very nervous knowing I wouldn't be taking Zachary to the clinic weekly to have him closely monitored. It was like stopping cold turkey. I was afraid of the unknown, the "possibilities," the "might come back" statements. NF was a complicated disorder. So much was unknown and there were so many complications that could arise dependent on each individual.

I guess this was where my faith and prayers would have to keep me positive in the belief that Zachary would be just fine. He had already proved how strong he was these past fifteen months.

I do have to admit it was great to have my seven day week back. I quickly adjusted back to a routine without having to go to the oncology clinic. After the chemo started wearing off, Zachary seemed to be less whiny and not fall asleep several times a day. It was a relief seeing Zachary act more like a healthy three-year-old, but in the back of my mind I still worried.

Zachary still had his port in. Dr. Moertel thought it made sense to keep it in since he needed lab counts ten days after his last chemo and he would be needing an MRI only a month after its completion. He said we could decide then, what we wanted to do. It wasn't harming him any.

Zachary's MRI scans basically showed no change in the size of the tumor from the last scan, but the blood supply was not there. Without the blood, the tumor was not fed and it could not grow. Dr. Moertel said he was hoping that we would still see a decrease in size of the tumor with the next couple of MRIs. All in all, it was good news. Nathan and I would sit tight, continue to pray and wait for the February MRI.

Zachary did have another neurosurgery appointment to reevaluate the neurofibroids on his head. I liked Dr. Robert Wood. He seemed very experienced and honest. After a consult we decided since the fibroids appeared smaller, Zac wasn't in contact sports and Dr. Wood said he personally would wait a while to see what happens with the lumps, we would give Zachary time to just be a little three-year-old. The surgery sounded gruesome and painful. Zac had enough pain and fear this past year and a half.

We dove into a fairly normal life for almost a year. Nicholas kept us busy with mite hockey, Jessica in club gymnastics, and school for all three. The doctor appointments were incorporated into our normal life. The underlying hidden fear seemed to lessen a little more as the quarterly MRIs came and went without any change.

Zachary had been stable for a while and Dr. Moertel and the social worker at children's nominated Zachary to be a "Wish Kid." They got the paperwork going to see if he qualified to have a wish granted through Make-A-Wish. Two representatives from Make-A-Wish came to our house for a visit. They basically came to find out what Zachary's wish was, not ours.

I do have to admit we had to sway him a little because he was only four. He didn't really understand what having a wish granted meant. I was a bit worried if I left it completely up to him we would end up with a year's supply of corn dogs (something Zachary had only wanted to eat while going through chemo).

Zachary loved Mickey Mouse, especially the movie Mickey's Once Upon a Christmas. We would watch it daily at times and not just in the winter. It was fitting that several months later, after a summer photo shoot for a send-off event - "Stories of Light," held at the Mall of America in December 2006, all five of us were escorted to the airport in a limo and flown to Give Kids the World Resort, in Florida, in January.

What an amazing gift! The resort was like we were in Candyland. It was so magical and life was carefree for those six days. We were told we had to let the kids have ice cream for breakfast at least once, which we did. The gingerbread house was where we ate breakfast and dinner most of the time. The food was great. They had a magical house were Zachary was given a star to Make-A-Wish upon. It was then put into a treasure box that shook and rattled and all of a sudden the helper pointed her finger to help us follow the blinking light as it traveled up to the ceiling.

"There," She pointed out way high up on the ceiling where a light flickered, "is where your star will go. And it will be there forever! So, when you want to come back and visit you can see your very own star."

"Woooww..." Nic and Jessica in unison said, dazed.

"I wish I could have a star," Jessica added.

I felt bad that Jessica felt a bit left out. At 6 ½-years-old, she still didn't fully understand. I tried to let her know we were all very lucky just to be here. "At least we get to be in this magical place because of Zachary, right?"

Nic unintentionally diverted her attention to a wishing well that Nathan gave them coins to throw in and to hear it burp and talk back to them. Zachary wasn't far behind.

We spent our days at the parks at Disney World, Sea World and Universal Studios. There was so much to see and do. It was actually hard some days to leave the resort we were staying at because they had so many fun activities planned there. Every day was full of fun and excitement.

I couldn't understand why Nathan and I started to argue when we were living in a magical place where we were able to set our worries, doctor appointments and needles aside. He ended up developing a severe headache and started vomiting.

"Are you sure you're not coming down with something?" I worried.

"No. I think it's a migraine."

"Do you want me to just take the kids and you can rest here?"

"Or you guys could hang here for the day?"

"I was planning on taking them back to Universal Studios. They had so much fun at Jurassic Park and Honey I shrunk the Kids. Nic really wanted to see that again," I explained hoping he'd be okay with my plan. "Besides, we don't get to do stuff like this every day."

"No, that's fine. I'll just stay back here and return some emails and try and get some sleep. I didn't sleep much last night."

Thankfully, Nathan felt better by the time we got back. He seemed to be in a good mood, just in time for the big mascot-type bunny, "Mayor Clayton," to tuck the kids in bed that night. It was so much fun watching the kids squeal as Mayor Clayton pulled the blankets off their beds and wrapped them up in them. The pillows were flying and Nic started getting into the whole un-tuck-in play. Soon he and Jessica were trying to jump on the big bunny. I had to call them off when Mayor Clayton looked a little worried. Nic, Jessica and Zachary forgot they weren't wrestling their dad, and for dad, there was no holding back. Poor bunny!

I was really sad to leave. I think I was mostly afraid of leaving this fairyland behind to return to the world of doctors and the fear of what was our reality.

It wasn't until we got home and Nathan finally opened up to me. "I didn't want to say anything before Zac's wish trip, and I didn't want to ruin your time while we were there by giving you something more to worry about," Nathan began.

"So you weren't telling me something! I knew it!" I was just glad it wasn't me.

"I'll just come out and say it - I'm being deployed again."

"What?!"

"Yeah, and I have to leave in a couple of weeks."

I wasn't expecting news like this, but I wasn't completely surprised either. Nathan had explained to me before that he didn't sign up to be in the Air Guard because he wanted to go to war, but it was always a possibility. It was what the training was all for. The extra money came in handy too.

I just stared at Nathan's depressed looking face. He was really not looking forward to this deployment.

"So you kept this kind of stressful information all to yourself?" I didn't pause long enough for him to answer. "That's why you got the migraine and were puking. It wasn't the noise or standing in the lines at Magic Kingdom, like you said - you were maxed out on stress. I really wished you would have confided in me."

"I didn't want you to be thinking about this when we were supposed to have fun."

"So instead we fought because you were stressed out and I was feeling your stress and anger and got mad and turned off by your behavior. I fed off of you. You know how that works?" I reminded him.

"I know now, I should have trusted you."

"I want to always know what's going on with you, Nathan. We have to keep talking. I can handle it," I reassured.

"So you are sure you will be all right with the kids by yourself again?"

"I've done it before, I can do it again."

Life more or less settled back down into the life we were becoming accustomed to.

Zachary was given the "green-light" to extend his MRIs now to every six months since he had been stable for almost a year. Things were looking up! I was pleasantly distracted by the exciting news that I was pregnant and expecting my fourth child sometime in November. Everything seemed to be going well. I was happy. How quickly life started to improve.

My first piece of bad news came when I went for my first prenatal appointment before my shift at work. My ultrasound confirmed no sign of a heartbeat. I was devastated! I wanted this baby desperately! How quickly a high can turn in to a low. Not only did I lose a much wanted baby, but Zachary's original doctor that we had been following with since he started chemotherapy, had left Children's of St. Paul. I trusted him and I would have to regain trust in another oncologist who specialized in NF.

It was May 31, 2007, six months since Zachary's last MRI. I went it alone with Zachary this time. I wasn't worried. He was also easier to reason with now that he was five. I was surprised when the new doctor, Dr. Bostrom informed me that there was a new tumor that was growing in a different part of his brain than the original one. This one wasn't "too big," and he felt it was safe enough to wait three more months before scanning Zachary again. The glioma remained stable, which was good. I took consolation in that.

I was very shocked by the change. Zachary had not exhibited any unusual behaviors. There were no indications that anything was wrong. I wished Dr. Moertel was still at Children's so I could get a little more information, but I decided I should trust that this new doctor knew what he was doing. After all he was a pediatric oncologist.

I made a mistake. Three months later Zachary had his follow-up MRI. It was August 29, 2007. After Zachary woke up from his scan we headed upstairs to the oncology clinic for the results and a brief exam. There had been no new symptoms so I remained optimistic.

Dr. Bostrom came into the small room where Zachary and I busied ourselves with some toy cars. He looked experience to me. He was fairly tall, lean, balding with a gray beard and wired rimmed glasses. "So has Zachary been feeling well?"

"He's actually regained his energy and only naps once a day. It's a nice change of pace," I replied.

I figured he was making small talk, but his next question raised some red flags.

"Has he had any problems with his balance, or seemed weak to you?"

Enough small talk. I came right out with it - "Did the tumor grow?"

Dr. Bostrom sat down at the computer and pulled up Zachary's scan from May and opened up today's. The pictures were side-by-side on the screen. "Well, it looks like it has grown a little bit from May, but I think we are okay to wait another three months before we do another brain MRI."

I stared at the pictures side-by-side. I'd seen enough of these to know a little better. My medical background helped too. I didn't want to sound like a know-it-all and I didn't feel it was necessary to tell him I was a nurse because I wasn't an oncology nurse, but I felt I needed to question him. "Are you sure we wouldn't want to do a scan, like, say- six weeks?"

"No. Three months will allow it time to declare itself and to let us know if we need to treat this or not." He sounded sure. He proceeded to examine Zachary, maybe not as thorough as Dr. Moertel, but he said Zachary appeared to have no new physical changes and so he was fine with waiting three more months.

I felt unsettled. My eyes kept darting back and forth at the scans sitting side-by-side on the computer screen. Dr. Bostrom was about to leave and I stopped him in his tracks. I quickly spoke up before losing my nerve to question authority. "You know, that looks doubled to me." I was a bit nervous second guessing his expertise. "I know I'm not a doctor, but isn't doubling in size a significant change?"

I could tell he didn't quite know what to say. He paused, "I still think three months is appropriate to wait, but if Zachary exhibits any symptoms of a headache, vision changes or weakness, definitely give us a call."

I was very surprised with the lack of concern. I left feeling extremely unsettled, but I reassured myself that he was a pediatric doctor working in oncology. He had to know his stuff.

I went about my business once I got home until I couldn't take it anymore. I called my sister Barb once I knew she would be home from work. I told her in detail what I saw in the scans and what this new doctor said. "I don't know, maybe I am overreacting, but I can't deny what I saw - and today's images were definitely doubled in size from May! It's plain as day!" I said.

"You're a nurse, Care, you need to go with your gut feeling!" Barb validated. "What is it that you want to do?"

"I want to find Dr. Moertel, but I was told he left Children's to go into research."

"I could try tracking him down," I could hear her as she pulled up information on her computer. After a couple minutes, she found what I needed.

"So what did you find?"

"He's working at the University of Minnesota - at the Masonic Cancer Center. It looks like he is the associate professor of pediatric hematology/oncology there. Do you have a pen? I've got a number here for you to call."

I finally got a hold of Dr. Moertel the following day. I felt an immediate sense of relief once I actually heard his voice on the other end of the phone.

"This is Chris Moertel."

"Dr. Moertel? This is Carol Ann Bartz, Zachary Bartz's mom," I said not wanting to take for granted he would remember who I was.

"Of course I remember you," Dr. Moertel politely confirmed. "What can I do for you?"

"I had to track you down - so I'm sorry if I am bothering you," I apologized. I hated that about myself, sometimes. I always felt if I needed something, I was bothering or burdening someone else. This time, my apology was only a halfhearted one. I was concerned about my five-year-old son and I would move heaven and earth to keep him safe - any of my children for that matter. "Well, back in May, Zachary was diagnosed with the new brain tumor..."

Dr. Moertel cut in. "I saw that. When Tammie told me about it, I took a look for myself. I was very bummed." I love that he talked to me like an equal.

"Well, Zachary had a follow-up scan yesterday because the doctor we saw in May said we could wait three months before rescanning," I explained. "Yesterday, Dr. Bostrom told me that it grew a little from May, but to me - it looks doubled in size! I know I am not a doctor, but it's plain as day. It's quite a bit bigger!"

I could hear Dr. Moertel fiddling around on his computer. "Bummer, I can't open it up from here. Could you call over to Children's and give them your consent to have Zachary scans and medical records released to here. I'll call too, so that I can view them and I'll call you back tomorrow."

I hung up the phone relieved for the time being that I put my concern into Dr. Moertel's hands. When he called me the following afternoon he asked if I wanted to come see him. I was shocked. "I thought you weren't seeing patients?"

"That was just for a short interim while I was wrapping up things at Children's and getting settled over here at the "U," Dr. Moertel informed. "I'm actually in the process of having a letter sent out to my previous patients letting them know of my new location."

Good, I thought. I wasn't imposing - not like that would stop me from bringing Zachary in to see him. "Yes, I would love to bring Zachary in to see you. How soon can he get in?"

Dr. Moertel made an appointment for Zac himself, to see him in two weeks.

I was hoping for sooner. When he told me he was concerned about the tumor and the rate at which it was growing, I became unsettled again.

While I waited for Zachary's upcoming appointment with Dr. Moertel, he consulted with other colleagues and a neurosurgeon. I was surprised when Nathan and I were at home one evening when he called our house.

"This tumor is very concerning and after having several different colleagues of mine review Zac scans, they all agree we need to do a craniotomy, and soon."

"What?" I couldn't believe what I just heard. A craniotomy is so invasive! I could picture a surgeon pulling Zachary's head apart. No. I don't want this. There has to be another way! "Can't you just start chemotherapy again? It seems to be keeping the glioma quiet," I asked.

"Unfortunately that wouldn't be helpful when we don't know what type of tumor it is," Dr. Moertel explained. "I know this isn't what you want to hear. It's a tough decision."

Nathan stood there leaning against the kitchen counter with a look of concern. "What is it?"

"They want to do craniotomy," I quickly whispered covering the mouthpiece with my hand. "Why can't you just do a biopsy?"

"The neurosurgeons discussed that. The problem with a biopsy is the extreme precision that is required when you can't visually see what is in front of you," he paused. "Carol Ann, the tumor is located 2 mm from the carotid artery and if it were nicked or any of the blood vessels coming off of the artery, Zachary could suffer brain damage or worse."

Dr. Moertel didn't have to spell it out. I knew what he meant. Tears flooded my eyes. I couldn't talk, so I stretched out my arm to Nathan and handed him the phone.

Dr. Moertel explained to Nathan what he just said to me.

"What if we didn't do anything?" Nathan questioned.

"If it continues to grow at the rate that it is, without treatment, Zachary could stroke and die," Dr. Moertel honestly replied.

"Doc, this is tough to take," Nathan admitted. "If Zachary was your son, what would you do?"

Without hesitation, Dr. Moertel said, "I would do the craniotomy."

CHAPTER 9

craniotomy

Several months after Zachary had fallen into the pond, Zac was faced with another life-threatening event and I was blessed with a life-giving event – I was now five months pregnant. In preparation for the upcoming craniotomy on September 26, 2007, I asked Father Al if he could come over for dinner and do the sacrament - The Anointing of the Sick, for Zachary.

Father Al was a unique priest. I loved him the moment he spoke his first time at our church - St. Bridget's in Lindstrom. He was a kind, gentle soul. He lost his wife to cancer years earlier and was told he could join the seminary once he raised his last child. He had five kids and fifteen grandkids. He had been in the military. He was an accountant, "a workaholic," he admitted, not proudly. He was a gymnast and a Golden gloves boxer at one time in his life. He was a hockey dad and a parent who struggled with the trying times of teenage years. He also had a daughter, Carrie, who had a brain tumor that was diagnosed when she was 19 years old.

I was drawn to Father Al because he was so knowledgeable of "real life." I could easily talk to him because he really understood me. And when I questioned God and my faith, he spoke to me in a way that made sense. Because of Father Al, my faith strengthened. I wanted to be a better person.

Nathan and I had him over frequently for dinner. Nicholas, Jessica and Zachary adored him. Many times they would call him "grandpa." He was more than a priest us, he was our family.

It was incredibly meaningful when Father Al anointed Zachary. He presented Zachary with an afghan - a beautiful blue colored child size "prayer blanket" that the women at St. Bridget's made for him. The tears rolled down my cheeks as I witnessed the sacrament being performed in my living room on my five-year-old son. I feared the unknown for Zac. Would he die on the operating table? Would he wake up from surgery and know I was his mommy? Would he become brain damaged because of the risky operation?

Zachary laid his hands out, palm side facing up as Father Al made the sign of the cross on each side blessing them with chrism oil. I thought to myself, *'How could something so beautiful be so horrifying?'* I had to put my trust in God. The "two Jesuses couldn't have saved him that day, only for God to let him die a couple months later, or would He?

I didn't sleep well for several nights before Zachary's brain surgery. The surgery, itself was risky. I was so nervous I was almost sick to my stomach. Nathan and I got Nicholas and Jessica off to school. It didn't make much sense to have them come to the hospital and sit through a six-hour surgery. They didn't fully understand the severity of Zachary's situation. Nathan and I decided to try and keep life as normal as possible for them.

Nathan finished throwing our bags into the car along with Zac's prayer blanket and Bear-bear before we were ready to make the drive down to the hospital. "That should do it. Anything else?"

"No, that should be it. I can always call you when you come back home to be with Nic and Jessica, if we need anything," I sighed. "I don't want to go. Can we just pretend this isn't happening?"

Zachary came out of the house and stood on the landing going into the garage. "Let's get this over with," he said matter-of-factly. He surprisingly wasn't afraid. I thought for sure we would have to drag him out of the house. Man, he sure matured in the past six months!

Zachary knew he had to do this. He knew there wasn't any choice in the matter. He didn't ask any questions. I hoped I had explained well enough to Zachary what was wrong, why he was going to have surgery and how it was all going to happen. I made sure he knew there was going to be medicine to take away any pain that he might have after the surgery. He seemed to understand. I stared at this little boy in amazement. He looked perfectly healthy to me. His blues eyes were bright on his slightly pudgy face, his lips were pink and his short blond hair lay neatly on his head. He looked mature for a five-year-old as he leaned against the door into the house, nicely dressed in his blue jeans - even if he was wearing a t-shirt with a dinosaur on it. I knew if Zachary could be so strong and brave, I would have to do the same.

"Yeah, let's get this over with. The sooner we leave the sooner we can come back home."

We were on our way to St. Bridget's Church to pick up Father Al. He said he had cleared his calendar for the entire day. I felt a sense of comfort knowing he was going to be with us.

My parents and sisters Marie and Barb, met us at the hospital. Nathan's mom and dad showed up shortly before Zachary was taken back to the OR. It was a good distraction for Zachary as well as myself. My stomach was in knots.

I held onto Zachary's hand as he was being wheeled down the bright white hallway to the operating room. Nathan was a step behind. "We'll be waiting right here until you are done. Just think of it as getting to take a nice long nap and if your head hurts when you wake up, the nurse will give you medicine to make it better," I reassured him.

We stopped. The OR doors were standing before us. I didn't want Zachary to go in. I squeezed his small, soft hand a little tighter as I leaned down to kiss it and then kissed his cheek. "I love you sooo much, baby. I'm right here." I tried fighting back the tears, but it was useless at this point. They dripped off my nose. I stepped back to let Nathan have his turn.

"Hey, best buddy. I love you. See you as soon as you're done." Nathan gave him a quick kiss on his forehead.

"We will take good care of him and we'll keep you informed as to how things are going," the nurse promised.

I stood helplessly staring as the OR doors shut and I couldn't see Zachary anymore. I continued to cry as Nathan wrapped his arms around me.

"He's going to be okay. He's going to be okay."

Nathan and I joined the rest of our family in the pediatric surgical waiting room. I sat down next to Barb and my mom. My mom patted my knee as Barb rubbed my back, neither knowing what to say. Nathan joined my dad, Marie and Father Al as they set up to play cribbage for a good distraction.

Twenty minutes went by and a doctor dressed in surgical blue scrubs and cap with his mask hanging loosely around his neck, approached our group. He must have determined I was Zachary's mom by seeing my red tear-stained eyes.

"Are you Zachary's mom?"

"Yes, I am. This is Nathan, Zachary's dad, "I said pointing him out at the cribbage table. Nathan excused himself from the card game and took a chair next to where I was sitting.

He introduced himself as he extended his hand to Nathan and me. "I'm Dr. Graupman. I just want to talk with you before we proceeded with the surgery. We have Zachary all set up and his brain mapped out as to where we want to take the biopsy from."

"He's asleep, right?" I interjected, wanting to make sure he wasn't awake to be afraid.

"He went to sleep without any trouble. We have him positioned in a special surgical chair for the best possible way to navigate around his brain. We have small screws inserted in four different places to keep his head completely immobile."

He must've seen the horrified look on my face because he quickly added, "This is standard for pretty much all brain surgeries. What I wanted to tell you is that I've consulted with a few other neurosurgeons and we were set on doing the craniotomy, but together we somehow came up with a route that we think we can get to the tumor without disturbing the carotid artery."

"So you aren't doing the craniotomy then?" I questioned with a bit of excitement.

"That's our hope, but it's not a for-sure-thing. The biopsy is a very tricky surgery, but it is less invasive," Dr. Graupman explained. "We think we can go in behind Zac's left ear, move his jaw muscle and zigzag our way up to the tumor. If there is any concern that we are too close to the carotid artery or its vessels, then we will stop, close that area up and proceed with the craniotomy."

I thought we were all set on doing craniotomy. I was a bit unsure about the change of plans, but I felt that Zachary's angels must have guided the neurosurgeons in this last-minute decision. A biopsy sounded so much less invasive and painful, that if Dr. Graupman thought this would work and save Zachary a lot less pain and a quicker recovery, I felt this was a better plan. I looked at Nathan for a sign of agreement.

I found myself looking at the clock frequently during the third hour. No one came out to let us know what was going on. It wasn't until around 4:30 pm, four hours after surgery started that Dr. Graupman came out. I held my breath.

"We are closing. Zachary will be moved to recovery pretty soon."

"Closing, meaning you're done - you are able to do the biopsy-way?" I asked unsure of what he meant.

"Oh, sorry. Yes, we were able to get a good-sized sample from going in behind the ear. Zachary did very well."

"What a relief!" my mom said.

"Praise God!" Father Al added as he clasped his hands loudly together in prayer.

There was a sudden release of tension in the waiting room. "Can I see him?" I eagerly asked.

"It'll be about another thirty to forty-five minutes before he is transferred to post-op. Someone will come get you once they get him in there and settled."

Zachary handled recovery without any complications as well. I couldn't believe how well he looked. The only indication of surgery was about five - one inch patches that were shaved into his head where his head was screwed into a device to keep his head still during surgery. Zachary also had about a 2 inch incision by his left ear where his hair was closely shaved, but not completely. For pain, he required Tylenol with Codeine for only two days once we got home from the hospital.

In the ICU, Zachary never complained about pain. However, the look in his distant eyes told me otherwise.

"Zac, does your head hurt?" I asked.

He said nothing as a tear streamed down both sides of his face. He didn't need to say a word. I called for a nurse for pain meds for Zac. I couldn't believe the silent suffering of this beautiful five-year-old boy.

We were quickly back to the routine of our usual activities. Zachary even went to church with us only three days after surgery. I was a bit surprised by an old lady's comment as we were leaving church that evening -"Oh, it looks like *someone* got a hold of the scissors."

I didn't quite know what to say. I didn't feel like explaining that he just had brain surgery, so I just smiled.

After a weekend recovery Zac returned to kindergarten. I didn't worry too much since school was only 2 ½ miles away. The bus picked Zac up at the end of our driveway at 12:40 pm and he rode it home with Jessica and Nic at the end of the school day. It was comforting to know that Jessica, a second-grader, also went to the primary school with Zac and could help him if he needed anything.

Zac really enjoyed kindergarten and loved his teacher Mrs. Krenz. I was glad that after Nicholas had her for his teacher, that now Zac did to. She was such a lovely lady. She was the perfect teacher for young kids. She was so kind, gentle, loving and organized. I knew she was drawn to Zachary immediately when she asked if it would be helpful to make a sleeping space for Zac if got tired. She explained to the rest of the class in the simplest terms why Zachary would be allowed to do this. They were all pretty good about it, with only a few questions. She was so protective of him. I knew he was in good hands with her. I was so pleased to hear her say that at school Zachary would come up to tell her, "I so happy."

A week later, Dr. Moertel called with the results of the brain biopsy. The brain tumor was called a fibrillary anaplastic astrocytoma. He said it was a completely different tumor. He also said he was unable to put a "grade" to the tumor because he didn't know if this tumor was related to the NF. If it was, it would be low grade, it would be localized and grow slowly over a long period of time. If it was not related to NF, it more than likely would be of high grade nature, which would mean it would be more aggressive.

At this point, Dr. Moertel felt, after reviewing with other doctors, oral chemotherapy would be Zachary's best treatment option. Radiation would potentially create the likelihood of Zachary developing more brain tumors which would be of high grade types, and surgery was not an option because of where the tumor was located and the risk of brain damage and death was too great.

I couldn't help but be angry with the lack of concern of Dr. Bostrom just a few weeks back, or maybe was it just stupidity? Had I not listened to my gut and stuck with my thought that I shouldn't question a specialist (one who appeared to be an authority of the situation and diagnosis of my child) Zachary would be in serious trouble.

I wanted to hear what Dr. Moertel thought about it, so I asked. "So what would have happened if we waited another three months like Dr. Bostrom told us to?"

Dr. Moertel sighed. "If you waited, Zac would have stroked or worse yet died at the rate the tumor was growing."

I was appalled that a pediatric oncologist could have given such destructive advice. I wanted him to know the error of his judgment and what his lack of expertise in Zac's situation would have meant. "I have to be honest, I'm very upset with the advice of Dr. Bostrom. I was unsettled a couple weeks ago and I'm really not okay with his lack of judgment," I boldly said. "Do you have the name of who I could write a complaint to so this doesn't happen again, to someone else?"

Without taking offense, Dr. Moertel said, "It's already been taking care of."

I was relieved once again knowing Dr. Moertel had my back and Zac's life was in his hands.

Although I didn't understand how oral chemotherapy could treat something that sounded so severe, I had to trust once again that this was the best treatment plan for him. So far Dr. Moertel hadn't steered us wrong. Zac began oral chemotherapy couple weeks after surgery and after Nathan returned home from his three-week deployment to Germany. I was allowed to give him the capsules at home, even though I was pregnant. It was a bit of a struggle at first. Zac would hide when he saw that I was mixing it up. I was instructed to glove, mask and gown to protect myself and my unborn baby from any possible contamination once I opened the pills. They were horse pills and there was no way Zac would be able to swallow one, let alone eight! Every night, for five nights in a row, I would pour the powder of eight capsules into applesauce or pudding and mix it in as best as I could without having to use too much food. Zac hated it! He would gag and cry and then gag some more. Five days on, and three days off, five days on… This would be the protocol for twelve to eighteen months.

Zac eventually learned how to swallow the horse pills. I was impressed! I had never heard of a five-year-old being able to swallow so many big pills. From working at the hospital, I knew plenty of adults that had to have their pills in liquid form.

Zachary was tolerating the chemo well and the every eight-week MRIs showed that the tumor was shrinking. Come March 2008 we were blessed with a healthy baby girl, Alexandra Ann. She was beautiful and Nic and Jessica were thrilled! Nic, now 10-years-old, was relieved because three weeks before I actually delivered he kept asking, "When will the baby come?"

"It can happen any time now, but my due date isn't actually for another four weeks," I told him. "Don't worry, it'll come."

"I'm worried," he confessed, "because I'm afraid it will die just like the last baby and the two babies before that!"

(After I had lost the baby over a year ago, I shared with Nic, Jessica and Zachary that they would have had two other siblings, but I miscarried twice before Nic was born.)

Needless to say, I was relieved too, when the baby finally came. We were all due for some happy news. Zac was a little unsure as to what he was supposed to do, so he followed Nicholas and Jessica's lead.

Nic, Jessica and Zachary all raced to my hospital room, my mom and dad close behind.

"Sooo… Is it a brother or sister?" I asked holding up the new bundled baby for everyone to see.

"Is it a sister?!" Jessica squealed with excitement.

"Nic?" I asked waiting for his guess.

"I don't know! He excitedly answered as if waiting to open up a Christmas present.

"It's – a – babeee - SISTER!" I announced.

Zachary looked curiously at the new baby and asked, "Can I pet her?"

We were all so happy. I stared at the joy in front to me - the smiles, the laughter. For the first time in my life, I felt complete. I was at peace.

9-21-08 Father Al performing the Annonting of Sick before Zac's craniotomy

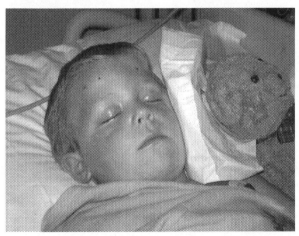

Zac resting after brain surgery 9-26-08

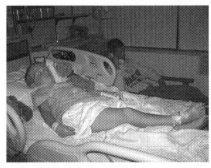

After the craniotomy - Zac and dad 9-26-08

Welcome baby Lexie! 3-7-08 Jessica (8), Nic (10), Nathan, Carol Ann and Zac (5)

CHAPTER 10

round three

The school year came quickly to a close and Zac started his summer off with an MRI on June 17, 2008. It was three months from when we were given the news that the astrocytoma type-tumor was gone. The carefreeness that I felt was wiped away when Dr. Moertel informed me that the tumor was already growing back. I was devastated! Talk about getting slapped in the face. Dr. Moertel admitted he and his colleagues didn't quite know what to do with him. "We don't have another case like him." With Zachary having the neurofibromatosis, it confused and complicated the way the tumors acted and presented themselves.

I researched what actually an astrocytoma was. I had when Zachary was first diagnosed with it, but something bothered me when I recalled the article referring to something about "five-years." At that time, Dr. Moertel thought Zachary's tumor was low grade. He never mentioned anything about putting a time limit on Zachary's life and I never asked.

There it was again in black and white, - "about 90% of children with low grade astrocytomas are alive five years of diagnosis." For high grade astrocytomas, it went on to say they "can rarely be removed totally because they often affect large areas of the brain by the time symptoms are obvious..." Blah, blah, blah... "Currently, the prognosis is poor in this group of patients. Survival rates of 35% to 40% after postsurgical irradiation with chemotherapy."

What does this mean? Zac has neurofibromatosis and that makes everything different for him, I thought, as I tried to convince myself. *Dr. Moertel never said that Zachary could die from this. I wanted to know, but I didn't. Dr. Moertel did tell me that the tumor was a grade three, out of four. It didn't matter. Zac was going to beat this - that's all there is to it! Zachary had a purpose. He had been saved before. His angels were with him - even when at times I think they must be busy.*

July 14, 2008 - Zachary had his port put back in in preparation for round three - to begin IV chemotherapy. He handled the surgery and his first treatment with high-dose carboplatin without any problems. Zac was such a trooper. I continued to be surprised as to how he didn't complain about what he had to go through. Nothing kept him down for too long. He had such a great spirit about him.

It became another new routine for Zachary, Lexie and I to drive down to the University of Minnesota Masonic Cancer Center for frequent kidney function test and monthly chemotherapy. The new clinic was pretty uninviting compared to the Children's hematology/ oncology clinic in St. Paul. The place seemed to always be about 90% adult patients. I occasionally would see a kid undergoing treatment. The clinic was lined with chairs, unlike all the toys at Children's, with the exception of a little corner that had a round little wooden table with kid sized chairs, a few toys and books. Sometimes they would have a volunteer there to do crafts with the kids while they waited to be seen. There is no "little door" just for kids - or adults like me who liked to use it once in a while to get Zachary to smile at my silliness.

Once Zac's lab results were read and we got the "all clear," a nurse would come and escort us to the chemo area. That was worse than the waiting area! There were about twelve or fourteen recliner chairs sectioned off by a curtain in a six by eight foot room. There really was no privacy and it was very uncomfortable being crammed in with little room left for Lexie's baby stroller, but we made do. At least they had small, square televisions on a white steel arm that you could maneuver in front of the recliner to keep Zachary entertained. They did have an activity cupboard where I could get DVD players, games or books and crafts for Zac to busy himself with.

The best entertainment was when the Wii gaming system was available. It was a bit challenging for Zac when he was sitting in a recliner chair. Eventually, he just stood up and moved as far as his IV tubing would allow him to go. He would play for hours. He wasn't about to sit back and waste his day away. It was a great distraction for him. It always made me smile to see Zachary socialize as he made his way down the narrow curtained hallway with his IV pole in tow when he had to go to the bathroom (which was usually three or four times).

Most of the curtains were opened at the foot of the recliners. If the people there happened to look interesting enough to Zac or something about them caught his eye, he would stop and chat after he introduced himself. Sometimes he would even pull himself up to the arm of the chair and peek around the television to see what they were watching on TV. That in itself would start up another conversation. He always had a wave and a friendly smile to pass out. He really spread the sunshine in such a dim situation. I was proud of this beautiful six-year-old boy who was my son.

I ended up volunteering to draw Zachary's blood at home to save us from driving down to the cities twice a week for his lab draws. It saved a ton on gas and hours out of my week, not to mention the hassle of getting a four-month-old baby ready to bring along with for the appointment. I was really nervous at first. I wrote down step-by-step what I was exactly supposed to do when the home health nurse came to show me. I was so afraid of doing something wrong. To me it was so much different than working in the hospital and it was more pressure because it was my own son. If I hurt him, I was worried he wouldn't trust me or worse yet - he would be afraid of his own mother!

I soon became a pro at being a peds oncology nurse. At times I thought maybe I should make the transfer from labor and delivery, but my gut told me – later - when Zachary was healed. Mentally, I needed a break from my reality and fear. I lived with being "on guard" with Zachary, I knew my work had to provide me with a different focus.

This new chemo regime had an accumulative effect and was supposed to "hit" him ten to fourteen days after the chemo infusion. Zachary would then have some time off to allow his body a chance to recover and then when he was feeling good, it was time for another treatment.

Zachary tolerated this type of chemotherapy with the reoccurring extreme tiredness. For a while Zac would ask me if it was "okay to lie down for a little bit?" It made me sad to have such a sweet innocent boy so incredibly tired, feeling like he had to ask if he could take a nap. After a few more times of getting permission for a nap, I would just find him crashed out on the couch or right in the middle of the floor. There was nothing I could do to make this better. Nathan and I just tried to make his life as normal as possible when he was awake and feeling good.

About four treatments into this new cycle of chemotherapy, Zachary started complaining of his tummy not feeling good as soon as he woke up in the morning. He started throwing up more, something that he hadn't done much of with the last types of chemo. Headaches became a regular occurrence as well. I started worrying more that the tumor could be growing.

The following MRIs remained stable. I knew with each MRI, my worrying was useless, but as a mother it was impossible to turn off, especially when I had been caught off guard one too many times already - and that was when Zachary hadn't complained of any symptoms.

At this point in Zac's treatment, Dr. Moertel felt it was time for him to have two big neurofibroids removed from his skull. They were getting bigger and Zac wanted to play T-ball coming up in May. Nathan and I wanted him to be included in the normal activities that little boys do. So we had another consult at Gillette children's hospital in St. Paul. Dr. Woods this time agreed that it would be wise to remove the fibroids. He said that if over time the fibroids would be rubbed up against, or the skin would open over them, they eventually could turn cancerous. A T-ball helmet could cause that and Nate and I were not about to make Zac miss out on yet another fun, normal activity.

Zachary had surgery April 16, 2009. The operation went well and Zac's pain was well-controlled. Surprisingly, he only had to stay overnight because he was doing so well. Again I was impressed. I thought it was a little too soon to be going home after cutting into my son's head, but I knew I could care for him at home just as well as in the hospital. Besides, I knew Zac would be so much happier at home with his brother and sisters.

Recovery went smooth with only the complaint of twenty-some stitches on the right side of his head and eight on his forehead, itching like crazy! Chemotherapy resumed the following week since Dr. Moertel said, "he was healing up nicely."

Zac even made it in time for his first T-ball practice. He was extra excited because Nathan volunteered to be the head coach of his team and Zac's buddy, Thomas, was on his team. They had spent a lot of time playing together before kindergarten. In the winter they would go sledding down the side of our hill, play PlayStation or eat corn dogs. It didn't matter, they always found something to do. I was so happy to see Zac play normally with a good friend. For those moments, it was as if all was okay. There was laughter, wrestling and plenty of farting. It was good!

June 23, 2009, Zachary had another routine MRI. We headed upstairs to the clinic to see Dr. Moertel and get the results like we always had done. This time Dr. Moertel came walking into the room asking, "Do you want to be done?"

I was a bit confused. I stared at him blankly because I didn't know what he meant. *"Done"* – because he thought Zachary had enough chemo and he was letting me make that decision or *"done"* – because he thought things looked good enough to stop treatment. "What do you mean? Is it completely gone?"

"Yes. Well, it is the same as the MRI three months ago - which basically means he is in remission."

I was happy, but at the same time I was nervous to be done when the MRI in April showed the tumor had shrunk to almost nothing. If this scan hadn't changed from April, then it still is "there." I didn't understand. I thought gone meant "gone," as in - "NOT there."

Dr. Moertel believed that the size of the tumor now was as small as it would ever shrink to. He felt it was taking on properties of something similar to scar tissue. I had to trust him. After all, we had been with him for five years now and he was doing a great job in treating Zachary up to this point.

7-14-2008 Zac, dad and Lexie in hospital. The restart of chemo for a brain astrocytoma.

Zac (7 years) and Thomas sliding before school 2-24-09 kindergarten

"So how do you think things might go for Zac since this was the third time he has been treated for tumors?" I asked wanting a prediction.

Dr. Moertel paused a moment as he rubbed his chin with his thumb and pointer finger. I know he didn't know quite how to answer me. "Zac is a difficult case," he stated. "He is quite odd, more or less. He's in a class of his own. What I mean by that is he is behaving completely different from other kids we are treating with neurofibromatosis. Kids Zac's age, with NF, don't get anaplastic astrocytomas. I've consulted with different doctors across the country and when I travel to conferences outside of the state. We are baffled with his case. Honestly, we, I, don't know what to expect - especially since he has sailed through all of this chemo and surgeries."

I didn't know if Dr. Moertel believed in angels, but I knew it was because of Zac's "Two Jesuses,"- "his" angel's. Zac had a purpose. I just wasn't sure what it was yet. So we left Masonic Cancer clinic with the plan of continuing what we had been doing these past five years. It was more "wait and see," but for now, we would rejoice in the good news.

CHAPTER 11

gone, but not "gone"

The rest of the summer was great. Zachary enjoyed a little golf camp and did a short session swimming lesson. I wanted Zac to stay involved in activities because I wanted so much for him to be like his brother and sister. I wanted for him to feel like he could do anything that they could do.

Nic and Jessica stayed busy with hockey camp and soccer. The days were spent playing with friends and swimming. It was a welcomed relief to not have to drive to the city so frequently for chemotherapy appointments. Zachary was slowly feeling better and naps became less frequent. I even ran a few local races and did my second triathlon. Life started to feel normal again.

In the fall, Zachary entered into first grade. They were well prepared to take care of him, giving him the best education they could. They had a program set up for speech therapy as well as help with reading and writing. His teacher, Mrs. Zupko, Nurse Debbie and the principal, Brenda, knew of Zac's battle with cancer and wanted to make school as accommodating as possible. Zachary adjusted well to the new all-day routine, but he started complaining of headaches on and off when school started in September.

I mentioned the headache to Dr. Moertel when Zac had an MRI on September 22, but his MRI appeared to be stable. I asked him if it could be from the strain on his good eye when he tried to read at school. He thought that was possible. I knew I wouldn't get a concrete answer. Soon the headaches began to occur at random times during the day, even outside of school and in no relation to reading. I tried alleviating his headaches with Tylenol or ibuprofen. I gave the school some medicine, to do the same.

December 22, 2009, Zachary was scheduled for another MRI. I was glad Zac had his field trip to the high school pool the day before. He would have been so mad if he missed that. As usual, we headed upstairs to meet with Dr. Moertel for the results.

The MRI confirmed my fear... There were eight new brain tumors! One happened to be on his left brain stem, which controls a lot of body movement and function and two others were on his cerebellum. The other five were scattered throughout the rest of his brain.

I had hoped that Zachary would still be in remission. It had only been five months since his last chemotherapy. *Why can't Zac catch a break*, I wondered? I was angry and extremely sad at the same time.

Dr. Moertel couldn't explain why Zachary wasn't slowing down on the constant regrowth of tumors. He had anticipated that by now, when his rapid growing years tapered off - so would the tumors. Not in Zac's case.

The new plan was for Zachary to begin chemotherapy again on January 12, 2010 - after another eye doctor appointment with Dr. Evan Ballard. Zac would go to the Masonic Cancer Center every other week for about a year.

"Side effects are pretty minimal with this new drug," Dr. Moertel explained, "but Zac will need to be on an antibiotic called Bactrim, for about a year as well."

"Is that because he will be more susceptible to infection because of a low white blood count?" I asked.

"Yes, so make sure you practice good hand washing, keep him away from sick people the best you can." Dr. Moertel shifted in his chair and leaned back on one elbow. "This new drug I want to use is called Avastin. It inhibits the activity of vascular growth which would then cause the tumor cells to basically die off."

"...Because the tumors are fed by the blood vessels, right?" I concluded.

"Right. Tumors thrive off of multiple blood vessels and Avastin has been showing that it is able to signal in on those vessels, stopping the growth of tumors." Dr. Moertel perked up. "I'm really excited about this drug. It is now being used in children that have not responded well to other chemotherapies and we are seeing good results."

I felt hopeful.

"So when can we get started?" Nathan asked trying to be proactive. I knew he wanted to combat the stubborn tumors as much as I wanted - and fast!

"There is one little problem, "Dr. Moertel added. "It is a new drug and some insurance companies are not covering it. It's very expensive!" Dr. Moertel grimaced. "It would cost you about $20,000 a month - and that would be for a year," Dr. Moertel solemnly informed. "I'll make the call to the insurance company. There will be paperwork for me to fill out - letting them know we've tried several other types of chemotherapy drugs so they won't think we are just moving on to the big guns of the chemo meds."

"Can we get started and pay later if it's not covered?" I asked not wanting to waste any time.

"That shouldn't be a problem. I'll work out the details and let you know what I find out."

"Mom, can we go, please?! Zachary interrupted. He was getting anxious about missing out on his Christmas party at school.

Nathan and I needed more information so I felt I had to give Zac some explanation as to why things were taking so long. "Zac, I hate to tell you this, but you're going to have to start chemo again." I didn't need to worry him more by telling him he had eight brain tumors. So I kept it simple.

Zac let out a little sigh, "Ohhh, great!" He pouted. He eventually left for the waiting room thinking he was getting closer to getting out the door to get to school.

I was so frustrated at this point. I couldn't believe we were here AGAIN. I cried into Nathan's arms after Dr. Moertel stepped out. "This is so unfair!"

I wiped my tears and tried to compose myself enough to walk out to get our jackets on. Zachary was a smart little boy. I couldn't hide my red eyes from him.

"Mom, why are you crying?"

I knelt down on one knee in front of him and with a little more honesty, whispered, "Zac, your tumors are back."

With a little more disdain, Zac grumbled, "Now I really am in a bad mood!"

All the way to school Zachary worried about what he might be missing for the Christmas party. We drove as fast as we could without getting a ticket.

Once we got to school and passed out gifts to nurse Debbie and his teacher assistant, Mrs. Nordahl, we finally made our way into his classroom. His classmates welcomed him with open arms.

"Zachary! You didn't miss the dice game!" They chanted excitedly as they gather around him.

"Where were you?!"

"We waited for you!" Another classmate reassured. The kids all stood around him and waited for him to speak. I could tell they were genuinely concerned.

Zac pulled down his shirt from the neck and showed his classmates the Snoopy Band-Aid over his port and disappointedly informed, "I have to have chemo again."

I didn't hear anything after that. The noise of chatter and laughter turned into a calming white noise. I only saw kids surrounding my tough little seven-year-old boy. Everything was okay for Zachary, right now. He was with his friends. It was Christmas time and there was a party in progress. No time for pouting, no time for tears.

Feeling defeated, I still clung on to my faith. I knew deep down that without hope, there was nothing. I refused to give up when Zac had so much love and life in him. If he could go another "round," I could too.

I lost it at work sitting around the nurse's station, talking to my coworkers. I was filling them in on how Zachary and my other kids were doing. I was a bit overwhelmed with it all and informed them that on top of everything, we were denied insurance coverage for the chemo drug, Avastin. It was now into Appeals and we owed $40,000 at this point, if our appeal was denied.

Once again Nathan and I regrouped. We knew we needed to keep Nicholas, Jessica and Zachary's life as normal as possible. Nic continued to play hockey. Zac was even inducted as one of the "coaches", by Mike Lizotte, the head coach of Nic's "A" Pee Wee team, just as Dale Lundeen had previously done and Coach Aaron would later do. Actually, Coach Aaron was not well received by most of the hockey boys on that team or their parents. He was extremely hard on the kids and not very encouraging. Nathan scoffed at me when I confidently said, "Just you wait. If anyone can change him, Zac will." It wasn't long after that Coach Aaron commented to Nic, "It must be pretty cool to have a little brother like Zac." The next game Zac was in the locker room giving the pre-game motivational speech. Coach Aaron was softening up.

Even though Zac couldn't play hockey, he took so much pride in watching his brother play. He was the biggest and loudest cheerleader! Zac was soon going into the locker room before games to give the boys their pep-talk. I don't know who looked forward to hockey games more, Nic or Zac, but when Zac was given the first place trophy for the Faribault Hockey Tournament, you would have thought by looking at his beaming face and bright eyes that he was the one on the ice who played his heart out for the big win.

Jessica kept busy with her gymnastics and piano and I signed Zachary up for martial arts through the school's Community Ed program. We continued to try and make Zac feel he was just the same as Nic and Jessica with the minor inconvenience of chemotherapy. Lexie, now 10-months-old, was easily packed up and came along to whatever event we had scheduled.

The Avastin was thankfully approved. At first Zachary seemed to be tolerating it and the other chemo drug (Irinotecan). Unfortunately, it didn't take long for him to feel the effects of it. He started complaining of a stomach hurting. I always knew when he wasn't feeling well because he would get pretty quiet. He rarely complained. I usually had to call him out on it. Zofran wasn't helping so Atropine was given and Zac started to perk up. The stomach pains continued at home along with headaches. The headaches always made me nervous and now I was told to monitor the headaches because if they became too bad it could be a brain bleed as a result of the Avastin. The chemo could also cause stomach bleeds, but Dr. Moertel didn't think that was why Zac stomach was hurting. He felt his stomach pain would be much worse if it was due to a bleed.

We continued on with our routine at home and Zachary went right back to school. He didn't want to miss out on anything. I was constantly amazed at his strength and zest for life. One minute he could be feeling sicker than a dog or barely able to keep his eyes open and the next, he was cheering on his brother's hockey team, running around having fun with his friends. Zac would take the bad news, dismiss it and then quickly join the party because he wasn't about to waste any of the time that he felt good - feeling sorry for himself. Every time I looked at Zac, I saw hope.

My hope increased when my father-in-law and my dad got a foundation up and running in Zachary's name... The Zachary NF and Cancer Research Fund. It is set up at the University of Minnesota to help support researchers in finding a cure for neurofibromatosis and its cancers. I began to feel that there was something I could do. If God wasn't going to bless Zachary with a miracle, I was bound and determined to find ways to raise money so researchers could find a cure that Zachary so desperately needed.

It took me a little while, but I finally got up the nerve to commit to holding a benefit at the Lindstrom community center. I was afraid people would think I was crazy to hold the benefit and ask for their money. I didn't want them to think I was asking for money for my family, but to find a cure for Zachary that would in turn help save others from the pain and suffering of cancers that had no known cure.

Meanwhile my dad held a pancake breakfast hosted by the Grantsburg's Knights of Columbus organization, that he was involved in. The counsel raised money in different ways to give financial support to families in need of money or for different worthy causes. Zachary's cause was definitely worthy. He even got to be a greeter and was happy to visit with those who attended.

My sister-in-law, Sandy also took up the project of putting together a cookbook -'Recipes for Research' which we also sold, and all money went into the Zachary fund. Slowly it was being built up.

Zac hated the disruption in his life because of the chemotherapy. He didn't like that it took him away from school, his friends or playing. We were at Masonic Cancer clinic, wedged into a little curtained cubicle and Zachary let out a sigh, simply stating, "I hate chemo. I don't want to be here." He wasn't mad or pouty, he was just being honest. As quickly as he spoke, he went back to coloring his picture as he watched his movie.

I looked at him blankly. What could I say that I haven't already said? I couldn't fix this and I think Zac was realizing that. Our hope was that Dr. Moertel and the researchers could stop these random tumors. We had hope, and together Zachary and I talked about our faith in God and that we would never give up! I knew we had to keep believing, keep positive and I couldn't let him ever sit alone with his sadness or disappointment. I could only walk over to Zac and stroke his soft hair. As I bent down to kiss his head the only words I could say in response was, "I know you do, baby. I know."

We tried to do fun things to break up the life we had, all of us had, with the constant doctor appointments, worries and just seeing Zachary tired and not feeling well. Nathan's older brother Greg, set up a stay in the suite of the Minnesota Wild hockey players – Backstrom, Schutz and Koivu. Zac was looking forward to the game for days. Even better yet, Zac was able to bring his buddy, Thomas, with him.

Through the clinic we were offered different family fun activities sponsored by an organization called Hope Kids. Hope kids provided ongoing events like baseball, hockey, football games, movie showings, picnics and waterpark outings, to name a few. It wasn't just for the child with cancer or other life-threatening medical conditions, but for their families who struggled as well. Their belief was like that of Nathan and mine - 'that hope can be a powerful medicine.'

May 18, 2010, four months after starting this new cycle of chemo, Zachary had another MRI. It was good news. Six out of the seven brain tumors were gone! The one on his left brain stem remained there, but Dr. Moertel said it looked like it was dying off. "We're on the right path," he said.

Because Zachary had been complaining of shoulder pain for the past six months, Dr. Moertel ordered an MRI to include images past his shoulders. He suspected something to be growing there. He was right. Zac had fibroids growing on both sides of his neck, more on the left than the right. Zac was also found to have fibroid growth around his heart. I was concerned, but Dr. Moertel said they see this frequently in people with neurofibromatosis and much bigger. At this point there was no plan to do anything different. They would continue to watch them. I was reassured it was nothing life-threatening at this point.

I was pleased with Zac's MRI results, but I felt most of the people I talked to wanted me to be ecstatic. I couldn't be. Yes, I was happy they were going away, but the tumors weren't all gone. I wasn't told, "After this cycle of chemo - he will be cured."

Zachary was always so upbeat. It started worrying me when he seemed more down.

"I wished I could be one of my friends, like Thomas or Austin or Kylie or even you, Mom." Zac quietly said.

I knew he was beginning to see that he was different from his friends, brother and sisters. He didn't understand why this was "his" way of life. This was all he'd ever known. He didn't have a choice in it. He hated it! He hated when he had to go to nurse Debbie's because he was so tired or his stomach hurt so much that he couldn't stay in class. He felt horrible when he missed out on fun things at school or if I had to come pick him up from school because he just felt awful. He always tried to gut it out, but at times, it was too much for him to power through. I hated having to pull him from his much looked forward to summer golf lessons to go for a chemo appointment. There wasn't very many of them to begin with. One day he got really mad when he forgot that he had to go to a chemo appointment.

He started to cry when we got in the car. "I hate this! Why do I have to do this?! I wished I was someone else!"

I was mad for him as well. "I'm sorry, Zac." I had nothing to offer him to make him feel better.

Finally after six months of stomach pain, which Zac's doctors were having me treat as constipation, they said it probably was ulcers. It didn't matter, the Zantac they put him on didn't seem to be helping much at all either. The chemo was wiping him out. He slept through most of the treatment. He usually looked and felt awful afterwards. He ended up vomiting on the way to the car and once again when we were in the car. (I was glad I asked for one of the blue emesis bags.) I was so mad! I wanted to bang my fist on the trunk of the car over and over. I couldn't help but wonder what purpose this was serving. *Hasn't he suffered enough? He's a little boy! Doesn't he deserve a break by now?*

More and more I had the sense that Zachary wasn't a regular eight-year-old boy. I couldn't quite put my finger on it. I couldn't say much to others because I didn't want them to think I was saying that Zac was more special than their child. It wasn't because he was fighting a battle year after year against cancer, but it was evident in how he fought. He bounced back so quickly from bad news, pain and disappointment. Sure he cried and screamed when he was two and three-years-old, but he didn't understand then. It didn't explain his goodness or pureness I felt and saw and how he interacted with people or how he found joy out of every day. He was never in a bad mood. He was all about "please" and "thank you," and when we talked about God and his Angels, he just seemed to really get it. I don't know, maybe I was reaching, but it really felt there was truth into what I sensed. I had a lot to learn from this little boy. I knew I had to live more like him.

The summer flew by quickly, as they always seemed to do. Zac struggled with a cough for about a month. It wasn't pneumonia, thank God, but it worried me all the same.

I was nervous and relieved at the same time when Zachary's next MRI came. I never knew what to expect anymore. This time on July 24, the MRI showed that the tumor on the left brain stem was almost completely gone! No other tumors were visible. Dr. Moertel felt that the two chemo drugs he was using seemed to be working. He did mention that it might be a good idea to stop the chemo altogether because he was concerned about the stomach pains Zac was having due the chemo.

"I don't want him to be incapacitated in any way for the new school year," Dr. Moertel admitted. "What do you think?"

It was a catch 22. "I hate to stop when there is something still there," I said. "Especially with his history of the tumors coming back."

"The rest of the brain tumor may not completely disappear," Dr. Moertel warned as he leaned forward in his chair planting his elbows on his lap while folding his hands together. "What we see could be turning into that scar-tissue we've talked about before."

"I hear what you're saying, and I hate that Zac has so much stomach pain and dry heaves, but I think I'd feel better completing one more round."

"That's kind of what I was thinking," Dr. Moertel sat straight up as he turned his chair to search on the computer for Zac's schedule. "We'll plan for four more treatments, with the last one being Friday, September 24."

With Zac not feeling well most of the time, it made it difficult to go anywhere. I'd have to bring emesis bags and his medicine just in case, wherever we went. I was nervous to leave home to take a trip out to Colorado with Nathan's mom and dad, to their mountain house. The kids were looking forward to it and up to this point nothing stood in our way of having fun. We left a few days after Zachary had his chemo treatment and returned the evening before his next one.

The trip started out okay, but the change in altitude from the plains of Minnesota to the mountains of Colorado took its toll on Zachary and Jessica. Zac's stomach pains intensified and he developed horrible side pain that wouldn't go away until shortly before we came home. He cried and didn't want to do much of anything. Jessica felt sick to her stomach and had a horrible headache. She thought she was going to die. She was so looking forward to this trip and after three days of feeling miserable she cried that she just wanted to go home. It ended up being altitude sickness and Jessica started feeling better by the fourth day. Zac, continued feeling sick, but not as severely. Who would have thought? I ended up calling Dr. Moertel out of concern, mostly because of the new side pain. He was surprised a little that the altitude affected Zachary so harshly and Jessica too. He couldn't explain it except for the possibility of the stress from the change in altitude on his already beaten down body. He encouraged them to drink lots of water and he reassured me that he just had an MRI shortly before we left and nothing should be growing - especially since he was still receiving chemo treatments.

I had to talk myself down. When the kids felt better, I felt better. I saw an immediate change in both of them, mostly Jessica, when we went down the mountain - one or 2000 feet, to go hiking on some state park trails. We did take a break from the mountains and Black Hawk and drove to Vail and into Grand Junction to visit Nathan's aunt and uncle.

Zac hated being tired, but more than anything he hated throwing up. I couldn't explain why he had to go through so much suffering or why he had to continually be sick when his friends would maybe be sick for a day or two and then they were "better." I felt he deserved an answer. I wanted an answer. The only thing I could come up with - that I wanted him to know was that it wasn't God doing this to him, it was the devil. I know some people might cringe at that explanation, but it made sense to Zac and me, for that matter.

"Zac, God loves you soooo much. You know that?" I told him.

"Yeah," he said as he looked up from his puzzle.

"You know how much daddy and I love you, right?"

"Yeah," Zac said as he flashed me a sweet grin.

"Well, I can explain it, but God loves you even more than daddy or I ever could."

"Like a hundred times more?" Zac put two puzzle pieces in and quickly jerked his closed fisted hand back and quietly shouted, "Yes!"

"Daddy and I never want anything bad to happen to you, Nic, Jessie or Lexie. We want you healthy - ALL the time. God does too. He could never pick any one and say - "You - get cancer," "you - get to be in a wheelchair," or "You - get to be in a car accident," I explained as I pointed my finger to imaginary people. "It's the devil that hurts people. I think he wants to try and make you and me hate God by picking on you. He knows you are going to do special things for God, that you are going to get more people to believe in God and the devil doesn't want you to do that. So he keeps picking on you, but you aren't letting the devil win! You are way too strong for him. You never give up. You are such a good boy, Zac!" I wanted him to know it wasn't anything he did that made him sick.

Zac turned his head and confidently said, "I'll never give up! I'll never let the devil win."

Zachary finished his chemotherapy cycle as planned on Friday, September 24. The appointment went as usual with the same complaints of stomach pain and the same meds were given that never really helped. The staff at the cancer care unit gave him lots of hugs as we went around saying our "goodbyes." They said they would miss him and that he always made them smile. It was a bittersweet goodbye.

Zac's stomach continued to hurt, but once we got home, he said, "That's okay, because it is the last TIME!"

I couldn't help but smile. At the same time I felt a gut retching pain because I couldn't fully believe that this was the last time. I didn't let Zachary know of my uncertainties. He was so sure. I wasn't about to accept any other alternative. We would never admit defeat. We believed in miracles.

"That's right, Zac. It's the last time."

CHAPTER 12

a new diagnosis

October quickly approached and Zac's flag football was wrapping up. He loved having normal, fun activities to participate in. He hadn't even been away from Masonic Cancer clinic for two weeks yet and it was time again for another MRI. It was good news. The last brain tumor, the one that remained on his left brain stem was completely gone! A sense of relief came over me.

"Completely gone?" I asked wanting to be sure.

"There are no signs of it or the other seven that were there," Dr. Moertel confirmed. "However, there is still a spot that shows up in the brain, right here," he said pointing to the light image on the computer, "but that has been there for quite some time. It hasn't changed in size for almost as long as it has been there."

"What is it? Is it an indication that a tumor will grow there?" I asked.

"No. We see this commonly in people with NF. They are referred to as UBO's or "unidentified bright objects." Dr. Moertel was pleased with how the last chemo worked in ridding Zac's brain of the tumors.

I wanted confirmation that Zac was all better. I wanted Dr. Moertel to say he had outgrown these tumors and the astrocytoma wouldn't ever come back.

"It's a little too soon to predict anything this close to completing chemotherapy," Dr. Moertel honestly spoke. "If we can get to five years without any further tumors, then we can safely say he is in remission."

I left the clinic that day thanking God for good news. What did all this uncertainty mean? I really felt I needed to make a difference. I was bound and determined to get the ball rolling for the benefit for NF and cancer.

The date was locked in, the down payment was made. March 26, 2011 was the date for the benefit. I had my work cut out for me. Now I just had to figure out how to get started. I had never done anything like this before.

Zac was preparing for his First Reconciliation, a sacrament in the Catholic Church given in second grade when one is old enough to distinguish between right and wrong. One confesses their sins to a priest with the intention of doing their best not to repeat that sin, to make amends by prayer and making it right - if that is possible.

Tonight, November 16 was the second graders first time in receiving the sacrament and receiving God's forgiveness through a priest. I was Zac's second-grade faith formation teacher. I felt I was doing a pretty good job teaching. I stressed to the kids that once they made their confession, they would be forgiven, if they were truly sorry, then they would be clean, with no more sin as long as they didn't commit another sin. I had hoped they would understand and not look at going to confession as a scary thing, but a blessing. Growing up, I knew, I didn't.

It wasn't a large crowd at church, it was a Tuesday and it was just the second graders and their families. The lights in church were dimmed and four priests sat in four different corners of the church. Scripture readings were read, prayers were said and Father Wehmann said a brief homily.

Kids and families were then given the go-ahead to one by one go to a priest for their confession.

Zac knelt next to me on the kneeler. He leaned over to me and whispered, "I'm a little nervous."

"It's okay. You're going to Father Al, right?" I verified knowing he was going to him because he knew him so well. "Father Al loves you. You can tell him anything."

Father Al's line shortened. "Go-ahead, Zac."

I couldn't help but turn my head just enough so I could see Zac talking to Father Al, with Father Al leaning into him so Zac wouldn't have to talk too loud. I was actually nervous for Zac. I hoped he would remember the prayer we had memorized. I hoped I had done a good job in preparing him. Father Al was smiling through the whole confession. What I wouldn't have given to have been a fly on the wall. I knew Zac didn't have anything too serious to confess, so I wondered why he was talking for so long. Two or three kids came back to their pew by the time Zac finished.

As Zac approached, tears were streaming down his face.

"Why are you crying?"

Zac looked up at me and innocently said, "Because I am so happy. I am all clean."

Thanksgiving came and went. The hustle and bustle of Christmas took over. We had Christmas parties to go to. In Mrs. Jackson's second-grade class we made tube-sock snowmen and gingerbread houses out of graham crackers with milk cartons. Zachary loved when I was able to come to his school and help out. It was challenging with Lexie, but the Christmas projects were so fun and Lexie was able to help.

I loved everything about Christmas. From cutting down our own tree, to making dozens and dozens of different kinds of Christmas cookies and candies, to the continual Christmas songs that I played, to the lights and decorations inside and out of the house, I had the Spirit of Christmas captured. Nicholas, Jessica and Zachary (Lexie was still not sure of what everything meant, not being quite two years old) felt the excitement as well. I loved watching them shake their wrapped

Christmas presents as they tried to guess what it could be. I didn't care that they ate a dozen cookies in a day. It was Christmas time!

I was always sad when Christmas was over. The magic seem to dissipate and most people lost the good cheer part. I always kept the Christmas music playing and our tree up until the end of January, if all the needles hadn't fallen off by then.

The kids kept life busy. There was always hockey, soccer and now Zac was involved in archery. Being blind in one eye (confirmed when he was 2-years old when the optic glioma had doubled in size) didn't slow him down. Just as the evaluators in Zac's preschool were amazed when they realize Zachary was the child they were assessing for visual impairment and couldn't believe this little boy zeroed-in on a tiny piece of lint on the rug and picked it up. Zac always exceeded our expectations. I guess that's why Nathan and I never downplayed his capabilities. He always tried, he never backed down from a challenge - well, except for not wanting to ice skate or ride a bike. When it came to those two things he was afraid of falling and hurting himself. Because of the blindness and the lack of balance, characteristics of NF, it made it twenty-times harder for him. We gave up on the ice-skating after putting on hockey skates several times and Zac saying, "I want my boots."

The skates came off and stayed off, but I was still bound and determined to get him to learn to ride a bike. I didn't want him left behind when all of his friends would take off down the road. When I explained why I wanted him to learn, he said he didn't care. I knew he did, but he was just afraid. There was always next spring and summer to learn, I would say.

In early January, Zachary started throwing up again. He threw up before bed, but quickly said he felt fine. The next day he said he didn't feel well before school, but he didn't say he wanted to stay home. I thought it was leftover from the effects of chemo and I figured it would pass. I ended up picking him up from school about two hours later. He was fine all day Saturday and then instantly said he didn't feel good and ran to the bathroom. It didn't resemble the flu to me. I wasn't sure what to think. I tried staying calm of mind. *"Kids get sick,"* I reminded myself. *Maybe it was the flu."*

A week later, Zac had another MRI. It was January 14, 2011. I had prayed that this new year would be better than the last. Zac was feeling better and I was hopeful by the news that the previous drugs he was on, was working for others who had NF and a brain tumor.

I sat in the MRI room at the foot of the scanner were Zac laid. There happened to be a television screen in the upper right corner of the room that I kept glancing at. I thought I would be able to read it myself and calm my nerves until I saw an obvious large white spot in Zac's brain. I panicked and my hands stated to shake, my chest was pounding so hard I could see my shirt move.

I knew bright white meant tumors. It looked all too familiar. I thought for sure it was another brain tumor, but I was no doctor. *Maybe this was someone else's picture that happen to be left up,* I thought hopefully, but I knew it wasn't. The pictures changed with the beating, pounding and clicking of the MRI.

I stopped what I was working on and began to frantically pray through the rest of the MRI.

While waiting for Dr. Moertel, a child life specialist came in and asked Zac if he wanted to play some games on an iPad. Zac was not one to refuse electronic games. Immediately I sensed it was a form of distraction. I wanted to cry, but I held my composure.

Dr. Moertel looked grim when he walked into our room.

"It's not good, is it?" I whispered so Zac couldn't hear.

"I'm afraid not."

The tears rolled down my face. Dr. Moertel put his hand on my arm. "I'm sorry it's not the news you were hoping for."

"Could that be why he was sporadically throwing up last weekend?"

"It very well could be. What I do know is that this is the same tumor he had when he was five. I wanted to be sure - that's why I took a while getting in here. I consulted with a few colleagues," he explained.

"How do you know without doing a biopsy of it?" I said wiping my nose with the back of my hand. *Where are the kleenexes when you need one?*

"Because it is growing in the same exact spot as the one he had there and it looks the same on MRI when you look at it in density and on different levels."

I didn't care what the results were. I just wanted it gone. "So what do we do?"

Zac picked up on the tension. It was kind of difficult to hide. "What's wrong?"

I hesitated and glared at Dr. Moertel. I didn't want to tell him the bad news. Dr. Moertel picked up on my ambivalence.

"Zacky, I'm sorry to tell you - but your tumor is back.

Zac looked up from his game he was playing and said, "Nooooo…!" He began to weep for a moment and then he was back to playing on the iPad.

After our conversation with Dr. Moertel, he sent us to see Dr. Dusenbury, radiation doctor that would be managing Zac while he went through radiation. I took a liking to her. She was kind, gentle and interacted well with Zachary. Once Dr. Dusenbury introduced herself to me, she immediately turned toward Zac and talked with him about fun, every day normal stuff.

Since Zac was squeezed into her schedule, Dr. Dusenbury said she didn't know the whole plan yet. "What I can tell you at this point is what I'll be managing. I know Dr. Moertel is consulting with other doctors to see if surgery is possible and I can tell you we are doing radiation. It will be for six weeks - Monday through Friday."

"Is that something we can do up at the hospital by us - Fairview Lakes?" I asked.

"No. It has to be done here at the University. We have a very precise machine called the Tomograph that we need to use."

"Okay," I was a bit in shock. I didn't care where I had to take Zac, I just wanted someone to fix him. Oh, how I wished Nathan was here with me instead of at home entertaining Lexie.

"Before we can get started, we need to fit Zac with a pretty tight, net-like mask to hold his head completely still during radiation. Once we get the mask made, we can get exact measurements and dimensions for radiation," Dr. Dusenberry explained.

"So when do we get the mask made? Today?" I eagerly hoped.

"No. Not today. We will have someone call you with the details." Dr. Dusenbery could have gotten up and left, but instead she sat a little a little longer, looking like she was trying to figure out if I was going to be okay or not. "Is there anything else I can do for you?"

I just wanted her to fix my son and promise me that everything was going to be okay. I knew she couldn't. I knew this was serious. Instead I simply hung my head and said, "No, that's okay."

I drove the forty-two miles home crying on and off. I hoped Zachary couldn't tell how upset and worried I was. The constant sniffling may have given me away. I didn't want to have to tell Nathan. He was going to be leaving on a military trip to Puerto Rico for two weeks. How would he be able to leave? How would I be able to let him go?

Zac fell asleep on the car ride home. I was beside myself with this horrible news. I had to call someone. I grabbed my cell phone. I was afraid to say the words because I knew once I did, it would make it more real.

"Moooommm…" My voice quivered.

"Hellooo?" she answered concernedly.

"Mom. Zac had his MRI this morning." I tried staying strong, but my voice broke. "It's not good. It's really bad!"

"Oh, no. I was waiting for your call. I had it on my calendar that the MRI was today."

"It's the same tumor he had when he was five years old! Dr. Moertel says that they will do radiation and then surgery or surgery then radiation."

"When will they know?"

"Dr. Moertel is consulting with neurosurgery and will get back to us after the weekend," I paused. "Mom, Nathan has to leave on his military trip next week!" I started to sob, forgetting Zac was in the backseat.

I woke up Zac. I was so mad at myself.

"Mom?" Zac groggily asked. "Why are you crying?"

"Zac, I'm sorry I woke you. I'm crying because I'm so sad your tumor is back," I honestly said. Hoping to distract him, I held the phone out to Zac. "Do you want to talk to Grammie?"

"Sure," he said grabbing the phone from my hand.

When Zac was done talking he passed the phone back up to me. "I'll call you when I find out more. I just wanted to let you know what's going on."

I was able to pull myself together for the most part until Zac got inside and was downstairs with Nic, Jessica and Lexie. Nathan was standing in the dining room by the sliding glass door.

"So, how did it go?"

I couldn't speak. My throat tightened as I rush towards him, throwing my arms around his waist. I started sobbing.

"What's wrong? What is it?"

"It's bad Nathan, it's…r-e-a-l-l-y b-a-d," I cried into his shirt.

Nathan waited for me to explain.

I tried to catch my breath in between sucking in gulps of air. As my breathing slowed down I felt ready to speak. I lifted my head up and took a step back. "The tumor that Zac had when he was five years old is back - the anaplastic astrocytoma. The one where there is no cure f-o-o-o--r-r."

Nathan held me close.

Nathan was silent for a minute taking it all in. "Did Dr. Moertel say what can be done?"

"They are trying to decide if they should do radiation first or surgery. Dr. Moertel said something about Zac taking that same oral chemo that he took last time, to work with radiation." I stood up straight and wiped the streaking mascara from my face and eyes.

"When will we know? You know I'm supposed to be deployed for that two week trip on Thursday."

Nathan and I were sick with worry all weekend as to what was going to happen and what Zachary was going to have to endure. We agreed that we would do our best to put on our happy faces so as not to worry Zac or the other kids, for that matter.

Monday came with no phone call regarding the plan, so I called in the evening thinking they were still busy trying to get a plan together. I left a message for Dr. Moertel to call back. He called about twenty minutes later.

There was still no plan.

"We are having our care conference on Wednesday when Zac's case will be discussed by several doctors, including a neurologist, radiologist and a few other specialists. We'll have a plan by Wednesday," Dr. Moertel stated.

"We really need to know because Nathan is supposed to leave on a military trip on Thursday."

"Is he going back over to Iraq?" Dr. Moertel asked.

"No. It's a two week trip."

Nathan motioned for the phone.

"Oh - Nathan wants to talk to you," I said quickly passing the phone off.

Nathan talked with Dr. Moertel for quite a while and hung up the phone.

"What else did he say?" I eagerly asked.

"Not much more than what you've already told me," Nathan vaguely spoke. "He thought that I would be okay to go on my trip because he thought they would more than likely do radiation first to try and shrink the tumor down as much as they could before they would operate. I don't know if I could get out of this trip anyway, this close to deployment."

"It's a family emergency! They would have to let you stay home," I shot back. "Wouldn't they?"

"I don't know," Nathan said running his hand through his hair. I could tell he was stressed out. "I'll let them know at the base and see if there is anyone on standby, just in case they decide to do surgery first. Dr. Moertel gave me his cell number. I'll call him if I need him to do anything or answer any questions."

It was my turn to be strong. I grabbed Nathan and hugged him tight. "It's going to be okay. It's gotta be. Zac is a tough kid."

Finally on Wednesday the 19th at 5 pm, Dr. Moertel's nurse coordinator called. All she could tell me was that we would not be doing surgery. I didn't understand why and she couldn't tell me. *Did they think they can get it by strictly doing radiation? Is it inoperable or would the risk of brain damage be too great if they did surgery?* I asked the nurse if she could have Dr. Moertel call us back to answer more questions. Until then, the only thing I could do was to pray with all my might that God would show mercy on my little boy and that Zac's spirit would hold strong and not be broken.

Since Zachary wasn't going to have surgery, I told Nathan to go ahead with his already planned military trip. I felt I could handle the upcoming appointments with Zac and the preparation that was required prior to starting radiation. Dr. Moertel told him there wouldn't be too much that he would miss out on. I also wanted Nathan to get the trip out of the way early-on in the radiation treatment, rather than later, when Zac might start feeling the effects of it.

I brought Zachary to meet with Dr. Dusenberry again the day after Nathan left. I asked her what the reason was for now deciding not to do surgery. The answer was not what I expected at all.

"From our conference meeting on Wednesday, it was determined that the tumor has grown too deep," Dr. Dusenberry paused briefly, "and-if surgery was done - Zachary would not be the same boy."

I knew without asking she meant that Zac would be severely brain-damaged.

"We will use Sinitunib/ Temserolamide, the oral chemo he used three years ago in conjunction with radiation."

"Will that really help being he was on it before and developed additional brain tumors?" I asked.

"It's standard protocol therapy and Dr. Moertel agreed to give it a go. He said, "It won't hurt him.""

Zac busied himself by coloring with markers on the exam table paper in the small examining room. I was hoping he was too intent on what he was doing that he wasn't paying attention to boring adult conversation.

Dr. Dusenberry shifted in her chair. "You know that radiation really isn't a cure, but it is more or less used to manage the tumor. The type of tumor Zachary has usually comes back even if surgery is performed."

I hesitantly asked, fearing the answer, "What happens if the tumor comes back?"

Dr. Dusenberry quietly said, "They usually succumb to it."

I couldn't believe what I was hearing! *'This isn't real! This isn't real!'* - throbbed in my head. *What is she saying?* I think I was in shock. Maybe the word "succumb" meant something else, but then again her voice grew more quiet when she said that.

"Dr. Moertel usually has something up his sleeve," Dr. Dusenberry tried to reassure.

That wasn't good enough. I needed something to work, NOW! Zac was nine-years-old. He has been battling brain tumors since he was two-years-old. I couldn't believe that we were being told for the fifth time in seven years that Zac had another brain tumor return. The severity of the tumors only seemed to be worse each time. I was so afraid. I was afraid of losing a life that was so full. Zachary's spirit was the most beautiful I had ever experienced. I was not about to admit defeat.

The remainder of the appointment was spent in radiology/imaging were Zac was measured and fitted for the radiation mask.

"Can you hop up here or do you need a lift?" Tim the radiologist tech asked Zac playfully.

"I think I can do it," Zac said backing up to the tomograph scanner.

I wanted Zac to feel at ease. I wanted to take away any anxiety or fear he may have in this untraveled territory. "I bet he can do it. He's really strong, you know? You should see his muscles," I joked around with him.

Zachary sat at the edge of the hard manila scanner and played along. "Do you want to see my muscles?"

"Oh, Zac! I'm not sure they can handle it. They might get jealous," I continued on with the charade.

"Okay, big guy," Tim cut in. "Let's see what you got."

Zac started to push up his sleeves, realizing he wouldn't be able to show off his muscles, justly, so he began to pull his arm out from one of the sweatshirt sleeves. Excited, he got a little twisted up, so I stepped in to help remove his arm from the other sleeve. I stepped back.

"Okay guys, you're ready?" Zac asked with a devious smile.

"Oh, we're ready!" Tim replied.

Zac flexed both arms up, one at a time, "Bam-BAM! F-i-i-rree POWER!"

"Holy COW!!!" Both men exclaimed at once.

"You better put them away before someone calls security," Tim got serious. "You know they don't allow guns in the hospital?"

Everyone laughed. The tension was broken, even if it was momentarily. I was just so glad that Zac was smiling and laughing in the midsts of such unfairness.

Tim helped Zachary position himself on the long narrow scanner bed. For an instant my mind wandered. *Is this what it looks like - my little boy lying ever so still - in a coffin?* I gasped for breath. I felt myself beginning to hyperventilate. *"What? Where did that come from?! Stop it!! Hail Mary, Hail Mary, Hail Mary, Hail Mary, Hail Mary,* I quickly repeated over and over in my head to chase away such an evil thought.

Zachary remained very calm and cooperative with the whole process. He sure had come such a long way from the two-year-old boy who would kick and scream and needed to be held down.

Dr. Moertel came by after Zac was fitted for his mask. I had questions. I wanted answers. He told me two different neurosurgeons looked at Zachary's MRI scans and they said, they wouldn't touch him. I wanted reassurance. I wanted Dr. Moertel to tell me Zac could beat this.

"I can't put a survival rate on Zac. I don't even know if it would be a 70% chance or 30% chance. I just don't know," Dr. Moertel solemnly admitted.

I wanted something to hang onto. I wanted something to strengthen my wounded faith.

"I'm just pleased that this type of tumor has stayed away for three years. Those three years have allowed for more brain development before, now, HAVING to do radiation."

So now, I guessed I was supposed to pray that the combination of radiation and oral chemo will keep the tumor away long enough until some new drug could be found for Zac. That's not a good feeling, but it was some hope. It's the only hope we had in saving Zac's life.

I had come believe that maybe God was using both of us to work together in finding "that" cure. So many people had already come to know and love him. In raising that money and with Zac's strong belief, faith in God and will to live, just maybe, a cure would be found. Maybe people were meant to see how the face of a young Christian boy could sustain a determined life - because he truly believed. I believed in Zac. I believed his "two Jesuses" saved him for a reason. He couldn't have lived only four years more to have it just end now. I knew I couldn't waste any more time. I had to get moving on the benefit!

Family and friends were concerned. We were receiving emails and a few phone calls about different surgeries, one even being where you sucked out the tumor. Even, from Puerto Rico, Nathan forwarded Dr. Moertel the emails. Dr. Moertel told Nathan it wouldn't work in Zachary's case.

"I will keep him going, I promise," he told Nathan.

I had to trust him. He was a great doctor and had never led us astray. I would not believe for a second that Zac's time was limited on this earth. This by no means was over! I would hold onto this hope as Nathan and I would explore other options and cancer treatments for Zac.

One day when Nathan was talking with our neighbor, Donny, he told him about a friend of his who had studied mushrooms extensively. Leroy said there are certain ones that have cancer fighting qualities and he himself felt his cancer was cured by these mushrooms. Donny said his sister also ate the mushrooms and was in remission from stage IV breast cancer. Leroy, the mushroom man heard of Zac and gave Donny mushrooms that he picked for him. He really believed in their healing properties. They were Shiitake mushrooms. Nathan and I did some more research and explained to Zac what their purpose was. He was agreeable to eating them.

At first he really liked them cooked up with butter, but it didn't take long for the novelty to wear off. Soon he started gagging on them. I changed up the presentation and put them on his chips and covered them with plenty of cheese. Zac tolerated this. We were willing to try anything! Nathan even went out with Leroy a time or two to hunt for these mushrooms. We would need a lot of them!

Driving home from the preparatory radiation appointment, a sense of fear came over me again. How well do I know my own child? I wanted to ask him one-hundred-and-one questions, but I asked him just one for now… "What are your most favorite things to do?"

Zachary had to only think for a second before answering. "Going to see Minnesota Wild (hockey team) play and talking to God every day."

I wasn't expecting the latter response. His heart was so good, but his answer frightened me. *What did he know? Was he already talking to God?* I prayed he would be content talking to Him from here.

Being alarmed, I had to ask, "You don't want to go to heaven and talk to God now, do you?"

"No, not right now," Zac casually said.

CHAPTER 13

"no penalties!"

I didn't know how I was going to do everything, especially with Nathan gone. With having to get Zachary down to the U of M, which happened to be a fifty minute-drive, if not more in the morning rush-hour, I would have to get up early to get myself, Zac and Lexie ready. I was not a morning person. With Nathan gone, I always stayed up much later than I should - cleaning up the house, getting the kid's stuff ready for school the next day and taking a little time to sit on the couch to veg for a little while, but not until I had brought kids to and from hockey and soccer.

It became overwhelming at times when I thought about just starting the process of radiation with Zachary and imagining week four or week five. *How could he do this?* I took a leave from work.

My alarm clock went off at 7:00 am, the morning of January 31. I lay in bed dreading what this day held. "Here we go," I whispered as I threw my covers back.

Zac, Lexie and I headed off to the hospital after getting Jessica off to school. Nicholas had already caught his 6:50 am bus for middle school. I had the gogurts, Eggo waffles and cups of juice for Zac and Lexie to eat in the car on the way. I wasn't about to wake up Zac or Lexie, for that matter any earlier than I had to. I felt bad enough waking Lexie up knowing she could easily sleep another two or more hours. I hoped six weeks of this wouldn't screw up her sleeping schedule.

When we got to the bowels of the hospital and were waiting in the waiting room, I grab Zac's hand and gave it a squeeze. "Are you nervous, Angel?"

"No," Zac simply said, then smirked his cute smile.

I hoped that he didn't think too much about the radiation. It was so hard to tell what was going on inside his head. He was always so compliant and just did what he was told. I didn't pry for more information because I wasn't sure if he was trying to cope in his own way or if he was trying to protect me from worrying. I worried anyway. He appeared quieter than usual. He wasn't his vibrant little self. He probably sensed my sadness and fear. I know he had seen me cry many times in the past two weeks. I probably scared him a time or two. I hated that I couldn't conceal my fear better from him, but this was just too big to be able to stuff.

As a mother I felt Zachary deserved a little of the truth. I told him what he needed to know and what to expect. Nathan and I didn't tell him the severity of the diagnosis. We were afraid that we would only scare him and change who he was and how he lived.

Zac had to have questions even though he hadn't asked any. I think he probably heard my telephone conversations or when Nathan and I would talk on occasion. It was hard to have any private conversations with four young kids around. I think he determined for himself that he wasn't going to let fear or medical procedures dictate how he was going to live his life. Just like a brave soldier, he does what he is told. He knew Nathan and I were trying to help him beat this terrible beast.

Zachary's name was called and we walked beyond the heavy steel radiation doors. Zac casually climbed onto the table that slid into the tomograph scanner. Carefully his white "Spiderman-like" mask was placed over his face and screwed into the table. Not a word. I wanted to cry, not because it was so scary, but I couldn't believe this was what we had come to. It was one more thing he "HAD" to do.

My prayer life quickly ramped up. I hoped my prayers were sincere enough for God and that I had done plenty of "thanking" because now, I definitely was "wanting." I wanted the radiation to work. I wanted the radiation to do more than just manage the tumor. I prayed for a miracle - for COMPLETE HEALING. I just prayed that Zachary would continue to surprise the doctors by conquering the unmentioned odds this time, as well.

The appointment didn't last long at all. We seemed to only be there about 30 minutes, including parking and waiting before we turned around to go home. Zachary decided he wanted to go to school. His life was normal there for the most part. He was with his friends and had a fantastic teacher, Mrs. Jackson. Being that this was his first treatment, I hoped he would feel okay. I couldn't imagine that he would feel the effects of radiation so quickly, but by the end of the day he seemed so tired. His retching and vomiting still continued from even before we started radiation.

In the middle of his third week of radiation, Zachary started doing really well - probably his best day since November. He came home from school with a little skip in his step telling me, "I didn't even go to nurse Debbie's today!"

Zac didn't even get sick once at home. This was a first. Most days he was completely wiped out. Usually by 7 pm he was hurting and wanted to go to bed. Tonight was no different. At least the nausea and vomiting didn't bother him today. Sometimes I would find myself looking at him amazed at who he was and how he was able to deal with such burdensome afflictions. I could only imagine how he must be feeling. Zac had been struggling daily with the whole nausea-vomiting thing for four months now. That's not including the nine months of severe stomach pain. Yet, he gets up when asked to do something, like a chore of some sort (unload the silverware from the dishwasher, empty the garbage or wipe the stairs) or he volunteers on his own. He tried so hard to get his homework done, but some evenings I had to just tell him, "We can do it later." Getting that permission was all he needed and then he would crawl into bed.

I brought Nic and Jessica to one of Zac's radiation appointments because I wanted them to see what Zachary actually had to go through. I felt out of six weeks, they could miss one day of school. Besides, we had Minnesota Wild hockey game tickets and VIP passes to meet the players after the game. It was made possible through Defending the Blue Line - a military organization whose mission is to ensure that children of military members are afforded every opportunity to participate in the game of hockey - one way or another. I hoped that by going to Zac's appointment, they would develop a sense of compassion now that they were older. I hoped that they could understand a little better by seeing what it was that Zac went through day in and day out.

I understood that Nic would get frustrated that Zachary was always tired and that he couldn't run, wrestle or play like other little nine-year-old brothers could. It always made me sad when he would push Zac into a chair that he was standing by, and yell, "Why do you have to be such a baby?!"

Many times Zac would cry out of hurt and frustration. I could see it in his eyes. "Nic, knock it off! He doesn't feel good," I defended.

"Yeah, well, he hardly ever wants to play!" Nic shot back.

"Don't you think he hates feeling sick and being tired all the time?" I wanted so badly to yell at him and say – 'How would you like to change places with Zac and see what it feels like?' - But I was able to control myself. Instead, I said, "If Zac rests for a while, maybe he'll feel like playing later."

"You always take his side!" and he stomped out the front door.

Jessica had her moments too. The year before when Zachary was going through chemotherapy, Jessica's happy, spunky attitude turned very dark. She was a very angry 11-year-old. I thought maybe it was hormonal. When I started noticing a lot of anger and harsh comments toward Zac, I started wondering what was going on.

Jessica came home from school one day crying the, "I hate school! I hate everyone there!"

"What's wrong?"

"I hate school. I hate being home and the only place that I like is at my piano teacher, Jennifer's, at least she understands me!"

The red flags were flapping in my face. I told them over and over that no matter how much Lexie and Zachary needed me, it didn't mean I loved them any less. Where did I go wrong?

"I thought you felt like you could always talk to me?" I calmly stated, putting my hurt feelings aside.

"Used to! Now you're too busy! Jennifer takes time to talk to me after piano lessons and she said I can come over and talk with her anytime I want," she paused, "if that's okay with you."

I didn't quite know what to say. I felt like I had to defend myself. "Jessie, you know how demanding Lexie is and how much attention she needs. You know I can't help it that I have to take Zac to the doctor and help him when he's sick. What I am I supposed to do?"

"I know," Jessica pouted. "That's why Jennifer could talk with me."

I wanted to help her. I had always wondered how Nic and Jessica were really coping with this lifestyle. It was finally bubbling to the surface. "Do you think you would rather talk to Father Wehmann or a counselor or Father Al, if he's not too busy with his new assignment?" I thought maybe someone with counseling experience would be able to get to the core of the problem and maybe I was a little jealous another woman was taking my place.

Later that evening I cried to Nathan. "I'm a horrible mother! My own daughter doesn't even like me!"

"Of course she does. Jessie is just going through a phase. She'll get over it," Nathan comforted.

I knew better. It was a cry for help. Like me, when I was young, we both needed attention. Instead of verbalizing my needs, I dismissed my feelings. Jessica on the other hand was strong enough to voice her problem.

I made a conscious effort to give her more attention, more one-on-one time and we started our ritual of reading Angel stories from the book, 'Angels Among Us,' before she went to bed each night. Within a week, things had started to improve. I was on the right track, I hoped. It was a little early to tell how things would go, but I at least now I was much more aware of how badly my other kids needed me too.

Lexie was even feeling the brunt of the chaos. She wasn't the sweet little toddler I once knew. She was getting to be demanding, at times rude and threw little temper tantrums. Nathan and I wondered how she could be so different when we raised Nic, Jessica and Zac all the same way. Many times Nathan would say, "I'm not raising a brat." I hoped it was the terrible two's but not happening until she was three.

Having Nic, Jessica and Lexie at the appointment with Zachary made a huge difference. It wasn't so somber. Nic raced Zac down the halls and then playfully roughed him up. There was giggling and teasing, but it was all in good fun. I had to tell all of them to settle down in the radiation waiting room so they wouldn't disturb the other patients. They continued to talk softly while I read Lexie a book.

"Zac," Laura, the radiation technician called out.

"Come on, guys. Time to go in."

The five of us stood up and walk together towards the room with the tomograph machine. It was almost as if we were part of Zac's Army battalion. He wasn't going this alone.

Upon seeing the big machine with a hole in the middle, Nic surprisingly uttered, "Wow, Zac, it looks like a big spaceship!"

Seeing such a foreign machine that their little brother had to lay on with a tight fitting mask that left netting impressions on Zac's face, softened Nic and Jessica. They began to gain more compassion and respect for the intimidating and scary things that Zac had to do. Often times I would hear Nic or Jessica admit "How do you do that?! I could never swallow all of those pills," or "Boy, Zac, you sure are brave. I could never have a needle poked into MY chest!"

Zachary was doing better in regards to the frequent bouts of retching and vomiting once he was put on the steroid Decadron. It alleviated enough of the swelling and pressure that was pushing on the center of the brain that controlled the vomiting. This was now caused by the radiation and not a growing tumor, according to Dr. Dusenberry. Zachary started gaining weight as well because of the steroid side effects. It was especially noticeable in his face. He hated it! The weight gain was happening so quickly, it made me nervous as well.

Dr. Moertel explained, "You could just be done eating dinner and you'll be hungry again. What you have to remember is that it is your head telling you that you are hungry - not your tummy."

Zac's radiation appointments wore on him as well. He missed half of every day of school. He was pretty upset after one radiation day. He wanted to get to school right away. When he found out that Dr. Moertel was an hour behind schedule, he was mad! He wasn't mean, just irritated. "No talking," he sternly warned me. "Let's just hurry up and go!" He was on a mission to get back to school. He had a spelling test that he was planning to "ace" and didn't want to miss it. He also said he didn't want to miss Phy-ed or lunch.

"If I miss lunch, I will be so mad!" Zac's voice rose in agitation. He sat *back* in the chair with his arms crossed.

I was a bit surprised because Zachary was usually calm and cooperative, as he got old enough to understand that no one was purposely trying to hurt him. I understood where he was coming from and even if he had a cold lunch today. It was the fact that he just wanted to be where the rest of his classmates were. I was glad he vented. I wished he would do more of it. I suppose he knew being angry and verbalizing it wasn't going to change anything, so why bother? I guess that's what made him so special. For a nine-year-old boy, he had already figured out how to live.

His happy bright spirit was contagious. He attracted children, adults and even strangers by his sunny smile and positive attitude. I could see the truth in the saying, "anger breeds anger and love breeds love." Zachary was a walking ray of sunshine. I had many adults pull me aside to tell me, "I could be having a really bad day, then Zac walks in the room and flashes me one of his smiles and genuinely asks me - 'How are you? Have a good day! He is the politest boy!"

As Zachary grew older he matured even faster. He appeared to understand people, God's love and how to live - all on his own. Sure, we prayed together, talked about God and went to church every weekend, but he seemed to have a greater understanding beyond his years. Many times I questioned if I had been blessed with a real Angel. *What was I supposed to learn from him?*

All of my kids were gifts from God. I knew it didn't mean I wouldn't yell or get mad at them. I just wanted to work harder on how I dealt with frustrating situations. I wanted to be a mom I could be proud of. I wanted to be a mom my children could love, trust and not be afraid of. I think Zac was trying to teach me patience and humility. I had my work cut out for me.

One day Dr. Moertel informed me there was a vaccine already underway and they just got the funding to add anaplastic astrocytoma to it. He said if it makes it past phase 1, it may become a possibility down the road to try on Zac. He felt that radiation would hold Zac longer than what chemotherapy did. Hearing this, it increased my hope that there would be more time for a cure to be found.

My sister, friends and I continue to work quickly towards our upcoming benefit. It was fast approaching and so much was left to do. I pounded the pavement, days on end, going to every business in Chisago City, Lindstrom, Forest Lake and Wyoming asking for something for our silent auction baskets. Calls were made to other cities for ski and hotel packages, donations were dropped off at my house by friends and acquaintances who wanted to help. We had to make this big. We had to raise money to find a much needed cure. I had to save my son!

With only a week left of radiation, Zachary's hair was really falling out in patches. I noticed a big difference when he was lying on the couch and turned his head. I had to hold my breath to keep myself from gasping when I saw a pile of his hair on the pillow. Up to this point it hadn't been too noticeable. The front right side of his head was bare, there were also large circular patches of hair missing in random areas on his head. It came to a point that his remaining hair look very odd, more so than if I would just shave it all off.

Zachary was sad and shed a few tears at first, but he turned it around and insisted on a Mohawk. Part of his hair was already missing and looking almost like one anyway, so I complied with Zac's wishes. The only thing that mattered was that he was happy. If he had to lose his hair, why not finish it on his terms?

Nic's hockey teammates made it to regions and all the boys, including Zac, decided to bleach their hair tow-head blonde. For many of the boys, it didn't quite turn out and Zac ended up looking a little like a skunk. I'm not sure if it was my lack of beautician schooling or if radiation had something to do with our mishap, but it didn't matter one bit. He was pleased and thought he looked like one of the guys.

With four more radiation treatments to go, Zac was really struggling. He was sick with random, frequent bouts of retching and vomiting. He had to carry an emesis bag with him in his coat pocket or backpack wherever he went. I hated seeing him race for the big garbage cans in the ice arena if we forgot his blue bag. He was incredibly tired, but somehow still managed to make it to the important events. He always chose to go even if it meant sleeping three-fourths of the way through church. He definitely wanted to be there for his big brother's hockey tournament. He made it to every game, even if most of it was spent sleeping on the wooden bleachers. Everyone was surprised how soundly and quickly he could sleep among the loud cheers and screams from the people in the crowd. That kid could sleep anywhere! It was so comforting to see several adult friends give up their coats for pillows or their blankets to cover him. He looked so peaceful and warm. That made it all the harder when I had to wake him up so he could get to the locker room to give the pep- talks before the games or at halftime. It was a big deal to Zac, and I think many of the players got a kick out of it.

Zac was given the opportunity to be one of the team - actually a coach. He would stand in front of the white grease-board and draw his strategic plan before the attentive players.

"Okay, so these are the other team..." Zac placed his X's randomly on the board. "... And you need to go a-a-a-r-r-r-o-o-o-u-n-n-d them." Zac was serious. "And another thing -," Zac added all fired up, "No-o-o penalties. Only hat-tricks!"

As the boys stood up and filed out onto the ice, Zac kept motivating the boys as he patted them on the back. "Remember - no-o-o penalties. All hat tricks! Whooh!"

Zachary would march right out behind the boys and sit next to me in the bleachers. He was so proud of the Chicago Lakes hockey team, especially his big brother. It was very fitting when after the opening motivational speech, his brother, Nic, went on to score 3 goals that game. Just like Zac instructed - only hat-tricks.

"That's my brother! That's my brother! Did you see that?!" Zac shouted excitedly.

Zachary finally completed his six weeks of radiation on March 14, 2011. I didn't know how we were ever going to make it. I frequently reverted back to my motto "one day at a time." My dear friend Carla also gave me a devotional prayer book, 'Jesus Calling,' which I read and reflected on daily. I quickly found the strength in two quick prayers that I would at times say over and over again until I could settle my mind down -"Help me Jesus, help me Jesus," and "I need you Jesus..."

I knew I had to trust in God, but I had a hard time keeping myself grounded and not look into the future. That angered me though. Weren't we allowed to plan for tomorrow or for that family trip we wanted to take, or for the next year or when our child entered into middle school, high school, college...? I know we are supposed to "live for the moment," so we don't die with regret. We also have the right to plan. For me, it changed. When someone would talk about next year, my heart would sink a little because now, I almost feared the future. I didn't know what it held for Zachary.

As for Zachary, he was so happy to be done with radiation.

"I hate you devil! I will always love You, God!" Zachary would proclaim.

Zachary would shout this when he was most overwhelmed with the countless episodes of retching and vomiting. He would sometimes be on his knees, clutching the toilet seat with his face staring into the toilet. Other times he would be sitting stiffly on the couch in dreadful anticipation of the next round of retching and heaving. He never blamed God. He would only occasionally make it known that, "I hate this."

We had to wait eight weeks for the follow-up MRI. I thought that was way too long. I wanted to scan him often and to be able to stay on top of any surprises. Moertel and Dusenberry explained that after radiation was complete it was still working. There would be lots of swelling on the brain as a result of the radiation killing off the cancer. Dr. Moertel said if we'd scan Zachary too soon after, I would just panic at what I saw. There isn't a definite way to tell by looking at the scans what was swelling and what was live tumor. I knew I had to be patient and go with what they recommended, but my patience was wearing thin when it came to waiting.

Dr. Moertel overrode Dr. Dusenberry's "eight-weeks" and made it six, instead. I agreed. Good Friday, April 21 was the plan date for the follow-up MRI. All I could say was if it was labeled as "Good," it better be good in Zachary's case too.

Again Dr. Moertel mentioned the use of a vaccine that they were using out East on adults with cancer. He said the basic concept of the vaccine was to cause the tumor to destruct. He hoped that soon they could start trying it on pediatric patients and Zachary would qualify.

Zac undergoing radiation 7-18-12

CHAPTER 14

"how much will a miracle cost?"

The benefit was fast approaching. All the activity helped keep my mind from the constant worry and "what-if's" that I was consumed with. If I wasn't on the phone (sometimes my cell phone and home phone at the same time) I was emailing, texting, meeting with one person or another. The chaos was not only felt by me, but by Nathan, Nic and Jessica. They were growing impatient with the lack of time and attention I had for them.

"You're always busy!" He shot at me in frustration.

"You know I can't help it. This is really important and it's actually like I'm running a business," I tried to explain.

Then there was Nic and Jessica who frequently reminded me, "You're always on the phone."

Yes, I was, but there was no way around it. I had a vision and I wanted this benefit to be a success. What did they expect? It wasn't going to happen on its own.

The day finally came. The meetings were done. The hall was decorated the night before, silent auction items, and raffles for the most part were displayed, and Barb was racing against the clock printing up the last of the silent auction forms and the names for the recognition board of our donors. It was mind-boggling as to how many pieces there were to putting on a benefit.

People started coming in before we opened the doors. I was anxious. I wanted it to be perfect when they walked in. The hall looked beautiful with the white lights and the tulle scalloped from the ceiling. The tables were decorated with flowers, candles and pictures of Zac that we had taken of him along his journey. Inspirational posters made by Jessica and her friends were hanging on the walls. For a hall that was dull and bare to begin with there was life now in this place.

Zachary was so excited for what I told him was "his" party.

"They are all coming for you Zac," I explained. "I'm hoping together they will spend lots of money and we can find your miracle."

"How much will a miracle cost?" Zachary innocently asked.

Once again, my heart skipped a beat. I didn't know how to answer. I would give Zac anything, even my own life to spare his. "I'm not sure, but we're going to try and get it."

I really felt I was on the right track. I could do a benefit each year and a run/walk somewhere in the middle. If Susan J Coleman could become a mega-race, raising millions for breast cancer research, why not us?

Zachary was extremely tired. He spent much of the day on Thursday and Friday, before Saturday's benefit, in Nurse Debbie's office, on the day he had already been sick six times and it was only approaching 5 pm. Zachary wondered where he could lay down before the party got started. The only spot that looked somewhat comfortable was upfront on the raised carpeted stage. He curled up in the fetal-position, resting his head on his rolled-up jacket. Father Al walked by a few minutes later and covered him with his jacket. *Let the holiness continue to sink in.*

The hall continued to fill up with people and more were coming in. We pre-sold five-hundred tickets and our caterer, the Old Log Restaurant, was prepared. I didn't want to turn anyone away. I wanted them to see Zac and know how important a cause this was.

Kerry, the Old Log manager said he could do fifty more people - so fifty more tickets were sold.

My sister Barb came back and asked, "Can you do fifty more?"

"Yep. Bring em' in," Kerry obliged.

This went on for a few more fifties. I was impressed that Kerry was able to accommodate so many more people than what I had planned for. Not everyone came to eat. There were plenty of other places to spend their money.

Our rifle raffle was done in twenty minutes and in thirty minutes the dozens and dozens of mystery envelope restaurant gift certificates sold out. Zachary even drew two beautiful pictures, a hunting one and the other of a fall-colored tree with a person standing underneath it. They were auctioned off bringing in $325 and the other for $275! Actually they were priceless, but they were going to good homes.

I was very pleased with myself and my team for pulling this off, especially when a friend of mine, who does a fundraiser yearly, commented, "Wow, you really have some good stuff!" Indeed we did.

The place was packed, at the highlight of the night we had seven-hundred people listening to Dr. Moertel and followed by, a researcher Dr. David Largaespada. I was so pleased to see Tammie, Zac's nurse practitioner, who works closely with him, and Laura from radiation who came to support us and our cause.

Then Zachary was up. He said he was nervous to talk in front of all the people.

"You don't have to if you don't want to," I reassured.

"No. I can do it."

"Just speak from your heart," and I patted him on the back as I nudged him center stage.

The lights were all off except for a big spotlight. The brilliant light surrounded Zac. I was excited to hear him speak. I was nervous too. Zac sat there for a moment. The crowd of people waited, and waited a little longer. I think Zac was taking it all in.

"He knew he was supposed to talk, right?" Nathan asked leaning into me.

"I thought so?"

Just as I moved closer to Zachary, he began to find his words. I let out the breath I was holding. "I just want to thank you all for coming. This is amazzzing!" Zac paused a moment to take a breath. "My angels are with you. God bless you."

Zachary radiated in the spotlight - if that was even possible. His spirit was so bright and his words simple, yet so honest and meaningful.

It was my turn to take the mic. I decided to start first before I would lose my nerve. "Wow!!" I said still in awe of how many people came. "I have to be honest, when I first decided to do this benefit, I wanted to have it be local because my main concern was if people would come. You came! Thank you for being here and supporting us in the ways that you have. If it wasn't for your prayers and kindness, Nathan and I wouldn't be standing here today. Today wouldn't have been possible if my sister Barb wouldn't have rolled up her sleeves and jumped in. What I didn't know about planning this event - she did. The rest of my friends and family who also gave of their time to help plan or put things together, and are still continuing to help out this evening, I am so grateful for. So thank you!" I continued on... "Just the other day, Zac's good buddy, Austin was over and I heard them talking. Austin told Zac, 'If you ever were in trouble and needed help, I would call 9-1-1.' Well, I think someone called 911 - because you all came!"

My brave front started to melted and I started to cry. I was so overwhelmed by the support of such beautiful caring people. I knew they loved Zac. I was so happy that they were here. "We are in a bit of trouble and we need to find a cure. I felt helpless waiting around, so I decided I should do something about it. So that's why we're here." I paused for a moment. "Zac just asked me how much a miracle cost. I told him I didn't know for sure, but we were going to try and find one... So spend your money! Thanks so much for being here!"

I felt like I could have talked forever. I had so much to say, but I had to give Nathan a chance. I passed the mic on and Nathan proceeded to talk about how Zac was his hero and how proud he was of him. He finished with his sincere gratitude for everyone's support. That night, I don't think we could have thanked everyone enough.

The hall cleared out to only a few close friends shortly after the silent auction was wrapped up. We did have a dance, but I think many were overwhelmed by the large number people and what ended up feeling like a small place - almost claustrophobic. There were plenty of people there to see some of Zac's dance moves. I couldn't help but think how good he looked. It was almost as if he wasn't sick. He didn't get sick the rest of the evening and he never complained of being tired. He was having the time of his life!

My sister, Barb had done some research and said for a first time benefit, to make $10,000 would be great. We were a small town, but it honestly didn't matter because we ended up making $24,000 - even after expenses were paid. We were thrilled!

We had Sunday to recover from the late night we all had after the benefit. Zachary slept on and off, but did well. By Monday he was so sick he couldn't get out of nurse Debbie's office. I ended up picking him up from school at noon. I knew he was feeling lousy when he wanted me to come get him.

"Poor baby," Nurse Debbie sadly said. "He is such a fighter. It breaks my heart to see him like this."

I agreed and I took him home where I tucked him in on the couch to watch movies – soon to find him asleep.

Zachary continued to struggle for weeks after he completed radiation, with bouts of retching, tiredness and now he developed a bad skin virus. *Really? What more can you do to this poor kid?* He was itching like crazy! Lotions weren't helping so I called the clinic. We had to go in and make sure he didn't have shingles. His doctor was afraid that it could be in his bloodstream. Thank God it wasn't that.

Zac was given another medicine that I had to put on all the bumps, leaving it on for four hours, soak in the tub and then use an emery board to file down or the bumps off. It was time-consuming, but Zac and I were willing to give anything a try. He was beside himself many times a day with itching fits. It was like watching a dog chasing its tail when I would watch Zac try to get relief from "rubbing" (turned into itching) his bumps. He continued to curse the devil and on occasion throw things out of frustration when he was completely beside himself. I felt so helpless. Sometimes I would just give in and have to use my fingernails to give him seconds of relief.

Zac's MRI got bumped a week later than what it originally was set for because Dr. Moertel was out of town for a conference. My anticipation grew, only to find that "it was stable." I think Dr. Moertel was expecting this or at least he didn't show that he was hoping for better and I didn't ask. There was still a lot of brain swelling that was referred to as "pseudo-swelling." Dr. Moertel wanted to wait three more months before doing the next scan because he felt the swelling should be gone by then. I didn't want to wait the extra month. I was so afraid of letting any time slip by if something new was developing and we could intervene earlier.

The plan was to begin a chemo drug, Avastin, which was previously used on Zachary, but this time it would be used to help decrease the swelling. We would wait three months unless the retching spells became too uncontrollable or he had too many headaches or difficulty with movement. The side effects of pseudo-swelling were basically the same as a brain tumor growing which was very unsettling.

Nathan said he was happy with the results because he was afraid that more tumors could have shown up - like the time Zac was faced with eight at once. I guess I wasn't even considering that option. I was really hoping to see a substantial decrease, if not a faint remnant of this ugly astrocytoma. *It has to go away by the mercy of God!* I was fighting the fear, every day of its possible regrowth. *If the doctors don't come up with something concrete…*

Zachary was listening to our conversation as he busied himself coloring. He started to cry.

"Zac, what's wrong?" I asked confused, turning to him bending down on both knees in front of him.

"My tumor is gone?" Zac excitedly questioned, thinking that was what he had heard.

I was distraught at having to burst his bubble. I couldn't lie and I couldn't candy-coat the fact that everything was the same as the MRI in January, before we even started radiation. I hoped he wouldn't think all the vomiting, extreme tiredness and itching were all-for-naught.

"No, it's still there, but it is the same size. At least it didn't get any bigger," I gently explained. I let Dr. Moertel take over hoping he could shed some light on such a tough, confusing situation.

Dr. Moertel tried to explain what stable meant in Zac's situation, but I still didn't think he really understood. Dr. Moertel told him that he was happy with the results, so Zac figured if Dr. Moertel's "stable" was good enough for him, it was good enough for Zac.

Zachary fell asleep and Nathan could sense I was on edge with the "stable" news. "Let's just live these next three months really happy. Let's have fun!" Nathan encouraged.

I knew he was right. I wished I didn't have to live three months to three months - MRI to MRI. I had to keep reminding myself to "live for the moment,"-wise words of the wife of Nathan's coworker and friend who had recently passed from brain cancer. Nathan and I struggled to find that balance between what had to be done and what we could set aside for the moment. I knew when I was inside watching Nathan outside with the kids, after dinner playing a game of baseball or soccer and I was still cleaning up the kitchen, looking out at them having fun, that "that was the moment."

Another important moment had come for Zachary in his Catholic faith. Second grade was a big year. First, Reconciliation and now his First Communion. Like Nic and Jessica, Zachary had been anticipating when he could go up for communion. In our faith formation classes, I, as a teacher, taught them what we believed as Catholics. Zachary was almost nine-years-old. His excitement grew as the day of his First Communion approached. He kept talking about it and saying, "I can't wait to receive Jesus!" His demeanor was different from that of being excited about Halloween, Easter or Christmas. He knew it was something extra special and there was no commercialism in it - like how Christmas and Easter have become for many.

Zachary knew he would have a party after, with grandparents and cousins to celebrate his special occasion. He knew he was going to get presents. I made sure he knew that they would be religious ones to reflect the sacrament, so he wouldn't be disappointed, to which he said, "That's okay, I like the holy things."

Zachary could not be more ready. He smiled from ear to ear as pictures were taken before the mass. During mass as we were kneeling down and the priest was at the part in the mass where he held up the host and said the words of Jesus, "This is my body...," Zachary leaned over to me and whispered, "It's almost time!" Zac's smile was so bright and his eyes spoke complete purity.

A chill ran up my spine. My heart told me something indeed was different about this boy, I called Zachary.

CHAPTER 15

good news

Zachary finished up his second grade year, having sudden bouts of feeling like he was going to throw up. He would run from his classroom, with a garbage can in hand, retching down the hall to Nurse Debbie's. I was getting phone calls again at least twice a day letting me know he was in her office looking pretty pasty. Most times Zac wanted to just lie down to try and sleep it off. He could sometimes nap for up to an hour and then be off to join this class. Occasionally, he would tell Nurse Debbie, "I want my mom."

It was then that I knew he was at his limit. I hated going into work not knowing if he was going to need to come home. Several times I would get "the" phone call right before 2 pm when I was planning on leaving for my drive into work. I would call Nathan hoping he would tell me to stay home, but he would instead tell me he would leave early, having Zac wait-it- out for almost another hour.

I wanted for Zachary to feel good. I wanted for him to not be so tired so he would have the energy to run and play and keep up with the rest of the kids.

The nausea and vomiting spells always made me worried that something more could be wrong other than the diagnosis of "pseudo-swelling," but Dr. Moertel and Tammie held firm. I tried to remain positive.

After waking up at 6:45 am one morning to Zac yelling, I couldn't sit back any longer and watch my son suffer day after day, month after month.

"I don't feel good! Oh, no, I don't feel good! Nic, hurry, get mom!" Zac said in a panic.

Again, the same thing at 8 am when Zac was almost ready to go to school for a field trip to the Minnesota Zoo.

This was enough! I thought. *Can't this kid catch a break and be given the chance to have some fun?!*

I thought of keeping him home, but I didn't want him to be sad because he would miss out on something fun once again. I put myself in the doctor's chair and made the decision to up his steroid, to hopefully get him through his field trip. I went as a chaperone so I felt we could work this out together.

It didn't quite work out the way I was hoping. Zac ended up having the dry-heaves on the bus on our way to the zoo and again later during the dolphin show. I was so mad for him. He did manage to get through the day, but crashed on the bus ride home back to the school. I did call the clinic and talk with Tammie and she agreed that his steroid dose should be increased to a higher level for six days before we would start to taper it off, AGAIN. She still thought Zac's symptoms could be related to the radiation. If I didn't see much improvement, she said there would be something else that they could try.

June and July 2011 passed quickly. Zachary spent most (at least half) of it sleeping. He was tired all the time. It broke my heart to see him sleep his summer away. He would take up to three naps a day each averaging thirty minutes to three hours. He could sleep anywhere. He wanted to be where the action was so every day he took a nap after breakfast then he would go on the deck to watch Nic, Jessica and Lexie swimming in our above ground pool, which was attached to our deck. Sometimes he would find the energy to run and jump and play, other times he would pass on the swimming and lie on a lawn chair, only to fall asleep.

I could see that Zachary was getting a little mentally worn down by the statements he started to make.

"I wonder what it feels like to be a normal boy."

The first time he said that, my heart just ached for him. I saw the pain and disappointment in his eyes. Yes, his life was different and he couldn't always keep up with the other boys because he was so tired, but he sure gave it everything he had to push himself until he couldn't go any further.

How I replied to his statement I felt was crucial to his motivation and determination to keep going. "Zac, you ARE a normal boy that just gets sick, sometimes."

What more could I say? Zac was smart. He knew he was sick and tired way more than his friends, but he still liked to play Xbox games, watch movies, shoot his bow, build bonfires and run and swim when he had the energy. Any chance he could, he invited Thomas, Austin or another friend to come and play. What Nic and Jessica were able to do we tried to allow for Zac as well, so he wouldn't think of himself as being different or start to label himself as "sick" and then take on the characteristics permanently of being a "sick" boy.

Zachary had so much life in him, even when he was so tired. It radiated from him. He definitely made up for his absence when he was sleeping by his quick wit and silliness when he was awake.

It finally came time for Zac's next MRI. The whole family came to support him. It was nice having Nathan and the kids. Zachary climbed on to the MRI table, a.k.a - "spaceship" and soon fell sleep without being sedated. He hadn't required the sedation since he was seven-years-old.

When the scan was done we all went upstairs for the results. Nic, Jessica and Lexie played around with Zachary. An appointment always had such a different feeling when the kids were together. For Zac, it seemed his apprehension gave way to laughter and silliness. As for me, I was still on pins and needles, but I welcomed the distraction.

Today the scan showed there was still a lot of swelling around the tumor, kind of a cauliflower-effect on top of it. Again, Dr. Moertel explained that this type of pressure was a big factor as to why Zac was still getting sick.

"I thought the swelling was supposed to be gone by six weeks post radiation?" I asked.

"Yes, typically it should be, but because of the intense radiation to the part of the brain that Zac had, sometimes the "pseudo-swelling" can last six months," Dr. Moertel explained.

"But the scan looks worse than in April, doesn't it?" I worried.

"Sometimes when tumors are dying off, more swelling can occur because the cancer cells are fighting against the efforts to destroy them," Dr. Moertel explained. "If you look here," he pointed to the tumor from April's scan, "the tumor is solid white in color - which means the tumor is alive. Now, look here at today's MRI. Do you see that most of the tumor looks gray? That is a good sign."

"So, it's dying out?" I cautiously asked.

"That's what it's telling me," Dr. Moertel confirmed. "And the three tumors that were present in April's MRIs are gone - with the exception of one, which is graying. My hope is that Zac can get three to five years before we have to do anything again." Dr. Moertel paused with a look of seriousness on his face. "However... It could be sooner, but if it should happen, with the advances in medicine and vaccines, we would use the best of what is out there."

We left the clinic a bit relieved, but still on edge. It was like we were constantly walking around with a ticking time-bomb.

I was given a prescription for Ritalin to start Zac on the next day. I thought it was just used for people with attention deficit disorder, but it can have the opposite effect on others who suffer from effects of being tired from intense radiation.

Zachary finished up his summer much the same as it began. He enjoyed his golfing lessons and pushed through his four weeks of summer school. I felt bad sending him to school in the heat of the summer. He didn't like going. It was one more thing that made him different from his siblings and friends. As a parent, I knew it was important he go because he had missed a lot of second grade, but had made up my mind already that I wasn't going to send him next summer. Zac's happiness was more important to me than him being smart. I could do the school work at home with him.

I did see a little improvement in his tiredness when Zac started taking the Ritalin. I wasn't paying attention and, Zac ran out of the pills and I couldn't get any more for four or five days. Surprisingly, even off the med, he actually seemed to have more energy. It was refreshing. I was hoping that it had finally built up in his system. As soon as I got the refill from the pharmacy, Zac started taking it again. Then he started saying, "I'm so tired." He was sleeping a lot more than he had the last four days. Could the drug level have dropped so quickly, I wondered. I didn't feel like taking Zachary in for a doctor's appointment to adjust his meds, so I decided to slip on my white doctor's coat and do my own experiment. I stopped the drug altogether and quickly, Zac seemed more awake. I concluded that the Ritalin wasn't helping Zac, but was having the opposite effect that Dr. Moertel expected it should have on him.

Nothing was quite as it was supposed to be when it came to Zachary and the cancer and symptoms. I was pleased when after Dr. Moertel completed his neurologic exam on Zac and he said, "It's funny, there are no findings of the classical symptoms I would expect to see from the brain tumors that Zac has, other than the vomiting and extreme tiredness - which are actually symptoms of the radiation."

"It's his Angels on his shoulders," I simply replied.

Dr. Moertel just smiled.

The little miracles were there. I just had to look harder and be grateful for them.

Zachary was so up and down with his vomiting episodes. We had it under control with the steroid, Decadron, and I, as well as Dr. Moertel, thought it would be good to get him off of it. Long-term use of the steroid could have harmful effects on him. If he didn't need it, why keep him on it? Zachary was six months post radiation so Dr. Moertel thought the side effects of radiation should be over.

A week before the first day of school, Zac began vomiting four to five times a day. There was no way I was going to have Zachary's new school year began the way it ended - with him in the nurse's office. I ended up putting him back on the steroid and figured we would wait to try to take him off of it depending on what the next MRI revealed.

Ideas were still being thrown around as to why Zac was still having such difficulty with the vomiting and tiredness. The thought now was from a screwed-up endocrine system due to all the chemo and radiation.

In spite of the beating Zachary was continuing to take on his body, he looked great. I was caught by surprise when I pulled up in the driveway one day after work. I saw the neighbor's grandson and another kid playing on our driveway. I did a double take when I figured out that it was Zac. He was really thinning out. He was looking more like himself again. I smiled. Maybe soon he would be "normal."

Zachary was doing well in school. He really liked his third-grade teacher, Mrs. Fredstrom. Like the other teachers Zachary had at Chisago Lakes Primary School, she was very attentive to his needs. Zac was feeling pretty good so far - he had only made two trips to nurse Debbie's office. He was excited about playing flag football and he was having a blast doing it - even if he rarely carried the ball or touched it, for that matter. He loved having his own sport and running around with all the boys. He was also looking forward to the start of archery.

October's MRI showed the brain tumor had shrunk more with continuing signs of it to be dying out. January's MRI followed suit and showed that the tumor shrunk yet some more. Actually, it was about a third smaller than what it looked like back in July and half the size of what it was in October. It was truly dying out!

Prior to his MRI, Zac enthusiastically kept saying, "I can't wait for my MRI! I know I am healed! I just know it!" We always drew on our faith to keep us positive. I wondered if I was faithful enough. I knew Zac was. I had to believe it could be the same for Zac, just as Jesus told the Roman soldier who came to Jesus, pleading for the healing of his dying servant, who was like a son to him. Jesus told him, "Because of your faith, your faith has healed him." And his servant was healed.

Nathan clutched his chest in relief. "Thank God! It's like I've got this five-hundred pound gorilla off my back again." He reached over and grabbed my hand pulling me in close. I turned to hug him. We both breathed a huge sigh of relief.

I could not predict how these MRIs would go any longer. There were rarely any indications for suspecting a tumor. Then out of the blue, when there were no symptom's we would be hit with the news that there indeed was something growing. When I would see Zachary vomiting, tired and complaining of a headache, I feared the worst, only to be told, "Everything was stable." It was like someone was messing with my mind.

"Zac did you hear that?" Nathan excitedly shouted to him as he sat on a chair by the window working on his math sheets.

"What?" It was as if he had shut everything out as a defense mechanism after hearing bad news one too many times.

"Your tumor is even smaller than last time! Isn't that awesome, best buddy?!" Nathan said turning to give Zac a big hug.

"Y-E-S!" Zac said elated clutching his fist and punching the air.

If only it could stay this way always. Maybe it could. I knew and believed with all my heart that anything was possible with God. Yet the black cloud lingered over my head as Dr. Moertel responded to my question of - "if the tumor could continue to shrink to the size of a pea or even a marble?"

"It will never go away completely. I'll just be happy if it shrinks again and we can stay at status quo," he honestly predicted. "Good news, though," Dr. Moertel changed gears, "the vaccine we've been working on has cleared phase 1, which means we know that it is not toxic to children. The problem is, as we enter into phase 2, we are waiting for $20 million so we can begin the research and find out if this drug works better in treating certain types of tumors compared to other conventional treatments, such as chemotherapies and radiation."

"Oh, is that why I see a camera crew has been following you around?" I asked curiously.

"Yeah, you know me, always in the limelight," Dr. Moertel joked.

I was excited about the possibility of the vaccine that could completely destroy tumors. This was what Zachary needed. It had to work and soon, but Dr. Moertel said these things take time and he couldn't predict how soon Zachary may need some other form of treatment. I felt that we were getting closer to a cure. Zac just needed to hang on and remain stable. Maybe it was time to do another benefit. I know $24,000 is small in comparison to $20 million, but you never know, someone out there could answer our prayers and write a check for that 20 million or even 5 million, I would take either. Zachary's name and story was getting around.

Through the Children's Cancer Research Foundation, funds are raised to support cancer research, and patient and public awareness of it. I happened to get a phone call from a woman named Kelly who was wondering if Nathan and I would be interested in sharing Zachary's story for the U of M newsletter and for us to be interviewed by Ryan and Shannon at KS95 - a local radio station. She went on to explain that they were interviewing kids and their parents to be played on the radio in December, in efforts to raise money for their annual radiothon for Children's Cancer Research and Gillette's Children's Specialty Healthcare.

I obliged. Anything I could do to help in raising awareness and getting people to open their pocketbooks to help in finding a cure for cancer, I would do. I also wanted people to know about Zac, his fight, his determination and the amazing boy that he was. I was complimented by many coworkers about what a great article it was and how brave and inspiring Zachary was. I was very proud.

I was nervous to meet Ryan and Shannon to be interviewed. They had given us questions to go over, but I still had no idea what I was going to say. I didn't want to sound stupid in front of thousands and thousands of people on the radio.

After the initial introduction, our mics were attached and we got to talking, I realized that I just needed to answer their questions and tell it like it was without being depressing.

Ryan and Shannon were very kind and seemed interested in Zac's story. It was more than just an interview. It was Zac's life, our life. I was hoping that telling Zac's story, would somehow make a difference.

Zachary did a great job with the interview. He was a good speaker. He talked easily with adults and was able to carry on a meaningful conversation at the ripe old age of nine. I couldn't help but get emotional when talking about Zachary's battle. When I talked about it, I was fine. I could give details and facts. It was when I really thought and felt what I said, that I would break down and cry.

I cried during the interview because as brave of a front as I put on, deep down inside, I feared for Zac's life. I wanted him to have the same chances as his brother and sisters. I wanted Zac to go to high school, to college... I just wanted him to live... To stay with me! To imagine my life without him, devastated me!

Nathan got choked up too. As tough of a guy as he looked – a military man and prison lieutenant, I knew he struggled with the same fears as I had. We didn't talk about the fear much because by doing that we felt it would take on more reality. Instead we focused on life.

I was surprised when Ryan and Shannon had already talked about their meeting with Zac on the radio the next morning. It only took meeting Zac once to be affected by him.

"He was such a positive light in that room!" Shannon confirmed. "He was so positive and his parents couldn't be more proud of him!"

Ryan went on to explain to the listeners his favorite part about Zac - "Zac ran for class president at his school and the platform he used was '*if you don't have anyone to play with on the playground, I will play with you*' - he was wearing a bracelet that even said, "NO BULLYING."

"Zac is awesome!" Shannon chimed in.

"I love his 'no bullying campaign,'" Ryan affirmed.

He and the other radio host went on to talk a little about bullying. "I bet Zac would let you jump on his coattails of that campaign. No surprise the kids elected him as class president. He is an aspiring nine-year-old boy!" Ryan said with conviction.

Zac was just beginning.

I don't know if it was the radiation or God, but Zac's tumor shrunk about half the size it was in January. Dr. Moertel said he thought we were on the right path. I was pleased and Zac was very excited by the news. He wanted to text his big brother right away to share the good news. I continued to hope for the day when Dr. Moertel would look at Zac's MRI scan and say in unbelief - "I can't explain it, the tumor is completely gone!"

Zachary's eye doctor, Dr. Ballard, who we routinely saw, said that since he wasn't going through chemotherapy treatment he could surgically repair Zac's left eye from "wandering." He made it clear that it wouldn't help restore any vision in his eye. It was supposed to be a pretty easy surgery that would keep him out of the loop for about four days. I gave Zac the choice as to whether he wanted to do this or not - since it basically was cosmetic. I figured he would say "no," but he surprised me when he said, "I want to do it."

"You do? How come?"

Zac became quiet and sadly spoke, "I don't like when other kids keep asking me, 'Why is your eye crossed?' or 'Zac, what's wrong with your eye?'"

I didn't even know it bothered him. I rarely noticed it myself. I suppose that's because I looked at him constantly.

"Ah, Zac, I'm sorry." I empathized. "I didn't know it bothered you. I'm sure the kids are just curious and don't mean to hurt your feelings."

Even though it wouldn't restore his vision, like Zac so often prayed for, he still wanted to go through with the surgery. It would be one less thing in making him different from his peers.

Zac and Mike Lizotte (Blake and Brock) The summer of 2011 when Zac was going through radiation, but not about to miss spending time with friends!

*Nathan, Carol Ann and Zac with Shannon and Ryan after
doing the interview for Kids Radiothon 3-13-12*

3rd grade super sticker day. Zac (10 years) celebrating after winning the tug-of-war. 5-29-12

CHAPTER 16

deadly miscommunication

Everything was settling down for once. Zachary was finally feeling good. His retching spells became more infrequent and he was having fun playing baseball. He even got a grand slam with bases-loaded! I was so excited for him. Zac couldn't stop talking about it.

I was a little concerned about having a birthday party for Zac because he had been struggling with being so tired and sick. I postponed it once and rescheduled it for June 30, 2012. It was a nice warm day for a pool party and the boys and girls really enjoyed themselves. Zac had energy and was able to keep going the entire time. This was how it was supposed to be.

Zachary's "feel-good" days came to an abrupt halt when he began having his retching spells again. Before this they usually lasted about two days, but this time he had been struggling on and off, all day for five days straight. Increasing his steroids and giving him his anti-nausea medicine had no effect. Nighttime offered little relieved and he was getting worn out with the constant running to the bathroom.

Nic was so good about getting up with Zac when he would panic, "Oh, no, N-n-i-i-i-c-c! I don't feel good again!"

After making sure Zac was okay and in the bathroom, Nic would come upstairs to get me for extra support and comfort for Zac. There was nothing worse for Zac than the uncontrollable, grueling bouts of vomiting or even the feeling of it.

After a horrible day of numerous episodes of Zac running back and forth to the bathroom, watching him in sheer agony as he held his head over the toilet retching and retching, I knew I had to call the doctor. I couldn't just sit there and rub his back and listen to him cry out - "God, please help me! I need you, God!"

I sat quietly on my heels, screaming at God in my head as the retching persisted. *"What are you doing?! Help him, NOW!"*

Zac turned his head away from the toilet and looked at me with vacant, sad eyes. He was worn down. "Why is this happening?"

This had to stop. I knew God wouldn't be so cruel as to do this to Zachary. I didn't want to sound like a know-it-all-Christian," but I knew at this point the comfort of God was the only thing that could help Zac. "Remember, Zac, it's not God doing this. It's the devil. The devil knows you're doing God's work and you are going to do so much more to help bring more people to God. And that scares the devil! The stupid devil is trying to stop you."

"I will never give up!" Zac protested.

"I know you won't. Just keep breathing. Slow deep breaths," I reassured as I continued to rub his back. My labor and delivery coaching was coming in good use. "I wished I knew why God won't step in and stop you from being so sick. I'll call the doctor as soon as you can get back to the couch."

I called the endocrine fellow how had no answers, so I immediately hung up and called the pediatric oncology fellow. She really didn't know what to say since Zachary didn't have any other symptoms except for the intense, persistent vomiting spells. The doctor on-call felt we should do an MRI to rule things out, on Wednesday, when Zachary had a growth hormone function test scheduled. I agreed, but wished we could do one sooner.

"Let's start him back on the omeprazole 20 mg twice a day, and if he develops any other symptoms - a headache, weakness, or loss of function - call back right away, the doctor said.

So for the next three days I had the option of fighting my worst fears of *What if the tumor has grown back?*, and get myself all worked up for nothing or I could remain calm, keep my prayer 'I need you Jesus, help me Jesus!' on my lips and help Zachary get through these next couple of days.

I did both.

In spite of Zachary's retching, he continued to say, "I know I'm healed, I just know it!" Wednesday, came. I felt much better going into the day because Zachary began to turn the corner Monday after 11 am and was not sick once on Tuesday. The acid relieving drug that Zac was now on seemed to be what Zachary needed. I felt confident that all the vomiting and retching was not tumor related.

Zac saw Tammie, the nurse practitioner, who worked closely with Dr. Moertel. We really liked her. She was attentive, kind, caring and knew her stuff - medically speaking.

"I've already spoken with Dr. Moertel about what was going on with Zac. I talked with him yesterday and he said that if Zac was better today that he'd most likely would want to hold off on the MRI for today."

"But wouldn't it be wise to just do it now and rule it out?" I questioned. "His next MRI isn't until mid-July. Three-months seem like a long time to wait.

"Let's first see how some of the test results from today look. Some of them can help determine if an MRI would be called for.

Shortly after Tammie left, Dr. Moertel came in to see Zachary. "What it looks like is that Zac is in the group of people who have gone through radiation and take longer to recover."

"But you'd said six weeks and then – six months and now we are at 15 months! That's a really long time," I reminded him.

"I know it is, but some things we don't know for sure as to how it will affect a person." He confessed. "It is common for people who have had radiation, stroke or brain injuries to develop gastric issues. I think Zac has some type of gastritis and that is why he is having all the vomiting episodes."

"What about the MRI?" I asked.

"I think we can hold off since the vomiting has subsided after restarting his medicine. Actually, I think we should wait until mid-August for his next MRI," Dr. Moertel said.

"Are you sure?" I asked. "That would be waiting four months since his last MRI. We haven't waited that long in between scans for five years."

I had to trust Dr. Moertel. He was an excellent doctor and one of the best in his field. He had many doctors from all over the country asking him questions, even doctors from Germany wondering when "the vaccine" would be ready. The problem with neurofibromatosis was there were so many variables to the disease and Zachary was afflicted in many ways doctors had rarely, if ever, seen before. Dr. Moertel was the closest thing I had to figuring out how to "fix" my son, while I continued to pray for a miracle.

It was July 6, 2012 and we were getting ready to drive up to Grantsburg, Wisconsin for the second annual brat feed put on by my dad and some of the Knights of Columbus members from his church. The money raised was going into the Zachary NF research fund. We were trying to find different ways, big and small, to add to the growing fund.

My sister, Marie and her five kids were there, which made it more fun for Nic, Jessica, Zachary and Lexie. We all pitched in, whether it was serving hotdogs or brats, working the cash register or holding up signs for people to see as they were driving up north for the holiday weekend.

Nathan had left for work early and planned to meet us in Alpha, the small town where the brat feed actually was. The rest of us were getting ourselves together and loading up our van.

"Come on Zac, we're almost ready to go," I called downstairs to him.

"All right, I'm coming." Zachary made his way up the stairs a little slower than usual. "I think I pulled my groin muscle."

"How did you do that?" I asked throwing in some extra snacks and clothes in a bag for Lexie.

"I'm not sure, but I think it happened when I got up too fast from the chair downstairs."

"Did it happen just now?" I wondered. "Show me where you pulled the muscle."

"You didn't pull your groin muscle!" Nic said thinking Zac was making it up.

"I did so, Nic!" Zachary insisted.

"Stop it! He obviously did something if he is limping around," I defended Zac. I hated that Nic and Jessica sometimes thought Zac was overreacting. "You just pulled it now?"

"No. It started last night."

I pressed on his leg not noticing anything different. "Does it hurt when you go like this?" I asked demonstrating a side lunge.

Zac tried leaning to one side and he hobbled off balance. "A little," he admitted.

"Well, you're going to have to be careful. Just walk carefully. Maybe Uncle Dan will be there and we can ask if he has any ideas how to make it better," I suggested.

Dan was my brother-in-law and a physical therapist at the Grantsburg hospital. I knew there wouldn't be much more he would be able to do for a groin pull other than show Zac a few stretches.

We arrived to the smoke rolling off the two big grills and the aroma of fresh cooked brats filling the air. I was pleased that my dad went through all the work to put on this fundraiser for Zachary's cause. My dad was a hard worker. He had been ever since I could remember. Before he retired, he was an electrician working long days and many times out of town and always came home beat. It wasn't uncommon that after dinner he would be off to help a neighbor who had called shortly after he had gotten home from work - needing a favor. My dad could never say "no" to anyone. It was much the same now.

He did everything he could to take care of my sisters and me. It was a struggle at times growing up with a special needs child. Therese required a lot of care, most of which became my mom's full-time job, but we managed by all of us pulling our weight. Our extended family continued to live like that. If there was a big job to do - we all were expected to roll up our sleeves.

Even if my dad, Dave, wasn't a sensitive man, I always knew it was there under the surface. The grandkids (there were eleven of them) could bring it out of him, especially Zac. Zac was probably the gentlest, loving person I knew and he rubbed off on everyone.

Zac went up to "Papa," ready to be put to work. "Hey, Papa!"

"Hi there, Zachary!" Papa Dave said giving him a side-hug as he turned the brats. "How's my best friend?"

"I'm good."

"I know you're good." Papa Dave joked. "You're the best!"

"Ha!" Zac smiled. "What can I do to help?"

Papa Dave sent Zachary to help my mom organize the giant rice crispy bars that she, my two sisters and aunts made.

The day was hot and Zachary was getting tired. Ever since radiation, he didn't tolerate the heat and humidity of Minnesota summers. At first I set up a place for Zachary to sleep in the back of the van, but even with the hatch up, he was too hot so I moved the blanket and pillow-pet under some shade trees.

Zachary got up at about the same time Uncle Dan pulled up.

"Hey, Zac!" I called trying to get his attention. "Did you show Uncle Dan your pulled muscle?"

Of course he didn't, Dan just got there, but I wanted Zac to check it out with him before he had to return back to work.

Dan was evaluating a few things with Zac so I walked away to help in the tent. Twenty minutes later Dan approached me. "That's not just a pulled groin muscle. Look how he's dragging his leg and he's not using his right arm," he commented.

"I stopped and *really* took a look. I tried not to get too worked up about little things. If I called the doctor on every whim, I would become labeled as one of "those" over-reactive moms. I always tried to stay calm, watch, wait and see. I was shocked that I had missed something so obvious!

Dan and I stood back silently watching Zac for a moment. He was not able to pick up his foot, he was stumbling around like he was drunk and he fell in between the long work tables because he lost his balance. He had stopped using his right arm on his dominant side. As he sat in a lawn chair, I watched as he leaned way over to his right side and reach for his can of soda with his left hand.

"Do you think it could be a stroke?" I asked waiting for Dan's opinion.

"How's his speech?"

"I haven't noticed any slurring or mouth droop." As I continued to stare at Zac, I could feel my heart begin to race, my eyes teared up. - *What if the tumor was growing?!*

After Zac fell a second time trying to help out and I caught him, I couldn't take anymore.

"Maybe you should call the doctor," my Mom urged.

"I was just thinking that," I said.

I walked away from the tent and stood by little shade tree to make my phone call. I was sweating, not because the small tree didn't offer any relief from the hot sun, but because I was so nervous to make the call.

After leaving a message with the front desk staff and not hearing back, I called again an hour later and was told that Dr. Moertel was in a meeting and asked if I'd like to talk with his nurse. Twenty minutes later Dr. Moertel's nurse returned my call.

I explained that Zachary thought he pulled his groin muscle and how my brother-in-law, who was a physical therapist, said it wasn't just a pulled muscle - that he actually was dragging his right leg, not using his right arm, and that he had fallen twice already.

"I will relay this to Dr. Moertel," she informed.

The nurse didn't seem to understand what I was telling her. She didn't verbalize any concern. "Maybe if your brother-in-law doesn't see Zac frequently enough, he might be seeing things that are normal for Zac."

"Nooo... He knows him. And Zac doesn't usually show signs when something IS wrong. Even when he was diagnosed with eight brain tumors at once, he never complained of a headache!" I explained. "This is W-A-A-A-Y-Y different!" I stressed that this was out of the ordinary for Zac, and I thought she finally understood.

"Okay, I'll tell Dr. Moertel – Oh, he actually just came in from his meeting and is standing right behind me," she said.

I could hear him talking in the background. I wanted to just say – *'Pass the phone to him.'*

Five minutes later the nurse called me back. "So what did he say?" I asked.

"I told Dr. Moertel what you said and he said 'wasn't too concerned about it' and that you could wait to see him on Wednesday and do an MRI then," the nurse stated.

I couldn't believe what I was hearing! *Didn't she hear what I just told her? What?! Today is Friday! Waiting until Wednesday is a long time to wait!*

"No, he said Wednesday would be okay," She reconfirmed.

I was frustrated and shocked at the lack of concern. *Was I missing something? Weren't these warning signs that warranted a much-needed appointment with the doctor?* I felt defeated, but thought I should trust their judgment. "Okaaay, if you're sure?"

I hung up the phone and walked over to my mom. "The nurse said she told

Dr. Moertel what I told her it and Dr. Moertel said we could wait to do an MRI on Wednesday. That's five days away!" My nerves were shot and I started to cry out of frustration and fear.

"Maybe you should take Zac to the hospital now," my mom suggested.

"I don't know. I don't want to make them mad by just showing up after they told me to wait." I took a deep breath. "I'll watch him a little longer and if I see any changes for the worse."

Zac had woken up from a nap under a few small shade trees. He still looked tired and hot. His cheeks were cherry-red. He got up and made his way over to the brat tent.

"Are you feeling okay?" I asked looking for any changes. I was on high alert now.

"I'm okay mom. Why do you keep asking me?" Zac asked.

I felt I needed to be honest with Zac. I knew he sensed my worry and withholding the truth from him would only make him more an anxious. "Zac, I'm worried about you." I placed my hands on his shoulders. "You're dragging your leg and are not using your right arm. That tells me something isn't right."

Out of the blue, Zac asked with panic in his eyes, "Is it something I can die from?!"

"Oh, no, Zac, but Uncle Dan doesn't think it's just a pulled groin muscle," I said trying to calm his nerves. "I did call Dr. Moertel and they want to do an MRI on Wednesday. So we'll just wait and see, okay? - But you have to make sure you tell me right away if you get a headache or anything."

I hated this! I hated seeing Zac suffer the most, but I hated having to rely on myself, my judgment. Yes, I was a nurse, and that helped with my medical observation skills, but I was also a very worried mom. I had been fooled once by a doctor's inadequate judgment. I was feeling that same uneasiness from five years ago. This was Dr. Moertel. I trusted his judgment. *Would he fail me too?*

By 6 pm the holiday weekend traffic had slowed. We helped pick up and I packed up taking my God daughter, Violet to have a sleepover, so Jessica and her, could have some "girl-time." Nic decided to go to my sister's to spend the night with his "brothers," Jacob and David, as he liked to call them.

By the time we got home, Zac's condition had worsened. He was sitting in the back of the van and was unable to stand up to move to the side door. He was able to slide his butt off the seat and down to the floor and scoot his way to the door. From there I stood on his weak side and together we hobbled to the garage stairs that led to the door to the house. Very slowly, Zac made it up the three stairs with my help, adjusting his foot after each step. When Zac couldn't even lift his foot over the threshold between the garage to the house, I knew I wouldn't be able to wait until Wednesday for him to be seen. *This isn't right,* I kept thinking.

I helped Zachary into the livingroom and got him situated in the recliner.

"Are you feeling okay?" I worried. "Any headache? Are you seeing okay? Does anything hurt?" I was looking for some definitive changes, even though he already exhibited several.

"No, I'm fine," Zac said disgruntled. I could tell he was bothered by his lack of movement.

I was very unsettled, but decided to wait it out. Violet and Lexie wanted to swim, so we went outside for a warm evenings when. Zac shuffled his way out onto the deck about a half hour later.

"Hey buddy, are you doing better?" I asked hopeful.

"Not really."

"Do you think you would like to get in the water?" I asked wondering if the distraction would lighten his mood.

"No, I just wanted to come out to be with you guys." Zac sat down in a reclining lawn chair.

I had been planning on spending some quality time with Jessica and my God daughter, but I couldn't let my mind relax. Zachary wanted to go inside and I wanted to be sure he got in without falling. Once again he dragged his right foot over the threshold from the deck into the house. He didn't say a word as the metal scraped across the top of his entire foot. I cringed.

My anxiety grew to the point I couldn't deny something was really wrong. I knew my son, and this wasn't right. He was getting worse by the hour. My gut was speaking so loudly that I was nauseated with concern. I needed a second opinion. I needed to be my son's voice. I picked up the phone and dialed the number to the pediatric hematology/oncology fellow. I spoke with the operator who took my message and told me if I didn't hear from the fellow in twenty minutes, I should call back.

Almost as soon as I hung up the phone, the phone rang. "Hello?" My chest tightened.

"Hey, babe. What are you doing?" My friend Shelley asked. - "Are you okay?"

Shelley was my dear friend who lived kitty-corner across the street from us.

"No," my voice quivered. "Something is wrong with Zachary. I'm waiting for a doctor to call me back right now." Just then my other line clicked. "Shelley, I think that's a doctor. I gotta go!"

I switched over to the other line and it was Dr. Jess Barnum, the pediatric oncology fellow. I explained everything to her from the "pulled groin muscle" diagnosis, to the quick deterioration in Zac's movements. I told her how I was told that Dr. Moertel was unconcerned and felt Zac could wait until Wednesday for an MRI.

"I'm concerned just listening to what you are telling me," Dr. Barnum calmly spoke, validating my concerns.

"This is way different behavior for Zac! He never has shown symptoms like this."

"And did they say why they wanted to wait until Wednesday for an MRI?" Dr. Barnum asked confused.

"No. I was very unsettled by that, but that's what Dr. Moertel's nurse told me he wanted to do."

"Well, I don't agree with that. I'm thinking you need to come down here to the ER and we need to get an MRI right away, but I'm going to call Dr. Moertel first. He's in-house through Wednesday. I'll tell him everything you told me and I'll call you right back."

I finally felt a sense of relief. I was being heard and I could hand over part of my worry to Dr. Barnum. "When you're done talking to Dr. Moertel, can you have him call me? I want to be sure he knows exactly what is going on with Zac." I hung up with her and called Nathan at work, to come home.

"Like, right now? Is it that serious?" Nathan wondered.

"Nathan, he can barely walk!" I whispered in the phone trying to conceal my alarm the best I could. "I'm waiting for Dr. Moertel to call me, but Dr. Barnum said we should plan to come down to the ER tonight."

Okay, I'll leave right now."

Just then, someone knocked on the door. I was surprised to see Shelley and her sister Lynne. "What are you doing here?!" I asked in my frazzled state of mind.

"You sounded like you needed some extra support so we decided to stop by and check on you," Shelley explained.

"Carol Ann, what's going on?" Lynne asked.

I quickly explained what was happening with Zac and then the phone rang. It was Dr. Moertel.

Relief washed over me at the sound of his voice. "Jess Barnum told me what was going on and I want you to know what I was told this afternoon was completely different than what you've told Dr. Barnum. If I was told what was just explained to me - this afternoon, I would have told you to drive right from Grantsburg to Amplatz Children's Hospital's ER immediately."

I was completely frustrated with the lack of communication! *Whatever happened to the closed-loop communication system that was supposed to be followed in the medical setting,* I thought. It clearly hadn't been used in this case. I think that's why I felt the nurse hadn't *heard* me. She never repeated back my exact concern. I didn't want to offend her and act all medical on her so I let it go. The medical system I had been working in seventeen years was failing me AGAIN!

"That's exactly the same as what I told your nurse, except, now - Zac's mobility is worse and he can barely move his right side!" I confirmed. "What do you think is going on? A stroke?"

"I need you to get to the Amplatz Children's Hospital. Do you remember how to get there? Children's hospital moved over to the west bank."

"Yes, I remember."

"I'll call ahead to the ER to let them know you are bringing Zachary, give them the details and make sure they have the MRI ready to go," Dr. Moertel urgently informed. "How soon do you think you'll be there?"

I had to throw a bag together for myself and Zac. I was frantically packing when Nathan walked in a bit anxious.

"We can stay here with the girls," Shelley offered.

"We can get them settled and bring them wherever they need to be tomorrow. Just let us know what you want us to do," Lynne reassured.

I was crying out of fear. It felt comforting to know I had such good friends to just read my mind and come over and willingly take care of my kids and goddaughter.

Nathan went downstairs to get Zac and carried him up in his arms. He was getting worse.

The fifty minute drive in the rain to the hospital felt like it took hours. I looked into the backseat and Zachary was lying there quietly. I wanted Nathan to drive faster for fear Zac would have a full-blown stroke at any minute.

Just like Dr. Moertel said, the ER team was waiting for Zachary. I stayed close without getting in the way as they hooked Zac up to all the machines. I was glad that I remembered to put the emla numbing cream on Zac's port before we left. It would be one less painful thing for him to worry about when they would start the IV.

The doctors came in and did their neurologic exam on him. The head ER doctor, Dr. Gage talked about unequal hand-grasps, facial droop and right-sided paralysis. I knew all of those were indicators of a stroke. Zac's blood pressure was also incredibly high at 146/94. I couldn't believe we were here, in this situation. I was glad I listened to my gut and called the pediatric oncology fellow when I did. My only regret was that I hadn't call sooner.

Before Zachary was taken for the MRI, they wanted to give him a medicine to lower his blood pressure. They didn't want him having a major stroke when he was in the scanner.

"It's going to be okay, baby." I told Zachary as I ran my fingers through his hair. "They are going to find out what's going on and fix you up."

Zac didn't say anything. He just held my hand.

Nathan and I walked quickly with Zachary as the nurse pushed him down the long dim hallway towards the MRI scanner. It was midnight and the hospital was quieting down. We walked in silence as fear began to overshadow us. There was no fighting it anymore. I knew something was really wrong. I just didn't know what they would find. I tried not to jump to that moment. I kept my focus on keeping Zac calm and feeling safe.

I kept whispering in his ear as I leaned over the metal gurney railing as we walked, "Hang in there, baby. I'm right here. I'm not going anywhere."

"Me either, best buddy." Nathan reassured.

Unlike all the other MRIs, I was not able to go into the room with Zac. I was upset that I had to stay back, but I knew Nathan needed me too. I didn't think he understood fully what was going on, but he knew it was bad.

Nathan never stopped pacing the forty-five minutes that the MRI took. I was up and down not knowing what to do with myself. When the MRI was over, Zachary was wheeled back into his glass door cubicle. He looked content, but tired.

"Do they know anything yet?" Zac asked trying to conceal his uneasiness.

"Not yet, but hopefully soon." I was anxious to know, yet didn't want to know.

After about twenty or thirty-minutes a resident doctor called me out of Zac's room. Nathan was getting a cup of water. "How do you want us to present the news?" She blandly asked me.

I felt a wave of terror wash through me. I immediately picked up on her casual, yet puzzling question. My eyes widened and my heart pounded frantically through my chest. I knew something was wrong. "It's not good, is it?"

She remained expressionless, only feeding my apprehension.

"It's growing already?!" My voice quivered with fear.

Her look said it all. When she spoke, I lost my composure.

"The vaccine isn't ready! It's not ready yet! It's not ready yet! What are we going to do?!" My voice escalated in panic the more I spoke.

Nathan was standing by the resident doctor and came to put his arms around me. I took a step back and pushed him away. "No! The vaccine isn't ready yet!" I was at a complete loss.

He reached out and quickly grabbed me, pulling me in close. I gave in, burying my head into his chest as he held my arms bent up against my chest as if I was trying to protect my heart. "No, no, nooo…" I pleaded as I cried falling to my knees. "What are we going to do? What are we going TO DO!?"

Nathan tried pulling me up to my feet, but I couldn't move. I was shaking uncontrollably.

"Maybe we should go into another room where you could have some privacy," the resident suggested.

I continued to moan in agony and in fear for my 10-year-old son's life. "We need more time. Nathan - what are we going to do?" I looked to him empty, searching for hope and I knew he didn't have any answers for me.

As I turned my tear stained face to the side, I clutched onto Nathan trying to find my legs, I noticed the ER staff sitting behind the nurse's station desk. For a moment I wondered how I must have looked to them as I sobbed and pleaded for my son's life. I didn't care, but when I realized I had been moved away from the door of Zachary's room, I cringed at the thought of him hearing me. I prayed he hadn't.

I wiped my eyes and took a few deep breaths as Nathan and I were led into a family room where a neurologist met with us. He pulled Zachary's scans up on the computer screen. Sure enough there was a massive tumor in his brain.

The neurologist said it didn't look to be an astrocytoma. It was a completely new tumor. As sick as it sounds, I was somewhat relieved. If it was the tumor Zachary just had radiation on, there wouldn't be anything they could do, but with a different tumor - they could fix it or so I thought.

"Can you operate and remove it all?" I asked calmer.

"I think so. It appears to be a meningioma - which is actually growing on top of the brain. It is creating so much pressure on the motor center of the brain that he has lost most of his function in his right arm and leg."

"So when can you do surgery?" Nathan eagerly asked.

"It's not that easy. The immediate plan is to try and shrink the swelling of the tumor by an IV medicine today and tomorrow. As long as Zac remains stable, we will do surgery to remove it on Monday," the neurologist explained carefully. "But - if he shows any further increase in loss of motor function or loss of consciousness, we will operate immediately."

A little hope flickered. We had more time. Nathan helped me wipe the stained mascara off my face and together we went into Zachary's room where he was playing on an iPad with a nurse. He seemed entertained. I hid my face as I search for some gum in my purse that I really didn't need.

"How are you doing Zac?" I casually asked hoping he wouldn't notice I had been crying.

"What's wrong? What did the doctor say?" Zac asked very concerned.

You couldn't hide a whole lot from Zac. He picked up on the prior tension in our lengthy absence while we were talking to the doctors.

"Zac," I carefully started. "There is another tumor. That's why I was crying." I had to be honest. He was too smart to hide the obvious.

"Oh, no!" Zac quickly gasped.

"But, Zac, the good news is - it is not the tumor that you had radiation on that's growing back. The doctor said he can take this one out by doing an operation." I said trying to reassure him.

None of us got much sleep that night. We settled into Zac's room around 3:30 am. Nathan slept on a fold-down couch and I took the chair next to Zac's bed. I dozed on and off, but woke up every time a nurse came in or when I tried to adjust in my chair and it would start folding back into its upright position.

Zachary was finally able to rest. I was glad he was able to sleep and put his mind to rest. His blood pressure was coming down nicely, which put me at ease.

It was still dark out when a different neurosurgeon resident doctor came in to speak with Nathan and me. The plan remained the same. These next two days were critical in that the swelling needed to go down enough to make surgery as easy as possible.

Zachary became more stable as the hours passed with the exception to what Dr. Moertel called a minor focal seizure. Zachary became afraid when his leg started twitching and jerking in a rhythmic manner. He couldn't stop it. It went on for about ten minutes. To prevent the generalized grand-mal seizure from occurring, he was quickly put on an anti-seizure med.

Zac was upset that he had to be in the hospital and that he was going to miss his golf camp which he had been looking forward to starting on Monday. He was devastated in the least at the news of yet ANOTHER brain tumor. He was so mad at the devil, but continued to bless God's name. I could only make sense of this tragedy thinking the devil is mad because of Zachary, my family and wonderful friends - and there are a lot of them, supporting us and helping us in trying to find a cure for cancer. So many people still needed to meet Zac and be a witness to his work.

Zac with Austin at Zac's 9th birthday. 6-30-12

CHAPTER 17
"i will never give up!"

It was Monday, surgery day. This was major brain surgery. Nathan and I had met with the neurosurgeon, Dr. Gillaume who was going to operate on Zachary. He said he was hoping that the tumor had not grown into the septal membrane (the line dividing the left brain hemisphere from the right.) He wouldn't know what he was dealing with until he got in there, examined the fluid in the center of the tumor and determined if it was fluid or hemorrhage. He anticipated surgery to last three or four hours.

Nathan, my parents, sisters, Father Al, Nathan's dad and I, all gathered around Zachary's bed to pray before he was taken to the operating room. I looked for strength in God and asked if everyone would pray the rosary with me. Zachary clutched his red rosewood wooden rosary that Father Al had given him the day before. He had gotten it from Rome, Italy years earlier. It was blessed by Pope John Paul II, but Zac insisted that Father Al also bless it. He held onto that rosary all night long.

The hours ticked by while Zachary was being operated on. My dad, sister Marie, Nathan and Father Al busied themselves playing cribbage at a roundtable in the corner of the room. The rest of us talked the hours away trying to keep the mood light. The presence of my family was a comforting distraction.

We ended up being the last family remaining in the waiting room. I fought my fears until Dr. Moertel and Dr. Guillaume finally approached us around 7 pm - six hours after the surgery started. The card game came to a sudden halt and all conversation stopped.

I scanned their faces for information. They gave nothing away. My heart was pounding out of my chest. "How is he?"

"Zac did very well," Dr. Guillaume said softly. I knew there was more that he was trying to figure out how to say. I waited nervously.

"Unfortunately, we were not able to get all of the tumor, because like I thought from looking at the scans, the tumor did grow into the septal membrane. Removing it at all would have damaged the motor center, leaving Zac permanently paralyzed on his right side - or worse."

"Is it a meningioma, like you thought?" I asked

"It doesn't look like the one that he had radiation on, but, no, it didn't have the characteristics of the meningioma," Dr. Guillaume informed us.

"The question is whether it is a sarcoma," Dr. Moertel added. "A biopsy was sent off and it began showing characteristics of one, but there are several types of sarcomas."

"Is it better to have a brain sarcoma than an astrocytoma?" I asked looking for reassurance.

"They are both types you don't want to see," Dr. Moertel admitted solemnly.

"When will you know for sure?" Nathan asked as I sat quietly processing the news.

"We won't know what type until Wednesday. We will have our conference meeting around 2 pm. The care team will come up with the best treatment plan for Zac then," Dr. Moertel determined. "I'm guessing he will have to undergo radiation and chemotherapy again."

I couldn't hold myself together any longer. I slumped over burying my face in my hands and let out a loud cry. "When is enough, enough? How much more does he have to take!?" I continued my rant in between my sobbing. "Where are you God? Where – are - you?!" I fell on to my mom's left shoulder as Barb grabbed on to my right knee as my body started to shake. I let out a long groan. "I can't do this anymore!"

I didn't care that I was making a spectacle of myself. I was completely lost in my grief and in the darkness I felt trapped in. Nathan was exactly right when he said, "we were in a living-nightmare." We were trapped in it and Zac couldn't catch a break for all of us to escape this unending horrifying reality.

I came to my senses and I reached deep down to find my courage to pull myself back together. I stopped crying and set aside my pity-party. Zac was the one suffering. If he wasn't going to quit, then I most certainly would not either. I would stand by him every step of the way.

I was praying that whatever type of cancer Zachary had that it would respond to some form of treatment because the alternative was something that would kill me. My heart was already breaking for Zachary.

Zachary had to spend the night in the pediatric ICU. He was doing okay even though his head was bandaged like a mummy, minus the bandages across the face. He slept most of the night and into the next day. He didn't complain once. He just wanted to be transferred out of the ICU and back up to his original room where it was more inviting.

Two days later and after another MRI, Zachary was clear to be discharge from the ICU. We got upstairs late afternoon and Zachary had already his first physical therapy to help him begin walking again. Dr. Guillaume and Moertel were very impressed with how fast he was regaining his strength after surgery. He could lift his arm, his hand grasp was much stronger and he could move his leg and wiggle his toes! Who would have thought something like wiggling your toes could bring such a smile to one's face? Praise God!

It was a lot of work lifting and lowering his leg and by the time he had shuffled out into the hallway and back into his room, Zac was tired out. Almost as soon as he lay back in bed he mentioned, "I have to go to the bathroom."

"Ah, Zac! Too bad you didn't think of that before you got all tucked in," I remarked. "Okay, I'll help you."

I was waiting for Zachary to make the first move when he was ready. He started lifting his head, and immediately began to cry. I thought he was in pain -"Zac, what's wrong?"

"Angels. They were just holding my head," Zac quietly whispered.

For a moment I thought he was making it up, but it only took a second to see how real the tears were. Zac never cried for no reason or to get attention. He hadn't even cried once about being in pain after having another major brain surgery. I sensed a sudden shift of peace in this moment. I knew these Angels were real and this time they brought comfort, strength and healing.

"What did they do?" I asked.

"They were holding my head with both hands."

"What did it feel like?" I wanted details. I wanted to know more.

"It felt - beautiful!" Zac said with a smile of an angel on his face as a tear streamed down his cheek.

I sat there in awe of the gift of this child. I was humbled by his strength and "never give up" attitude. I could only hope to learn from him and be more like him. He was my hero. He fought like a Navy SEAL. I now really understood why a friend of ours, Pat, gave Zachary his son Nick's Navy SEAL Trident pin a few days after his son's funeral. Pat said he and Nick talked about Zac being the toughest person they knew. Nick heroically died August 6, 2011 after being shot down in a Chinook militarily helicopter along with thirty other military personnel in Afghanistan. Zachary was also a fighter, a warrior in every sense of the word.

We had a meeting with Dr. Moertel, Dr. Guillaume, Dr. Jess Barnum and Tammie. My sisters and Mom came to support Nathan and I as we were to learn of the type of cancer Zac had and the treatment plan. The tumor was what they had feared - a sarcoma. It was extremely rare, highly malignant and fast-growing.

At first they thought radiation would be too dangerous a second time, but Dr. Dusenberry decided it would now be possible and they would be able to prevent any radiation from crossing over into where Zac had been radiated last year. If it were to happen there would be serious consequences for Zac. Dr. Dusenberry and Dr. Moertel wanted to start as soon as possible and not wait until Zachary was completely healed from surgery because they were afraid that this tumor would grow rapidly. He would then have a scan two weeks after his six weeks of radiation and then begin on two different types of chemotherapy.

Searching for hope, I asked Dr. Moertel if he had taken care of any kids with brain sarcomas and how they typically did. He said, "Yes, but the outcome is not very good." He admitted that he had never taken care of a child with NF and a brain sarcoma. "The NF piece complicates things. I am not sure how this chemo will work or if the tumor will grow in spite of all the medicine, but my hope is that it will work."

The meeting was done and the plan was made, and now I had to face my son and renege on the comment that he wouldn't have to go through chemo again if he had brain surgery. I couldn't be the one to break his heart. I asked Dr. Moertel to be the one to tell him. I could tell that he didn't want to either.

Zachary was sitting on the edge of the bed when Dr. Moertel came in. "Hey, Zac. I need to tell you something," he began as he sat down in the chair next to the bed. "We couldn't get all of the tumor so now we will have to do radiation again."

Zac solemnly and quietly said, "Okay."

"Zac," Dr. Moertel paused as he moved his chair right up to his bed so that his knees were almost touching Zac's. "I know we didn't think we needed to, before surgery, but it is also necessary that we start chemotherapy again."

Zachary look shocked and quickly shut his eyes and sat there very still. He didn't say a word. The one tear streaming down his face said it all, then more followed at a faster rate. My heart was breaking for him. This wasn't part of the deal. Without complaining, he went through brain surgery, now he has to go through what he hates most of all - ALL OVER AGAIN!

Zac suddenly opened up his eyes. "Now, wait - am I going to get that nausea and that - you know - sick feelings?" He was so dreading the side effects of the chemo.

"It might not be as bad as last time because the tumor isn't as deep," Dr. Moertel said trying to be reassuring.

Everyone in the room felt Zac's discouragement, pain and frustration. We all crowded around Zac, on and by the bed and held him and told him how brave and strong he was, but he didn't have to always be. We told him he could still be mad and sad.

"The bravest of men cry," Barb added.

He seemed to have calmed down, but kept his eyes closed as all of us sat silently with him - even Dr. Moertel. What else could you say? There was nothing any of us could say or do to make it better. He wanted guarantees too.

Zac opened up his eyes and firmly spoke, "I will never give up!"

After seven days of being in the hospital, Zachary was able to come home. He was very happy to be back with his brother and sisters, back to his own bed where all was normal and good. He was worried about what was to come. He knew the plan, but still every time I would talk to the doctors or family or a friend about it, he would just shut his eyes. It was like he was trying to shut himself out of the world - to escape to someplace else. If he was talked to about the plan, he would answer simply, letting them know in a word or two what they needed to know... end of conversation. Zachary would get so quiet at times, it began to worry me that he might become depressed.

Zachary began radiation only six days after being discharged from the hospital. He was tolerating it this time around so much better than the last. He had gone seven or eight weeks without retching or vomiting - the longest stretch in close to two years.

The steroids played a big part in keeping the swelling off of the motor center of the brain, but because he required such a large dose, he quickly started to gain weight - especially in his face. He looked like he had put on ten pounds in a matter of days. He was hungry all the time and if the drug was given too close to bed, he was not able to sleep. Unfortunately, because of the busy long summer days, I forgot his evening dose until it was too close to bedtime. So two nights in a row, I held it, hoping instead Zac would get his much-needed rest. Bad move. Zac began complaining of his right leg feeling heavy. I quickly learned this was one of many meds that he needed on schedule.

I knew many family members and friends felt helpless as Nathan and I fought to do whatever we needed to do in our efforts to save her son. My brother and sister-in-law, Greg and Sandy organized a golf tournament to raise money for the Zachary NF and Cancer Research Fund. It was a beautiful day for golf. Zachary participated as much as he could and the evening concluded with a nice dinner of filet Mignon and crabcakes. For a first golf fundraiser, $5000 was made. It was $5000 closer to finding a cure.

Neighbors and friends generously made us meals, gave us gas cards, financial support, helped us with our other kids and continued to pray for Zachary's healing.

Nathan and I really tried to keep Zachary busy with fun things to do, to keep him excited about life and to have things to look forward to so he could remember the summer as a really fun one and not one of brain surgery, radiation and more chemo. Nathan finally took out his boat after having it stored away for three years. He took Zac, Nic and some other friends fishing and started planning more days to go out. They had so much fun. Zac's kindergarten teacher, Debbie Krenz and fourth grade teacher, Mr. Krenz took Zac out mini golfing and a couple, about 70-years-old, who were like grandparents to Nic, Jessica, Zac and Lexie (Lynn and Riley) took them to a movie and to Stars and Strikes to bowl and play laser tag. Poor Riley volunteered to jump in the game and wear Lexie's laser vest because it was too big and heavy for her 4-year-old little body to wear. Zachary and Jessica got him good, so they said.

My prayer life grew and I was strengthened by the words I read in my prayer books. I knew my relationship with God was what was holding me together. Each time I went to church I left feeling "filled-up." The music spoke to me on such a different level. I listened intently to the word our priests spoke during the homily. I searched for meaning and answers everywhere and in everything.

I hoped and prayed that each one of my children would learn from the example I was trying to set up. They were great kids. I was proud knowing they prayed. I could hear Nic through his and Zac's bedroom door, on many occasions as he read to Zac from a military Bible that Nathan gave him. I was pleased that I didn't have to pull teeth to get them to come to church. They just knew it was the right thing to do.

I was given a new prayer to St. Peregrine, the patron saint of those suffering from cancer. As I was reading it out loud to Zachary for the first time, a tear rolled down his face. When I asked him why he was crying, he remained silent. I wished I would have read the prayer first myself.

"Did the prayer make you sad?" I asked.

He turned and hugged me tightly as he continued to cry. "It just isn't fair," he wept.

I really wanted him to talk without upsetting him more so I cautiously asked, "What do you mean?"

"I'm just tired of having to do this over and over again."

As soon as I heard the word, "tired," I froze. I had never heard him say that before. I had been deathly afraid to hear him say something like that, but even more afraid for him to mean it, literally.

We talked a while until he calmed down. I did ask him a question I never wanted to, for fear of his answer. "Do you not want to do this anymore?" I wasn't sure if he actually knew what the end result would be if he "stopped," but I knew.

"I will never give up!" Zachary assured me in a very determined voice.

I don't think I could have let him even if he wanted to. I loved him so much and selfishly needed him with me.

How disturbed Zachary was by that prayer really bothered me. I continued to think it was because of a certain word and how it was used in the prayer...

'O great St. Peregrine, you have been called "The Mighty", "The Wonder Worker" because of the numerous miracles which you obtained from God for those who have turned to you in their need. For so many years, you bore in your own flesh this cancerous disease that destroys the very fiber of our being. –'

I asked him the next morning if the prayer scared him because it had the word, "cancer," in it. He confirmed what I was thinking. Needless to say, I told him he didn't have to say that prayer. There were other prayers, and his own words were just as good.

With only two weeks left of radiation and chemotherapy, Nic decided to tag along with Zac. Nic was being his normal "goofy-big-brother" self - chasing Zac and trying to spank him if he wouldn't go up or down the stairs fast enough. Boy, did he get Zac laughing. I couldn't help but smile as hospital staff had to dodge them in the hallways.

In the room where Zachary received his chemotherapy, they played games on the DS and iPod that was given by generous friends - talk about hours of entertainment. While they ate lunch, side-by-side, they watched a movie. Nicholas couldn't believe what Zac's stay involved or how long it took. It had been a while since he was able to come along because of school or sports. Zac was so pleased that he had his big brother's companionship.

It took four weeks for Zac's hair to fall out again. I was hoping maybe he would get lucky this time. He was pulling it out in clumps.

"Zac, don't do that, I sadly said.

"Mom, look!" Zac said showing me a clump of his short blondish-brown hair in his fingers. "I'm worried, Mom."

I was kind of shocked myself. It happens so suddenly. It was like a really dry Christmas tree that you dared not touch because when you did, the pine needles showered down like rain all over the floor. Zac sat up after lying on the couch and I looked down the back of his black T-shirt. It was covered in hair and there was now a big bald patch on the side of his head where it had rubbed up against the pillow. Patch by patch Zac's hair started to fall out. A couple of days later, I ended up having to shave the rest off. When I finished, Zac started crying. He reached for the mirror. I held his hand for a moment and asked if he was sure he wanted to look. I was afraid for him to see. I was afraid he would be even more scared of his appearance once he looked. I have to admit, I kind of was. He didn't look like the 10-year-old boy that he was. At first Zac, said he didn't want to look, but then I came to my senses realizing that he would eventually see himself in the mirror. Now I thought he should take a look when I was right by him. He ended up looking and began to cry again.

Once a week during radiation, Zac had to check in with Dr. Dusenberry. He was still doing pretty well with a short bout of nausea and retching. Of course I immediately worried that it could be related to tumor growth, but I quickly tried to dismiss the negative thought. I had time to remember he had recently switched steroid meds. It probably wasn't strong enough.

I struggled daily with the terror of what we were facing and the hope that Zachary could overcome this, but a conversation with Dr. Dusenberry kept haunting me. She told me in her twenty years she had only seen about three patients with the brain sarcomas. "It is very rare."

I dared to ask if "those patients" did well. She stammered a bit before saying, "Hmm… I don't remember."

I didn't like how that sounded. No one seemed to be able to offer any hope. But with the way Zac responded to his last radiation, she said she was very optimistic that he would respond well this time too.

I searched so hard for the hope that Zac would be able to beat this. I suppose that's why I kept asking questions of everyone. When I saw Dr. Moertel after one of Zac's radiation treatments, I asked him about what Dr. Dusenberry actually knew.

"She knows, doesn't she? She just doesn't want to tell me," I said trying to get the truth out of Dr. Moertel.

"She was just copping out," he admitted. "I'm sorry I don't have any reassuring words for you. I just don't know."

Maybe I kept asking for answers because I couldn't comprehend what was being told to me without someone being brutally honest. At the same time, I don't think I could have handled brutal honesty. I couldn't wrap my head around this. Determine as I was, I couldn't let anything, but life, be the only outcome for Zachary. The alternative was unbearable to me!

I battled back and forth throughout the day and while I tried to sleep, that the visions and scenarios I feared may come to pass. I swear the devil was trying to wear me down. It would be easier to give in and admit defeat and stop praying, but I knew that would please the devil, so I hung on and prayed even harder. God is my strength. He is good. As my devotional prayer book writes - *"having sacrificed my very life for you, I can be trusted in every facet of your life."*

I had no one else that could promise me that Zachary was going to be just fine. I had to trust God's plan. Zachary had a purpose. I just wasn't exactly sure what it was, but I was seeing how people gravitated towards him and how happy people were just to be around him. I continued to call on Jesus to keep me strong and to help chase away the frightening thoughts.

Radiation was completed right before Zac was going to start fourth grade. It helped Zac tremendously to have Nic come with him to his appointments or when Jessica and Lexie would tag along and have their "movie theater" day and eat the hospital lunch. Those days went by quicker and felt more like a party. Zac was happier and so grateful to know he wasn't going through this alone.

The first day of fourth grade went smoothly for Zac. He really liked Mr. Krenz, who his sister Jessica had three years earlier. He was happy to be back with all of his friends and doing something normal that all the other kids did. He came home with a big smile and changed into his swim shorts. It was a warm day and the summer-like days were numbered. Nathan would soon be closing up the pool for the impending winter.

With me to keep him company, Zac jumped into the pool, swam around briefly and had me count how long he could hold his breath underwater - something he always liked to challenge himself and then he was done. Tired out from no nap all day, he made his way to the driveway where I later found him sleeping on the warm cement. He was so exhausted. He slept about an hour until Jessica thought it would be funny and she put a caterpillar on his back. Nice way to be woken up!

September 12, 2012 - Zachary had a follow-up MRI. The day didn't start out very well when his nurse was unable to access his port due to the extra weight he had put on because of the steroids. The port site was puffy and irregular looking, making it a difficult stick to begin with, but after several attempts the lidocaine cream wore off. With tears in his eyes Zac said he wanted her to stop. The nurse was teary eyed herself, she felt so bad. We ended up getting another nurse to access it and he was ready.

Even before Dr. Moertel got into Zac's room, Nathan nervously asked him how things looked. He said, "Things look pretty good." In comparison to his last MRI the tumor did not grow which was the main concern, because in spite of radiation these tumors come back doubled in size. Unfortunately, it is also not unusual for cysts to grow in place of the tumor. That was what Zac was dealing with.

For now, he would continue to watch him closely since the cysts can act like a tumor and cause the same problems. If the cyst did grow, Zac would need a shunt placed to divert the fluid. So Zac would get a two week break to continue to recover and we would meet after Dr. Moertel discussed Zac's case with Dr. Guillaume and other colleagues. He expected he would start up a new type of chemotherapy. He also informed me that Zac "has maxed out on radiation and can never have it again in his lifetime."

Those words sounded so final, almost punishing. I asked, "But if it comes back, can you still do something?"

With intense thought in his eyes, he said, "I can do a lot of things."

He also told me that the researcher, Dr. Largaespada asked if he could have a section of the tumor that was removed from Zachary to study. His hope was to come up with cross treatment possibilities (something along those lines.) I say, *HURRY UP!*

The researchers were wonderful. They met Zac a few times when he came to help feed the fish and mice that aided their research efforts. They were instantly taken by him. They all had a picture of him on their desks saying they are trying to find all different cures without knowing the people behind their work. With Zac, it became personal and they had a new drive. *Pretty cool*, I thought.

So, yet one more thing. It's hard not to get discouraged in the face of disappointment over and over again, but in the big picture I knew this was good news. The tumor hadn't grown. We had more time, but I still felt like someone was standing on my chest - maybe not with all their weight. I just wanted to hear the words, "Zac is healed." I hated the "lurking-in-the-bushes" feeling.

Mentally, I sometimes crumbled many times throughout a day. I never knew with Zac because he always walked around with a smile on his face. He was incredibly positive. He didn't focus on the negative. He would think about it for a few minutes, process it, sometimes get a little mad when he was at his limit of feeling sick, but he always let it go. It could be school, getting together with a friend, a football game, going to Minnesota Wild or Gopher hockey game or family night that helped him live to the next day.

One particular day Zac received a letter in the mail from Matt, who was a Navy SEAL. He had been friends with Nick Spehar a fellow Navy SEAL who perished on the Chinook military helicopter on August 6, 2011 when it was shot down killing all 38 people on board. Zac was very found of Nick and because of him was bound and determined to one day become a Navy SEAL. His admiration intensified after our family visited Nick's dad a few days after his son's funeral when he stated "Nick and I talked about you a lot. Nick said he thought you were the toughest guy he knew." Pat paused a moment as he choked back the tears as he stepped closer to Zac. "Do you know what this is?" he asked as he held up a SEAL trident as the sunlight reflected off of the golden insignia.

Pat went on to explain it was a much sought after badge issued only to enlisted members who completed the year-and-a-half SEAL training. It represented what a Navy SEAL stands for – the old anchor symbolizes the Navy, which reminds them of where their roots come from – the accomplishments of the Naval Combat Demolition Units and Underwater Demolitions Teams. The trident symbolizes a connection to the sea. The pistol represents the SEALS capabilities on land, it is cocked and ready to fire and should serve as a constant reminder that you must be ready at all times. The eagle symbolizes the SEALS ability to swiftly insert from the air. Normally, when the eagle is placed on military decorations, its head is held high. On the SEALS insignia, the eagles head is lowered to remind that humility is the true measure of warrior's strength.

"I thought long and hard about this. This trident was given to me by Nick's commander." Moving yet closer to Zac, Pat reached out and pinned the trident to Zac's t-shirt.

My eyes widened as I starred in astonishment.

"I know Nick would want you to have this," Pat admitted wiping tears from his eyes. "You earned your trident."

Zac held the trident to the highest respect from that day forward.

Matt had previously met Zac and our family a few months after Nick's funeral and continued to pray and support him along with his Navy SEAL brothers who had learned about him. It excited and inspired Zac even more.

Matt was currently in Afghanistan preparing *"to do the job that we do...which is to make sure bad men do not harm the people we care about back home in America."* He went on to say... *"We train hard for this mission and put in a lot of time in order to increase our chances of mission success. We have millions of dollars and hundreds of people dedicated to help us prepare for our mission. However, what blows me and the guys away is that you never received any training to complete your mission, but have had success in beating the cancer once already. Your strength hasn't been built by trainers or years of work, instead, you possess an inner strength that has been forged through the adversity you have experienced during your fight with cancer. You are a motivation to us all here at the team and we are behind you all the way."*

Zac was all smiles as Nathan read it out loud to him. He never looked at himself as doing something extraordinary. To him it was what he had to do because he wanted to live. Yes, he was frustrated at times and he was sick of having to live year after year receiving chemo treatments, but there was so much he wanted to do. Matt and the seal team motivated Zac. He saw them as incredibly tough warriors. They were strong and they set their fear aside to take on the mission at hand.

Many times Nathan would encourage Zachary to get through a difficult moment, be it a difficult needlestick, working through pain or taking medicine, by saying - "Come on Zac, you can do it! Be a Navy seal!" Knowing he was like a Navy seal, it empowered him to push through.

The next appointment we met with Dr. Moertel. After discussing Zachary's case with the team they came up with what they felt was the best plan for him right now. There were two different drugs that they felt could work to combat the incurable brain sarcoma with the least side effects. The problem was they were very expensive. I didn't ask how much, it didn't matter. We would have to wait to begin treatment until Dr. Moertel submitted the request to our insurance company. He warned us that they might deny it because it was extremely expensive, but we would appeal it. One way or another we would get it. Dr. Moertel hoped to start Zac on it sometime next week.

More hoops to jump through with the news that our insurance company denied our request. Sure the new drug was expensive, but it wasn't like we were asking for the "really expensive" stuff right away. Dr. Moertel would have to supply them with all the previous chemo drugs Zac had been on these past eight years.

I couldn't understand how a group of dignified business people could deny a child or anyone for that matter, medicine (trial or not) that potentially could be the answer in saving their life. I swore if they denied Zachary this time, I would go wherever they were and demand a meeting. (Maybe I'd barge into one already in session. At this point I would do anything for Zachary.) I would ask each and every one of them who had a say in the decision which child of theirs they would choose to put a death sentence on - or if I could pick. I would have them look into Zachary's eyes and tell him what their decision would mean for him. *Can you tell I had put some thought into this?* I was angry! There was no way it would end here.

While we waited, Zac eagerly looked forward to Chicago Lakes High School football game. He had been chosen to be honorary captain for the game. Two weeks prior to the game, eight boys, including Danny (Thomas's older brother) stopped by to give Zac a football skullcap that was signed by all the players. They told Zac the news of him being captain. Zac couldn't wait for game day. He started off with "the coin toss" to determine which team would receive the ball first. (We should have practiced flipping the coin.) Zac was announced in the lineup and was the first to run out onto the field and break the banner, leading the rest of the team. Zac was pumped! You could see the intense energy pouring from his entire being.

"Yes! Yes!" Zac chanted in sheer excitement and delight of "THIS" moment. He punched his fist in the air as he ran.

What an exhilarating, proud moment for me, to see how happy and full of life as Zac was. I was touched by the thoughtfulness of the football Association, coaches, players and Stephanie (Thomas and Danny's mom) who coordinated the event. It may have not been a big deal to the team or the parents and students in the bleachers, but it meant the world to Zac. Zac lived and I literally "lived" for days like these. It lifted him up and carried him through the difficult days.

October 12, 2012, Zachary had an MRI to check on the cysts as well as the rest of the brain. The cysts were smaller so we did not have to meet with Zac's neurosurgeon to talk about a shunt being placed. The swelling had also gone down more in his brain and the tumor site was also smaller. A bit of relief for now, but I was still not able to take a "deep breath."

Dr. Moertel also informed me that the insurance company agreed to cover the new expense of chemotherapy drugs for Zac. I was relieved to say the least. He would start the infusion today and provided he would not have liver or kidney damage or develop a certain rash, he would be on it for at least six months.

"If these meds work and the sarcoma is not visible on the MRI - would it stay gone forever?" I asked looking for reassurance.

I wanted more than anything to be told this type of tumor could disappear, to never come back if so many years went by or if certain drugs dissolved it. I asked questions expecting answers that I wanted to hear, but instead got answers that left me fearing for Zachary's future. In those moments, I clung to my faith and believed so strongly that God could override anything. There was always hope.

"These tumors come back quite quickly. That's why I wanted to get this drug approved and get started on it right away," Dr. Moertel explained, half-heartedly answering my question.

In my head, I heard what he was also fearing, but quickly dismissed any finality of his words. Dr. Moertel didn't know for sure Zachary's fate. He said so himself that he has never dealt with a child or an adult with NF and a brain sarcoma. Zachary was a fighter. He had already overcome so many obstacles. *Why would this be any different?*

And yet there was something different about Zachary that I haven't seen in other children. It was the way he treated other people. You could tell how much he loved them by how he made everyone feel special. He always prayed for others who he saw suffering - It was the little girl who had no hair or the boy in the wheelchair or the old person walking with a cane or Sophie, from church who was ninety-three years old or Tony who confessed to Zac that he was scared for his upcoming surgery. That day after mass, Zac went into the sacristy with Tony who was to receive 'Annointing of the Sick.' Turning to Tony, Zac maturely said, "Don't be afraid, God will be with you." Without much hesitation, Zac would walk away from me and approach the unfortunate person he saw before him. "I will pray for you," Zac would tell them and return back to where I was standing.

He was good as gold, through and through. I can honestly say he "never" did anything bad on purpose. The incident with hitting his brother with the baseball bat was purely an accident and I don't really count when Nathan would asked Zac if he had washed his hands before dinner and he would say "yes," but he really didn't, as being so horrible. He was a child and he was probably really hungry that day!

Aside from those things, I started looking at Zachary as a "mini-Jesus," loving, greeting and getting people to follow him. He was a walking ray of sunshine. He had a message. *How many needed to hear it? Hundreds? Thousand? Millions?* I hoped millions because then it meant Zachary had a lot of years of work to do here on earth.

Zac and Dr. Moertel. NF Hero award presented to Zac for the most courageous and positive kid going through NF and cancer treatments. 5-15-12

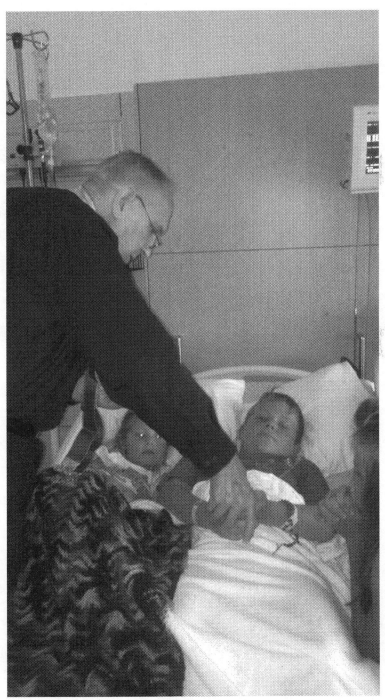

Zac (10 yrs old) in hospital praying with Father Al before brain surgery (with Lexie(4) and Jess(12)) 7-8-2012

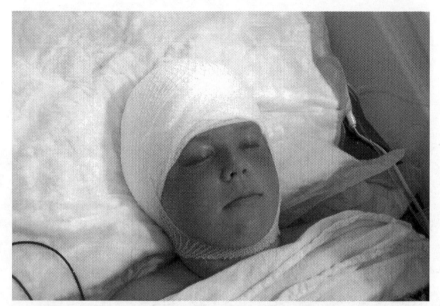

Zac after brain surgery for a rare sarcoma. 7-9-12

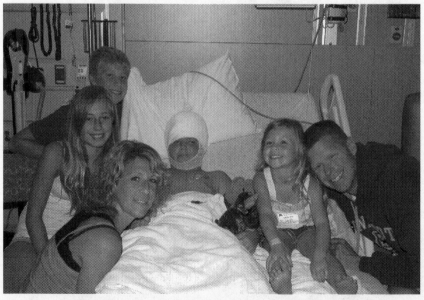

Zac, Carol Ann, Jess, Nic, Lexie and Nathan after unexpected surgery. 7-10-12

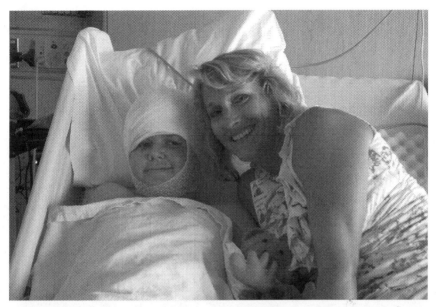

Zac and Aunt Carla a day after brain surgery. 7-10-2012

Zac -The Beast wearing his new skull cap given to him by the Chisago Lakes HS football team when they came to ask if he would be a co-captain. 8-17-13

9-24-12 The Chisago Lakes football captains! Zac with
Danny and Bradee. Let the game begin!

CHAPTER 18

on a mission

The new chemo drugs were quickly affecting Zac. His platelet and white blood count dropped quickly. He could be more susceptible to infection when his white blood count was low. He also started vomiting again and was beside himself with uncontrollable itching from his oral chemotherapy. At times Zac would lay on the floor and rub his back up and down on the carpet to get relief, other times it looked as if he was frantically trying to remove a swarm of mosquitoes from his back, stomach and arms. I felt helpless once again. Lotion gave only a mild temporary relief. It was worrisome when it showed up red and raised on the side of his face, under his eyes, the corner of his eyes and on his eyelids. It looked as if someone punched him in the eye. Of course the Zac didn't complain much. He just itched and asked for help putting lotion on.

On a positive note, Zac was pretty excited that he was slowly losing the steroid weight. We adjusted his diet, limiting sweets - he agreed to only eat one sweet a day - maybe two. Nathan and I had learned that cancer fed off of sugar. It was so hard to hold Zac accountable to limiting his sweets when his sisters and brother could pretty much eat them whenever they wanted. I didn't feel it was fair to restrict Nic, Jessica or Lexie though. They were already struggling with the attention that was continually focused upon their brother. They handled it better now that they were older, but I still saw moments when their anger would spark because of something related to Zac. It wasn't because of the "things" given to Zac, but I knew it was the lack of attention that was really the reason.

For such a young boy, Zac understood we weren't trying to be mean by withholding sweets. He knew it was a chance at beating cancer. Many times he would come home and say, "I didn't have any sweets at school today and it was Katie's birthday. I told her 'no thank you,' when she was going to give me her birthday treat."

"Oh, honey! You should have had it. It was a special day," I said feeling regretful for him.

"That's okay. I wasn't sure what I would want for my sweet at home," Zac explained.

"You could have had Katie's birthday treat and one at home too. Remember that having extra sweets are okay once in a while, just not all the time."

"I want to be healed so I'm only going to have one sweet a day..." Zac paused, "maybe none."

After only a few treatments, Zac's blood pressure was pretty high. It always ended up coming back down, but we had to wait at the hospital until it did. His vomiting episodes were controlled by the drug, Zofran. His body was fighting so hard.

"How much longer do I have to be on this chemo?" Zac asked a bit distressed.

I didn't have the heart to tell him, hopefully, four or five months. I think he would have crawled out of his skin, but he deserved an answer so I replied, "A few more months, I think - I'm sorry sweetie."

Zac was blessed with many wonderful friends and friends of friends who heard about Zac and wanted to do nice things for him. Many times Nic, Jessica and Lexie were able to benefit from the gifts. This time Nic and Nathan were able to go with him on a guided bear hunt in Butternut, Wisconsin. (The girls and I could have gone, but decided to stay back. I'm not a hunter and I know Lexie would have gone nuts staying in a small cabin with no Max and Ruby to watch.) Actually the first bear hunt Zac and Nathan went on to the same location, they didn't see anything. Their guides felt bad that they didn't have the dogs to aid them in tracking a bear so they invited them back a few weeks later.

Nic was able to make this hunt and it was a good thing he did. This time they had the dogs that they needed to track a bear. They chased it right up a tree. As the dogs barked uncontrollably, Nic and Zac ran with the guides to where they came upon a two-hundred-plus pound bear. Zac was given permission to take the shot. Nathan steadied the platform for the gun, held his breath and without hesitation Zac fired his rifle. You wouldn't have guessed that Zac was legally blind in his left eye. He shot a perfectly executed shot and dropped the bear right out of the tree.

Immediately Zac started shouting "YAHHH! YAHHHHH!!!," in excitement. He raced over to one of the guides, Chad, and gave him a big hug. Off to the bear he ran to see the efforts of his long, cold days that he put in to get this bear. He was a true hunter. Like father like son.

Two months later, in November, Zac was invited to go on a special deer hunt through Wilderness Whitetails in Rosholt, Wisconsin. It was set up through United Special Sportsmen Alliance (USSA) a nonprofit wish granting charity that specializes in sending critically ill and disabled youth (and veterans) on the outdoor adventure of their dreams. Someone through Zac's archery club spread the word about Zac's love for hunting and before we knew it, Zac was asked if he would want to go on the special hunt. Needless to say, he didn't have to be asked a second time.

Nathan and Zac left late at night after Chisago's football game. They drove about four hours to the camp where they slept a couple of hours before getting up to get in position to begin their vigil. I was a bit worried sending Zac who was already tired, out in the cold and leaving his dad in charge of all his meds. I knew when Zac's body became stressed, he got sick and the vomiting episodes would fire up, but I couldn't deny him from doing the things he loved to do. Opportunities like this gave him something to focus on and look forward to. It helped him get through the difficult times.

After his second night, right away in the morning before sunrise, Zac spotted his first attainable deer. As Nathan helped steady Zac's gun, he prayed that Zac would make a good shot and not just wound the animal. Zac took a deep breath and held it as he fired an incredible shot, dropping the deer in its tracks. Zac was elated! With tears in his eyes, his smile extended from ear to ear.

"Nice shot, dude!" Then Nathan jokingly said, "The bad news is - you're going to get beat up. The good news - YOU JUST BAGGED A MONSTER BUCK!!!"

Zachary re-called, before the trip that Nic, half-jokingly warned him, "If you get a buck before me, I'm going to pound you!"

Without flinching, Zac toughly yelled in a military voice, "I'M GONNA TAKE THE PAIN!"

To Nathan, Zac and their guide's surprise, Zac just shot a massive nineteen-point buck! The deer ended up weighing in at over three-hundred pounds, one-hundred pounds more than his bear! Nathan was just as giddy as Zac . He had been hunting for many years and the biggest deer he ever shot was an eight-pointer.

Right after the hunt, Nathan and Zac drove straight to the ice arena where a game was just finishing up. Zac carried his giant buck antler trophy into the locker room to show his brother and his teammates before their practice. They were all stunned, but not more than his brother Nic. Oh, how happy they were for him! The pats on the back and words of congratulations were so uplifting as the players and their parents stood in awe of such an amazing accomplishment of someone so young and struggling with his health and eyesight.

Zac was glad to be home after a tiring, cold, exciting trip. I was more relieved to have him back where I could keep my eye on him. I felt better knowing I could see him, touch him and hug him. It was hard to step back and let him go to do adventures, normal activities without me close by.

Back to the routines of home, Nathan and I knelt beside Zachary's bed like we always did and prayed to Blessed Pope John Paul II, St. Peregrine, as well as our own prayers. Zac started to cry. Right away, I knew why he was so sad. I knew prayer time made him think and pray more deeply. I could see it in his face as he laid on his back, eyes closed and hands folded.

I asked if he was crying because dad used the word "cancer" in his prayer.

Through his tears, he sobbed, "Yes."

That evil word frightened him. I tried never to say that ugly word. It was easier for Zac and myself to use the less ugly word, "tumor." As evil as the devil was, he was continuing to try and sneak his way into Zac any way that he could. It sounded gruesome, I know. I didn't say that to Zac, but that was what it was comparable to. We would not accept it by name or by disease. Zac was more powerful than ever. Our prayers were bigger and stronger than ever. People were praying for him all over the world and I believed, his "two Jesuses" were "pushing" him through the tough times and "pulling" him over the hurdles that were set before him.

It was December 4, time for Zachary's next MRI that morning. He had been in an extra good mood with St. Nicholas Day only days away.

"You know how I know this is going to be a good St. Nicholas day?"

"Why?" I asked with Zac barely waiting for me to speak.

"Because I already know what I'm going to get it. I am going to be healed!" Zac spoke with such confidence and no hesitation.

I wanted to do the same, but I wondered as a parent, punched in the gut one too many times, if I would be irresponsible for not shielding myself from past blows. In our house we would continue to speak good and holy words. I would continue to battle against the evil that crept into my mind. Zac didn't need to know of my apprehension. His belief was what helped him to live so fully and so freely. Nathan and I would not take that away from him. I had never heard him speak a single negative word on this roller coaster of a life he had been on for the past eight years.

I was apprehensive about doing another MRI right before Christmas. The results of our past two December MRI's were not good and made it difficult to celebrate in the darkness of the situation.

I was trying to stay positive, but it was hard when Zac started getting sick again the week before. He was sick to his stomach seven to eight times during the night and started up again in the morning before school. When he says he wants to stay home from school, you knew he didn't feel well. I was noticing that he seemed more tired lately and on top of that, he was still limping.

The limping began about five maybe six weeks earlier, with Zac saying that it was a pulled muscle. I thought it was, at first because he had been running around the perimeter at school, during recess to get the steroid weight off. He was so proud of himself and the results of his hard work. Lakeside Elementary school even started a Mile Club that kids could join and keep track of their weekly miles. This pushed Zac even harder. So far he was the leader with the most miles and he had tiny little rubber shoes that he would receive for each several miles that he ran, that he could put on his shoelace as proof of miles accumulated.

For the last several weeks Zac had to resort to walking because of his leg. It didn't seem like his leg was improving so I questioned if he really did have a pulled muscle. I continued to mention it to Dr. Moertel and Tammie at the clinic, but they didn't have much to say about it.

I didn't want to overreact if it was just a pulled muscle, but I kept thinking back to July at the brat fundraiser when I thought that Zac had a "pulled muscle"- and it wasn't. What quickly transpired was horrifying. His limping was suspicious and it was very unsettling that a pulled muscle would take this long to heal.

One evening Zachary lost his balance while walking across the kitchen after dinner. He fell down hard, but got right back up. I wanted to call Dr. Moertel then and there and say, "Let's do the MRI now!" My uneasiness grew. I hated the resemblance to July, but it wasn't completely the same. There were no other symptoms. I ran the drill on Zac... no headache, no vision changes, hand grasps were strong and equal, he was sticking his tongue out straight - not deviated to the side. *I just might go mad*, I thought.

I prayed that all the prayers said up to this point, would work in Zac's favor. The MRI showed that the tumor was still there, but surprisingly it was smaller by over

25%. Dr. Moertel said the tumor looked like it was filled with some kind of "gunk." I think he called it "protozoa gunk" which was supposed to disappear with the tumor.

Because we never get upstairs after Zac's MRI's when we are supposed to, we are always late for our scheduled appointment times, but they room Zac and begin the process to start chemotherapy all the same. Dr. Moertel had to leave after a brief visit with us for the weekly brain tumor conference. He said he would review Zac scans with the other doctors and alter his treatment plan if needed.

When Dr. Moertel returned, he confirmed that Zac would remain on this chemotherapy as long as he could tolerate it. Still six months to a year. He was a bit concerned that the chemo was causing high blood pressure and high cholesterol and could prevent him from continuing this course of treatment, but for now, he would watch him closely.

Again I mentioned Zac's limping. Dr. Moertel thought it could be the result of the massive amounts of steroids and the length of time he had been on them and that it could be affecting his joints. He went on to explain that steroids can decrease cartilage around the joints. The plan would be for Zac to have an x-ray the next time he was in. *Finally!*

Zac's story that we shared with Ryan and Shannon for the upcoming radiothon was ready to be aired the following two days when they would be broadcasting from the Mall of America. Friends had called us to tell us they heard our story on the radio. I really hoped in our own little way that we would help raise money to cure cancer in kids. So when Shannon asked if we would come down for a live interview, in addition to our pre-recorded interview, I accepted. Zac wanted to. I felt it was important and wondered – *maybe this is part of what Zac was supposed to do in reaching more people and to help create awareness and raise money.*

I was so nervous, but I knew what I had experienced with Zac needed to be shared. I held together pretty well until Ryan asked me - "What is your Christmas wish?"

Without hesitation I said, "I want Zac to be healed. I want him to be like a normal boy. I want him to go to high school - to be like his older brother, to just be normal." I paused for a second thinking how different Zac's life was from every other boy I knew. The struggle for life was intense. The fear of the possibility of no future was terrifying. "I just can't imagine my life without my child." My voice cracked and the tears came.

Zac sat in a soft red chair next to where Shannon and I sat on a couch. He looked so mature for a 10-year-old, headphones on and microphone in hand.

Ryan turned to Zac. "What are you thinking over there?"

With a quiver of emotion in his voice he said, "I hope people call-in." And like a pro, he read off the 1-800 number for people to call in to KS95 with their pledge. Zac wanted more than anything to be healed. He knew the listeners were his hope in putting their money together in efforts to raise money for research.

"Are you a rockstar at school?" Ryan jokingly asked.

Zac just grinned. He didn't quite know how to respond so I asked Zac my own question. "What are some of the boys doing for you at school?"

"Shaving their h-e-e-a-a-d-s..." You could hear the smile of approval from across the radio.

I went on to explain Zac's battle with cancer. I wanted listeners to know the randomness of cancer. I wanted them to know how one person alone couldn't raise enough money to save a child.

"Why are you here?" Shannon's pre-recording asked Zac, when we were interviewed from his hospital bed, played on air, as we took a break.

"I have to get some medicine. The chemo. And I'm just sick of being in the hospital. I wish I could go home."

"Do you ever worry?" Ryan asked Zac.

"No." Zac reevaluated his answer. -"But sometimes when I'm just going through this, I worry." Zac was trying to fight the tears. You could hear it in his voice.

We cried, we laughed a little, but we stressed how much we needed people to step up and help in finding a cure. We wanted Zachary around for years to come. We needed help as well as so many other kids out there who were also battling cancer.

Nathan sat quietly most of the interview, because I knew every detail of Zac's condition, and I had a difficult time sitting back when anyone talked about him or the need for a cure.

Nathan wanted people to have a glimpse of who Zachary Bartz was. "He is my best friend, my hero. I'm just so proud of him. He inspires so many people and his kindness is such a light. It doesn't matter what happens - his attitude never fails," Nathan's voice was shaking as he wept.

There was not a dry eye in that corner of the Mall of America where the radiothon was aired. Ryan and Shannon were wiping away tears. Our plea was desperate for our son, but at the same time for the other children.

Zac repeated the 1-800 number again and all the phone lines lit up!

"Zac, do you see that?!" Shannon excitedly pointed to all the volunteers taking calls for donations. "You did that, buddy! It was all you!"

Zac started to cry. I wasn't sure what was going on. I hoped what I had said didn't scare him, but I needed the listeners to know that this was real. "Zac, why are you crying?"

"I'm just so happy that people are calling in."

I was amazed at his pure unselfish heart.

"Someone just called in and donated $5000 and said, 'That's because of Zac!'" Shannon proudly relayed.

The phone lines all stayed lit for quite some time.

"You did it again, Zac!" Shannon confirmed. "You know, everytime we aired your story today, all the phone lines lit up. No one else has ever done that."

I was so proud of him. I knew Zac definitely was on a mission. It was just the beginning. Without people seeing or meeting him, he was still able to inspire them.

KS95 ended up raising over half-a-million in two days for cancer research and Gillette Children's Specialty Healthcare. It was a success.

Zac and Thomas - baldies. Just hanging out. 3-10-13

*Zac and Dean O'Brien with the deer he shot. Dean surprised him
with it during a 4ᵗʰ grade presentation at school 3-25-13*

Zac's turkey hunt with USSA guides 5-5-13

CHAPTER 19

metastasizing

As Christmas time was approaching, Zac's pain was worsening and he was limping even more. Climbing the stairs became more difficult for him as well. His doctors didn't want him to wait any longer for a scan to check things out. I asked Tammie, if they suspected they would find a tumor.

"Having the MRI is the next step since his x-ray was clear," Tammie said.

I prayed and asked people to pray that these symptoms Zac was experiencing were related to all current and past steroid use. What kept me calm was hearing from several different people, from church and the schools, telling me "I have a saint on my hands" or "Zac is a very special child" or how inspiring Zac was.

Shortly after Zac and I got home from having his MRI I received a phone call from Tammie telling me they wanted Zac to come back in for another MRI the next day. My first thought was they had found something suspicious. The preliminary report showed the spinal nerve roots were inflamed, but probably as a result of having NF. Tammie didn't think the sarcoma spread to the spine, but wanted another MRI with contrast because the previous one wasn't ordered with it. She and Dr. Moertel wanted the clearest picture they could get - to be sure.

I was frustrated that they hadn't ordered an MRI with contrast right away. It seemed like we were down at the hospital so often, Zac was missing school and I had to work the evening shift during the time Zac was scheduled for his MRI. I passed off my responsibility of taking Zac myself, to Nathan, only because it was of his spine. Had it been of his brain, I would have canceled my shift. I was barely working as it was and with Christmas coming, I thought I'd better keep my shift.

Christmas had come and went. I was disappointed yet again that all the preparation and excitement leading up to Christmas was done once relatives departed, and our heads hit the pillow. My hope was strengthened knowing that one of our worst fears was not the reason for Zac's extremely sore leg.

Dr. Moertel had called and told me that all the doctors in the patient care conference agreed that there was no evidence of the cancer spreading to his spine. They saw many fibroids in his sacrum that they thought could be compressing on the nerves - enlarging them - causing Zac's pain and hence, the limping. They really didn't know. No one had a good explanation. I just wanted them to fix it. Zac was getting very frustrated and cried every once in a while because he was sick of the pain and limitations as a result of it. This was not typical behavior for Zac.

Zac had resorted to sitting on his butt when going downstairs. He could barely carry anything in his arms because he needed to support himself. I felt so bad for him on Christmas day because I encouraged him to go outside to play with his cousins. I didn't want him to be left out. Once he got out there, he stood on the edge of the frozen lake watching them all skate around. Oh, how my heart ached for him! I just wanted him to be able to keep up with the others and to do what they did. Moments later, Olivia who was three months older than Zac, came to help him step down onto the ice. Soon afterward I peeked outside again and I saw the two of them sitting on a small snowbank playing with his snowball thrower he got from Santa. I was glad that someone recognized his limitations and stayed by his side making the best of the situation. My heart lightened.

This couldn't continue on without doing something, I thought. Someone needed to figure out how they would fix Zac's newest ailment. Dr. Guillaume said he could try and do surgery, but he wouldn't even know where to start. There was talk of painful "unpleasant" EMG testing to find out if his pain was coming from the enlarged spinal nerve roots or if it was damage resulting from his brain surgery in July. The other option was to try a new medication that was supposed to help with nerve pain. I chose the medication first before subjecting him to anything "unpleasant."

After about a week, Zac said his leg was feeling a little better and as luck would have it, two minutes later, his brother Nic surprisingly grabbed him and threw him to the kitchen floor, wanting to "rough-house" with him. Instantly Zac was crying out in pain.

Nic thought he was overreacting. I didn't understand how Nic and Jessica still couldn't grasp the severity of their little brother's condition. They didn't seem to believe me when I warned them about his diagnosis and what it could mean. (I only told them because I didn't want them to any regrets if something should happen. I wanted them to have the chance to say things that needed to be said or time to change how they treated him. It wasn't that they couldn't fight with him once in a while, but to try and be a little more patient and understanding of what Zac was really experiencing.)

"What were you thinking?!" I screamed at Nic, watching in panic as Zac lay on the kitchen floor grabbing his leg.

"It doesn't hurt that bad!" Nic shot back. "He just said it was feeling better."

"Yeah, until you knocked him down and caused his leg to bend back. His leg just started feeling a little better because of his new medicine."

"You always take his side! I am so sick of it!" Nic yelled.

I was losing my patience at his blind selfishness to Zac's pain. "Okay, you ask Zac how his leg feels. Does it look like it feels better to you?"

There was silence as Nic stared at Zac whimpering.

"Ask him!" I demanded.

"Zac, your leg doesn't hurt that bad, does it?" Nic asked sounding a little remorseful now that he was actually looking at what was going on.

"Y-a-a-h-h-H! What do you think?!" Zac said brushing the tears off his face with the back of his hand.

"Help me get him in the chair," I said to Nic as I slowly moved Zac's leg to a straighter position.

Nic bent down to help lift Zac up from under his armpits as I guided his leg. "I just wanted to wrestle with you, Zac. Sorry."

With true acceptance of Nic's apology, Zac said, "That's okay."

"From now on, can we agree to no more rough-housing until Zac's leg is better? It doesn't mean you can't wrestle around a little bit when he's sitting on the floor - just realize how much bigger and stronger you are then him. Tone it down a little, okay?"

Zac had a pretty rough start to the New Year. On New Year's Eve, his leg was getting worse. We were at the neighbors for a party and Zac wanted to go outside and slide with the other boys. It looked like so much fun. I wanted him to be able to join in. My heart was breaking as I peeked out the back window in the garage. The other boys had already been down the hill three times and Zac was still trying to just get on the sled and get himself positioned for the run. I wanted to go out and help him, but I didn't want him to feel like I was babying him. After what seemed like forever, he was off. About fifteen, maybe twenty feet later, the sled veered right and he tipped over with the sled. He still had at least another hundred feet he could have gone. I continued to spy as he literally crawled up the hill to try it again. I admired his determination. Not once, in what was supposed to be a simple task, did he complain or sit there and pout.

Finally one of the boys came to the top of the hill. I secretly hoped he would give Zac a hand. With a puzzled look on his face he asked, "Why are you crawling?"

"My parents said that I wasn't supposed to walk on my leg. I hurt my knee."

Zac continued to crawl up the hill and started the long process of trying to position himself back on the sled. The second attempt at going down the hill ended abruptly. In the same exact spot, Zac's sled curved to the right and he tipped over - again! I was getting mad for him! Something that was supposed to be so fun became so challenging. I couldn't take it anymore.

Finally, I cracked the door open and yelled out so he knew he wasn't alone. "Hey, buddy! How's it going?"

The other boys had now gone down to the bonfire at the bottom of the hill.

"How do I get down?" Zac asked.

"Grab your sled and go the rest of the way down the hill."

He was done trying that so he asked, "Can I roll the rest of the way down the hill?"

And that's what he did. I knew he would be all right sitting by the fire. I stayed just long enough to see him off. I couldn't bear to watch any longer at what my child had to resort to, so I went back into the house.

I thought of my sister, Therese who was confined to a wheelchair. There was no way I was going to go through that again with my own child. I knew it sounded selfish, but to sit back and watch life being taken away, little by little, was unbearable. I could now understand my parent's heartbreak when they thought they had a healthy baby to only be quickly replaced with one who would need total care into adulthood. I hated that Therese could only watch us play. I would not accept the same fate for Zac. This was NOT going to be Zac's life.

As Nathan and I lay in bed New Year's Eve night we talked like we did many times. It was one place where things were quiet and there were no interruptions by children since they were tucked into bed. Before we drifted off to sleep I commented – "I pray that this year will be better than this past year."

"Amen to that," Nathan said.

Come New Year's Day, Zac couldn't get out of bed without Nic's help. My concern grew. I took him to his schedule chemotherapy appointment on January 2, 2013. Dr. Moertel and the fellow, Dr. Jess Barnum saw him and was a bit concerned about his decline in mobility. I was getting extremely impatient, mad, actually. So they both reviewed his recent MRI scan and x-ray and agreed that he should have yet another MRI. Their thought at this point was it could be a tear.

Meanwhile, Zac was instructed to stay off his leg and he went to physical therapy to get fitted for crutches. Zac was so frustrated. He was crying on and off. Dr. Moertel ordered morphine for him while he was getting his chemo treatment. Zac's demeanor changed and the crying stopped. There was finally some relief.

Zac had his MRI the next night and Dr. Moertel called me the following day. I prayed that they would know how to fix it. Dr. Moertel said what Zac had was a "bone stroke" (AVN). There was a significant lesion in his right distal lower femur. They usually see it in leukemia patients who are on massive doses of steroids.

"The steroids finally caught up with him," Dr. Moertel said.

Zac would need to get a leg immobilizer to stabilize his leg. He was not allowed to bear any weight on that leg for fear that his lower femur would collapse. An appointment with an orthopedic surgeon that Dr. Moertel said was one of the best around, was made for Monday, January 7. Dr. Moertel predicted surgery would entail extracting bone marrow from Zac's hip and injecting it into his femur.

We would have to wait until Monday for Dr. Cheng's recommendation. In the meantime, I was throwing a pity-party for Zac all by myself. His summer was taken from him because the radiation made him sleep it away and now - no playing in the snow?! *When would he get a break?*

Monday's appointment was supposed to be a twenty-five minute physical and consultation. Zac, Lexie and I waited forty-five minutes to see the doctor and waited another hour and a half after that. During the wait, almost right after we got there, Zac had a five or ten minute episode where his leg shook uncontrollably. It really scared him because this was the second time it had happened and he couldn't make it stop. Zac said his leg felt numb after the shaking was done and he had less control of his leg movements. On top of that, Zac mentioned he had another headache (his third in a row!) I did call for a nurse to observe what was going on. I wanted the doctors to have every piece of visual information. I was already furious that it took the doctors over two months to diagnose what was going on with Zac's leg. Dr. Cheng didn't really have anything to say about Zac's "episode." He seemed perplexed when looking at Zac's scan and latest x-ray.

I didn't like the silence and the look on his face. "Dr. Moertel says it's a bone stroke. Is that right?"

"Umm, I wouldn't say that," Dr. Cheng offered no further information.

"What is it then? It's not - cancer?" I tried to whisper so Zac wouldn't hear while he was coloring with Lexie.

Zac looked up. *Oh no!* Had he heard me?

"It's cancer?!" Zac shrieked. "What's wrong?"

"No, no, Zac. He's not sure what it is," I tried to calm his anxiety and cover up my poor effort at whispering.

Dr. Cheng, without emotion in his voice said, "I haven't seen anything like this before."

Great! What was that supposed to mean? I felt my anxiety and frustration grow. I thought we had already diagnosed this and now we were still guessing at what it was.

"I think I would like to do a biopsy to see what we are dealing with," he paused for a moment. "I suppose you would want to do this sooner, rather than later?"

I could feel my heart pounding as the hair stood up on my head. "I know you would have to squeeze Zac into your schedule and make someone else wait, but to be selfish - I don't care!"

Dr. Cheng sat up in his chair and said, "I understand. I'll see what we can do."

I sat in the doctor's office with Zac and Lexie for quite some time waiting for a date and time for the biopsy. My mind was racing. Finally, I couldn't take it anymore. I went out and around the corner to Dr. Cheng's office where he was sitting.

I took a deep breath and quickly asked my question before I lost my nerve. "Do you think its cancer?"

"It could be one of three things. I ruled out an infection because Zac isn't showing signs of infection." The other was something related to NF, but he was most worried about it being some type of cancer in the bone.

The following day, Zac was scheduled for a biopsy. It would take about a half an hour after getting a sample of the tissue and running a frozen section microscopic lab test to determine if it was cancerous or not.

Nathan and I waited nervously for surgery to be done. It was taking longer than the anticipated hour.

"Should I order that biomat?" Nathan asked breaking the silence.

Nathan and Zac met someone on their first attempt at getting a bear on their hunting trip who wanted them to meet a man who had beaten a cancer. At his house, he told Nathan of this special heating pad-like-mat, but wasn't "just" a heating pad. It had amethyst crystals in rows from top to bottom, along with other structures that NASA had helped design that created ionization, which in turn promoted cellular change. It was used for things from stress, arthritis to cancer. You adjusted the heat accordingly. It was a complex process and expensive, but Nathan and I were willing to try everything at this point.

First it was the mushrooms which we now omitted, because Zac couldn't tolerate them, and instead started using different vitamins, changed Zac's diet, added more vitamins, said lots of prayers and positive talking - and now - the Biomat.

"Yes. Order it now."

I think we already knew what the outcome of the biopsy was without Dr. Cheng's confirmation.

We were called to a conference room. We sat on a coach waiting for Dr. Cheng to enter. He was still in his scrubs with the surgical hat still tied behind his head and mask hanging loosely around his neck as he took a seat in a chair.

I waited patiently for him to speak. The seconds were killing me.

"It's not a bone stroke, but it is some type of tumor. In doing the frozen preliminary section, we still are not sure what type it is. We scraped out what we could, but remember, this wasn't a treatment. The surgery was just to do the biopsy," Dr. Cheng explained.

Nathan and I were silent for a moment until I asked, "Will you know for sure what we are dealing with in seventy-two hours?" I asked knowing it took several days for tissue to grow.

"We should know by Thursday. We have to wait a few more days for it to grow. Then the doctors at the patient care conference will meet to discuss how they want to treat it."

I was furious! One – for waiting so long to finally diagnose it as a tumor, and two - for still not knowing what we were dealing with. I held out for the hope that the tumor was benign. It was a possibility since some tumors can resemble both benign and malignant properties.

After we were done talking with Dr. Cheng, Zac was getting settled in the post op recovery room. I wanted to hurry and be at his side when he woke up. Right away, I could tell he was in pain. The nurse had already given him something, but it wasn't working. Zac didn't say anything until I asked if he had a little pain or a lot of pain.

Groggily, he mumbled, "A lot of pain."

I hated seeing him in pain. It was so unfair that he had to go through all of this. I continued to wonder when he would get a break from chemo, pain and the inability to walk. The postop nurse continued to give Zac pain medicine. I was surprised that they were sending Zac home in such a state. I knew he would prefer to be, so after he was painfully fitted for a leg immobilizer and we got his oxycodone, we left the hospital.

I knew Zac would still have some discomfort two days post-surgery, but at least I thought he would have less pain than he had before having the surgery. Unfortunately that was not the case. He was worse. He seemed to be in even more pain than when he had brain surgery. He cried out in excruciating pain when I was trying to get him up from a couch (where I had him set up to sleep until he was more mobile) to go to the bathroom.

"Just stop! Just stop!" Zac kept yelling as the tears rolled down his face.

I started to cry myself because I had barely moved his leg. I didn't know how I was going to move him to be able to get into the bathroom.

We sat for a few more minutes to regroup and he decided to give it another try. It was horrible, but we did it. He didn't get up the rest of the day. I continued to medicate him around the clock. I even set my alarm to get up every four hours to give him his medication in the middle of the night. It didn't seem to help in easing his pain and now he was saying he couldn't bend his knee.

Dr. Cheng said Zac needed to work on his mobility by bending and straightening his leg, several times a day. He also wanted him to wear his knee immobilizer.

Zac agreed that we should try. "I can take the pain," Zac said. First he had to find the song on his iPod that he called, "Mike's song," – 'I Want to Live Like That,' by Sidewalk Prophets. He played it to calm himself whenever he had to do something unpleasant.

Mike was Nic's hockey coach a few years back and passed away unexpectantly in his sleep about a year-and-a-half ago. He held a very special place in Zac's heart.

Zac played the song constantly. I waited patiently for Zac to give me the green light to move his leg. I had only inserted two fingers from each hand underneath his leg in preparation to move him when he started screaming. Immediately he cried out for Mike. "Mike! I need you! Mike - help me!" Zac yelled over and over again. "Why did you have to eat the apple, Adam and Eve?!"

Something wasn't right. Zac was the toughest person I knew and this behavior was way out of character for him. *For God's sake, this isn't even a repair - it was a biopsy with some scraping,* I thought. I didn't see the point in having Zac wear the hinged leg brace when he couldn't even move. I wasn't about to force him to move or get up when it literally tortured him.

The following day I called the orthopedic clinic to talk to the doctor or a nurse to find out if this was normal. I called again a few hours later after not receiving a return phone call and still, I hadn't heard from them. I ended up calling Zac's oncologist to see if I could increase his pain meds. Tammie agreed that I should. She said that she and Dr. Moertel would be looking at the biopsy sample again today for more definitive results. I was relieved when in answer to my question, she reassured that they rarely amputate any longer, but do extensive bone grafting. The results had to be good and there had to be answers as to how they were going to repair Zac's leg.

The following day my friend Carla was coming with her youngest daughter to visit Zac. I knew that wasn't the full intention of her visit. She knew that I was expecting Dr. Moertel to be calling with the final results of Zac's femur biopsy. Because she had such a big heart, she wanted to be with me for support when I got the phone call.

I was sick with worry all morning. My heart raced every time the phone would ring. Shortly before noon the phone rang. It was Dr. Moertel. I left the kitchen and walked down the hall into my bedroom to talk so Zac wouldn't be able to hear our conversation. I wasn't sure how this was going to go.

Dr. Moertel didn't sound his usual upbeat self.

"It's not good news, is it?"

"No, I'm sorry, it's not," Dr. Moertel apologized for the impending bad news. "I had a national expert, as well as other specialists looking at Zac's biopsy and it is confirmed to be an osteosarcoma - and it's malignant."

I didn't quite know what to say. I sat there on the phone searching for the next question. I had so many, but I was so lost in the devastating news. I swallowed hard trying not to cry because once I started crying, I had the hardest time talking and making my words understandable.

"So what's the next step?" I asked sniffling.

"I am involving two sarcoma experts who will be treating Zac, as well as myself, but before we develop a new treatment plan, I am scheduling Zac for a complete bone scan, lung X-ray and an MRI."

"Why? Do you think there's more?"

"We just want to cover everything. We aren't sure why Zac developed a sarcoma in his leg and usually when you have one sarcoma - it's originating from somewhere else," Dr. Moertel continued. "It more than likely is coming from the brain, as its primary site, but the neurofibromatosis confuses the issue."

I was confused! I was so angry and I didn't know how to deal with this information or what it meant. I wanted to call Nathan at work, but decided against it. What good would that do? He wouldn't be able to focus at work and by telling him, there was nothing he could do anyway. I decided I would keep it to myself until after he got home.

When I hung up the phone, I let out a wail. I fell to my knees and bawled my eyes out. I let it all out. Snot was running from my nose and I wasn't able to get myself to move to get a Kleenex from my bathroom. I cried until I realized Zac might be wondering where I was and what was going on. I pulled myself up off the floor, blew my nose and tried to hide the fact that I was just crying.

"I'll be down in a minute, buddy," I shouted from the top of the stairs in as normal of a voice as I could muster. "You doing okay?"

"I'm okay."

Good. He didn't sound like he suspected anything. A few minutes later Nathan called from work to check on Zac. He asked if I had heard from Dr. Moertel. I lied and told him, "Not yet." He didn't suspect anything from my voice.

I walked back into my bathroom to check my eyes to see if they were still red and puffy. There was a knock on the door, Carla and Laura were here.

As soon as Carla stepped into the house she asked as she hugged me, "How are you?"

I couldn't hold in my despair and with brutal honesty I sobbed, "Not good." I held onto her tight and just cried until my body began to literally shake. I pulled myself together enough to say, "Now I've probably scared Laura. Sorry," I wiped the tears from my already puffy eyes. *Zachary heard me for sure this time. How would I cover this one up?*

Laura went downstairs to see Zac while Carla and I talked. I was glad she had insisted on coming. Earlier, I had told her I would be okay at home by myself when I got the results. She knew me better than I knew myself sometimes.

I had been posting on and off on Caringbridge, a site that helped friends and family stay connected through journaling about Zac's story, for years. These past few weeks, I was writing more and more. I felt compelled to share Zac's story because we had met so many awesome friends and they all cared so much. I owed them information because they worried too and I needed them to pray. It was comforting to know how many people out there cared. I believed in the power of prayer and we needed it more and more. I was grateful to have a place to purge my feelings, get words of encouragement and not have to take my time away from Zac or my other kids to call every single person. As it was, it took me usually an hour to journal.

Sometime after 7 pm Tammie called to give me an idea of what to expect in Zac's new treatment plan. She said, "Zac's treatment will be intense." She went on to predict that he would begin a new sarcoma chemotherapy on Monday, January 21. He would be hospitalized for three or four days, then come home for 19 days to allow his body to recover. His white blood count was predicted to drop to almost nothing after a single treatment. Then he would go back in for three or four days, home for 19 and repeat for 10 weeks when she anticipated that they would do a bone graft on his leg, either from a cadaver or metal. He would resume the chemo schedule after he recovered from that surgery.

I couldn't believe this was what our lives would be. In all of Zac's eight years of dealing with this we were able to get by, with outpatient treatments. By doing inpatient treatment there was less and less of a way to delude myself of the severity of Zac situation. I began to fear the unknown lifestyle we were about to embark on and how it would change us all. I hoped in some way it would bring us closer together as a family. I hoped all of us would really "look" at what and who was most important in our lives and ALWAYS act in accordance to that. *Could a 13-year-old and an almost 15-year-old be capable of that type of maturity? What would it do to Lexie who was still four-years-old? She was already showing effects of what the diverted attention was doing to her.* My heart was shattered.

That weekend, Nathan and I tried to be as normal as we could. We watched movies, played games and tried to laugh. Monday we shared enough with the kids to let them know about the cancer in Zac's leg and what the new treatment plan would entail. Of course Zac was the most devastated. There was no way to sugarcoat it.

Tuesday after hours of scans and an x-ray we met Dr. Moertel for results back in the Journey clinic. Dr. Jess Barnum was with him. Neither of them were smiling. The news was bad. The cancer had now metastasized to his lungs, but thankfully had not spread anywhere else in the bone. Nate and I were shocked, to stay the least. Zac was so angry and sad, to put it mildly. At this point there were no words to describe the grief that he was feeling - only tears. I knelt down by the wheelchair he sat in and held him as we cried together.

How much more, Lord? How much more can he take? I thought. My heart was so heavy. Little by little, I began to feel myself dying inside. *We can't take anymore!* I shouted on the inside. Whoever came up with the saying, "God only gives what you can handle,"- should be shot! I couldn't take anymore! And most importantly, Zac doesn't want ANYMORE!

Two days later, Barb was going to meet me outside of the Discovery clinic where Zac had his post-surgical checkup with Dr. Cheng. Although Zac's pain was a little better, he could barely move his leg without instant tremendous pain.

I was sweating trying to get Zac upstairs by myself. I could only move him a centimeter at a time and it had to be S-L-O-W. I really don't know how I got him up all thirteen stairs, down the two steps from the house, into the garage and into the van. I had Zac's leg propped up on a pillow and one behind his back against the van door so that he could sit crosswise on the seat. Let me tell you, it was an ordeal, but we made it work.

I was thankful Barb met me, to help us out. Zac's school borrowed me the wheelchair they had so when Barb saw me parked in the front of the Discovery clinic she pulled in behind me to help get Zac out with the least amount of pain. I hated moving him because it was my fault every time he screamed out in pain. I unloaded the wheelchair and explained to Barb how we were going to get Zac out as she listened intently not wanting to make a mistake.

It was like we were moving a very fragile package, with a ticking time bomb inside. I had Barb carry Zac under his arms since I knew how to move Zac's leg and pillow as if they were connected. In spite of the sting of the cold January air, Barb and I moved Zac gingerly until we carefully set him in his seat. I continue to hold his leg straight out with the pillow underneath until Barb adjusted the leg-rest to where Zac could tolerate me setting it down.

I suppose growing up with a handicapped sister was good preparation for Barb and me in transferring Zac and working as a team to get him in the wheelchair. The pain part wasn't something we grew up with though. Apparently we must have done pretty well because Zac didn't cry out once. He even said, "That didn't hardly hurt."

Once inside we waited an hour and a half to see Dr. Cheng. Instead, Dr. Moertel came in and filled me in on what the doctors discussed at the patient care conference earlier that morning. The sarcoma experts felt certain that the tumor Zac had brain surgery on, this past July, was the same type of tumor in his leg and lungs. They believed the brain sarcoma unexpectedly came first, metastasized to his lungs and onto his femur.

Dr. Moertel said they had treated many pediatric patients with femur and lung sarcomas, but unfortunately not brain. They wanted to use the chemotherapy meds that are protocol for leg and lung cancer and hoped that it would also take care of the brain tumor. Dr. Moertel believed the radiation was still working, five months later, on Zac's brain tumor, but that the current chemotherapy he had been using had not been effective. If it had been, he explained, the other two areas in his body would not have been affected.

The plan was for Zac to go into the hospital Monday, January 21, 2013 and begin treatment with two very powerful chemotherapy drugs. We were warned that Zac would struggle with nausea and vomiting and he would lose his hair that had almost all grown back in. I asked if radiation could be used on his leg or for the lungs. Dr. Cheng said it couldn't because of where the tumor was which was located in part of the growth plate and it would impede the bone from healing as well as ever being able to grow. As for the lungs, Dr. Moertel thought the chemotherapy would do a good job. He also mentioned it would be a possibility to remove the spots if they got smaller and remained stable for a time.

It was explained to me that the reason for Zac's horrible leg pain was not because of the surgery, but rather from the cancer. It was at the base of the femur and rubbed up against the tumor every time Zac's leg was moved. I now understood the excruciating pain that cancer could cause. It "was" the devil.

After two rounds of this chemotherapy, Zac would have another MRI to find out if this treatment was effective. It had to be! I would not accept any other answer. We were going to win this war!

Zac didn't have much to say after leaving the doctor's appointment. I think he was absorbing the realization of what was to come and what it would mean for him. I didn't know how much I should talk to him about what was going on. I wanted him to be informed, but I didn't want to scare him. He would make it so much easier on me if he would ask questions, but he didn't. He just seemed to accept it. It was like when he was a few years younger and I would be talking to someone on the phone or to him about his chemotherapy and he would quietly put his hands over his ears and say, "I don't want to talk about it." That was my clue that "it" DID bother him. Shutting it out was the way he coped.

Zac was so afraid of going in the hospital. It showed in his demeanor. He wasn't smiling much. As I was tucking him in bed he told me, "I don't want Monday to come."

"I don't either," I said as I leaned over and hugged him tightly.

This was the worst nightmare - and not just for me. I was awake and the nightmare continued because I saw Zac still in so much pain. I saw his worry and felt mine swallowing me up. My mind was getting more difficult to control. I tried to shut it off from what I feared could be Zac's outcome, with my hope and trust in God's healing, but it didn't last long. Hope and fear fought each other continuously, while I was awake and when I tried to sleep.

Friday morning came and I wanted to do something to take Monday off of Zac's mind. It had been three weeks since he had even left the basement. He had been very weepy lately because he was scared and was getting tired of not being able to walk around. I was able to talk Zachary into going to school for just a short visit. It was tough getting Zac upstairs. We almost decided to call it quits because Zac's pain was unbearable! I was sweating trying to move him without hurting him, but nothing was working. Zac and I were both crying at this point. We were stuck at the top of the stairs. I couldn't lift him and support his leg at the same time and I couldn't pick him up and carry him like a baby because that would mean he had to bend his leg.

I prayed my neighbor, John, would be home. Sometimes he worked from home. I was in luck! He came right over and together we lifted Zac up and into the van. I was never happier to see someone and so grateful for his help.

I thought I had ruined my chance at giving Zac a good experience by going to school. He was so good for agreeing to try this difficult task. We managed to get into school with Nurse Leslie's help and everything turned the corner from that moment.

Everyone in the office insisted on seeing him and giving him hugs. He ended up visiting more than he did actual schoolwork. To top off his day, he even got a standing ovation by all the kids when they wheeled him into the cafeteria. What an awesome moment for such a wonderful, most deserving child! Zac ended up staying for a few hours and he said he was so happy that he did.

CHAPTER 20

leaving home

Monday morning was the beginning of a new journey. I opened my eyes and wished I could just roll over and deny that Zac and I would have to begin a routine of hospital stays, family separation and unknown responses for Zac to even harder chemo drugs. I was feeling a little at ease, partially because Nathan and I got Zac settled into his room and he wasn't nearly as teary-eyed as he had been all day. I also felt some relief that we were finally starting to do something to combat what was trying to destroy my beautiful son.

It wasn't easy leaving home, but it did help tremendously that Zac's good friend stayed the night, giggling it up, picking on each other, Nic picking on Thomas and Thomas and Zac giving it right back to Nic. Everything felt so right - so normal. Jessica helped Thomas set up his iPod so he and Zac could stay in touch by texting. It would help him feel less isolated the more ways he could get in touch with others.

Thomas was a great distraction for Zac. He was a patient, kind and gentle soul who I knew genuinely cared about Zac. He always took the time for him, even when he had other friend invites. He never ditched Zac to do something that may have sounded more fun. He wanted to be with Zac. For a ten-year-old, he was more grown-up than most other kids I knew.

The night before coming to the hospital and even when getting ready to leave home, Zac cried on and off when his mind had a chance to wander. "I don't want to go. I just want to be normal."

What could I say? I didn't want to go either. I wanted to ignore this whole situation and pretend it might go away on its own. For a second, I thought about doing that.

Once at the hospital and unpacked, we waited around. We saw a few different resident doctors who checked Zac over and asked lots of questions. Even though we arrived about noon, Zac's IV fluids didn't start until around 4 pm. With the type of chemotherapy Zac was getting, he had to have four hours of IV hydration prior to starting it to protect his kidneys. The first chemo med started at 9:20 pm and infused over three hours. Shortly after that the other chemo would begin and run over twenty-four hours and be repeated every twenty-four hours for the next couple of days.

I was so worried about Zac having his "sick feelings." I knew he was too, but after talking to one of the nurses, I felt more reassured. She said the kids seemed to do pretty well with having the IV Zofran and dexamethasone prior to starting the chemo's. I prayed Zac would be one of those kids.

Zac was experiencing pain in his ankle for a few weeks and with recent scan result, Dr. Moertel ordered an MRI since he was in the hospital. I knew he was a bit suspicious and wanted the full picture of what he was dealing with.

Nathan, Nic, Jessica and Lexie came for a visit and left at 6 pm when Zac was called down for the MRI. Zac had tears in his eyes. He wanted so much to go home with them. After a few more, "I hate this," and a few more, "I just want to be normal," Zac was headed down for his scan.

I jumped right in with transferring Zac from wheelchair to the MRI table. Normally in a hospital setting, the employees insist on doing it for liability reasons, but I didn't get any flack. I think when they saw how slowly and carefully I was moving him to prevent him from a sudden jolt of pain, they knew it was in Zac's best interest.

"It looks like someone should hire you here", Joe, the x-ray tech joked, but was actually serious.

I smiled. I didn't throw it around that I was a nurse and that I actually worked in this hospital. I didn't want them to think I was putting myself on a "power-trip" list. I also didn't want people to expect that I knew everything that was going on. I was a labor and delivery nurse - far different then pediatric oncology, although I felt I was beginning to be an expert in the field - to some degree.

"Actually, I already do work here," I admitted. "I'm a nurse on the birthplace." I was thankful that I chose nursing as my profession more times than I could count lately. All the training and knowledge I had from starting out in patient transport, to a nursing assistant, to a nurse came in handy. As Zac's mother, I felt so helpless many times, but at least I was able to anticipate what he needed before he needed it because of my background.

It was a rough first night. Being the first room by the unit entrance doors was extremely annoying for a light sleeper like me. I could hear the click of the door every time someone came in. I lifted my head each time to look at our door because I thought it was someone coming in to see us. After about twenty times I tried challenging myself not to even bother looking, it didn't always work.

Zac was up so often - every forty-five minutes to an hour-and-a-half throughout the night, needing to pee because of the high rate of IV fluids, running in constantly. I thought that was why he was so tired the next morning, but it was the chemotherapy already kicking in. He slept and slept.

I did wake him up to an unexpected phone call the next day. I whispered loudly, "Zac. Matt, the Navy seal, is on the phone! He's calling all the way from Afghanistan! Can you wake up to talk to him?"

"Hey - Matt!" Zac's grogginess quickly gave way to wide-awake excitement. And their conversation went on...

What a great wake-up call and it couldn't have come at a better time!

Dr. Moertel came in midmorning and was in long enough to see Zac have another "leg seizure." He thought it was because Zac's anti-seizure med was being compromised by the chemo drugs. I wanted to do a brain MRI. I was afraid of how quickly the cancer had been spreading. I wasn't convinced the seizures were happening because of the chemo drugs lessening the effects of the seizure med since Zac had three "leg seizures" before he was even restarted on his anti-seizure med.

The fear Nathan and I sat with, day in and day out, waiting and wondering if the chemotherapy would be effective was becoming too much. That was why we explored other treatment options. I had brought the biomat to the hospital and we were using it fifty minutes - three times a day, every day. I researched more about the metabolic cancer diet once we suspected the cancer spread to Zac's leg. I didn't see how a child could possibly follow something so strict.

It is stressed in a metabolic cancer diet that sugar be completely omitted as well as processed foods, starches and milk. Drinking alkaline water to raise the body's pH and give the immune system a better chance to fight off viruses and bacteria. Eating raw vegetables, particularly spinach, Kale, cruciferious leafy greens, carrots and fresh fruit was also recommended. The suggestion of eating frozen liver cubes for the high iron was a little more than what we felt we could get Zac to try.

After calling St. Jude's Hospital for information on diets that helped beat cancer not, having any information, Cancer Center for America saying they only dealt with adults and at Amplatz Children's dietitians not have any advice, there didn't seem to be anything in any one oncology program that could prove or deny that following a metabolic diet worked.

Dr. Yoshimizu, who was instrumental in treating patients with the biomat, had the only information of certain a diet without sugar or processed foods, which could be beneficial to cancer patients. Nathan was adamant that we follow it. I felt we had to try, if Zac was willing, because I wanted to know we had tried everything. This could be the piece that would heal Zac of this spreading cancer.

The day before, lunch and dinner had been unappealing to Zac. With all the fun food choices on the menu, he only got turkey, salad and a vegetable. Lunch was no better. The look on the nurse's face made me feel guilty for making my son eat it. Thank goodness for our recent purchase of our high-performance Vita-Mix blender that I brought, to make him a smoothie loaded with fruits and carrots. That was as close to a treat as I could give him.

By lunch or should I say, breakfast (at 1 pm, because he slept all day) I asked what he wanted to eat.

"Something healthy," Zac replied and started to cry.

He was so frustrated with not being able to eat what he wanted and at the same time wanting to follow "the mission" that Nathan talked to him about - to beat this cancer. It was so unfair to put a child through this! I was angry.

Shannon from KS95 and I became friends after meeting almost a year ago when we were first interviewed for the radiothon. She told me later that when she first met Zac, "She fell in love with him and had to get to know us." I was pleased. She came for a visit after work and brought pizza for her and me for a late lunch. I could see Zac eyeing the pizza as his tray of a salad, raw carrots, grapes and eggs sat in front of him. I couldn't stand it any longer.

"Zac, you want some pizza?"

"I shouldn't," Zac said sadly.

"Zac, you can have pizza if you want. You've been doing really good with your food. You deserve a treat now and then," I reassured.

"But Dad will get mad."

"It's okay. Dad doesn't have to know."

Zac nodded his head "yes." I passed over a giant piece of Divanni's pepperoni-pineapple pizza to him. The smile on his face was priceless. He was happy, I was happy. *Why did this have to be so hard? We would figure it out, I told myself, but not at the expense of Zachary's happiness.*

Earlier, Dr. Moertel had said he hadn't had a chance to review Zac's ankle scan and he had a meeting he needed to get to. He returned for a second time that day to go over the MRI results with me. I didn't feel anything. No hope, no fear. I just wanted to hear what he had to say.

"I had to take a deep breath before looking at the scan," Dr. Moertel confessed. "The ankle is clear."

Hallelujah! Finally some positive news for change. "So what do you think the pain is from?"

"It appears, and makes sense, to be the result of the past two-and-a-half months of walking "funny" on his one leg," Dr. Moertel explained.

As long as the cancer hadn't spread, I was content with his answer.

It was surprising how it quick the days went with the doctors and nurses coming in and out, the phone calls and visitors. Zac enjoyed the visits when he wasn't struggling to keep his eyes opened. I had been in the hospital with Zac for three days now, and aside from him being so tired, everything was going well.

My friend, Stacy, brought Nic so he could see his little brother, along with her three kids. Zac was happy to see them when he woke up. He needed to use the bathroom before he started playing Xbox, so I got him up and took him into the bathroom like I had many times before. Unfortunately, this time as I was trying to pull the IV pole into the bathroom so I could close the door, Zac got tangled up in the IV tubing and lost his balance. He suddenly fell sideways and into the shower. His bad leg became twisted and bent behind him (something he couldn't do because the pain was so horrible). He started screaming and crying and pain.

I tried to squeeze in close to help him, but I couldn't lift him and straighten his leg at the same time. Just knowing I had to reposition his leg terrified me for the additional pain I was about to cause. Stacy instantly got up but didn't know what to do and there wasn't enough room for two of us in the bathroom. I quickly pulled the emergency cord hanging on the wall in the bathroom.

"Go get a nurse!" I instructed.

I tried to move him, but he cried out louder in pain and if I just left him lying there while we waited for help, he cried in pain. I feared he broke his already fragile leg from the way he was screaming.

Just then my sister, Barb showed up. The look on her face was one of sheer horror. I can only imagine what it looked like from her point of view.

Suddenly, Zac's pain diverted to his port site. "My port hurts, it hurts!"

Barb had the kids go to the teen game room with Stacy to allow for more room to help Zac. By the time Zac's nurse came in, I was crying. Fatiyah had a look of panic on her face as she saw Zac on the bathroom floor.

Somehow between the three of us we got Zac into bed. Once in bed, we couldn't seem to get Zac comfortable. He was still complaining of his port and I noticed it was looking much more puffy. The needle which was still taped securely to his chest had somehow pulled out and poked back into another spot in his chest, outside of the port.

Zac just closed his eyes. I could only imagine what he was thinking, what he was wishing... to be any place but here. Fatiyah stopped the chemo, took out the port needle and reinserted a new one. Zac didn't have much to say. He got a short reprieve of happiness when Nic, Hunter, Ben and Olivia came back into the room to play a very short Xbox game before he was taken to x-ray to see if he had any further damage to his femur.

There was no fracture or break, just additional swelling. And luckily Zac's chemo was stopped before too much infiltrated where it wasn't supposed to go. Thankfully he dodged a bullet on that one. Well, kind of...

Zac needed to have his pain meds increased because of the fall. He started settling down. I actually had to keep waking him up so he would eat a little something. Eventually, I gave up realizing he needed to sleep more than he needed to eat.

It wasn't before long the nurses started coming in to Zac's room to look at his port site. They were trying to determine if Zac's port-site looked a lot more swollen than usual. I continued to insist that it looked much more puffy than before. It probably wouldn't have been as big of a deal, but the chemo drug was infusing when he fell and when his port needle came out and re-stuck him outside of his port the infusing chemo could deaden Zac's skin tissue.

Eventually the nurse stopped at Zac's IV and tried drawing blood from the port. It wasn't working like it was supposed to. Zac was getting frustrated and annoyed with the doctors and nurses poking at his puffy chest. He was reaching his limit. The tears welled up in his eyes and he continued to whisper, "I hate this, I hate this."

It was around 1 am when his nurse came in explaining that she had to put a solution on and around Zac's port to prevent the tissues under the skin from dying. Within a few minutes of applying the solution, Zac started crying saying, "It burn's! It's burning! It's itching!" He was crying and writhing in pain!

I felt horrible having to hold his hand down so he wouldn't grab or scratch at his chest and contaminate the area. It looked as if he was trying to get out of his body. At first I was hoping this was a "typical" reaction. I warned the nurse that his skin became excessively sensitive and itchy because of the previous chemo that he had been on. I began to wonder if the old chemo medicine was not yet out of his system.

I told her to give Zac a break. I thought she was done, but she turned around and grabbed more swabs from off the counter behind her and continue to enlarge the area. Soon Zac had a seven inch circle that looked like someone had laid a hot iron on his chest. It was unbearable listening to Zac's crying. I could only sit there, squeezing his hand and absorb the helpless cry into my soul. I couldn't believe something that was supposed to be so easy turned into an excruciating nightmare of an event.

Finally the nurse went out to get a doctor to look at the burn as she said, "I'm not sure if this is a normal reaction. I'll check with pharmacy."

Oh, it's NOT normal, I muttered under my breath. Are you kidding?! I could see plain as day that this couldn't be a normal process to put a child through. Didn't she hear him cry out? Zac was not one to cry and complain going through the actual event of things. He didn't like it, but he usually shut himself out from what was to come or what he was going through.

"The policy says that this has to be repeated every couple hours," the nurse told me without remorse.

I couldn't believe she would even consider doing it again seeing the massive burn on Zac's chest. "We're not doing this again," I told her. "You can write down that 'Mother declines further treatment.'" I knew as a patient advocate, I had the right to refuse treatment, it was part of the Patient Bill of Rights. I felt like a rebel, but it felt good to be able to stand up for my son. I knew Zac was relieved, because I felt it.

As a compensation for not continuing with the "AFO" wash, the nurse was in every hour to turn on the lights and inspect Zac's port-site and hang IV medicine. In between that, Zac needed to go to the bathroom - so it was sleepless night for the both of us.

There were no smiles, come morning, until Zac was informed his five hour kidney function test had been postponed and Dr. Moertel gave Zac the all clear for discharge saying, "We better send you home before anything else happens."

We finally made it home. Zac was starting to smile again and color was coming back into his cheeks. My old Zac was back!

After a beautiful snowfall, Nic tried to convince Zac to go outside. He wanted someone to hang out with. He hated spending so much time by himself. He wanted to do normal things with his little brother. Nic told Zac he would pull him on a sled and take him down to the lake.

Zac got teary-eyed and said he didn't want to. I thought maybe he was just tired. He sometimes got weepy when he was, but I knew something was worrying him. After a little crying, I found out that Zac thought Nic was going to push him down the big hill to the lake (something a big brother would do to get a kick out of scaring his little brother.) I reassured him that Nic was going to pull him and be careful that nothing would happen to his leg.

To be sure that was Nic's intention, I asked in front of Zac if that was indeed his plan. Nic sincerely promised. After I was finished drawing Zac's blood - something else he didn't let on about being nervous about, especially with his past week) I got him suited up the best I could, leg immobilizer and all. I said a quick prayer as Nic and I loaded him in the big black sled. Off they went.

Over an hour later Zac came back, full of snow and rosy cheeks shouting, "That was so much fun!"

Zac ended up sitting on his butt, on the shoveled off ice rink that Nic and a friend made and played goalie. He did something "almost" normal for the first time in a long time, other than watch movies and play Xbox. It was a good day!

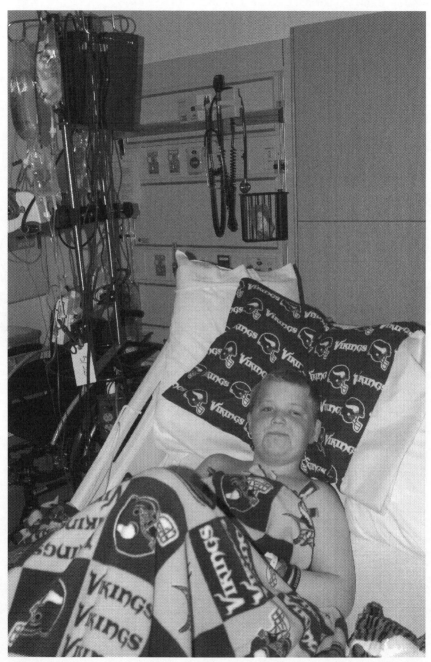

The beginning of intense chemotherapy for Zac 1-22-13

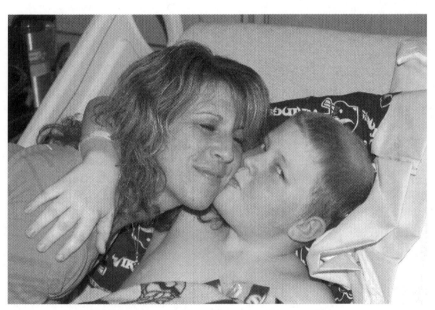

*A kiss from my angel. Zac and me 1-22-13 at start of intense
chemotherapy at Amplatz Children's Hospital.*

CHAPTER 21

the jake parenteau award

January 30, 2013 - two weeks and a day since Zachary's last MRI and chest x-ray, Zac had a brain MRI follow-up this.

"So - any predictions about the results?" Nathan asked me.

"I can't do that anymore," I flatly said. "I am numb to the process at this point and my heart can't take it anymore either."

Zac sat and played on his iPod as we watched him. Dr. Moertel came in and began carrying on a conversation with us about hockey when he was pulled away to a phone call. A few minutes later, Emily our social worker called Nathan out of the room. At first I didn't think much of it. I figured she was talking to him about financial paperwork. All of a sudden, I felt a stab of fear. Something didn't seem right.

There they all were in an office room of cubicles and computers. Dr. Moertel, Tammie, Kathy (Dr. Moertel's nurse), Emily and Nathan were standing in front of a computer.

"What's going on?" I asked. I waited for an answer. It was like they didn't hear me, so I asked again, but louder this time. "What's going ON?"

The silence and their looks told me something was very wrong. There was not one, but two tumors now in Zac's brain! His scan on December 5th had shown that the original brain sarcoma was still shrinking. Today, it was larger and showed an area of swelling. The second tumor sat closed by. Unbelievable! Zac's condition was getting more serious by the week.

I was in complete shock! I felt instantly so hopeless. It was like the cancer was taking over his body and there was nothing I could do to stop it. I broke down and cried. What started out as a relatively quiet cry, quickly turned into wailing.

"No, no, no!! This can't be happening!"

I could see Tammie felt my pain as she approached me and wrapped her arms around me with tears in her eyes. I was visibly shaking with fear - something that seemed to happen when I was engulfed with grief and the loss of hope.

"You have to save my son! You HAVE to save my son!" I pleaded in despair.

Nathan stood back with his head hanging down in silent shock. Emily stood by him with her hand on his back letting him know she was there for him.

"Please, oh please, save my son. Please, please, ple-a-e-a-z-zzz," I moaned, begging for Zac's life.

Tammie just held me as I felt my knees trying to buckle underneath me. There was not a dry eye in the room. Everyone stood silently as I tried to pull myself together. As my sobs gave way to sniffles, I found my voice with a little composure.

"What are we going to do?" I asked as I thought of Zac sitting with Lexie in the other room, a few doors down the hall.

We were NOT giving up on Zac! We had to find a way to cure him once and for all. He had so much life in him - so much hope, so much belief in God's healing power. I was not about to take that away from him.

"The cancer is so smart. If we block one pathway, the cancer just finds another route to invade," Tammie explained.

"But there's still something we can do, right?" I asked looking at Dr. Moertel.

Nathan and I talked with Dr. Guillaume, the pediatric neurosurgeon, Dr. Moertel and Tammie. We decided against doing brain surgery at this time because Dr. Guillaume said that doing brain surgery would not cure him, only alleviate symptoms of the brain tumor (such as Zac's leg seizures) and that wasn't even guaranteed. By doing surgery, it would interrupt the chemotherapy treatment and right now it was too soon to know if it was working. Nathan and I did not want to take that chance.

"It is encouraging that Zac's leg is feeling so much better. That could be a sign that the chemo is working," Dr. Moertel said. "It is also a possibility that the swelling on the first sarcoma could be a reaction to the chemo working on destroying it."

I didn't think I could get any more sad than I already had been. I was wrong. I didn't know what else to ask for. I didn't know how to fight the fear that was trying to consume me. Yes, it was easy to say the words of prayer, to go to church, to try my hardest to be good and do the right thing, but I literally felt like my child was slowly being taken away from me. I didn't understand how God could permit this to happen. *Where was He? Why wasn't He helping Zac?*

I dried my tears, wiped off the stained mascara (I was going to have to resort to wearing waterproof from now on) and took a deep breath as I entered Zac's room where he, Lexie and Liz were working on a painting project and making glue.

"Where did you go?" Zac asked looking up to see me digging in my purse. I was trying to hide my puppy eyes from him by pretending I was looking for something so I wouldn't have to look him in the eye.

"Oh, the doctors just wanted to talk to us about the chemo plan and insurance. I'm just really frustrated," I said hiding the real story. I didn't see any point in telling him he had another brain sarcoma.

Nathan and I decided not to mention the new tumor to Zac. We probably would tell Nic and Jessica later so they might be able to realize the seriousness of Zac's situation. As for Zac, Nathan and I did not want him to feel defeated. I believed there was always hope. We wanted Zac to be happy and wanted him to have a happy life. I didn't think that would be possible for Zac or our family, if we gave in to the notion that Zac wouldn't or couldn't beat this.

I grew up believing God could heal my sister, Therese from being confined to a wheelchair. Every night my parents, sisters and me would gather around in a circle and pray the rosary. Sometimes we would pray the rosary for one specific intention and other times it would be one intention per decade (section) of the rosary.

The summer before ninth grade, my whole family went all the way to Italy, because a friend of my mom's was going to be ordained a priest by Pope John Paul II and wanted my parents to come. We didn't have a lot of money growing up, so originally my parents were just going to take Therese, but later decided we should all go because it was a chance of a lifetime. They made it work.

My sister was blessed by the Pope, as well and was invited to sit up by the altar during the ordination mass, with my dad at St. Peter's Basilica. What an honor, especially now knowing that Pope John Paul II was recently canonized a saint!

Since we were so close, my parents thought we should travel to Lourdes, France, to the grotto where many documented miracles have occurred. After a discussion with a very holy man, it was decided not to go. The man told my parents, "It is not her time." I remember walking down the many steps of the Vatican crying.

I also struggled through an intense eating disorder for 14 years of my life and probably should have died. I wanted to at times just so I could escape the claws of starvation, obsessive exercise, the loneliness and depression. Through that, as well, I never gave up my faith or love for God. I prayed that somehow I would see the light of day and that I could be happy once again. After all those years, I can only attribute climbing out of that deep, dark pit with the help of God. To have survived that, I had to have a purpose, but what was it? - Which leads me to where I was with Zac… *Were Zac and my other children, my purpose? Was I being tested to prepare myself to get to this point in my life - Zac's life? How strong was my faith and belief in the one true God? I never stopped believing that God could do anything. He could heal anyone. He could override any decision. Nothing was impossible so as long as you held tight to your faith - so I believed.*

I wondered if we should take Zac to our Lady of Lourdes in France. What if his healing awaited him there? I worried about the expense. I wasn't working that much, but more importantly, what if we traveled all that way for only the same disappointment I went through with my sister Therese?

I talked to my Mom about it and she said, "Zachary could be healed here, just the same. You don't have to go all the way to Lourdes to be healed."

We decided to stay home and I would continue to pray for God's will to be my will. More and more people were reading Caringbridge and all of them said they were praying for Zac's healing. Many of them had Zac on their prayer chain at their church. Even people who knew or had just heard of Zac were passing on their request to their family and friends to pray for him. I truly believed in the power of prayer. I hoped God would hear us.

Zac and I ended up driving back to Amplatz Children's Hospital on Friday, February 1 for another appointment. I drew his blood later than usual, that morning because I decided to let Zac sleep in. I didn't want to wake him just to have to jab a needle into his port. The chemo really tired him out. I was hoping that this far out from his last treatment, his hemoglobin would be higher than 7.0 - anything under that was a ticket for a blood transfusion.

When Zac woke up I could see the writing on the wall. He was pasty white. I knew his hemoglobin would be low. He seemed so tired, even after sleeping in. He was quiet which frightened me even more. I worried that this continual beating of bad news would destroy his bright spirit. I couldn't bear to see that taken from him.

"*Please God,*" I prayed, "*help me to help him.*"

"What do you think about going to school for a little while when I drop off your blood at the clinic? It usually takes a couple hours before we get results," I explained.

"Yeah, I guess."

I knew he was tired, but I was afraid if he stayed home with me, he would just watch TV and sleep on and off and worry silently. "Zac, I have to be honest, but I think you'll only get to go to school for about two hours because I think your hemoglobin is low. You look pretty pale and you're pretty tired, aren't you?"

"Yeah, I'm just so tired," Zac admitted with tears of frustration welling up in his eyes.

"At least if your hemoglobin is low, they can give you the transfusion and you'll end up feeling so much better almost right away. Then you will have lots of energy for the Jake Parenteau Award ceremony tonight before the high school varsity hockey game," I said hoping that would lighten his mood.

"Oh, yeah! That's tonight!" Zac perked up and I saw a spark in his eye. He had something to look forward to. "I almost forgot. I can't wait for tonight! It's going to be so awesome!"

Zac's mood completely changed. In spite of his paleness, the bounce was back in his step - if he could walk without crutches, that is.

My intuition was right. Zac needed a transfusion. It was late by the time they drew more blood to send to the lab and then the blood didn't get ordered, so we waited even longer to get started. I glanced at my watch and was getting antsier by the minute. Zac was not going to miss receiving the Jake Parenteau Award - not if I could help it.

Tammie came in to check Zac over and talk with me. "And how are you doing?" She asked.

I didn't hide or sugarcoat my worry. Tammie had already seen me at my worst. "I can't sleep. I eventually fall asleep seeing visions and worrying about what could happen, and then I sleep only to have a nightmare, then I wake up and realize I am living that nightmare," I explained, trying not to sound like I was complaining. But she wanted to know...

"I know you have a strong faith, otherwise I wouldn't be suggesting this, but walk around your house with Nathan and pray out loud –'all evil leave this house at once! This is a place of peace and healing. May God and his angels watch over, guard and protect Zachary. Cancer, I command you to leave his body and fill it with health' - something like that. You would be surprised," Tammie said.

"At this point I will try anything. Thanks. It sounds very comforting and powerful."

Deanna, Zac's nurse finally came in with Angie to get the transfusion started.

"Hey, guess what?" Zac playfully asked the nurses.

"What?!" they both said in unison.

"I get to receive the Jake Parenteau award tonight, before my brother's hockey game!" Zac was all smiles. He could barely keep contain himself.

"Wow! That sounds like a cool award. What does it mean?" Deanna asked.

Zac went on to explain a little about it. I filled in the rest telling them that even though Zac has never been able to play hockey because of his balance issues, due to NF - he loved it, supported his brother and his teammates by going to as many games as he could and cheered on the Wildcat hockey players - all of them! He was nominated and chosen to receive the award from Jake Parenteau, himself - a former Chicago Lakes Wildcat hockey player who went on to play for the University of Minnesota Gophers. The award was given for outstanding sportsmanship, both on and off the ice. Zac was chosen for this award for his inspiration, for his strength, dedication, kindness and positive attitude - all words that the kids used to describe Zac. And true they were!

"Is there any way to speed-up the blood transfusion?" I asked knowing they usually ran it in at a slower rate.

"Of course. Zac never has had any issues with the transfusion before, has he?"

"Nope." I was relieved, thinking we could make it if traffic wasn't bad going home.

"I can speed up the flush too," Deanna offered.

"Mom, I'm so excited! This is gonna be so awesome. I can't wait!" Zac repeated over the course of the next couple hours and all the way home.

Zac and I drove straight to the Chisago Lakes ice arena and arrived shortly before the start of the game. The award would be presented before the game and we didn't miss a thing. The arena was packed.

When Zac was called for, Nathan and a friend of his carried Zac in the wheelchair down the many cement steps of the arena and pushed him around the rink to where they had an opening for him to go through onto the ice. Other awards were presented to other kids first. Everything was casual and timely until a brief description of what the recipient of the Jake Parenteau award stood for was read, as well as a short summary of Zac's battle against cancer.

Zac eagerly awaited the announcement with a look of anticipation.

"The Jake Parenteau award goes to...ZACHARY BARTZ!!!"

Nathan passed Zac off to the two captains of the varsity hockey team, Danny and Bradee. They pushed him only about three feet where Jake met them and together they began their walk to center ice. Immediately Zac raised his hands in utter joy and excitement at the announcement of his name. The people in the bleachers cheered as they stood giving Zac a standing ovation. Zac wildly waved his hands back and forth acknowledging the audience. He was so happy! I don't think I have ever seen him with a smile on his face so big and for so long. If he could have, Zac would have jumped out of that wheelchair to jump up and down. Instead, as the cheers and whistling grew louder and louder, Zac started pumping his right fist in the air. "Yah!" He shouted. "Yah!!" Zac continued on as he raised both of his hands in victory.

The cheering went on and on. Jake was clapping and Danny (Thomas's older brother, was actually wiping tears from his eyes with his big black hockey glove.

Bradee continued pushing Zac across the ice towards the crowd as he bit his lip in efforts to keep himself from crying. Jake stood proudly by Zac's left side. I was crying at the beautiful moment that freed Zac of all pain and agony and replaced it with pure joy. The award was more than just an award for Zac. It was a priceless gift of love, acceptance and recognition for a boy - fighting for his life - not wanting to be left behind.

After everyone was tucked in bed, I told Nathan what Tammie shared with me about walking around our house - calling out loud in prayer into the winter cold night for the Angels to help us. He agreed to it. We slipped on our winter boots and bundled up. It was midnight. I was a little intimidated praying out loud even though Nathan was the only one who would hear me. We trudged through the untouched blanket of snow - praying for the evil that loomed over us to leave – it was NOT welcome! And in its place – fill the void with peace and healing...

That night as a lay my head on my pillow, I slept uninterrupted, without a nightmare for the first time in a long time. I felt peace.

Zac receiving the Jake Parenteau award with Danny, Bradee and Jake Parenteau 2-1-12

CHAPTER 22

a big difference

The hospitalizations, unfortunately, were becoming a routine. I had a system of preparing for the hospitalizations by washing clothes and sheets, making beds, cleaning the house, grocery shopping and sometimes even made a batch of cookies for the kids. I tried to squeeze in a shift or two at the hospital before it was time to go back to Amplatz for the next treatment.

After a hospital stay, I would start all over again. It was exhausting - if I could complain for a minute. I hated packing for the next week when I still wasn't caught up on sleep or chores from being in the hospital with Zac. Nights in the hospital were not for sleeping. I routinely was woken up by Zac about every forty-five minutes to an hour and a half, saying - "Mom? Mom?! I have to go to the bathroom!" And when Zac had to go, he needed to go! There was no taking my time in getting up from a brief, comatosed sleep. I wouldn't have had it any other way, I was his mom and I wanted to always be there for him, but it was very trying at times. As tired as I was and as frustrated as I got some nights, I whispered to God as I lay back down, *"Lord I will do this as long as I live. Please give me the strength to keep helping Zac. Please, let him live."*

Zac took about a month off of school until his leg pain was more manageable. I let him wake up on his own, figuring if he was so tired he wouldn't have fun and enjoy his friends and teachers. To me, that was more important for his mental health than the actual learning. When Zac woke up, he would call my cell phone from the phone that I left on his bedside table. "Mom, I'm awake," Zac would say.

He usually had to go to the bathroom really bad, so without a moment to waste, I quickly scooted out of bed and ran downstairs to where he and Nic shared a room in the basement. It was reassuring to know that Nic, without complaining, would help Zac up to the bathroom or to use the urinal if he needed to go in the middle of the night. I hadn't needed to set my alarm recently to wake myself up every four hours to give Zac pain medicine, so it was a welcomed break.

Once the pain subsided a bit, Zac figured out how to use the urinal that was left on the floor by his bed. He would either use crutches or scoot on his butt, propping his right leg on top of his left ankle as he made his way down the hall to the family room. He turned on the biomat for his fifty minutes of "mat-therapy" before having a piece of toast or sometimes just a glass of juice to wash down all his morning pills.

"I'm so full after all my pills," Zac would mention unsatisfied at the tasteless "breakfast".

I usually got him to school by 11 am and he made it through the rest of the day. I felt like things were somewhat normal knowing he was at school, doing what a ten-year-old boy should be doing. He still didn't ride the bus home because of the fragility of his leg. Instead, Mrs. Nordahl, a para in his classroom, offered to drive him home in her car. Since she lived closeby, I welcomed the help and Zac felt safer not having to maneuver the stairs of the school bus.

The hospitalizations also seemed to go a little better, although the leg seizures were occurring more often. The doctors didn't have any definite answers as to why this was happening, so they continued to increase the Kepra (anti-seizure med). Zac was much happier being allowed to order what he wanted to eat versus us trying to omit white bread, processed foods or sugar from his diet. I felt it was too much for a 10-year-old to handle with everything else that was being taken away from him - from his running, his walking, being removed from his home and school every two-and-a-half weeks, to lay in the hospital. Nathan and I didn't know that changing his diet would affect him as severely as it had. We both were just so deathly afraid of how out-of-control this cancer had become. The literature that we had been reading told of how several cancer survivors stressed the importance of eliminating all sugars, if you had cancer. The information said - the sugar you eat just feeds the cancer. I could only picture my hand feeding the ferocious cancer beast that resided in my beautiful little boy. The diet was something Nathan and I felt we could have control over, but at what cost? Zachary was only 10 years old! Something as simple as a cookie or ice cream cone, that could put a smile on a child's face, could also be the cause of sadness and depression, if denied.

Zac was compliant to the diet change. We actually omitted sugar for three months when Zac was five years old, thinking that would make a difference when we were fighting the astrocytoma. Easter was approaching and I questioned - how do you allow your other kids an Easter basket that the Easter Bunny always brought, and deny the youngest? You don't. Or do the other kids have to suffer, and none of them get Easter candy? Absolutely not. So the Easter bunny came like he always did. But in spite of the no-sugar diet before Easter, Zac's astrocytoma tumor resolved and eight new brain tumors surfaced.

It was incredibly frustrating because there was no guaranteed science at how to beat cancer. It was different for everyone. I realized whatever I did, I could not be a part of inflicting pain on my own son. Zac was so much happier since we let him eat what he felt like, but in moderation, of course. Zac maybe had a sweet a day, if not every other day (that was his idea). We tried to get him to eat more fruits and vegetables which, was difficult because he got so full so fast from all his medicine.

I bought a Vitamix high performance blender at the Minnesota State fair with the intention of making high antioxidants smoothies every day. And we did. I felt keeping Zac's spirit alive was so much more a key in beating this then only the 'possibility' of being cured if he followed a perfect diet. We would just have to incorporate other approaches that seemed beneficial and more tangible. Zac also did a shot of straight lemon juice, daily, and I started learning about Pure Essential oils and he was using them as well. I took Zac to a few healing touch therapy appointments in Pine City until I realized I couldn't afford to spend that kind of money without knowing for sure it would help rid the body of cancer. He took more vitamins and supplements that helped support his immune system. We were trying everything we could think of.

In the hospital, Zachary had visitors other than the usual friends and family that stopped in. Jake Parenteau made frequent visits after his initial meeting at the award ceremony. For his first visit Jake brought fellow Minnesota Gopher hockey teammates - Justin Holl and Zac Buddish. Throughout the day Zac kept telling me, "I am so excited for today! I can't wait for them to get here!" He was beaming.

It was fun for all of us. Nic and Zac played a few games of NHL 13 with the guys. Jessica just stared at them, calculating how old she'd have to be before she could date them. The room got a bit loud with all the cheering. I went out to the nurse's station to apologize for our loudness in advance, before someone would come in to "shush" us. I was relieved when the nurse said the noise was fine, "we love to hear the laughter in here."

Zac loved people. He loved his elementary school friends, boys as well as the girls, but he had such a mature connection to adults. He could carry on an extensive conversation without this silent awkwardness that usually happens with kids.

Nick, the fallen Navy SEALs brother, Jacob came by our house one Sunday afternoon to introduce Matt, Nick's friend who was also a Navy SEAL. Matt flew to Minnesota to send his condolences to Mr. and Mrs. Spehar. In the loss of their son, Mr. Spehar formed a close bond with many of the SEALS. It was mutual. They would visit him from time to time.

This visit, Matt traveled alone. He wanted to meet Zac in person since he had only been able to get to know him over the phone. Matt knew Zac was struggling. I think without realizing it, he brought some of his determination, courage and bravery with him. By taking time out of his day to come see a boy who had been beaten down one too many times, he recharged him. Zac by his own nature radiated the same qualities as a Navy SEAL - just in a different way.

I was reminded again how one person could make a difference in a life. Zac, my other kids, Nathan and myself included appreciated the continual care, concern and time people took to help us - small ways or big. We valued the friends that God put in our life at the right time. I don't think it is by accident when people come into our lives. The possibilities are endless as to how we could affect someone. Maybe it's more about - how far would you go to bring someone happiness or get something out of life that could make a difference?

February 26, 2013 was a big day. Zac had the longest MRI he has ever had - almost 4 hours! This was the MRI that would confirm if the chemotherapy protocol for the osteosarcoma was also working on his lungs and brain.

I went into the MRI with Zac as I had done since he was seven years old when he decided he could go into the "spaceship" without being put to sleep. He could lie completely still for the fifty minutes his scan took. He never had any trouble staying still, even now with the longer MRI's. Recently he had to have them stop because he needed to go to the bathroom and his back was killing him lying on the hard plastic table. The technician said she really didn't want to move him because she would have to start the series all over again. Really?! He has to pee! I could see the ambivalence and agony on Zac's face as he was asked to wait.

"Do you think you can hold it?" I asked almost hating myself for suggesting such a thing.

"Yeah, I - - guess," Zac said unsure through clenched teeth.

I changed my mind. I knew how incredibly uncomfortable it was for me to try and "hold it," hoping I could make it to the next rest stop when traveling. The nurse in me came out.

"Do you have a urinal?" I asked the technician.

"Yah, I think so," she said as she opened cupboard door after cupboard door to look. "Here's one."

Without moving Zac, I helped him to go to the bathroom lying flat on his back. I'm not sure who was more relieved. The last thing I wanted was for him to have to endure an extra hour of scanning because he moved. He was almost done.

As I sat in the MRI room watching Zac lay there so obediently, I couldn't help but wonder how what Zac was going through – brain tumor after brain tumor – could be for any "good." Nine years was a lifetime of suffering for a child. It was for Zac, anyway. It was all that he knew – except when he would get little breaks in between new diagnosed tumors and having to restart chemotherapy. I prayed and prayed for Zac's healing. One day, something in me started feeling like I was fighting God. I know I was supposed to trust Him, but how could I come to accept God's will if His will was for Zachary to be with Him? I didn't want to say "those words." It hurt me and scared me to my core. I felt that God wanted my complete trust – no matter what it entailed. I kept pushing that nagging thought to the back of my mind.

As I sat wondering what Zac's MRI results would be, I remained hopeful, but guarded. I recently read a book that my Mom gave me. I was looking for hope and for stories of miracles to keep me focused. The book 'The Porter of Saint Bonaventure: The Life of Father Solanus,' was about an American man, born in Minnesota, who became a Capuchin priest. He was referred to as saint Father Casey Solanus by thousands and many attributed cures of sickness that seemed beyond medical science, including doctors. He died in 1957 with documentation of thousands of miracles. (He is currently in the process of being canonized as saint.)

If we were alive today, our family would take a trip to visit him. I imagined him being able to heal my Zac. His book inspired me and we began to pray to him daily to intercede for Zac's healing. His life message I wrote down and taped to my kitchen cupboard so I would pray it and remind myself throughout the day not to fight the One I was supposed to trust:

"That confidence in God is the very soul of prayer and becomes a condition for supernatural intervention in our lives. God condescends to use our powers if we don't spoil His plan by ours."

Was I spoiling His plan? Was I getting in His way? Who was I to be able to stop God? I was nothing next to him. I was trying very hard to have confidence in God and believing that He knew what He was doing. Maybe He was waiting for me to just say and believe "those" words…"Not my will, but Yours." This was the hardest type of trust I had ever known.

As he walked in, I scanned Dr. Moertel's face for any indication of good versus bad news. There was nothing. I waited not sure I want to go into that dreadful, painful place of knowing. Nathan made a comment to which Dr. Moertel replied in a quiet voice, "It's good."

I opened my eyes wide with surprise. I wasn't sure I heard him right, so I waited quietly as he opened up Zachary's scans on the computer. He confirmed what I heard.

The brain tumor had already shrunk 0.5 cm. Dr. Moertel said, "that was a big difference in their world." The other brain tumor was also smaller and the cancer in the lungs was improved. As for the femur, it looked worse, but Dr. Moertel explained that we didn't start chemotherapy until three weeks after finding the osteosarcoma. Because of how aggressive the cancer was, he said, it probably grew quite a bit during that time.

Finally, a little breathing room once again. Zac would be rescanned after two more chemo cycles - in six weeks - more time to give the chemotherapy the chance to show us what it could do.

Round three of inpatient chemotherapy brought a few interesting and fun visitors. Shannon from KS95 came after work to play some Yahtzee with Zac. She explained how she didn't have the best luck with games, but she scooted up her chair to the edge of Zac's bed where we had the game ready to go on the bedside table.

Right off the bat, Zac rolled a yahtzee - five dice, all fives! Shannon looked defeated even before she rolled the dice for the first time. It didn't matter, Zac was happy, we were laughing and having fun as Zac was kicking her butt.

Later in the evening Jake Parenteau, his girlfriend and Justin Hall, came back for another visit. NHL 13 was the game of choice to be played on the Xbox. More laughter and chatter filled the room. I haven't seen so much smiling in one hospital day from Zac. The visits were a bit tiring, but so much fun. Zac didn't feel left out from the outside world, not when the outside world came to see him.

Again the next day the visitors came. Zachary napped on and off throughout the day which was good, because Jake came back to play Xbox with him and Nic. While Jake was still there, the 2013 - St. Paul Winter Carnival royalty all showed up. Zac's room was packed wall-to-wall. He was surprised by such a visit. King Boreas actually visited Zac's fourth grade class where he was awarded a special royalty. He came home that day super excited!

Later, King Boreas shared with me how drawn to Zachary he was and how touched he was by his vibrant, positive spirit. He wanted to stay in touch with Zac and do whatever he could to help. So in a thoughtful gesture, he had the Winter Carnival Prime Minister, Matt Wallace call me to set up the surprise visit - if I felt Zac would be up for it.

What a treat for Zac to see them all dressed up in their fancy clothes there in his hospital room just for him! Talk about smiles.

After all the visiting, Zac was tuckered out. He couldn't stay awake to watch a movie with Aunt Barb and myself. The chemo was taking a toll. I was also quite concerned when he was weighed and had gained 10 pounds overnight. The scale was accurate. I had the nursing assistant try different scales. No one could figure out where the weight came from. Since his lungs were clear and he didn't have swollen hands, ankles or feet, no one seemed bothered, but me. I just didn't want any more unexpected surprises, especially after he was just treated for pneumonia.

It wasn't always fun and full of visitors in the hospital. Many times it was just Zac, myself and Aunt Barb who visited in the evenings - most of the time. Before we came in on Tuesday, Zac was sitting at the kitchen table and began quietly crying. He looked so glum, almost lost.

"I don't want to go back to the hospital," Zac whispered.

"What do you hate about it the most?" I asked wanting him to share his pain, knowing we still had to go to the hospital.

Hanging his head, he said, "Not being with my friends."

Before we were to leave the hospital, Zac's orthopedic doctor was supposed to stop by to give me the results of Zac's x-ray. He never came. I called the clinic from home in the morning and had to leave a message on his nurse's voicemail. By 4 pm and I still hadn't heard anything. It was important for me to hear what Dr. Cheng had to say. Much of Zac sadness was due to the fact that he couldn't walk, let alone put any weight on his right leg. It was now three months that he had been on crutches and it was getting old. I wanted to know what we could do to move towards walking again.

I debated if I should call again. I tried waiting patiently, but with the weekend approaching and the clinic closing at 5 pm, I felt I deserved some sort of answer. I spoke with the triage nurse who reassured me my phone call would be returned at the end of the day. *Okay then...*

When it was 5:35 pm, I had the feeling like I had been blown off once again. I called one more time - "The clinic is now closed..." *Lovely!*

In the scheme of things, it wasn't that big of a deal, but to me, I felt like my concerns were basically disregarded. I haven't had a great track record with "really" being heard, and in some of those instances, Zac would not be alive had I listened to them and what they were telling me. I just wanted to feel like Zac's situation was important enough to get a return phone call. I was extremely frustrated.

It was important for Zac to have attainable goals, plans that were possible - even if they were down the road. His spirit thrived on that. I knew the doctors and nurses were busy, but this was not just about a broken bone, but a child's life. My child.

I was very surprised when Dr. Cheng called at 9:05 pm. We were in the middle of celebrating Lexie's 5th birthday (a little late for a 5-year-old, but Nic had hockey and I wanted the whole family to be there.) I had to excuse myself from our family party for the long awaited phone call.

Dr. Cheng did apologize, which was nice, but it didn't change how I felt about the neglect. He went on to say the x-ray actually looked worse and the outside of the femur was cracked. He didn't know how it would heal while Zac was going through chemotherapy.

"We will have to wait and see. And I hear Zac doesn't particularly follow the rules," he said meaning Zac was a complicated case.

Dr. Cheng went on to say Zac could begin to weight-bear, using two crutches. "He has to be careful," he stressed.

I didn't quite understand his way of thinking. Yes, I wanted him to give us the "green-light" to start walking, but at what expense? "We'll do what you think is best, but if you think it's better to wait, I don't mind having Zac wait longer to bear weight. I don't want to risk him breaking his leg and needing a bone graft."

"No, I think he he'll be okay."

Really? I thought to myself. It didn't sound right.

When Zac needed another blood transfusion, I thought I would run by what Dr. Cheng advised, to Tammie. She was a bit shocked. "He should NOT be putting ANY weight on his leg. I'll talk with Dr. Cheng."

CHAPTER 23

home to reality

With the news of the brain tumor shrinking, less spots in his lungs and the debate of whether Zac's leg was better, worse or the same, Nathan and I decided to take a break from life and travel to Mexico for a week with my best friend Carla, her husband Tom and another couple who were friends of theirs. Nathan and I had planned to go months earlier, but with the constant bad news, change in Zac's treatment and blood transfusions, I resigned myself to the fact that we couldn't go. Married life was incredibly tough when fighting to stay positive in the light of ambivalent news that constantly pounded in my head – *your little boy is probably going to die, your little boy is going to die...* It was tough enough trying to keep Nic, Jessica and Lexie's life as normal as possible while trying to keep my nursing job at the hospital and find quality time with Nathan.

I wasn't about to leave Zac's side since I knew him best and I was constantly on high alert for any changes in his health. I was afraid to step away, but I also felt myself struggling to keep my head above water. Trying to keep up with the housework, the grocery shopping and other commitments, there seemed like there was little time for Nathan and me. I didn't have much left to give. When things became too overwhelming, and there hadn't been any time for either of us to sit down and have a real conversation because of the kids constantly interrupting, the arguing and pointing fingers would begin.

Nathan and I talked about how many couples going through a similar journey probably divorced because of the stress and lack of communication. I knew from the past deployments when Nathan was gone and I was left to care for three small children months at a time that I never wanted to be a single parent, let alone go through this battle without him by my side. For the most part, the way we communicated held us together along with our love for each other and our children. We fought to get the most out of life and we, both competitive by nature, were not about to give up. We were tired of this, but we reminded ourselves, not nearly as tired as Zac was. He was the one suffering!

Nathan and I were on a mission to save Zac, but we needed to be strong for the battles that waited. They were there, you could feel them thick in the air. I just didn't know exactly what they were or when they would jump out at us. That was one of the reasons I finally agreed to go on the trip. I wanted a break from real life - even if it was only for a week. I cried thinking how unfair it was that I physically got a break from the life and Zac didn't. Nathan needed me also and I needed him. I knew the trip would help us reconnect and since Tammie and Dr. Moertel said they thought we should go - the permission slip was signed - I would go.

Zac had been out of the hospital after his inpatient chemotherapy, I had drawn his blood twice and brought him in for his blood transfusion that he always seemed to need a week after being out of the hospital. He was feeling good and would only need his Grandpa Harvey to bring him to the hospital for one blood draw.

Nathan's mom and dad had agreed to stay with the kids while we were away. They were very involved in our children's lives and were always willing to help out.

I cried on the way to the airport and I cried during take-off, but I was also relieved to escape. The trip was awesome! A week later, we came back refreshed and extremely tan. Still guilty for what people would think of us leaving Zac and spending the money, which had been given by Nathan's parents, I hoped our real friends wouldn't judge us, but understand.

The morning after we got back from our trip, Zac was lying on his biomat and said when he woke up he couldn't wiggle his toes on his right foot. "I don't know if I had a leg seizure when I was sleeping or not."

Here we go… We came home to reality - literally. It sometimes took a little while for Zac to regain the strength of his arm or leg after what the doctors were now calling "seizures." I didn't panic, but when three hours passed and he still couldn't wiggle his toes and he didn't have the strength in his foot to flex it up and down, I started to worry.

I ran through the usual neuro drills… "Do you have a headache? Does your arm feel different? Squeeze my hands."

I waited it out, but remain bothered by it all day. Finally at 8 pm, I called the hematology/ oncology fellow on-call, at the hospital. I didn't want to be missing something and I definitely did not want to be responsible should anything develop.

The fellow was glad I called, but said if anything should change (headache, further numbness…) go to the emergency department. She called to check on Zac Sunday mid-morning and we decided to hold tight until Zachary's upcoming inpatient admission for chemo, on Tuesday.

Zac continued to baffle the doctors. There were no definite explanations, no answers, only "maybe this" or "it could be…" I hated being left hanging. *Why couldn't Zac for once have something they knew about and could have a "fix" for?* I knew worrying was useless. It says so in the Bible and in my devotional book, Jesus Calling –

"Rehearsing your troubles result in experiencing them many times, whereas you are meant to go through them only when they actually occur. Do not multiply your suffering in this way!"

"But you don't know what will happen today, much less tomorrow. Our path may take an abrupt turn, leaving you away from those mountains. There may be an easier way up the mountain than is visible from this distance…"

"Do not give into fear or worry, those robbers of abundant living… and many difficulties on the road ahead will vanish before you reach them."

What made it difficult in controlling my mind to stay positive was when the doctors could only throw out possibilities of what could be the reason for Zac's ongoing and new ailments. I wished I had the choice to pick out the reason.

1. It could be his femur collapsing more.
2. It could be tumor related.
3. It could be the brain tumor dying, causing more swelling in that area which was creating the swelling on the motor center that controls his foot movement.

I choose number three.

No change in treatment plan, just as I thought. We would wait and see ortho, neurology and physical therapy. Maybe they would have some answers, but I wasn't going to hold my breath.

Easter was approaching and Zac and I were missing out on Holy week. I tried to stay focused on the importance of the week's events leading up to the Resurrection, but something about being in the hospital made it almost impossible. Instead of reflecting on Jesus's sacrifice for us all, I continued to watch my own son suffer. My motivation was different. My heart felt different. Zac was the closest thing I had come to knowing Jesus. He was also so good and pure, so faithful in his love for God. When asked how he stayed so strong, he said, "God gives me strength." He's almost eleven!

I prayed God was using Zachary in a way that included complete healing. I wanted to get back to what everyone considered a normal life with the little things to complain about like money, fighting kids, car problems or the pressures that jobs demanded. I wanted to hear Zac's feet walking up the stairs again, I wanted him to be able to run around and wrestle his brother and dad again. To be able to be free of daily and weekly needle pokes, transfusions and hospital stays so he could focus on playing with his friends, baseball, golf and archery was what I wanted for Zac.

The little things were a big deal. Zac gave me hints that he thought about them too, with occasional comments – "Mom, it's gonna take me a lot longer to find Easter eggs since I'm on crutches."

If Christmas was the time for miracles and Easter was the time for new hope, new life and new beginnings, could it be possible to have both, for Zac? I continued to believe so. The doctors hadn't sat Nathan or me down yet to tell us we were fighting a losing battle, so hope was still alive.

It had been a "routine" hospital stay until nighttime when Zac's nurse was questioning the look of his port. He was lying down so it was not that noticeable to me, but she thought it looked puffier than usual.

Something had happened about five years back to the skin on and around his port that caused the skin to be raised and a bit discolored from the surrounding tissue. I always questioned "why?" but no one ever had an answer.

In the morning it was brought up during doctor rounds. The port area did look odd and the skin color was a little darker than before.

"Let's stop the chemo and get an x-ray and do a dye study just to be sure it is infusing right."

The port was indeed broken and had been leaking chemo out into Zac's tissues, which was very damaging.

Prior to using the AFO wash (that had previously created burns on Zac's chest) the doctor felt it was necessary to try and aspirate the fluid pocket that they felt had built up just under his skin and on top of his port.

Zac cried and cried as they repeatedly poked a long needle into his unanesthetized skin, attempting to remove the pooling chemo. No fluid was retrieved. They finally agreed that his port site needed time to settle down and heal. At 5 pm they would surgically place a pic line (a catheter that sits under the inside upper arm for long-term use of IV meds).

When it came time for the AFO wash, Zac was nervous. I told him it would be better this time because he didn't have the old chemo in his body any longer to make his skin react to the treatment like it had last time. I was wrong. The burning and itching was much better this time, but about two minutes after the nurse left, Zac's upper left chest started to blister. I quickly called the nurse back in. Soon doctors were back in observing Zac as if he were a science experiment.

Today happened to be "Superhero Day." Zac was filmed earlier stating who his heroes were. I was pleased when on his own, he said his brother Nic and deceased Navy SEAL, Nick Spehar were his heroes. I urged Zac to go downstairs were all the festivities were taking place in the Amplatz Children's lobby, hoping to take his mind off of getting the PICC line.

His sadness quickly turned into surprise when he saw superheroes all over - Minnesota Wild hockey players, the Minnesota Twins and Wild mascot's, music and balloons. I pushed Zac in the wheelchair closer to see as hospital staff and pediatric patients took turns going down an open runway of people clapping and cheering on either side as they processed down through the tunnel.

A staff member saw us watching and asked if Zac would like to go down the runway. His eyes brightened. As usual, Zac was able to quickly switch off his frustration and tears for a smile. Off he went down the open tunnel, smiling and wiggling (dancing) to the beat of the music.

Once back settled in his room, Lexie came running in with Grandma Janet and Grandpa Harvey right behind. Zac and I hadn't seen her, Nic, Jessica or Nathan for a few days, so you would have thought it would have been a happy reunion, but Zac started quietly crying. He missed his family so much!

"I hate when Zac's crying," Lexie matter-of-factly said. "It makes me so mad!" She didn't want to kiss Zac, but after a little forceful encouragement she gave him a little hug.

That only made Zac cry more. He just wanted to go home and be with his family and pretend none of this was happening.

I felt the stress of separation too. I hated that life stopped for a week while I knew everyone else was out there in the "real world" going to work, eating family dinners together or attending the sport activities of their children. Our real-world meant every two weeks, Zac and I would be confined to the hospital while everyone else "lived." Many times I didn't see my other kids an entire hospital stay because of their sports and school. We didn't live close enough for a quick visit. Nathan had to work to keep a roof over our heads and was the one who kept our other kids lives running.

I didn't sign up to be a mother "part-time." *How was I supposed to be mother to all of my children when I couldn't leave the one who needed me the most?*

We made a break from the hospital on Good Friday without Zac ever regaining movement in his foot or toes. No MRI - "it wouldn't change their treatment plan at this time." So we would have to wait and see...

As soon as I got home, it was a mad dash to get things prepared for Easter. The dessert and appetizers were made to bring to my parents. We had a wonderful Easter spent with family, but it was painful watching Zac try and find the Easter eggs. When you are rooting for your ten-year-old to hurry and beat his five-year-old sister – something is amiss.

Zac had a difficult time, as he predicted – looking for Easter eggs on crutches. He never complained he just crutched his way to and fro doing the best he could to spot an egg. At one point he dropped his crutches and quickly fell to the floor on his butt, just to get to an egg he happened to see before anyone else (ie. Lexie) might snatch it. Nic and Jessica were wonderful in that they let Zac find as many eggs as they could without Zac suspecting their help.

4th grade field day - The 100m (wheelchair) dash. Zac was not about to become a bystander! 6-3-13

Zac hunting for Easter eggs. Crutches are not about to stol him! 3-31-13

CHAPTER 24

going nowhere fast...

April 9th, 2013. Zac had another three hour MRI, followed by a platelet and blood transfusion. Dr. Moertel came in to deliver the news. He said Zac's femur lesions looked better although it appeared that the bone collapsed more and there were less spots in his lungs. This seemed like good news, but I was concerned what "the femur bone collapsing" meant.

"I'm not a very good bone doctor. That will be a question for Dr. Cheng," Dr. Moertel said as he pulled up the brain scan on the computer.

The brain tumor looked the same with the exception of some gray hazing radiating off of the tumor. Once again Dr. Moertel did not know what it was. "It could be a radiation reaction."

I was confused. - "This many months after he has completed radiation?"

"With having NF, it could be. I'll have the radiation doctor as well as Dr. Guillaume review it."

There was talk about doing a biopsy or possibly removing it, which he said was unlikely because of how it was spreading out. It was not typical of a sarcoma, I was told because when they grow back they grow back in a solid round mass.

The stress of uncertainty ate away at me. The fear of the unknown was almost as bad as the fear of knowing. But as long as there were treatment options, I still had hope that Zac could beat this.

The day after Zac's MRI, Tammie called. She informed me that they had a care conference with all the brain doctors and they definitely agreed that one of the brain tumors that had the hazing coming off of it, "looked different." They were debating if it was something called "radiation necrosis" or something else. They wanted to do a profusion image, but then Dr. Moertel said "no" because he wasn't going to change up the treatment plan when it was working on Zac's femur. Same story, different day... so frustrating.

We knew Zac's leg looked better, but now Tammie said that the cancer was almost gone from his leg! That was encouraging! She explained that as the cancer was leaving Zac's leg, it was leaving holes in his bone making it weaker, causing it to collapse. Unfortunately the effects of the chemo were not allowing his bone to regenerate. There was mention of doing bone marrow injections into his leg, but it wouldn't be possible until chemo treatments were completed.

The plan was to do the profusion MRI and CT scan before Zac's next chemo admission, the following week. He would also have his broken port removed and allow the site to heal before replacing it.

The weekend went by quickly and it was already time for Zac's surgery to remove his broken port. Tammie stopped in briefly to give Nathan and I Zac's CT results. The spots in Zac's lungs were almost gone and the ones remaining were smaller. It seemed the chemotherapy was working. Nathan, Zac and I were ecstatic. Good news had been hard to come by lately. With that, Tammie said it looked like he still had some sort of infection brewing in his lungs so he would need to start on an antibiotic.

While we were talking, the radiologist text paged Tammie and said "so far the brain scan didn't look worrisome in comparison to the previous scans." Nathan and I were breathing a little easier.

Surgery went without any complications and once Zac was settled in his room the hematology/ oncology fellow, Dr. Jess Barnum came in to see me. She asked if I understood what Tammie had said in regards to Zac's brain scan. I repeated to her what Tammie had told me. Dr. Barnum told me that wasn't exactly true.

I could sense an unsettled concern. "So, you are not thinking it is radiation necrosis?"

"We still aren't sure and the radiologist is still reimaging his scans."

Going from good news, only two hours earlier, to this ominous, ambivalent conversation, I could feel the heaviness squeezing at my heart and throat. "Haven't you seen others with something that looked similar to what is going on with Zac?"

"We have, but what Zac's looks like has similarities of radiation necrosis and – "the other," Dr. Barnum carefully said. "The doctors are meeting tomorrow at 12:30 pm and will know more then. Dr. Moertel, Tammie and I will see you after the meeting tomorrow."

I didn't know what to think. I was struggling with the vagueness of diagnosis, let alone prognosis. I wanted to ask more questions, but I didn't want to mentally go there. I swear I was on the verge of going insane! I was trying to stay in the here and now. I began feeling sick to my stomach.

The following morning only brought added confusion to Zac's scans when Dr. Moertel came in to check on him. When I commented on how happy Zac and I were when we were told that the cancer was almost gone in his leg, he looked at me blankly.

"No, I wouldn't say that," Dr. Moertel replied.

"What do you mean? I thought that's the reason why his bone was collapsing - because the cancer was leaving and in the process - leaving holes in his femur," I explained myself.

"That's something we'll be discussing in Thursday's meeting. Dr. Cheng will be there, as well as sarcoma doctors."

I was taken aback. We were given good news. *You can't take it back!* My faith and confidence in the different doctors I was dealing with was dissipating.

When Dr. Moertel set me straight on the lung CT - telling me that the cancer "wasn't almost gone, but improved," I was ready to throw in the towel. *God can override anything the doctors say. That's what a miracle was, wasn't it?* I had to believe in that because I was getting different stories from the same scans. I trusted Dr. Moertel, but I still felt in the dark.

Dr. Moertel came back again in the evening to relay that the team of doctors were still not sure what the "hazing" was in Zac's brain. We were getting nowhere fast. My frustration was building. I wanted someone, anyone to tell me with certainty what was going on with Zac - and fix it! Now we had to discontinue one of Zac's chemo meds because he had the most that he could ever have of that particular drug. It could cause irreversible heart damage if continued. Discontinuing one chemo med and adding one that Zac had been on previously made me nervous. If it didn't work before, why would it now? Dr. Moertel said he wanted to give the "possible" radiation necrosis a jump-start and see if it would work in dissolving the hazing.

"I've seen radiation necrosis go away in three days." Dr. Moertel said.

Zac would start the drug in two weeks. In the meantime, we would wait for yet another meeting the next day when Dr. Moertel felt there should be enough experienced doctors to put everything together and come up with a solid plan.

It was still dark out the next morning when the orthopedic doctor, Dr. Cheng came into Zac's room. As I wearily sat up, smoothed down my hair and rubbed my eyes from my few hours of sleep, I could see his face although I had to strain my eyes to make him out from the shadows in the room. It was only 6 am.

"I was told you wanted to see me?" Dr. Cheng nonchalantly said. "You have some questions for me?" He sat in the orange vinyl chair between Zac's bed and my fold-down couch.

I felt very unsettled with Dr. Cheng's opening question. *"Yah! Duh?! I've been wanting to see you for weeks! Pardon my lack of politeness, but I've been told my son now has two brains sarcomas that are so rare that they may see one case in every five years, and he has lung cancer as well as an osteosarcoma in his femur. He was also in his fifth round of chemotherapy, maybe six - I've lost count since each round has lasted at least a year, AND he has been on crutches almost 4 months! Dr. Cheng has spoken to me twice since he biopsied Zac's leg early January. He's STILL on crutches! DID I MENTION THAT?! - Yah, I have questions.*

At this point with the lack of communication and differing opinions in Zac's condition, I was beyond frustration. It didn't get any better after my conversation with Dr. Cheng.

Now I was being told that Zac's leg is not almost cancer free, but it "looks worse." He saw more spots and said he doesn't think the chemotherapy was working. Radiation was discussed in conference, but if they did use it, Zac's femur would not grow. Dr. Cheng wouldn't do surgery or knee replacement because it would also stop the bone growth. Even scraping out the tumor wouldn't cure Zac's leg of the cancer, only stunt the bone growth.

I felt like there were no options. Where was the hope in all of this?

"He's at high risk for his leg breaking," Dr. Cheng informed.

"But when will he get off of the crutches?" I didn't think he would be on them forever. I looked over at Zac. He was still on his right side facing away from us and was quietly sleeping.

"If you factor in Zac's quality of life and life expectancy - which may be seven years at most, I think he should get a special knee brace and get him walking on one crutch for a few weeks and then possibly progress to a cane," Dr. Cheng said.

What!? I was a bit shocked. The words "quality of life" and "life expectancy" and "seven years" rang in my head. What did he mean by that? No one had ever talked to me like that before. Those words have never been used in reference to Zac's condition. Dr. Cheng's whole way of thinking made no sense to me. Yes, I wanted Zac to start walking without crutches, but if he breaks his leg he would be in so much pain and have to wait even longer for his bone to heal. How would that benefit his "quality of life?!" It wouldn't! Zac would then require surgery and his leg would be done growing.

I peeked over at Zac again, fearful he was listening to our conversation (that's why I wanted to go in the hall). He still appeared to be sleeping. I hoped he wouldn't understand what "quality of life" or "life expectancy" meant if he did hear us talking.

I was out of questions. Without saying it, Dr. Cheng painted a death sentence. He didn't know him like what Dr. Moertel or Tammie did. He had to be wrong. I would not lose my son.

Almost immediately after Dr. Cheng stepped out of the room the darkness gave way to the light that was filtering through the shades with the rising sun. Zac rolled on to his side and turned his sweet face towards me. "What did he mean by seven years?"

Oh Great. He did hear! I scrambled for a believable explanation. I knew what Dr. Cheng meant, but I wasn't about to burden my 10-year-old son with even more devastating news that may not even be true. I was out of explanation, I cluelessly said, "Nooooo, he didn't say anything about seven years. I'm not sure what you heard."

Changing the subject, I asked "Did we wake you? I thought you were sleeping?"

"I was dozing when I thought I heard him say something about seven years," Zac explained.

From now on, I would have the doctor's talk outside his room. I needed to protect Zac from the confusing conversations and be able to have time to decipher what he should and should not know.

I sat uneasy with the morning's conversation all day. I tried to lighten up by playing a few games of Yahtzee with Zac, but it still ate at me. I couldn't hold back my frustration and tears when Emily, our social worker, came in to check on Zac and me.

As Zachary busied himself with Xbox NHL 13, I unloaded on Emily. She sat and listened and sympathized with the impending doom I was left with. "Am I crazy in believing Zac could beat this?" I asked.

"Of course not. Look at what he's done up to this point."

"Dr. Moertel and Tammie - no one, for that matter has ever talked about life expectancy, have they?" I asked looking for confirmation. I didn't want to appear to be "way out there."

"No. I have never heard any of them say anything to that effect in clinic conversation or in meetings I have been in," Emily truthfully reflected.

Before Emily left, she gave me the name and number of patient relations. I could sense from her that she felt the un-organization and mixed messages were unacceptable. I felt relieved I had her to talk to.

"It's your right," Emily reminded me.

"I know, I just don't want to get anyone in trouble or to have them later look at me or talk differently to me for calling them out," I explained.

"You're not getting them in trouble. You're trying to get them on the same page."

"I'll wait and see how things go with Dr. Moertel when I talk to him today," I paused. "I know Dr. Cheng is a skilled doctor, but he doesn't seem to have been at the same meeting. I am just sick and tired of all the mixed messages and disorganization. I will probably call so no other parent will have to go through the same painful chaos."

I tried waiting patiently for Dr. Moertel to stop by like he had said, but something nagged at me to call his cell phone. It was 4:30 pm and he would be leaving soon for the day.

"Oh, I'm just on my way out. I won't be able to come until tomorrow morning," Dr. Moertel said.

Really? I didn't know what to say. I couldn't sit with the news Dr. Cheng delivered to me in so I quickly filled him in on my unsettling conversation.

Dr. Moertel through crackling, because of the lack of reception, said something about Dr. Cheng not getting the final radiology report.

More confusion. Was he not in the morning meeting with Dr. Moertel?

After I hung up with Dr. Moertel, I began to question the answers to previously asked questions. I wasn't sure who I could trust in knowing what was really going on with Zac. Dr. Moertel hadn't steered me wrong in the past eight - almost nine years, but I wouldn't be seeing him until tomorrow. Dr. Jess Barnum was in-house and I liked her as a person and in her way of handling Zac.

She stopped by Zac's room, sat and talked with me and showed me some of his scans again.

Bottom line - Zac's lungs looked a "tiny" bit better, but the cancer was not almost all gone. Zac's leg looked a "tiny" bit better, but had two new small spots that were not previously there. The cancer was in the growth plate making it very difficult to treat. Zac's brain was otherwise stable with the exception of the hazing, which no one had yet identified, one way or the other.

With brain sarcomas being rare and Zac using so many different chemotherapies, Dr. Jess Barnum said, "I'm worried."

I knew deep down what she was worried about, but she didn't say "it" and I was not going to let myself go there.

I knew all about God's will, but that didn't mean I was going to throw in the towel and give my son to Him. I know that sounded selfish. Maybe I was a disappointment to God because I wasn't fully surrendering my son (back) to Him. But what mother could easily and willingly hand over one of their children to God. Yes, I have heard the saying that all of our children are on loan to us, but it didn't matter, Zac was mine to love and to take care of here on earth. I would do anything and everything to save him. I hoped I wouldn't be punished for thinking this way. I was really working on trying to be more faithful, but I struggled with my faith on and off. Today, I struggled on.

CHAPTER 25

storming heaven

In my efforts to "do something" in spite of my helplessness concerning Zac's health, I decided to hold a "Healing Prayer service" at our church in Lindstrom. Father Wehmann and my good friend Lisa came by the hospital to help me plan it.

We picked the readings, Father Wehmann picked a gospel he felt was very fitting, Father Al agreed to do the homily and Zac and I picked songs that either empowered or comforted us. Lisa designed the program for me, and Karl, our music director/pianist worked with those in our community who volunteered to offer up their musical talents in our efforts to storm Heaven.

We were close to being ready for the big day. I figured Zac should be feeling well after being out of the hospital for a week. We actually were able to celebrate his eleventh birthday after being discharged from the hospital at my parents on May 12th. We drove straight to my parents since that was where Zac wanted to go for his day. He loved it there. He had his PICC line removed and a new port placed and was feeling good.

After Nathan drove the forty-five minutes to pick us up from the hospital, we headed home to unload our bags, then reload to spend a long day "at the cabin" with cousins and all. Zac was so grateful for his gifts and to be able to blow out his candles after being sung "Happy Birthday."

I had a difficult time trying to stay focused in the here and now. I couldn't help but wonder how many more birthdays Zac would have. I glanced over to where my dad sat next to Zac to see him crying. I knew he was thinking the same thing.

The following week I could tell Zac had taken a beating from the new switch in chemo medicines. He looked a bit more pasty and his lips were pale. The nausea and vomiting had returned, but the two added anti-nausea meds and scolpolomine patch seemed to be finally working.

"We're going to have to plan for your 'friend' birthday party, huh?" I said as I put the A&W rootbeer in a brown paper bag to take later that day to Zac's fourth grade classroom for his rootbeer's float birthday treat. It had become a tradition for us when the kids were in fourth and fifth grade.

"I think I will wait until I can walk without crutches to have my birthday party," Zac replied.

"You don't want to have a pool party?" I absent-minded said. "You could still get in the water and swim." I knew it was a bad idea as I was suggesting it. Of course he could be in the water, he just couldn't jump off the deck into the pool or get himself out of the pool – like everyone else. I knew Zac was thinking the same thing.

"Not really."

"What about going to a movie?"

"Naaa. There aren't any good movies out," Zac declined.

"Are you sure you want to wait? I don't know how long it will be before they will let you walk without crutches. Remember, Katie from PT said we have to strengthen your leg muscles first - so that when it's safe to walk you'll be good and ready." I knew it was going to be a while and I didn't want him to miss out on what was supposed to be a fun day. He always looked forward to his birthday parties.

"Yeah, I'm okay to wait. It'll be more fun for me when I can walk."

I was heartbroken for Zac. How disappointing. Nothing more was said about his party.

Nathan and I didn't have extra money to throw at trying anything other than what we were already doing to help heal Zac. My hope lied heavily in God and the doctors. I hoped that the added holistic approach was working in conjunction with the chemotherapy. I prayed that the prayers around the world were being heard and taken into consideration for the miracle Zac so desperately needed. I always had big crazy ideas, so it made sense to me to put out a request on Caringbridge for anyone who could make it, to join us at St. Bridget's Church in a nondenominational prayer service. (I didn't want to offend anyone and I wanted everyone to feel welcomed.) I thought maybe if a lot of people joined us, together under the same roof, our prayers would be that much more powerful. Maybe Zac's healing wouldn't be right then in the church, maybe not even the next day, but maybe sooner rather than later.

Sunday, May 19, 2013 was a warm bright sunny day, a good day for Zac's healing. I wanted to get to the church extra early so I could spend time in adoration, (prayers said before the Blessed Sacrament) but my morning was thrown all off when Zac sat at the kitchen table with a bloody nose.

I had just started making everyone an omelet for breakfast. Lexie ran to grab Zac some Kleenex. Zac had been getting bloody noses more often lately. I always knew his platelets were low when he got the nosebleeds. Usually they would stop after a minute or two, but not today.

"Pinch it a little harder and don't tip your head back - you don't want that blood draining in your stomach," I instructed Zac.

I continued making Zac's omelet then I turned to see how Zac was doing. Within thirty seconds the Kleenex was saturated with blood.

"Mom... It's not stopping," Zac said a little nervous.

"Ohhh... Gross!" Lexie shrieked and ran out of the kitchen. "Zac's got a bloody nose! Zac's got a bloody nose!"

I replaced the Kleenex with a wad of paper towels. As I removed the Kleenex, blood came running out of his nose. I had never seen a bloody nose like this before.

Before long I had piles of bloody paper towels lying on the kitchen floor.

"Whooh! What's going on? Nic asked, surprised as he came into the kitchen. "It looks like a murder scene in here."

Zac sat quietly as I continued to pinch his nose to the point my fingers were getting tired. "Nic, go ahead and eat Zac's omelet. I'll have to make him another one when we get the bleeding to stop."

I released the pressure from Zac's nose to see if it stopped, but within seconds it started dripping again.

"Whoa! What's going on?!" Jessica asked as she stepped into the kitchen staring at all of the bloody paper towels and me on my knees next to Zac pinching his nose.

"I hab anodder bloody nose. What does it wook wike?" Zac said with a little irritated sarcasm.

I gave Jessica "the eye" in hopes that she wouldn't make a comment that would push Zac over the edge. I knew Zac was frustrated and worried that his nose bleed wasn't stopping.

After forty minutes and the nosebleed was still not clotting off, I decided to call the oncology fellow at Amplatz. The prayer service was only two hours away and we were not going to miss it! I was hoping she would tell me I could take Zac to the hospital that was ten miles away and they could cauterize his nose.

"Zac, I think the devil is doing this because he doesn't want you to go to the healing prayer service. He is afraid you will be healed. He doesn't want you to be able to continue your work," I rationalized.

"Get Nic, Jessica and Lexie and walk around the house in prayer. Call out to the Angels to stop the bleeding!" I shouted to Nathan in a last effort to stop Zac's nosebleed. I wasn't going to let a bloody nose stop us from going to the healing prayer service. Yes, people could gather without Zac there to pray, but it wouldn't be the same.

"I'm on it!" Nathan was out the door.

When the oncology fellow called me back, she told me to draw Zac's blood saying "He may need to come to the hospital, be admitted and given platelets."

I couldn't believe this. "Could we wait another ten minutes to see if it stops? We have a healing prayer service for Zac at 2 pm."

She agreed, as long as I got Zac's blood drawn to make sure he had platelets left. "But if it does stop and he has another bloody nose, he needs to come in right away."

As the oncology fellow was finishing her sentence, Nathan came in from praying the prayer around the house and Zac's nose stopped bleeding after an hour.

We made it to church in time to greet friends, family, teachers, classmates - even friends I hadn't seen since high school! I was touched by the selflessness of everyone who took time out of their Sunday to go back to church for Zac - for us.

For most, people in crisis asked for prayers from others, for weeks or perhaps months, but people continued to pray with us in our struggle - for years! I was overwhelmed by the support.

The prayer service turned out beautifully, except for a minor incident when the statue of the Blessed Virgin Mary was almost knocked over when Lexie tried to lay flowers at her feet, to honor her. It was a quick save (it almost felt to be in slow motion) as Lisa and I ran for Mary at the same time before she tipped over and broke. Father Wehmann and Father Al did a beautiful job in the way they spoke of Zac. The music was what I was hoping it would be and Zac did great, sharing his story about his "two Jesuses." It was a story he wanted to share with those who didn't know, because like he said, "They are always with me."

I held it together pretty well during the service. I did almost lose it when Zac started crying as he told everyone about his Angels. My initial thought was *Oh, no what did I do?* I was afraid I forced him to think about the possibility of death in front of all these people. My intention was to empower him and make his experience as far from a funeral as possible. *I can't cry*, I told myself. *I have to stay strong for Zac.*

Later, when I asked him why he was crying he said, "Because whenever I think about my Angels it makes me so happy - and like, everything is going to be okay."

There was not a dry eye in the church.

CHAPTER 26

"nothing worth having comes easy"

There was speculation that the damage to Zac's foot (for which he had to wear a special AFO brace) would be permanent. I refused to believe that, although the possibility haunted me. It was painful for me to sit back and watch Zac's independence taken away, little by little. I never thought Zac would be on crutches for this long. It had already been five months. I was beginning to worry that he would never run again.

A few weeks later – Zac had another MRI and another brain tumor conference. This time one of the doctors was able to see the area of the brain that controlled the function of Zac's right foot. He determined that area of the brain was not damaged by the radiation. He believed that once the radiation necrosis resolved, as well as the left brain hemisphere swelling, Zac's function should return.

After Dr. Moertel saw the increase in strength in Zac's right leg and that he could slightly move his big toe, he said he needed to take back the comment about "permanent damage."

I know for many it may not have seemed to like a big deal to move one's toe, but it was for Zac. It was something positive and it was a sign of hope - no matter how small. I couldn't accept the comment about "permanent damage." Yes, it stung, but to admit defeat was more painful. Zac hated the crutches. He hated having to sit back and watch all the other kids run around and play. Kids weren't made to sit.

Having kids of my own changed me for the better. I knew being a mom would be hard. I watched my mom in caring for my handicapped sister. I witnessed the sacrifices my parents made to give her the best life she could have. I never really realized how hard it must have been on my parents. I never envisioned I would struggle in a similar way one day.

My sister, Therese cheated death when she was a baby, but the trade-off was permanent damage that would affect her for the rest of her life. I on the other hand continued to fight the fear of death possibly taking my child. I would rather take Zac with disabilities then to not have him at all.

The mind is a complicated thing. I was always competitive by nature. I didn't like to lose. This was one race we were going to finish with a victory. I couldn't accept anything less.

Zac started having more seizures while we were in the hospital for his week of chemo. He hadn't been hungry since shortly after the chemo started. He finally had an appetite when Nathan, Nic, Jessica and Lexie came to have family night in the hospital. We were just about to eat our pizza and watch a movie when Zac mentioned that his arm felt numb. A few minutes later his arm started jerking. It took almost ten minutes for it to subside.

Zac took a couple bites of pizza then commented that his "butt felt tingly." Nic and Jessica laughed and cracked a few jokes, but I knew it was something more, as odd as it seemed.

A few minutes later his torso started jerking in a rhythmic manner. I called for the nurse to have another set of eyes on what was going on. Of course the seizure was done by the time she got hold of the resident doctor. After a few questions and restating what Zac's protocol for seizures were, he left.

It wasn't even two minutes later when Zac said his throat was feeling "bubbly" and he felt the tingling in his butt and belly again. I didn't want to appear like I was overreacting, but I was nervous something impending was about to happen with his airway. I wanted Zac safe from harm and I was worried what my other kids might see.

I found a nurse in the hallway and asked if she could grab the doctor again. He did manage to make it into Zac's room in time to see the end of Zac's head, neck and torso jerking. I'm not sure what I wanted him to do about it other than be there should Zac go into a full grand-mal seizure or worse. I wanted him to see that these "seizures" were different. I wanted them to stop.

After three more very short mild seizures the next morning, the doctor increased Zac's medicine. He was now taking fifteen pills a day.

Once we were home and away from the poisonous chemotherapy that had been pumped into his veins, the seizures resolved. A relief, although I never left the house without his seizure medicine and I gave a supply to the school nurse to have on hand, as well - just in case.

Zac made it through the last four days of fourth grade, but I could see him tiring out. I knew his hemoglobin would be low once again. It was becoming quite routine. His face looked pale as well as his lips. I didn't realize how white Zac's lips were until I actually "looked" at all of Zac's classmates on that last day of school. They had pink lips. Zac really fought being tired. Even when his hemoglobin would be six-something (normal is between 11.0-13.0) he would force himself to ignore how tired he was (to a certain point) and be able to be a part of life. He hated missing out!

So for his first day of summer vacation, we headed down to Amplatz for a blood transfusion. I told him his consolation prize would be the energy he would quickly regain.

It usually was immediate. He would leave the Journey clinic saying, "Man, I feel way better." Unfortunately, not this time.

Sunday we were at Zac's buddy, Thomas's, for his brother's graduation party. There were lots of kids running around, but not Zac. He crutched way over to me sitting in the garage at a table. Through tears, he quietly whispered that there were a few boys going swimming. I thought he didn't think he was allowed to swim. "You can go swimming, I'll help you get changed and into the water."

Zac's eyes continued to fill up with tears and exhausted said, "I just don't *feel* like it. I'm so tired."

My heart ached for him. To see something that looks like so much fun and you want to do it, but at the same time are so physically tired that you just can't make yourself - really stunk! I was surprised by his honesty. He always had been able to make himself do the "fun things" and crash right after.

The only advice I had for him was to continue to visualize his leg getting stronger and healing, and picture himself walking and running. "We'll get there."

"I kinda forgot what it looks like to walk without crutches," Zac said.

We would fix that. I started hearing the song playing in my head – 'We're not gonna take this. No, we ain't gonna take this. We are not gonna take this—anymore!'

I wasn't about to sit back and let the "cancer-thing" take Zac over little by little. I couldn't let doubt or defeat become the core of his being - or mine. If we chose that as Zac's fate, our current existence would be over.

I removed the "get well" poster that I had taped up on the wall in our play room/workout room that my friend Stephanie had made for Zac when he was in the hospital almost a year ago when he underwent brain surgery. It had several pictures of him playing baseball. He was running, he was standing on his own two feet - without crutches. I found a few more pictures to add and then Nathan stapled the poster right above Zac's bed on the ceiling. This way he could see and remember what it looked like to walk and run. This would be the first thing he would see when he woke up in the morning and the last thing before he closed his eyes to sleep.

Nathan and I would talk and envision what we wanted out of life, on how we wanted to live - and for the most part we were accomplishing many of those dreams on a smaller scale, for now, but it was happening, little by little. If what we wanted was that important in having, we worked hard for it. The saying - "Nothing worth having comes easy," was true. It wasn't any different in Zac situation. Zac's mind at this point had to be stronger than the physical aspect of his body. It was Nathan's and my job to keep him mentally strong. We constantly fed him words of strength when despair and frustration would set in. Sometimes it was difficult remaining positive when it felt like the devil, at any chance, would try and tear Zac down, but it was even more frightening to admit defeat.

With the help of daily physical therapy sessions while in the hospital and continuing to exercise at home, Zac's leg was getting stronger. What we took for granted, like the simple lifting of our leg, straight up and down while lying face up on the bed or while lying face down and trying to bend our leg to touch our butt, was incredibly difficult for Zac. His right quadricep and glute muscle were severely atrophied. He had to master these challenges before he could attempt to walk.

Many times it was difficult for Zac to do the exercises at home because he was so tired. Everything took so much effort and the progress was slow. Because he wanted so badly to be back in the mileage club at school and just be able to walk from here to there with ease, Zac was driven to do his exercises three times a day.

It was Fourth of July, one of Zac's favorite holidays. Ever since he was a couple years old, he was enthralled with bonfires, sparklers and fireworks. He loved being around people and the array of food, particularly grandma Darlene's candy dish filled with miniature candy bars.

I could tell Zac was struggling with a low hemoglobin before we went to my parent's lake place to spend the day. He slept in, which was unusual for him and he looked pasty white, but Zac insisted on going. He wasn't about to pass up on the day's festivities.

It was gut-wrenching for me to watch him sleep in a patio chair outside on the lawn while his cousin swam and ran around with boundless energy. I asked if he wanted to swim for a bit, but he didn't feel up to it so he hung out with us adults and listened to our silly antics as we reminisced. Zac even laughed with us even when he didn't understand what we were laughing about. It didn't matter, he just liked to laugh. It could be a lame part in a movie and Zac would be the only one belting out a hearty laugh.

After Zac took another nap and had some food, I was able to entice him in the bean bag toss game. He was a little reluctant at first, mostly because he was tired, but also because of the crutches.

"Howz' this going to work?" Zac asked a bit confused.

"Could you hold onto one crutch and just throw the bean bag as far as you can?" I suggested hoping it would work. I wanted him to be able to feel like he could do something other than sit.

The first couple throws made it only halfway to the other side.

"Could you hold onto the back of a chair for better support?" I quickly added not wanting him to be discouraged so soon.

Zac threw a little further, but because he couldn't take a big step forward while throwing, the beanbag wasn't landing on the slanted board with the hole in the center, which still sat another ten feet out. Finally, after moving the boards closer together, without making Zac feel to babyish and agreeing to let him stand without using his crutch and allowing him to put some support on his "bad" leg, he was landing the bags on the board.

Zac smiled, but quickly found the game to be either too tiring or boring since he couldn't play to his full ability. "I'll just sit and visit," Zac said.

I felt defeated. I couldn't stand to sit back and watch Zac watch everyone else have fun. I knew he was tired, but if he found something that he could do that held his attention, he usually was able to push past how tired he was – for a little while longer.

Zac ended up swinging his golf clubs standing on one leg. He did pretty well. His cousin, Jack, who was two years younger than him patiently waited for the golf ball to be hit so he could retrieve it for Zac. It got interesting when Zac asked if he could hit the golf balls into the lake. He had over a hundred of them so he wasn't too worried if a few couldn't be recovered. I didn't care, I just wanted Zac to smile and play.

Jack quickly volunteered to be on the search and rescue mission in finding the golf balls in the lake. It became a fun game. Soon Olivia joined in. My mom, dad, sisters, Nathan and I laughed as the golf balls ricocheted off of the birch trees. We cheered with each "kerplunck" of the balls into the lake.

Zac was giggling. I knew he was having fun when it turned into his hardy, deep-belly laugh. This time Zac was part of the fun and kids were coming to join him. I felt comforted by the simple beauty of laughter and Zac was right in the middle of it all.

The long weekend came to an end and as I suspected Zac's hemoglobin was very low and he had barely any platelets. I prayed he didn't cut himself or get a bloody nose, at least not until we would be in the hospital the following day.

Monday morning Zac was sitting at the table eating a bowl of cereal with Nic when with a heavy heart in anticipation for another week of separation from his family said, "Nic, I don't want tomorrow to come."

"I know what you mean, bro," Nic sympathetically replied.

Even though Nic didn't often speak openly about Zac's illness, I watched him internalize the toll it was taking on Zac. Occasionally he'd get mad at Zac for not being able to or not wanting to participate in boy-type games, but he loved the time he spent with his little brother. It wasn't so much that he was angry at Zac that he couldn't play, but that his normal rambunctious little brother was stolen from Nic.

Nic was awesome with Zac. One day he came up with a game where Zac and his friend Thomas stood on the deck that overlooked the side yard by about fifteen feet with loaded airsoft guns. Zac and Thomas were instructed to shoot Nic and his friend, Kyle as they ran back and forth down below them, without shirts on - to make it more "intense"- so I was told. Before I knew it, Thomas was recruited down to the yard to be a running target to help lessen the blows that Nic and Kyle were taking by the two snipers. I shook my head and couldn't help but smile. What was that saying? - "Boys will be boys!" Zac was one of the boys and they were having fun.

Many nights I would listen outside their bedroom door when they talked more deeply. Other times Nic would read out of his military Bible while Zac listened lying on his back with his hands folded in prayer on top of his blankets (okay, I peeked sometimes too.) Many nights I would listen to them roaring in laughter so loud that I had to go in and tell them to settle down and go to sleep. One night the smell of horrendous gas seeped out as I cracked open the door.

"You guys!" I said alarmed at the sudden shock of the smell.

"Mom, hurry! Close the door!" Nic panicked amid the laughter.

"Are you kidding?! It's toxic in here. You need to air it out before you suffocate!"

"No, mom - really! You gotta close the door! This is a man's room, "Zac instructed. "We like it this way!" And they both started to giggle uncontrollably.

"You guys are sick! I'm not coming in here to kiss you goodnight – so GOODNIGHT! I love you boys." I quickly shut the door as I unplugged my nose. *If only it could be like this all the time,* I wished.

Everything changed for me when we would separate as a family. I think Lexie felt it the worst. She was getting more clingy and would whine that she didn't want me and Zac to go to the hospital. It hurt to leave her behind, but I couldn't leave Zac either. Too much was at stake with Zac and I needed to be with him to pick up on any subtle changes. Many times it was a warning sign for something bigger to come. I knew Zac's routine. I knew the system and I knew Zac was comforted by my presence. We had formed a very special, close bond. He trusted me and I wanted nothing more than to give him comfort, happiness and nothing short of normal.

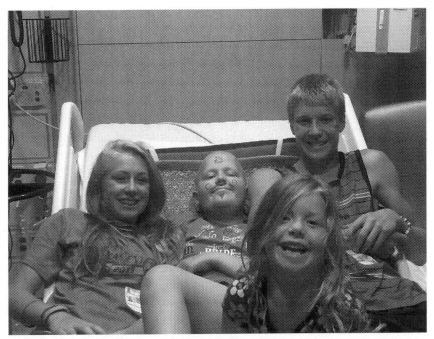

Family time at the hospital - Jess(13), Zac(11), Nic(15) and Lexie(5). 8-1-13

CHAPTER 27

my best day ever!

Back to clinic for a quick look-over before being admitted for the week of chemo. I was a bit concerned the night before when I noticed his new port site looking like it was splitting open. It didn't look normal, but since we were coming in to see Dr. Moertel that day I didn't worry too much.

Dr. Moertel took a quick look and stepped out of the room, returning with Tammie. Before long, the doctor who put it in (back in May) came up to look at it. I was afraid it was infected, which would end his summer of swimming, but Dr. Sidel decided that the port could remain in and continue to be used. It was splitting because of the Avastin drug that he was on for radiation necrosis. The drug was making Zac's port site difficult to completely heal, and in Zac's case, causing something that was healed - to open up.

The incision was reinforced and Zac was taken off the Avastin for a couple of weeks. I was nervous about withholding the medicine when it seemed to be working. Zac had recently started to wiggle his toes and began moving his foot. It was another disappointment, but I couldn't allow Zac or myself to dwell on it. Since we were waiting for Zac's IV fluids and chemo to be sent up from pharmacy, I asked Zac's nurse if it was okay to take Zac outside before he was hooked up to all the IVs.

It was a hot day and I knew the freedom of being outside would make being trapped in the hospital later a little more tolerable for the both of us.

The hospital lawn sprinklers were on, spraying a thick mist on the grass especially in one particular area over the sidewalk. I had an idea. Zac must have been reading my mind.

"Do you think I could maybe go through the sprinkler?" Zac wondered, expecting I would say "no."

"I think that would be a good idea since it's so hot outside," I replied.

"Ohh-k-k-a-y-y?" Zac grinned, preparing himself for the impending cold.

As I pushed Zac closer, the mist swept across his face as the warm breeze blew. Zac welcomed its refreshing relief on his hot checks. "Would you ever just push me in the middle of the sprinkler and leave me?" he playfully asked.

"I don't know? Maybe-e-e…" I honestly joked back.

"Mo-o-o-m-m! You wouldn't!" Zac shot back, surprised.

"Well, if I did push you in the middle of the sprinklers and run off there would be nothing you could do. You would get soaking wet!" I teased.

Zac smiled. Before he knew it, I was running him through the sprinklers. Not only once, but five times! He just laughed and begged to do it again. It didn't help Zac that a coach from Augsburg College and two of his players egged me on, as they crossed the street.

On the last run through, I stopped Zac dead center in the middle of the sprinklers and locked the wheelchair brakes into safety and ran from the cold water.

"Mom! You wouldn't!" Zac squealed in delight with a touch of panic as he grabbed his head and tucked in his legs trying to shield himself from the soaking water.

"Sucker!!" I quickly pulled my phone from my jean short pocket to take a picture. This was a moment I wanted to capture. "Zac, I'll quick get a picture and then I'll get you out," I promised starting to feel a little guilty that he was getting drenched.

We laughed all the way back into the hospital. Laughter at any given opportunity was a welcomed gift.

It was Friday, July 12, 2013. A few days earlier, Zac was told that the Chicago Blackhawks hockey player, Nick Leddy was coming to Ampltz Children's Hospital – bringing the Stanley Cup! Being the huge hockey fan that he was, Zac could hardly contain his excitement. He talked about going downstairs to the lobby hours earlier to "tailgate" – so he could get a good "seat." The plan was in place until Melissa, the Child Life Specialist came in to Zac's room that morning while he was finishing breakfast.

"I'm sorry to say, Zac, that the hospital promotions team said that you would not be able to wait in the lobby for Nick Leddy," Melissa paused with a gleam in her eye. Zac's smile quickly faded and the look of disappointment washed over him. "But instead - they personally chose you to be the official greeter when Nick Leddy's limo arrives in the front of the hospital!"

The second half of Melissa's sentence did not register for Zac. He remained sullen. He was stuck on hearing that he "couldn't wait in the lobby."

"Zac! Did you hear what she said?!" "You get to be the first person to see Nick Leddy and the Stanley Cup! I explained waiting for the light bulb to go on.

"Zac, you will be front and center waiting for the limo to pull up in front of you! Would you like to do that?" Melissa rephrased feeling a bit guilty for trying to trick him.

The lights went on!

"Oh, Yah! Oh, WOW! – I thought you were telling me I couldn't be downstairs because of my chemo or something. Wheww! I was worried for a second. This is going to be so awesome! Zac livened up. "I can't wait!"

It was about 2:30 pm when Zac was escorted, followed by his brother Nic and his friend, Hunter, his dad, Uncle Greg and cousin Jace, downstairs to get in place before the halls and lobby became crowded with patients, visitors and hospital personnel. This was a big deal for hockey fans!

I thought Zac had a big smile on his face as he waited for the limo to arrive, but when Nick's over-sized limo pulled up right in front of him, his smile grew twice as big. He could hardly contain himself. There were so many people now gathered all around the sidewalk and in the hospital lobby. And there Zac was - front and center. I was honestly more excited watching the joy and excitement Zac was experiencing than seeing the Stanley Cup.

Once Nick stepped out of the limo, he walked right over to Zac where he was leaning forward on his crutches. Zac politely shook Nick's hand and welcomed him. He was the perfect kid to greet him. After the "hellos," Zac asked, "So, what did it feel like to win the Stanley Cup?!"

"Like a dream," Nick replied.

"Yah, right now I feel like I'm dreaming too," Zac agreed.

People crowded around and strained to see and hear what Nick and Zac were doing and saying.

"Say, how would you like to touch it?" Nick asked.

Zac hesitated. He seemed confused. I instantly knew he was reflecting on his brother's conversation with him only moments before Nick arrived. "Whatever you do, Zac, do NOT touch the Stanley Cup!" Nic warned. "It's a sign of disrespect if you do.

"Zac," I whispered loudly, "it's okay. Go ahead! Nick is giving you permission."

Zac's eyes brightened and his smile widened - if that was even possible. He looked squarely into Nick Leddy's eyes. "I can? Really?!"

Zac carefully placed his hand on the silver shiny cup that was awarded annually to the National Hockey League (NHL) playoffs winner after the conclusion of many games. It was unusual among trophies because it has all the names of the winning players, coaches and management on its chalice. Sometimes it is even referred to as the Holy Grail. It was a sacred moment for Zac. Even though he couldn't play hockey, he loved the sport as much as his big brother who was looking on in disbelief as he was touching THE Stanley Cup.

Nick Leddy had to get inside Amplatz to set the cup down for display and to take pictures with the many fans who were waiting patiently for their turn. Zac watched in amazement as Nick walked through the revolving door. "I can't believe this! This is so awesome!" Zac said in a daze. "This is my best day ever!"

Another best day for Zac. He had a lot of those days tucked away. Days like these sure made a difference when you looked at the big picture and what he had to go through just to stay alive.

We went back inside to get in line to see the Stanley Cup again and get more pictures. There were plenty of camera flashes, new stations filming and reporters, all eager to capitalize on such a grand event. Even though Nick Leddy played for Chicago Blackhawks, he was born and raised in Minnesota and played briefly for the Minnesota Gophers college hockey team before being traded. That made the event just a little more special.

Nic brought Zac's Black Hawk baseball hat from home and got it signed. Zac, in his innocent playfullness casually asked Nick if he would sign his bald head to which Nick asked for my permission.

I didn't hesitate for a second. "Of course!"

"Front or back?" Nick asked Zac.

"Right on the scar..." Zac replied with a chuckle.

Nick glanced at me one last time to make sure it was okay. I shrugged my shoulders letting him know that if it was okay with Zac, it was okay with me.

With a black permanent sharpie, Nick signed his name a little back from the six-inch scar on top of Zac's head, from his brain surgery a year ago. News crews were filming and a reporter interviewed Zac and I for an article in the St. Paul Pioneer press. Zac had no plans of washing his head anytime soon.

Although this hospital stay was filled with fun and excitement, Zac was happy to be back home in familiar surroundings. Just hanging out downstairs playing Xbox with his big brother or sitting outside cutting up sticks for a bonfire with his hunting knife was enough to make home life desirable. His friends could easily come over to play. Zac could come and go without being tethered to an IV pole. He was free.

Zac's kindergarten teacher (Nic's, as well) and his fourth grade teacher (Jessica's too) Debbie and Tom Krenz quickly became close to our family. Like many others, they wanted to help, whether it was to stop by with pizza and play some Yahtzee with the family or to take all the kids to movie so I could have some "me-time" or to just take Zac to have his own afternoon of fun.

Debbie had a calming effect on me with her gentle nurturing disposition. She was a slender dark-haired woman who looked much younger than her age. She hadn't aged a day in the last ten years. Tom was a fitness buff, very slim with thick, dark wavy hair. He was another one of those people who didn't age. He loved his summer triathlons or winter cross-country skiing races.

Debbie thought out the situation before calling me to see if her and her husband Tom could take Zac out for a day of golfing. She knew from talking with me on a regular basis that Zac quickly tired the week after he was discharged from the hospital. We picked the Monday, two days after he got out because we thought he should still be feeling pretty energetic.

Tom later disclosed to me that he was a bit leery taking Zac out golfing with his limitations. He didn't know how it would be possible, but not wanting to break a promise they loaded up to go golfing, the hottest day in July. As Tom told me, he was bumped from the driver seat and had to walk the yardage, not wanting to overcrowd the cart. One more time Zac overshadow Tom when he was in the company of them both.

Zac and Debbie tested Tom's patience with slow play, casual prepping between shots and blatant lack of awareness of time. Tom's game and his attitude suffered. His frustration soared with the countless comments from his wife about "good shot," when the ball would travel ten yards and Zac's ambition to correct his compact backswing had him plowing chunks of sod. Tom confessed that *profanity was poised upon his lips!* The words were ready to fly. *"Why not?"* Tom thought. *"Zac's old man works at a prison."*

Tom was ready to uncoil the granddaddy of them all when Zac piped up, "Keep your spirit, Mr. Krenz!"

The heat of the day must have been taking its toll on poor Tom. At this point, he felt like wrapping "big Bertha" around both of their haloed heads, but he didn't.

Enough golf and they went to Tom and Debbie's for a pontoon ride on Green Lake, with the intention of going for a swim. As soon as they got out into the middle of the lake, Tom strapped a life jacket on Zac and threw him off the boat into the water. He half expected Zac to rise slowly above the waves and climb back on board. Nothing.

While bobbing around in the chop, Debbie and Zac would play games and soak in the glorious rays of the sunshine. Tom, on the other hand, "was determined to see if this kid was for real." Stealthily and without warning, Tom shark-tailed up behind Zac and dunked him underwater. This probing continued even after he was scolded by his beautiful wife. Tom just wasn't convinced "the kid" was mortal. He had to know.

Then came the challenge: Who could hold their breath longer. Zac was bragging about his so-called feat-of-strength at his own pool. Forty-five seconds! Tom called his bluff. Down Zac went and Tom chirped "one Mississippi... two Mississippi..."

When Zac got to fifteen, Tom felt pretty confident he'd be up in no time at all. Motionless, he laid spread eagled like a fallen angel to earth. When he got to twenty-five seconds, Tom began to question whether he had passed out and made a panicked suggestion to Debbie to pull his head up out of the water. *"Boy, this would be a black eye on the Krenz family if we let him drown under our supervision,"* Tom thought. Without warning, Zac shot up a thumbs-up that he was still alive with a degree of brain activity. *Unbelievable! His lungs were supposed to be riddled with tumors and chemo. He held his breath for forty-three long seconds!!!!* Tom knew it. *The kid had been sandbagging! Either that, and there was no better euphemism here or he was ZacStrong!"*

(Very fitting that Tom ordered and paid for seven-hundred orange ZacStrong bracelets to give to each kid at Lakeside, the remainder would be sold and the money donated to the Zac Fund for NF and Cancer Research. The schools were a huge support of Zac and seeing the bracelets around in the community was an amazing statement.)

Zac and Debbie came home laughing and smiling. "That was my best day ever!" Zac exclaimed. "That was so much fun, thank you!" As for Tom, he still looked like he needed a beer.

Another best day. We were on the right path. The more "best days," the better.

Only four days after his golf outing with the Krenz's, Zac was invited to go to the USSA camp. Actually our whole family was invited to attend, but because of a prior family reunion commitment the rest of us delined. This was the same non-profit national wish granting charity that Zac went through for his bear, buck and turkey hunt. This time it was going to be like a big camping party with all kinds of fun activities.

I was very hesitant to let him go because I felt I needed to be there with my x-rayed vision to watch Zac diligently in case something should happen. But Bryan, a friend of ours reassured he would take good care of him. Knowing there was a medical team on-site and my sister Marie and brother-in-law, Dan suggested that "Maybe it would be good for Zac to get a break from you guys." I rethought my reasons for holding him back.

Of course I was on high alert with Zac, being his white blood count was almost non-existent. I was told that if he would develop a fever, he would need to be in the hospital getting a particular antibiotic within one hour. The nearest hospital was fifty miles away. Zac was instructed not to swim in the lake because of the potential for infection with his low counts. I worried about what would happen if he had a big seizure or if he didn't remember to take all of his medicine.

I was concerned about his physical health, but the deciding factor was my concern for his mental health. I had to do whatever I could to keep his spirits up.

If he had no physical limitations, Zac would be begging to go to a fun camp. This could be good for him to experience the struggles other kids dealt with so he wouldn't feel so alone.

I packed his bag and sorted out all of Zac's pills into baggies labeling them with dates and times. I explained to Bryan the anti-seizure med and how it was to be given if it should be needed. I felt that was overwhelming him, but between Zac and Bryan, they said they could handle it.

After Zac had a blood and platelet transfusion on Friday, we met up with Nathan at Bryan's work to drop him off with all of the instructions and items he needed for the weekend. I prayed he would be safe and nothing would go wrong. Zac would drive the three hours to the camp with Bryan, his wife Jan and his two children, Halle and Ried.

They talked the entire way up. You never had to worry about Zac, he was quite the conversationalist. When the conversation changed to the Minnesota Vikings football team, things became heated. Zac made it no secret that he loved the Vikings. He had high hopes that they would have a better season this year and go all the way to the Super Bowl. Halle sided with Zac. Bryan, on the other-hand favored the Green Bay Packers. He had been a die-hard fan all his life.

Zac sneered when he realized this undesirable difference. "Pull the truck over," Zac instructed Bryan, "I'll crutch it from here!"

The playful banter continued until Zac and Bryan made a bet that if the Vikings won the next game against the Packers, Bryan would have to wear a Viking shirt all day, but if the Packers won, Zac would have to wear a Packer shirt. Zac was praying for a BIG Vikings win.

Zac came back home saying he had the best time. He met a girl who so far had forty-one surgeries - mostly brain. She was nineteen-years-old. He shared stories of this awesome camp that Bridgid, the founder and owner, sets up on her acreage trying to give some hope and happiness to kids with serious illnesses. There were so many fun things to do - fishing with a pro-fisherman (who Zac proudly announced that he out-fished), racing in a special race truck that Dean Patterson, a pro racer gave kids exhilarating rides around in at G-force speed, (well, almost - but Zac said it was FAST!) archery, rifle shooting, a bon-fire, outdoor movie, a night dance and even jumping out of the scoop of a crane or from an attached rope into the lake below.

I was so glad I agreed to let Zac go with Bryan and his family. I didn't want Zac to miss out on anything. Zac needed his life outside of the hospital to be as full of fun as possible. It recharged him.

Chosen Amplatz Greeter, Zac with hockey player Nick Leddy and the Stanley Cup 7-12-13

Zac left in the sprinkler while going for a walk with mom. 7-12-13

CHAPTER 28

baby steps

On July 23, 2013 Zac had a full day of testing with a lot of waiting around. I hated waiting around. At first I felt like there was so much that I could be doing with that time – especially when I lost two weeks a month, being in the hospital with Zac. But then I came to realize that it wasn't wasted time, but time I valued because I got to spend it with Zac. All the other stuff could wait. There was enough food in the house that Nathan, Nic, Jessica and Lexie wouldn't starve and when the laundry piled high enough, Jessica or Nathan would wash some clothes.

As Zac and I waited for his three hour MRI, we decided to go outside for a walk and enjoy the warm sunshine. When inpatient, in between chemo's we liked to go out for long walks around the west side of the U of M campus, down the cobble-stoned sidewalks and crossing the street to walk around Augsburg College campus. Today it was much easier without an IV pole, although I was pretty skilled at pushing a wheelchair and pulling an IV.

Zac and I covered a lot of ground and talked about our wishes and plans for the future. In the back of my mind, I prayed they would come to pass. The fear always lurked there. I wanted Zac to be able to plan for his future and his dreams. He wanted to be a professional golfer, and to visit sick kids in the hospital once he was healed. He planned on being a Navy SEAL and to publicly speak across the world about how he beat cancer with his belief and hope in God, but most of all he talked about how he couldn't wait to walk without crutches.

The MRI was finally done, but I worried that we would not get the results until tomorrow since Zac was bumped back so many times and Dr. Moertel had to leave the hospital by 5:30 pm. It was 5:15 pm.

I was relieved when I saw Dr. Moertel round the corner into the radiology waiting room. I was so grateful that he didn't leave me to wrestle with the demons in my mind that try, on a daily basis, to suffocate the hope.

Zac's lungs were "stable" from the last MRI which Dr. Moertel said was much improved from his diagnosis on January 15. Back then there were eleven or thirteen spots in each lung and now there were five in one lung and one spot in the other! His leg was also "stable" with a few less spots and no further collapsing of the knee joint. This was also good news, but not enough for Dr. Moertel to say his leg was strong enough to walk on it.

As for the brain, there was no new growth. There was still swelling on the left half and Dr. Moertel said it looked like Zac had a small stroke which was evident by a hole in his brain (over the motor center which controls the function of his foot and toes). He couldn't understand why he was regaining his movement. I sat quietly as he pondered the findings. Later I told Zac, "It's because he doesn't know what we know..."

Wasn't it Jesus who said, *"Go. Your faith has healed you?"* Well, I don't know anyone else who had more faith than Zac.

Dr. Moertel also mentioned that it looked like there was a radiation war going on in Zac's brain because of all of the radiation and some of the two separate treatments ended up crossing over a section of the same area in the brain. Zac's case would be discussed the next day with the possibility of using a hyperbaric chamber to help treat the necrosis. Dr. Moertel still wanted to hold off on using the Avastin since Zac's port-site began splitting open a second time.

"All in all," Dr. Moertel said, "for a sarcoma patient, Zac is doing very well."

It was decided against to use the hyperbaric chamber and resume using the Avastin that Zac was on before, for the necrosis. The brain swelling looked better in spite of not using anything to treat it within the past month.

Zac felt good enough to participate in our second annual golf tournament for the Zac Fund at the White Bear Dellwood Country Club. Nathan's brother, Greg and his wife, Sandy did a good job in organizing it. With the support of KS95 radio, Ryan and Shannon from the morning show promoted the event on air and Shannon and Icky came to work the day of the event. It was a success.

The support was awesome. Friends, coworkers, teachers and newcomers who heard of Zac's battle were there to do what they could to get us closer to our goal – saving Zac's life. Zac mingled with the golfers and dazzled them with his pure, genuine goodness. He even conned Mr. D., Chisago Primary School's Phy Ed teacher for twenty dollars for a "special" golf ball (as Zac put it) which Mr. D. ended up hitting a hole-in-one with.

After a nap on the golf cart (Zac could sleep anywhere) and a fall on his way up to the microphone to thank everyone for coming, Nathan added a little more excitement to finish out the evening when he made a special announcement that Dr. Moertel had told him shortly before dinner that the doctors further reviewed the scans of Zac's leg and they saw new bone growth! They agreed that he could start to walk! (Tammie later told me at a following appointment that the doctors all cheered at the conference when they saw the new results.)

We had been waiting to hear those words for eight months. Everyone at the golf club gave Zac a standing ovation, the second time in five minutes. Zac was thrilled beyond words! His tears said it all.

July 31, 2013 was the day that Zac was given permission to begin walking. It was almost like watching a baby take his first steps. Katie, Zac's physical therapist, came before breakfast and s put his knee brace on. Up he went. At first Zac was hesitant to put weight on his leg. He had been told for so long not to. Between Katie and I, we reassured him that it was okay.

Because Zac's right leg muscle had atrophied so much, he was unsteady. Two crutches would be necessary for the time being. He had to really think about everything - from lifting his leg up high enough to allow his droopy foot to clear the floor, to properly planting his foot straight on the floor so it wouldn't roll to the side. There was a time or two I watched with panic as he barely straightened his foot in time and it looked like he was about to snap his ankle. I just held my breath and trusted Katie to do her job.

After he started getting the hang of it, the first baby steps turned into what almost looked like he was walking with a prosthesis, something I secretly feared might be a possibility in the future. I quickly dismissed those negative thought and praised his determination. He was walking!

Before long, we headed down the hallway towards the stairwell. Katie had Zac working on climbing stairs. It was slow going, but when I asked him how it felt, Zac looked up and with a big smile ecstatically said, "It feels awesome!"

Zac still remained positive and kept up with his strict and unusual routine of having to do the biomat, pure essential oils and his exercises. Even scooting up and downstairs on his butt was becoming a normal way of life. He didn't like it, but he didn't say much about it. He filled his summer days hanging out with Thomas and another good buddy, Austin who lived just a few houses down from us. He was another boy who was so kind and patient with Zac. They would spend time breaking and stacking sticks and branches in the fire-pit out back or on the driveway and try to light a fire using leaves and a magnifying glass. (They weren't using matches at least - I couldn't take all their fun away.) They would color at the patio table, dig and build in the sand or play in our above ground pool.

Zac invited girls to come over too. Kylie, Kendra, Abby and Halle were a few that enjoyed hanging out with him. It warmed my heart that these kids came over and brought with them so much more than just a way to fill time for Zac. They brought genuine friendship. Without them even knowing it, they were learning a lot from Zac...compassion, patience, positive attitude, strength, bravery, love and not to feel sorry for yourself.

I was grateful when Zac had days he could play and not be in the hospital. It was as if all was right with the world and life felt as it should be.

Zac seemed like he was having a more difficult time recovering from his chemo treatments. He started complaining of bad headaches which concerned me enough to call in to speak with the hematology/oncology fellow one night. When he mentioned his neck hurting, I knew I had to check it out with the doctor, especially since he had just been released from the hospital after spiking a fever from some unknown infection.

"I trust you Jesus, I trust you Jesus," I whispered over and over again to help keep my mind in check. I feared the unknown constantly.

Since the fellow wasn't sure what the headache would be from, she instructed me to give Zac some oxycodone. By morning he was feeling better.

I was a bit surprised when Dr. Moertel called me at home the Monday after Zac was discharged from the hospital. He told me that after he and Dr. Cheng reviewed Zac's CT scan of his leg, they both felt that it was a good idea to do a surgical procedure – sooner rather than later. Dr. Cheng saw a very weak area in the bone of his leg and was worried he would fracture it, especially now, since he started putting weight on it. There was a large area by the growth plate, by his knee, that was either filled with tumor, dead tumor or empty space. Either way, the area was extremely at risk.

Dr. Cheng wanted to scrape the area out and fill it with acrylic cement to strengthen the bone. The only problem was then there was the high possibility of his leg not growing.

"A fracture and the aftermath would be far worse," Dr. Cheng emphasized. He said the surgery would probably be as painful as the biopsy Zac had back in January. I hoped Dr. Cheng wasn't taking into consideration the pain that was later attributed to the cancer.

The risk of Zac fracturing his leg and putting him months and months behind with treatment, not to mention the excruciating pain he would be in far outweighed the concern of halting his leg growth. I figured it must be really concerning if they changed their mind from the winter when they said "no" to surgery because they worried it would impeed the bone growth.

Surgery was scheduled for Tuesday, August 13th at 11:00 am at Amplatz Children's Hospital.

Dr. Moertel even said in regards to my concern in the disruption of the bone growth, "Zac has had small miracles. We can cross that bridge when, and if we get there."

I know Zac had had small miracles, probably some big ones too that I was unaware of. *All things Possible,* just like the Christian song by Jeremy Camp. Christian songs were regularly played on the radio in the house or car. I even kept the radio on in my bathroom all night long. I always said it was like having prayer constantly surrounding me.

I wasn't surprised when Dr. Sadak said after rounds one day that "Zac is doing far better than what we ever expected." I was a bit concerned with his actual words and what he meant by it once it registered. I knew Zac would continue to have his miracles. More would come to see and believe. I was more and more convinced that Zac's purpose was to make believers in God.

When I explained to Zac the necessity for doing the leg surgery, a sudden look of panic washed over his face. His main concern was if it was going to hurt like before.

I told him "No." I explained to him again that a big part of his uncontrollable, horrible pain from the last leg surgery was mainly due to the fast spreading cancer.

As I helped Zac get out of the tub and dried him off, he started to weep. "I'm scared for tomorrow," he opened up.

Nathan, Zac and I headed into the hospital early because Zac did not recover well after his last blood and platelet transfusions and required stable counts going into surgery. Zac was still so tired saying, "I think they should have given me two of those bloods."

Surgery went well and the pain seemed to remain under control until 4:00 am. The nurse forgot to give Zac his 1:30 am pain med. Prior to that, Zac was given something every three to four hours. Since we were both sleeping, I think she figured he didn't need it. BIG mistake! He remained very straight faced and quiet all morning. I knew he was in more pain than he was letting on.

Later that day I caught him quietly crying. When I asked where his pain was on a scale of one to ten, he replied, "five." When he sheds tears, it's NOT a "five," more like an "eight or nine."

For some reason, Zac thought he was troubling us if he mentioned he had pain. He was too young to be stoic.

The orthopedic resident came in a little after 7:00 am and said after quickly looking Zac over, "Everything looks good. We'll be sending him home on oxycodone and Tylenol."

I was stunned. He was so nonchalant in regards to Zac's pain.

"Oh, Zac's hemoglobin dropped a little from yesterday to 7.3. Ortho doesn't feel he needs a blood transfusion, but oncology can make that decision."

I was a little perturbed. *You have a boy in a whole lot of pain and a low hemoglobin – so you're going to send him home?!* I planned on making a new plan with the oncology team.

Needless to say, Zac ended up with a blood transfusion. I figured if athletes can have a pint of blood to improve their race performance, then I could argue to have my son receive blood to just improve his daily life.

Katie from physical therapy came by to evaluate Zac and get him up and moving. She had worked with Zac regularly and knew him well. Just by looking at his face she knew he wasn't himself.

Katie left the room saying she was going to talk to a nurse to get him something more for pain. The look of relief on Zac's face was clear. Zac's meds were increased and we continued to play "catch-up" to find the comfort he had the previous day.

The plan was to wait another day before going home. I think that drove Zac to forcing himself to try and get up when an occupational therapist came in shortly after Katie left. I knew Zac thought if he could work through the pain of getting up to the bathroom to wash his face and brush his teeth, then he could go home.

I was stunned by his tenacity, but agreeable to give it a try only because he was so determined. He tried so hard, but could only make it to the side of the bed after ten minutes. He cried some more. I wasn't sure if his tears were of frustration, defeat or from the pain. Probably all three.

"I just want to be healed. Please God, heal me!" Zac pleaded.

The next morning when the orthopedic resident came back to check on Zac, I informed him that I hadn't seen a change in his pain level. This time I wanted to make sure he understood – *"There is NO change in his pain!"* It was unacceptable to me. He left ordering Atarax which really isn't for pain, but more to help Zac sleep. I could have used some for my anxiety!

Zac's blood pressure had remained high (indicating he was in pain –huh?!) He slept and slept until a nurse who we had never had before came in and sternly told Katie she should get Zac up.

"We were just discussing Zac and how he recently got Atarax and is finally getting some much needed sleep," I explained.

"He really needs to get up and get moving so he can go home," the nurse instructed coldly.

It didn't take me long to realize how much I didn't care for this nurse.

Zac was finally able to escape the pain for two and a half hours and now because it was important to "get moving" (which I knew as a nurse caring for cesarean section patients was important but not to be pushed if pain was excessive) she wanted him up so she more than likely could discharge Zac to lighten her patient load. Where were our regular nurses?!

The nurse's military façade wasn't going to be broken, so with regret, I woke Zac up with the reasoning that if he could tolerate moving, we could pack up and go home.

Zac was discharged around noon with the words written "Pain well controlled" in his discharge notes. *Really?!*

At home, Zac continued to be in terrible pain even though I was administering narcotics every three hours around the clock. After four days of being home from the hospital we were back in the Journey Clinic for an appointment with Dr. Moertel before being admitted for Zac's chemo week. It didn't take Dr. Moertel long to see how much pain Zac was still in and the amount of swelling he still had around his knee. He decided to delay his chemo week until next week to allow his leg more time to heal, saying the chemo would only destroy his platelets and further slow-down his healing.

Although Ibuprofen had been forbidden because of Zac's low platelets Dr. Moertel suggested he start using it. What a difference after one dose! Within a couple of days, I was able to space out the narcotics and three days after seeing Dr. Moertel, Zac started baring a little weight on his leg.

Zac finished up his last week of summer vacation in the hospital. The in-and-out of the hospital and the time spent alone was taking a toll. It was incredibly difficult watching the other kids running around and jumping into the pools and lakes. All he wanted to do was be like them and doing what they were doing.

I was able to get him out of the house to sit on a blanket to watch Nic and his friends play. I figured that would be better than being completely excluded. I had to rethink my bright idea when I looked outside only to see that Nic and his friends had already taken off leaving Zac sleeping under the shade tree with our dog, Hazel lying right by his side.

I stared for a brief minute. He was peaceful. He appeared comfortable and he was NOT alone. I sighed heavily and turned to go back into the house. It had to get better.

CHAPTER 29

no harm done

Finally...some encouraging news! The pathology report came back on the tumor that Dr. Cheng had scraped out of Zac's leg, prior to cementing it. It was ninety-nine percent dead! Hope filled the air and I breathed it in deeply.

I was excited to see what Dr. Cheng's reaction was going to be when he stopped by for a brief visit to see how Zac was recovering. When I asked him if he had seen the pathology report, I didn't wait for his response. I informed him that it was ninety-nine percent dead.

Dr. Cheng without much emotion said, "I was very surprised by that. I thought it was going to go the other way."

He warned me, "It doesn't mean that it can't come back and there are people that don't survive this."

My excitement was turned down a notch, but I wasn't going to let him take away the "good" in our news.

I was beginning to understand Dr. Cheng was a "matter-of-fact guy." He was one of the best in his field and he went strictly by the medical diagnosis and there was not much room for possibility – let alone hope, with him.

I think Dr. Cheng saw how he burst my bubble and felt some compassion because in his next breath, he said, "We are here now and it is good."

Our second benefit was fast approaching. In my spare time, if I wasn't on the phone, I was texting or emailing in preparation for the big day. I was determined to raise more money for research than we had with our previous benefit.

Barb and Carla spent a lot of time with me trying to get everything organized and finalized. It was a good distraction from my worry of the frequent headaches that Zac was experiencing. In the past two weeks, he had more headaches than I could count. From a kid who never complained of headaches, they were not normal for Zac and they weighed heavily on my mind.

When his arm started going numb and stayed numb for hours at a time, happening at the same time as his headaches, I became unsettled.

While in the hospital, Zac happened to have one of these "spells," as the neurologist called them. I watched nervously as they examined him over and over again. I wondered what they were seeing. I continued to watch as they were critiquing a picture that Zac had been working on for the past few days. They weren't talking about the creativity of it, but the way he was coloring it. I wondered what they were thinking. I wanted to ask what they suspected, but I was afraid of what they would say. They were deep in conversation so I sat back and held my breath.

Lately our life had been relatively stable in a not so stable way, but we were functioning with our new normal. I really didn't want any more surprises. I wanted improvement. I wanted to start hearing doctor's say - "We can fix this."

I asked if this warranted a brain MRI. They agreed that it would, even though it hadn't been very long since his last one. They also suggested they do an EEG/EMG.

Not long after the head neurologist and resident left, the EEG tech was in Zac's room pushing round electrodes into his bald head. Zac was very quiet.

I knew something wasn't quite right with Zac. "Are you doing okay?"

Zac started to cry. I didn't think he was crying because it hurt to have the electrodes put on, but because he hated the continual poking and prodding. I figured the long visit with the doctors and the undecisivness was really worrying him.

As tears rolled down his face, he said in a loud whisper, "I'm sick of this."

The smell was icky with each electrode that she poked in and glued on to Zac's head. I took over plugging his overly sensitive nose with a towel to at least shield him from the strong stench. I kept asking him if it hurt because I wasn't convinced he was being straight with me or the tech.

Finally he said it was a lot of pressure with each electrode. "Yah, it really hurt bad," Zac admitted after all twenty-seven white life-saver electrodes were securely on.

"Zac, you have the right to tell someone –"I need a break" or "Stop.""

For some reason Zac felt he shouldn't say anything. I didn't understand why he was so afraid to. It wasn't complaining, I told him. It was informing.

"Zac, I wanted to say something for you, but I don't know how it feels – what you are going through. You have to be your own voice, but when you can't or you want me to say something – let me know and I'll be your voice," I explained.

The EMG was cut short because after neurology reviewed the last twenty-two hours, they concluded that in spite all of Zac's painful headaches plus the arm numbness, none of it showed it to be related to seizure activity. This was good, I thought.

After Dr. Moertel said he wanted to hold off on the MRI because he suspected it would look more worrisome with an increase in swelling as a result of the radiation necrosis and lack of Avastin (used to combat it). He felt Zac's symptoms were not related to the brain tumors.

By 3:45 am, Zac began having constant severe headaches. They increased in intensity when he sat up to take his pills and then again as he lay back down, until the pressure equalized. It was now decided to do a brain MRI.

Prior to the MRI and added angiogram (a test that uses special dye to see how blood flows through the brain to help detect a blood clot or aneurysm) Zac was given decadron in hopes that it would allow him some relief from all the pain and pressure he was experiencing.

It worked and after he was given several hours of much needed rest, Zac quietly asked, "Why does this have to happen?"

I had no answer. I was asking God the same thing.

The angiogram showed the arteries in his brain were all normal – so the fear of stroke was also eliminated. The MRI showed more swelling than the one done a month ago, like Dr. Moertel anticipated, but the area where Dr. Guillaume removed most of the tumor a year ago, showed something questionable. The doctors pondered if it was additional swelling or if it was new tumor growth.

The scans were sent across the Mississippi River to the University Campus Hospital to have "numbers run" and calculated to determine the density of the indeterminate area.

Frustration was mounting. I didn't understand why it seemed EVERYTHING that was happening to Zac was inoperable, unfixable or inconclusive.

The plan to wean Zac from the decadron didn't seem like it was going to happen. After loading him up with oxycodone, more decadron and morphine, Zac had a better night. We were given the news the following day that they already had the results. It looked like further radiation necrosis and the pressure in his brain was high.

Zac was discharged home on high amounts of the steroid and an appointment to return Friday to resume his Avastin treatment.

And so Zac's summer vacation came to a close with him getting ramped back up on the steroids that puffed him up. I hated when he had no control over how his body looked. There was no amount of eating spinach, kale or collard greens that could maintain his weight. I continued to reassure Zac that we would take care of the weight issue later. He knew the relief from the debilitating headaches was the priority. I didn't have to convince him of that.

It was a chilly sunny fall morning on September 3, 2013 and Zac was able to make the first day of school, right along side his five-year-old sister, Lexie who was starting her first day of half-day kindergarten. I was sad to see my baby all grown up and starting school for the first of twelve more years. I couldn't help but be a bit excited for her as well, as she eagerly anticipated her big day.

I rushed around the house frantically trying to get the two of them out to the end of our driveway on time. My nerves escalated wondering how it would go for Zac to be riding the school bus again. He hadn't been on the bus since after Christmas vacation in the fourth grade.

I was taking pictures of Zac and Lexie at the top of our long driveway when the school bus driver drove past our stop at the end of our driveway. Without slowing down, she drove up the hill to the next stop. I freaked out! I really wanted Lexie to ride the bus for her first day – EVER!

It was partially my fault for not having them waiting at the end of the driveway.

It took more time then I allotted for since I had to draw Zac's blood that morning and Lexie woke up to a rats-nest and she wanted it styled into a French braid.

I quickly ran into the house and called the bus garage to ask if they could radio the bus driver to swing around and pick up Zac and Lexie.

A few minutes later, Heather, who was our bus driver the year before apologized saying she was so used to skipping our house since Zac didn't ride the bus the last five months of school. No harm done. I was glad she was there and the kids were ready to go.

Lexie, bright eyed and with a beaming smile, quick kissed me goodbye and skipped up the bus steps and found herself a seat right next to her friend Julia.

Zac was next. I didn't remember the bus steps being so tall and I forgot there was only a railing on the left side of the steps. After eyeing the situation, I decided it would be easiest to lift Zac up to the first step. From there he worked incredibly hard to get up the remaining steps. His strength was so diminished in his right leg and there was no railing at the top of the steps for him to grab onto to support himself. I could tell he was nervous. I was nervous for him. I could see the concern in Heather. The kids were all staring. I wondered if I should have driven him to school, but I wanted this year to begin differently than how last school year ended.

I jumped back on the bus and lifted Zac up once more. There was no turning back at this point. Zac worked his way slowly down the narrow aisle using his crutches as I held my breath.

There could not have been a more perfect time, but Zac's good friend, Austin stood up and started to cheer and clap for Zac in his victory. The other kids joined in. I was touched by the display of compassion of the bus full of kindergarteners through fifth graders. At the same time I was so sad having to watch Zac struggle to do something so easy for most kids. His whole life had been a struggle in some way, shape or form – up to this moment.

With every fiber of his being he conquered that mountain. Not one word was uttered, not even "I can't."

The weather held long enough to keep our pool open into the first week of school. It was about to change so as pool closing tradition would have it at the Bartz's, we took the big four steps out of the pool and sat them on the deck that wrapped halfway around the pool.

One by one the kids would jump off the top step to the water below. Spread eagle, can opener, cannon ball, half-split jump – it didn't matter.

I looked at Zac curled up on the lawn chair covered in his beach towel watching his sisters jumping and laughing in the fun of the once a year event. I could see the longing in his eyes as he continued to stare. I couldn't help but wonder if he would ever have the chance to do the traditional jump again. My mind was gearing into over-drive. I couldn't help but wonder if he would have a next year. I didn't know what reality was anymore because I had so much hope and faith in God that I really believed anything was possible. I really felt Zac would "beat this."

Nathan must have been thinking the same thing. He hollered from across the pool to Zac. "Hey, Zac! Do do you want to try jumping off?"

"Naa."

"Come on bud, it'll be fun! It's your last chance before I close it up for the winter," Nathan said trying to be convincing.

Zac thought for a moment like maybe he wanted to give it a try. "Yah, but how would I do it?" Zac was never one to miss out on fun.

"Ah - Nathan…I'm not so sure it's such a good idea." I reluctantly spoke. "He could break his leg if he hits the water wrong. I hoped Nathan would listen to my voice of reality.

Nathan was a bit perturbed at my sensible reasoning. "He's not going to break his leg! He's got cement in it now! He's a Navy SEAL! Right, Zac?!"

I couldn't decide whether to give my son an opportunity to be included in one last summer *hurrah* or hold him back in protection for fear that he very likely could break his leg.

I set the camcorder down and knelt down next to Zac. "Do you want to give it a try?"

"It does look like fun, but how will I do it?" Zac said.

"If you want to do it, we'll make it work. Dad and Jessie will help you up the steps and then dad can hold on to you until you fall into the water," I explained hoping I wouldn't regret this.

Zac perked up. "Okay! I'm going to do it!"

Nathan was trying to give Zac as much independence as possible in getting up the pool steps himself. "Come on, use your arms," Nathan militantly encouraged, "put some muscle into it, buddy!"

I could see Zac's uncertainty rising in the process. It wasn't as easy as I made it sound, especially when Nathan was using this difficult time as one of his "teaching moments." His frustration was building, as was mine.

Nathan and I argued on several occasions over whose way to do something was right. When it came to Zac, I usually came out on top. I was the medical professional in the family and I was his mother. That trumped everything – well, most of the time.

Just then my friend, Denise and her daughter, Lizzy came around the backyard and up the deck carrying wrapped baskets for our benefits silent auction. The look on Denise's face said it all. "What's going on here…?"

"I know, I know! It looks bad, but Zac said he wanted to give it a try. I couldn't deny him this chance of happiness – if he doesn't break his leg," I said feeling like an inadequate parent.

Zac was finally standing at the second from the top step with a look of panic. His back was toward the pool and he was contemplating how to turn his body around on one leg with only one railing to hang on to and Nathan was monkeying with the pool a couple of feet to Zac's left – nowhere near where I thought he should be standing. Sometimes he could be clueless!

"Nathan! Please, go stand right by Zac," I paused the camcorder so in the playback it wouldn't sound like I was nagging. I was so nervous for Zac and really started regretting my decision to allow for such a stunt.

"Oh, boy," Denise muttered as she watched the daredevil act before her. You would think we were watching someone jump from seventy-five feet in the air to our pool below.

After I yelled instructions to Zac on how to support his bad leg, he gathered up his courage and fell to the water below. I waited in anticipation until his head came above the water to conclude if this was a good idea or a bad one.

"That was so awesome!" Zac shouted with his first breath of air as he shook water from his shiny bald head.

"Did it hurt?" I had to double check.

"No, I'm good!" Zac was all smiles, relieved too.

"You want to go again?!" Nathan asked with a convincing tone for another jump.

"Ya-a-a-h-h!" Zac assured.

The process was a challenging one – from trying to get Zac out of the pool, without any steps and up to the top steps to jump back in the water. Between Nathan wanting Zac to do most of the work getting himself ready to jump and me wanting to make it easy on him and give him all the help he wanted, I was surprised after the few tears that Zac wanted to go again and again.

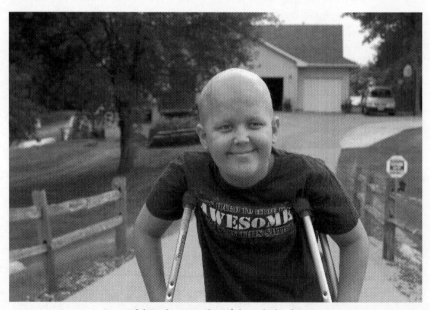

Beautiful Zachary on the 2ⁿᵈ day of school. 9-4-13

Zac's leap of faith. Closing up the pool for the winter - Bartz's style! 9-9-13

CHAPTER 30

zac's pack

The big day for the benefit had finally arrived. Once again many people and businesses generously donated wonderful items for our silent auction. I was excited about having a larger venue and working with the manager's at Star's and Strikes. It was a relief knowing that they had everything under control with the food, drinks, wait-staff and hall. Barb, Carla and I at this point only had to set up all the silent auction items and prepare for the evening to go as smooth as possible.

Carla laid out all the pens on the bidding sheets for the silent auction items and walked up to me and said, "Strangest thing when putting out the pens for the sheets, but I had the exact number! I believe it's a God-thing. It's not just a coincidence."

By choosing a larger venue, I hoped more people would come. It didn't feel as claustrophobic with the high ceilings and a large open room that was adjoined to a bar where we lined up our silent auction items. There was plenty of room for games and people. We had a raised stage where Andy Wilkerson, our emcee and good friend would host the event again. Once the tables were set up with mirrors, candles and pictures of Zac and his journey – it looked stunning.

The doors opened and people started filing in. It wasn't before long the place was packed – wall to wall, with a line of people wrapped around outside waiting to get in.

Even though our pre-ticket sales had been about seven hundred, I was still worried that people may have decided to stay home or go hunting instead – it happened to be deer hunting opener which was the only available date when I decided to reschedule after getting the news of the metastasized cancer to the lungs and second brain tumor. I wanted this benefit to be bigger and better. So far it was. I was desperate to make a difference with the communities support in raising money that would help us get closer to finding a cure or maybe it would be in the gathering of people out of love for a special boy that would save him.

I stood back to take it all in. I was in awe of all the blue and orange Zac-Pack: Never give up t-shirts intermingled among the hundreds and hundreds of people. My friend Kirsten designed the print for the t-shirts for our first benefit, and two years later we changed the design a little, as well as the colors and made them available for purchase, on-line. Many people bought the t-shirts to show their love and support – and hence – one of Zac's pack. Before long, we had packed in one thousand people!

The night was incredibly busy visiting with all those who came. I didn't sit once and I heard the food was delicious. I didn't care that I didn't get the chance to eat. I didn't want to take away any time from talking with as many people as I could. I wanted everyone to know how grateful I was for them taking the time to come and support our cause. But it seemed bigger than that. I knew it really was about Zac and everyone who knew him or knew of him wanted to do something that made a difference in his life. They wanted to save him. How could I possible thank them for that?

I only saw Nathan once that night and that was when our family went on stage. Before lifting Zac up the three steps to the top, I reminded him as he gazed upon all the people, "They are all here for you, Zac! Look what you did!" Zac grinned.

In the back of my mind, I thought of his eleventh birthday party he wanted to postpone until he could walk without crutches. I knew this wasn't a birthday celebration but it was a huge party because of Zac. I hoped it brought him some peace and satisfaction.

With his charming, debonair-self, Zac stood before the crowd and smiled his sweet smile. With no evidence of pain or fatigue he joyously thanked everyone for coming. He told them how much it meant to him that they came. And like he so often ended many of his speeches, he earnestly said, "My Angels are with you. God Bless you!"

Everyone clapped as they gave him a well-deserved standing ovation.

I took the mic next. I wanted to make sure that this time Nic, Jessica and Lexie were recognized as part of the family. Many times over the years they were, not intentionally, in the background. Zac was the one who suffered the most. He was the one who had to go through the physical pain and he was the one who needed the healing. But I wanted everyone to know Zac's brother and sisters and to see they were in this with us. They loved Zac and suffered right alongside their brother. It was tough on all of us.

I referred to my Caringbridge entries and reiterated how thankful we were for their generosity and support in the past and today. "The rain couldn't have come at a better time – it brought all of you inside here with us!" I thanked them for helping Zac, Nic, Jessica, Lexie, Nathan and myself for not feeling so alone in such an isolated lifestyle. I could have talked for an hour, but I needed to share the stage with Nathan and I had yet to introduce Dr. Moertel to let him explain how a cure was getting closer with the support directed towards research.

I kicked myself later when I realized I hadn't acknowledged my sister, Barb personally for the hundreds of hours she put into helping me organize the benefit – Carla too. I couldn't have done it without them.

About two months before the benefit, the mom of a friend of Zac's, Claudette emailed me to ask if she could donate a jewelry item from the company Oragami Owl. It was a jewelry line where you can personalize your jewelry by adding different pieces to a locket of your choosing. Zac got to be the master creator. He chose everything that was symbolic to him.

He ended up creating a beautiful necklace that encased a pair of hockey sticks, United States flag, a (Wild) cat paw, a cross, an emerald stone (May) a topaz (November for my birth month) and a "diamond" (for pure goodness – like Zac's heart). The chain it hung from had a pair of angel wings and another larger emerald-like stone. A shorter chain that could be worn with it (or separately) had a smooth silver dog-tag with the word "BELIEVE" engraved on it. A round emerald stone hung to the side. It was exquisite! (Claudette insisted she make an exact replica of it for me!)

It was one of our live auction items. The bid climbed to $610 before it was sold! Carla's husband Tom was the winner. I thought it was awesome that he won it for my friend. Later Carla told me that she told Tom she wanted him to make sure he outbid anyone. I was happy that she got a little piece of Zac.

Our other priceless live auction item was a painting my sister did with Zac when he was in the Journey clinic receiving blood and platelet transfusions. Since angels were so important to Zac, I drew a picture of a simple angel which she then drew on to a canvas. With many different colors, Barb dipped Zac's fingertip into paint until his colorful fingerprints filled the entire angel. With Zac's signature to complete it, it became an amazing piece of art. It was sold for $700! Denise, the mom of another one of Zac's friends, confided in me that she told her husband that she had to have it and her husband gave her the "okay" to spend whatever it took.

Another man who happened to be from our church had heard the bidding going on and walked around the corner of the bar and right up to the stage with a signed check in his hand for an item that was being auctioned off. He wanted to give me the check even without knowing what he was buying. Unfortunately the bidding was going higher than his check was for. I felt bad. I wanted to give him something for his loving gesture, but he refused saying "No, it's okay. It's all for a good cause – I didn't even know what was being auctioned off!" He smiled and walked away. He had a big heart.

Before everyone got up to mingle, King Borealus, Ted Natus of the St. Paul Winter Carnival introduced his entire royal court. After anointing each of us into their royal family they presented us with a large check for the Zachary Fund for NF and Cancer Research. I was thrilled!

The night was everything I hoped for. Andy did another outstanding job working the crowd, as well as Shannon from KS95, who worked the crowd from the floor. The selfless efforts of everyone working together or spending their money had a huge impact in the success of that night.

We ended up clearing $38,000! Not too bad for a second benefit.

School seemed to be going well for Zac. Everything was close to the same as the previous year. It was like we were stuck in some type of time warp with the strict constant hospital routine that we had become accustomed to. The only new change was Zac's fifth grade teacher, Mr. Maahs – another awesome teacher at Lakeside School.

Zac continued to miss a lot of school and would get overwhelmed at times with the homework when his hemoglobin was low and he was extra tired. I encouraged him to talk to his teachers, which he did. They were very understanding and accommodating. I saw a difference in his stress level go down immediately. Zac handled the stress of everyday life and the situations thrown his way very well for an eleven year old. He rarely spoke in depth of how he felt about his condition. I thought maybe it was because we always talked about beating the cancerous beast and how we were going to spread God's message of what faith, hope and persistent prayer could overcome and he knew that he had to do "this" to get to that point.

One particular day in the hospital Zac hesitantly told me that a boy at his school told a friend of his that "Zac would be dead in a year." This friend asked Zac if that was true. I tried not to look alarmed. I quickly scanned Zac's reaction after confiding in me. I didn't ask him if he believed it or how it made him feel. I wished I would have. It probably was my window of opportunity to get him to open up, but I was caught off-guard. Instead, I tried to do damage control. I worried what that type of comment did to his spirit. I never wanted Zac to entertain the idea of dying. Heaven knows I fought that darkness daily.

I knew the comment was said because of the lack of maturity of the fourth grader who said this. I knew he didn't understand. I wasn't mad at him. I was just horrified that Zac heard that callous statement and those words came off of his lips in retelling it to me.

On Tuesday, September 24, 2013 Zac was scheduled to start his day of testing at 11:30 am. He was going to get an hour and a half of school before I would pick him up. He wanted to stay on top of math.

Unfortunately Zac had woken up Saturday morning while still in the hospital with his right arm feeling heavier than it did on Friday evening. This morning he wasn't able to get to the bathroom by himself because he couldn't grasp on to his crutches. He was unable to feed himself or work a pencil.

Typically after chemotherapy was done and we got back home, Zac's arm would regain its feeling and strength. It wasn't happening this time.

Because he couldn't control his crutches, I ended up giving him a piggyback ride down to the end of the driveway to catch the bus. I didn't know how else to get him there. I felt rushed as the bus sat idle and I didn't want the bus to have to wait too long. My anger escalated and my chest tightened. I didn't know how I was going to do this. I finally realized I couldn't carry Zac, his backpack and crutches all at the same time, so halfway down the driveway, in haste I threw the backpack and crutches to the ground. *So let the bus be late! I screamed in my head.* I cursed out loud, regretting it immediately.

To Zac, he probably thought I was mad at him, but I wasn't. I was angry at the whole situation! I was worried about today's scans. I had fought the battle in my head all night at work and once I got home and tried to sleep a few hours before getting up for the day.

Once Zac and I were back in the journey clinic, Dr. Moertel informed us that his lungs and femur were "stable."

"I called Dr. Guillaume to go over Zac's brain scan because I'm not sure what's going on," Dr. Moertel conceded.

I grew anxious. "What do you mean?"

"The mass that has been present and was measured a few weeks ago has now grown from one inch to three inches. I'm not exactly sure what we're looking at," Dr. Moertel admitted.

Dr. Guillaume came up to where Zac and I were talking with Dr. Moertel. After reviewing the scans together they both felt that the mass was a combination of fluid and swelling related to the dying tumor, but they were not certain. They believed that it was causing his arm to be numb.

The plan quickly formed to doing brain surgery to draw out the fluid, remove as much of the mass as safely possible and biopsy it to be sure it was not a new tumor. Dr. Guillaume wanted to do surgery in the next couple of days, but Dr. Moertel reminded him that Zac had Avastin this past Friday. Because of the interference in healing after the use of it, they both felt they couldn't safely do surgery for ten days – and that was pushing it.

In the meantime, Dr. Moertel planned to greatly increase the steroid that Zac was on to contain the swelling. I hated that drug as much as Zac. It would really puff him up and he wouldn't have control over that. The last time he was on high doses of the steroid I barely recognized him.

I was seeing so many unpleasant similarities to over a year ago when Zac suddenly became paralyzed because of the rapidly growing tumor. Every different change in his physical being, I questioned. I prayed that the steroids would keep him functioning and contain the pain until the set surgery day of October 10, 2013 at 11:00 am.

The weekend before Thursday's surgery, Zac started complaining of his back hurting. Zac never said anything about pain unless it was getting bad, I knew then that I needed to pay attention. At first he said it was because of his bed – not having a box-spring. I thought, *shame on us for not getting him a boxspring sooner*. I was going to tell Nathan we needed to get one within the next day or two.

Quickly the back pain became unbearable. It reminded me of the back pain he had while in the hospital after lying flat on his back for about three days. While getting a blood and platelet transfusion, Tammie said it was more than likely "steroid pain." *Great! Another side-effect from something that is needed to cover a different side-effect*. Thank God he improved after he was given a narcotic.

The backaches continued to the point where I would have to take him home from Jessica's soccer game, and he wasn't even able to kneel, let alone sit in church during Saturday evening mass. He was beside himself, but didn't want to leave church. I tried rubbing his back and even an older couple kneeling behind us felt helpless to Zac's pain that they took it upon themselves to rub his back when my hand got tired.

Relief was nowhere to be had. The narcotics I had at home weren't helping. I couldn't just make him deal with the pain and tell him to try and go to asleep. I finally called the hematology/ oncology fellow on-call at Amplatz. She suggested giving him another dose of oxycodone and if the pain couldn't be controlled by the dose, I should bring Zac in to the ER to be evaluated and given IV antibiotics.

"It could be an inclination of the tumor further spreading," The fellow warned.

I couldn't entertain that thought. Zac just had an MRI. *Could the cancer spread that fast?!*

After hanging up the phone I gave Zac some pain meds. I finally sat down to update Caringbridge and no sooner than I typed my fourth short paragraph, Zac called my cell phone. My stomach dropped. *He couldn't sleep. The pain was back and now into his legs! The pain had to be from the steroids.*

Little by little I was seeing Zac's physical abilities taken from him, but I would never admit that he was handicapped. This was temporary! Maybe that's why I refused for so long to getting a handicapped parking card. I wasn't going to accept this as his fate. We still had the hope of physical repair and that he would be walking and playing like the rest of the kids - soon one day.

The spinal MRI was clean for the most part with the exception of fibroids growing along the vertebrae. The pain was said to be related to the prolonged massive steroid use over the last year and a half.

The steroids were needed, but the effects were taking their toll physically as well as mentally on Zac. The weight gain was almost as bad as the physical pain. In recent weeks, I told Zac not to even bother looking in the mirror - it upset him every time he saw himself. I reminded him the weight gain was not his fault and it WAS temporary.

But today after Nic's cross country meet, he caught a glimps of himself in the mirror and started to cry. How do you fix that? Continued love and words of encouragement seemed empty at times. I could only hug him tight and kiss his soft cheeks.

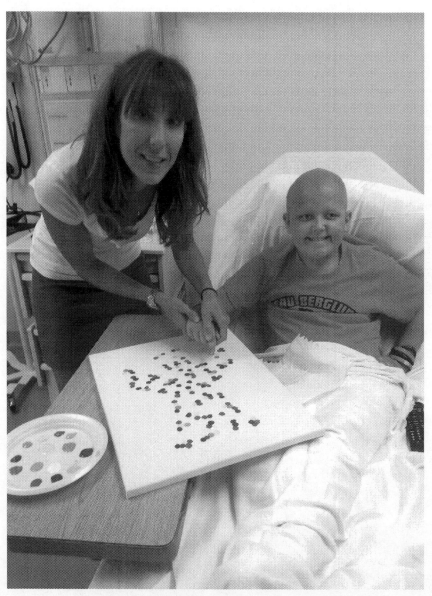

Aunt Barb and Zac working on angel painting for upcoming benefit,
while getting blood and platelet transfusion. 9-6-13

CHAPTER 31

zacstrong!

Tuesday October 8, 2013 was Jessica's fourteenth birthday, but it was designated by Lakeside Elementary School's principal, Sara Johnson, as ZacStrong Day. Sara and the teachers planned for a big rally for Zac to lift him up as he prepared for his brain surgery on the tenth.

The kids were alerted to wear their Zac Pack t-shirts or a blue one to show their support for Zac. Posters were secretly made and hung on all the walls of the school.

The fifth grade class was informed that they were being given a second recess for "good behavior" and "hard work." Little did Zac know everyone was actually preparing for the rally.

Outside, Mr. Maahs's fifth grade class began to chant - "WE ARE...! (they paused) "ZACSTRONG!" Over and over again they chanted.

Back in school the halls were lined with third, fourth, fifth graders and their teachers. When Mr. Maahs pushed Zac in his wheelchair, back into the school, he pushed him underneath the extended arms of all the children that had formed a bridge. The kids and teachers began chanting – "ZAC –ZAC- ZAC!" over and over again. Zac smiled from ear to ear surrounded by their love and support.

Down another hall and another hall, Zac was pushed to where yet more children continued to rally and strengthen him as he prepared to go into battle.

When I picked Zac up at the end of the day, one of the paras came up to me to tell me through tear-stained eyes how inspiring and special Zac was.

"I asked him how he was able to stay so strong and positive and he told me – *'God gives me strength.'*

"That sounds about right," I said so proud of my brave little man.

"He's not like other kids," Barb went on to say. "He's so pure and so good." She stepped in a little closer to me as if to share a secret. "Do you know other kids are following his example? Being a public school, we are not supposed to talk about God, but Zac has brought God back into the school. When other kids don't feel good or they hurt themselves they will say, *"If Zac can be strong, I can too! God will help me! I'm ZacStrong!"*...then they will turn and walk out of Nurse Leslie's and back to class. You can't take that away. It's good,"

As I drove Zac home from school, sitting in the front seat, he turned to look at me. "The devil is done," he matter-of-factly stated. "He can't take this anymore. I'm too much for him! He can't handle this!!" Zac confidently spoke by his empowering revelation.

The rally was a success! Zac was filled with a newfound strength. I could see a determination to help Zac that was built by all of his prayer warriors – and there were many and Zac contained it all within himself. He held fast to it and planned to use it as he entered into his next battle where the beast continued to linger.

Bright and early Zac and I left for the University of Minnesota Hospital for an early MRI that would be different than the ones before. Dr. Guillaume needed to have all the areas plotted out for points of speech and motor function so he would know specifically which points to avoid.

As soon as Zac was finished, we drove over to the Amplatz side for labs to be drawn and his other appointments. It was a long day in preparation for an intense surgery which was scheduled for the next day.

I was nervous that Zac was having surgery too soon from his last dose of Avastin but I knew Zac needed it to relieve the incredible pressure that was continuing to build in his brain. I also had the utmost respect and faith in Dr. Guillaume.

I thought we were all set for tomorrow's surgery, minus the packing, when I got a phone call at 5:30 pm from Dr. Guillaume. I was quite surprised that he had personally called. Uneasy, I waited for him to explain his reason for calling.

"Have you spoken with Dr. Moertel about Zac's MRI since you left the hospital?" Dr. Guillaume asked.

A red flag popped up. Something was wrong. I stopped getting dinner ready and walked out of the kitchen where Zac was sitting at the table. I was alarmed by Dr. Guillaume's vague question and I didn't want Zac to overhear any of the conversation.

"No, we just got home about a half hour ago. What's going on?"

"I had six other doctors review Zac's MRI of today and they all felt he should NOT have surgery tomorrow." Dr. Guillaume paused as I remained silent. "We can't explain why, but the tumor is dramatically smaller than it was three days ago."

My first reaction was disappointment because by doing the surgery, I wanted Zac's arm and leg to regain its full function so he could once again write and feed himself with his right hand. I was having a difficult time processing what was being said.

"I don't understand."

The MRI had some technical problems and there was a lot of artifact making the MRI very difficult to read."

Great. We just got home and now Dr. Guillaume was going to ask me to bring Zac down for another scan, I predicted. Not without a few more questions.

When I asked what the artifact was, Dr. Guillaume simply said "I don't know. That's never happened before."

"I understand, I think, but how did the tumor shrink so fast?" I asked wanting verification for my answer.

"We're not sure if it's dying out, and if it is, we don't want to risk anything by going in and disrupting whatever the process that is going on, that is shrinking things. It would be dumb to do surgery when the tumor is shrinking on its own," Dr. Guillaume flat out said.

The doctors felt by waiting longer, it would give Zac more time to rid his body of the Avastin and if he still needed surgery in another four to six weeks, it would be more ideal. Dr. Guillaume admitted that after stopping avastin it is recommended to wait four to six weeks before doing any type of surgery. "But in Zac's situation we were pushing it because of how fast the tumor had grown. If we would do surgery too soon – it's – NOT good."

"I don't want to do more harm than good," Dr. Guillaume admitted. "Once Avastin is stopped, usually the swelling gets worse – and it did, for Zac, but now, things are markedly improved."

Still trying to comprehend the sudden changes, I asked if the high dose of steroid that Zac was on could have helped in decreasing the swelling of the tumor.

"Steroids would not cause the tumor to shrink as much as what it has. We just aren't sure."

"It's God," I told him.

"You're probably right," Dr. Guillaume said without hesitation.

I know this had to be a miracle in itself. I believed all of what transpired was God's way of saying – "STOP! I don't want you to go ahead with surgery. WAIT! It's too close to the last Avastin treatment. Surgery is NOT safe now." I believed God then decided to step in in yet a bigger way to stop the doctors by dramatically shrinking the tumor. I was elated at the awesome news that was finally sinking in. God was good. The Lakeside rally was a form of a powerful and pure prayer and God saved my son today and from death tomorrow. A little crazy? Maybe, but there was no other explanation.

I hung up the phone with Dr. Guillaume and I walked into the kitchen where Zac was still sitting at the table reading his new 'Dog Tag's' book that a Lakeside librarian bought for Zac.

I started peeling off the white spongy cheerio-like markers that were all plastered to Zac's head.

"What are you doing?!" Zac asked shocked I would do such a thing.

"We're not doing surgery," I said. "the tumor shrunk quite a bit!"

"What?!" Zac could hardly believe his ears.

"Yep! The tumor is smaller and the doctors don't want to do surgery now!"

Zac's eyes welled up with tears of happiness and relief as he started to cry. He reached out to me for a hug and I wrapped my arms tightly around him. "It's a miracle," Zac whispered.

"It's a miracle," I confirmed.

The following morning I called the school to alert them that I would be bringing Zac in because surgery was astonishingly cancelled. With Zac's schedule, allowing him to sleep until he woke up and then lay on the biomat, we always got to school after it had already started. Today would be no different.

When we got to school the ladies in the office were so glad to see Zac. They fought over who would wheel him into class. I had to admit to Sara, the principal that I was a little embarrassed that they went out of their way to make posters, had the rally and the teachers made the uplifting video on Vimeo for Zac and now he was back in school. I figured the kids would be confused. I hoped they all understood how everyone lifted Zac up even if he wasn't going to have surgery. I hoped they believed in what a miracle this was.

"I think you all were a part of Zac's miracle. There is no other reason especially when the neurosurgeon had no explanation as to why the tumor and swelling changed so dramatically."

"I bet you're right," Sara said.

I hugged her and thanked her again.

Shortly before the end of the school day, I received a phone call from Leslie, the school nurse. I hated when I got "those" phone calls. I held my breath in anticipation for what she was about to say.

I was relieved to know that Zac didn't have a severe headache, vomiting episode or a seizure - instead it was a fall.

"He's okay though," Leslie reassured. "Zac was standing up, leaning forward trying to pick up his backpack when he lost his balance and smacked his face on his desk. Unfortunately he chipped his front tooth and bruised up his right cheek. I put ice on it right away."

"Is he complaining of anything else hurting? Any headache?" I always worried about his head.

"No. He says he feels fine. I just wanted to let you know and Michelle Nordahl wanted to make sure you were okay with her still bringing him home."

Zac was a sight to see! He looked like he had gotten into a fight. He started coming up with some far-fetched stories to explain his battle wounds. "I got in a fight, but you should see the other guy!" or "There was this bear in my backyard and it started to attack me until I took out my Swiss Army knife..."

After a phone call, I transferred Zac into the van and off to Hauge Dental we went. I was glad our friend Tom was a dentist and he was able to squeeze Zac in to his schedule right away.

Friday, Zac was up and ready for school - new tooth and all. It never really mattered where we were going we always were in a rush. Zac tried to be as helpful and independent as possible. I could tell he didn't want to slow down or burden anyone. I think he saw either the stress radiating from me or the sweat glistening on my forehead and figured he would do what he could to save us some extra minutes.

I was in the house getting ready while Zac was waiting on the garage landing when I heard a loud thud and Lexie came running into the house screaming.

"Mom! Zac fell! He's hurt! Hurry!"

There at the bottom of the three wooden steps laid Zac crumpled in a heap.

"Zac! Are you okay?! What happened?!" My heart raced as I jumped off the side of the platform and tried to move him. I don't know why, but the next question out of my mouth was – "Is your tooth okay?"

Once I checked Zac all over and determined that the most important bone, his leg – wasn't broken, I got him to sit on the bottom step to get his bearings. His face was scraped up and bleeding a little and his eye started turning black and blue.

"Zac, you're really gonna have to come up with a better story."

CHAPTER 32

barely hanging on

The plan was for Zac to have a break from chemotherapy for a couple of weeks and start weaning him from his steroids. All of that changed when Dr. Moertel called on Friday October 14, 2013. He wanted Zac to resume his chemo treatments in order to keep his lungs and leg stable. He believed his brain was acting separate from them and he didn't want to chance any unforeseen surprises.

I understood what his thought process was, but I was mad all the same. I let my guard down for just a day and half thinking – maybe pretending was a better way of putting it, that Zac was kind of in remission. A word I hadn't spoken for eight years. I secretly was planning how Zac and the rest of the family would get to live, somewhat normal, even if it was for a few weeks.

A quick slap in the face and I was back to reality. I would willingly live the lifestyle we had been living for the rest of my life if it meant having all of my children under Nathan and my care. I let Zac have a carefree weekend and broke the news to him that he needed to go back into the hospital tomorrow for a week of chemo.

It didn't sit well, but as Zac always would do in unpleasant and disappointing situations, he opened up that old rugged beat-up trunk and pulled out his armor and slipped it back on.

Zac's stay in the hospital was uneventful for the most part. Since it was the week of conferences there was no school three days that week and he had friends from school come to visit and play UNO. He had fun and was joking around talking and laughing about farting and such talk that make eleven-year-old boys laugh. Casually he mentioned a headache and that he was getting tired. Eventually he had to call it quits and Andrew and Grant left with their mom.

It was the night of October 18th when I began to grow uneasy as I helped Zac to the bathroom. He seemed very unsteady. I atttributed it to being tired from the past three days of PT and that his leg muscles were getting tired and sore. It hadn't been all that long since he had his leg surgery and Zac really worked hard for Katie during his therapy sessions, but something wasn't quite right.

By 7:30 am Friday morning, Zac woke up saying his arm was feeling heavier. *Here we go...* I was hoping we would escape this hospitalization without the toll the chemo seemed to take on his right side. Zac was just regaining function in his arm and leg and starting to do more for himself again. Now he couldn't lift his arm.

I was mad! We were just making a little progress and now it was snatched away.

Along with the numbness, Zac started having more headaches. By Friday evening they grew worse. If he stood to use the urinal or lay on his left side, it got increasingly worse. Brushing his teeth in the bathroom became unbearable and I had to quickly get him back to bed where it took a minute or two for the pressure to subside.

He had one more chemo treatment before we would be going home tomorrow. I worried what it would do to him. I began to wonder if he should even have the final one. If the tumor shrunk drastically – even the swelling from the chemo or the IV fluids shouldn't create such a disability.

I ran my concerns by the nurse and she said the doctors might investigate a little further in the morning to see if there could be another explanation for his headaches – other than the swelling. I'm sure they wondered I was vying for another MRI.

It was after midnight and I laid down praying that Zac's headache would resolve and he could finally drift off to sleep. It wasn't but a few minutes later that Zac called out in a loud whisper that his head really hurt. His breathing became labored and intensified.

"Squeeze my hand, baby. I'll call for the nurse."

When the nurse came in, I was disappointed that it wasn't one of our regular nurses who really knew Zac. She saw Zac lying flat on his back, motionless except for the steady breathing that helped him to deal with his bad headache. Shortly after explaining what was going on and asking to see the doctor, she came back with a resident doctor that I had never met before.

Quickly I explained Zac's condition to her and told her he needed something for pain.

"How about we try some Tylenol?" She casually suggested.

"Tylenol is not going to touch him. The last time this happened the only thing that finally helped him was Decadron," I explained.

"Well, without knowing if Tylenol is going to work, I would rather not start out with the Decadron," the resident rationalized.

I tried to reason with her. She could clearly see the distress and pain Zac was in, but out of respect, I agreed to try her way.

Fifteen minutes, then twenty minutes passed and Zac grew worse. The pain was one continuous wave after another. It reminded me of a laboring woman – contraction after contraction, breathing intensifying at the height of one, pleading for the release of the pain and to catch a break, only to prepare for the next.

Earlier when I had asked Zac where his pain was at on a scale of one to ten, he said "five." I suspected higher.

"Where's your pain at now, baby?"

"Nine," Zac weakly admitted.

By how he was acting, I knew it was probably an eleven. He was always so stoic.

I reached for the call-light and called the nurse in again.

"He needs something stronger. The Tylenol isn't working at all and he says his pain is at a nine.

Back came the resident. She wanted to try yet another medicine. My patience was wearing thin. "I want to speak to the doctor," I firmly said.

"I AM a doctor," she strongly affirmed.

I didn't know what to say. Inside, I wanted to scream – *I want Dr. Moertel or Sadak or Barnum! Now!!* – but I wasn't a forceful person by nature. As a nurse, I handed out and explained the 'Patient Bill of Right's' many times. In my own dire situation, I completely forgot my own rights, especially the right to request a new doctor. Eventually I convinced her to give him the Decadron. She seemed oblivious to Zac's incredible pain and walked out of the room.

The pain continued to increase to the point I started worrying that the pressure in his brain might become so intense that his brain would rupture or he might stroke. I didn't understand why no one could see what was going on and that this was out of character for Zac. *Why weren't they concerned?!*

The resident doctor and nurse would occasionally come in and see if there was any improvements, but they left twenty seconds later, not batting an eye after I told them that there was no change.

I grew angrier and more frustrated and more fearful with each deep breath Zac took. The twenty or thirty seconds of relief he had in between each "contraction" gave me time to utter a desperate prayer – *Please God help him. Please stop the pain!*

Every sixty seconds of excruciating pain, I continued to coach Zac to "breathe, breathe…hang on baby, hang on." I had no idea what I was encouraging him to hang on for – for someone to come in and see and then provide relief?

Every so often Zac would cry out – "God - Please, PLEASE help me!"

I was helpless. I was in a hospital full of doctors and nurses with medicine that could take away pain, diagnostic equipment that could give an indication of what was wrong and yet, there was no help to be given,

By 6 am, Zac couldn't take the pain anymore. He could not contain the horrific pain any longer and as he motioned for help, he threw up all over me. He was now listless, but trying to turn his head. I knew the pain was incredible. I grabbed a bucket and dumped the contents out on to the counter top and raced over to help Zac position his head in the right direction and press the call-light for help as he continued to throw up again and again.

Fatiyah, one of Zac's regular nurses came in once she heard my desperate cry for help. Immediately a sense of calm came over me. I knew she would listen to me and take action.

"You're here?! I wished I would have known you were here!" I said knowing if she was Zac's nurse, she wouldn't have let it come to this point and let him suffer unnecessarily for almost seven hours. "Can you grab me some more wash cloths?" I asked as I quickly tried wiping the vomit from Zac's neck and arm.

Finally a little help arrived. The right shift nursing assistant jumped in to help clean Zac up as I slipped into the bathroom to clean myself up. The reprieve to be able to step back and just be his mom was a much needed break – even if it was for

5 minutes. Once I closed the bathroom door, I grabbed onto the sink and wept. This was bad.

Fatiyah came back with morphine and Zac was beginning to show signs of comfort. His breathing slowed to an occasional sigh and then - quiet sleep. Finally sleep.

I lay down and barely had time to shut my eyes when Dr. Moertel and Dr. Jess Barnum came in. I quickly sat up, exhausted and disoriented.

"I've ordered a brain CT," Dr. Moertel said with a look of concern on his face as he stared intently at Zac sleeping. "He looks comfortable."

I wanted to be sure he wasn't fooled by Zac's recent bout of sleep so I gave him and Dr. Barnum a replay of the last seven hours.

Zac started lightly moaning after Dr. Moertel and Dr. Barnum left the room. I quickly asked if he could have more for pain and there already in Fatiyah's hand was morphine.

"They are coming for Zac in a few minutes and Dr. Moertel wants to be sure he is able to get through the scan comfortably.

Zac had a large brain bleed and that was the reason for the severe headaches and more than likely the reason he lost function of his right arm. We quickly packed up our room and loaded up a cart with as much of our belongings as we could and were transferred to the third floor – the Pediatric Intensive Care Unit (PICU).

Zac's blood pressure was very high, his sodium levels were low and his pain was increasing. The ICU doctors and nurses were quick to respond. I was caught in a whirlwind of chaos. Just the day before we were playing Yahtzee - and now – doctors were buzzing around him.

I wanted so much to have Nathan for support, but figured it would be best to call him once I knew more and the kids were taken care of. It was still early and I didn't know what all this meant.

With Zac's increasing pain, I asked right away for more pain meds. He had suffered enough and I couldn't bear to watch him go through another horrifying moment like the past seven hours. My heart sank when I was told they had to stop the morphine, but would give him Tylenol along with a massive loading dose of IV Decadron. Their reasoning was they wanted to see how he would respond neurologically to questions and commands. Narcotics would mask that and they would not be able to tell if his bleed was worsening. They wanted to be ready if they had to run to surgery. The next couple of hours were critical.

The minutes felt like hours. The day seemed ten times longer when I had to continue to watch Zac suffer in pain. Tylenol and cold packs could only do so much. This just seemed cruelly insane! I wondered if they would be able to withstand such pain. I was on the verge of demanding they give Zac morphine, but I also understood their reasoning.

Soon the pain extended into his back and radiated into his legs. It would last for hours at a time, in the same type of continual contraction-like pain as before. No amount of rubbing and massaging seemed to help. Eventually he was given lidocaine patches for his back which seemed to offer some relief.

Surgery to repair the bleed was not a possibility. If they did do any form of surgery, it would be to drain off the blood that was coming from the tumor. They still didn't know if the bleeding was because the tumor was dying out or if it was due to something else. We were in a holding pattern until Dr. Guillaume reviewed Zac's scans and checked the OR schedule in the morning, provided Zac didn't take a turn for the worse – if that were possible.

If I wasn't dosing, I was praying. Zac's pain began to increase around 6 am, Sunday. The pain meds that were previously controlling his pain no longer gave him the same relief. His blood pressure remained high all night until they loaded him up on Hydralazine. He was stable, yet critical.

Another brain and spinal MRI was ordered to see if there was a visible reason that would now explain the debilitating pain that Zac was having. His platelets continued to drop even after having a transfusion the day before. I prepared myself that Zac would have surgery sometime soon.

Watching the nurses hang more platelets concerned me. I wasn't sure what having a brain bleed meant for Zac. I knew it was bad, but I also believed they could stop it or the bleed could self-absorb. My brain was having a difficult time shutting off the "what-if's." It had been intense in the PICU ever since Zac was rolled into the center of the sterile white and cream room that was decked out with medical equipment. It was so much harder to pretend in this environment, especially not knowing when I would be able to take my son home.

Zac went into surgery, four days later, when he was more stable, a little after 2 pm on Tuesday the twenty-second. Dr. Guillaume sat and talked with us after the surgery and said everything went well. He was able to insert a drain with minimal bleeding. The fluid pressure on the brain was very high, but came down quickly after the drain was in and working.

If fluid would build up too high, now, Zac would have a way for it to be aspirated without surgically opening his head each time. Everything was dependent on what the biopsy Dr. Guillaume sent off to the East Bank, would show. He said, "It was too early to tell, but the area looked angry…like there was a battle going on. There was dead tissue seen, but other areas looked suspicious."

So far the surgery was indeterminate at this point.

After three-and-a-half days of not eating, Zac was enjoying a chocolate malt that Nathan insisted the doctors allow him to give to his starving son. When Zac was asked what he would want to eat when his dad came back the next day, he thought for a moment and casually said, "I actually feel like crab legs and a kitty cocktail."

My Zac was back!

Surgery was behind us, but Zac was still having occasional headaches that were not related to surgery. He also was continuing to have high blood pressures, low sodium levels and was requiring blood and platelet transfusions daily. He was on so many medications. Discharge from the hospital was not in the near future. I was excited that at least Zac was able to lift his right arm about six inches off the bed. I would take any sign of improvement.

The morning of October twenty-fourth, I was informed that Dr. Moertel and Tammie wanted to have a meeting. At first I thought it was going to be in regards to Zac's treatment plan, but I began suspecting that there was a little more to it.

"Is Nathan going to be here today?" Emily, our social worker asked.

"No, he went back to work today for the first time all week," I said looking at her suspiciously. I immediately began to feel very uneasy. "We could conference him in, though."

Emily was a little less chipper than usual. I wondered why they were asking for Nathan's presence. They rarely asked if he was coming, in the past. I was going to dismiss my suspicions, but something inside my gut kept twisting and turning.

I finally came out with my burning question, "Is the news not very good?" *They couldn't have the biopsy results back yet? It was still supposed to be another one to three days.*

"I don't really know," Emily replied.

I had no reason to doubt Emily. She had always been straight with me in the past. I took a deep breath and fought to remain calm. The more I tried to fight my rising fears, the more nervous I became about the upcoming meeting. I quickly called my sister, Barb to let her know what was going on.

"Do you want me to come? I can be there after I bring Jack back to school after his appointment."

"Well, Emily will be there with me," I paused for a second trying to anticipate what would develop out of the meeting. I didn't want to inconvenience her. She had dropped so many things with her family to come support Zac and me already. I felt like a child trying to be a big girl. "I should be okay."

My strength crumbled and my voice quivered as I began to cry. "I'm sorry," I whispered in the phone trying to hide my concerns from Zac. "I'm just really afraid of what they have to say."

"I'll be there as soon as I can," Barb affirmed.

I wouldn't have to stand alone. My pillar of strength would be coming to support me once again.

My heart pounded as Emily and I walked down the hall to the small green conference room. I was glad she was with me. I had grown to rely on her for a source of comfort and support, as well as Barb. Dr. Moertel, Tammie and Dr. Jess Barnum entered the room and sat down. I waited in silence. The calm before the storm...

Dr. Moertel called Nathan's office. "Nate?"

"Hey, doc. What's going on?" I could hear the tremble in Nathan's voice. I wished he was sitting beside me.

"I won't beat around the bush," Dr. Moertel began. "Zac's brain bleed is the result of the extensive chemotherapy treatments he has had over the last nine years, plus radiation," Dr. Moertel spoke slowly and steadily – almost like he had rehearsed what he was going to say. "His brain is very fragile and he won't be able to tolerate any further chemotherapy or radiation. It would be too dangerous and would more than likely cause more brain bleeds." He paused only to take a quick breath. "The biopsy showed more cancer cell tissue throughout a new large brain tumor. There is dying tumor as well, but as I said, the chemo is becoming very harmful to Zac."

I was shocked and at loss for words. What was he saying? Without any chemotherapy and the cancer still infesting Zac's brain – he would die! I waited for him to continue as the tears welled up in my eyes. There had to be something he could do! He always had something else to try.

"The reason Zac is requiring daily blood and platelet transfusions is because of the current bleed. He is using up the platelets he is given to stop the bleeding, but the bleeding is severe," Dr. Moertel went on to explain.

"So what do we do?" I asked feeling my sense of hope being sucked out of my soul as I wiped the falling tears from my eyes.

"There is this trial drug called Mekinist that I would like to try, but I am not sure what the side effects on Zac would be. It also is extremely expensive and could take weeks to get because there is a lot of paperwork involved and the company has to first agree that Zac is a candidate."

Nathan and I felt we had to try. We didn't want to sit back and watch Zac die knowing there could be something out there that could possibly save his life. Maybe Zac came this far to be the first child to use this trial Mekinist drug and it would be the breakthrough in medical science that would provide a cure to many suffering from neurofibromatosis and cancer.

Just then the door opened and Barb came in quietly and slowly sat down next to me on the vinyl couch. "What's going on?" she whispered.

Nathan was asking Dr. Moertel some questions about the Mekinist drug over the speaker phone so I quickly whispered, trying to contain my tears, "There is no more chemo to try, but possibly a chance at trying a trial drug." It didn't take her long to reach for the Kleenexes as she put her arm around me.

Tammie looked at me with tears in her eyes. I knew she was struggling having to give us this news. She and Dr. Moertel had known Zac since he was two-years-old. They were more than Zac's doctors, they were our friends.

"This is going to be an important decision for you and Nathan to make – but because Zac has a pretty significant brain bleed that is slowing down, our fear is that Zac could have a new large brain bleed at any time," Tammie said with her eyes remaining fixed on me. "You guys need to make the decision if you would want to go ahead with surgery or just make him comfortable – and let him be."

I couldn't believe I was in this conversation. Nathan was completely silent on the other end of the phone. With a lump in my throat, I asked looking at Dr. Jess Barnum, "Couldn't Dr. Guillaume go in and stop the bleed?"

"With the bleed he has now and if he had another severe bleed, surgery would be very difficult with his brain as fragile as it is," Dr. Jess Barnum gently explained.

My mind raced at a loss as how to process the unexpected information.

"Carol Ann," Tammie spoke, "Under those conditions, Zac would not be left the same boy."

There was not a dry eye in that conference room. Dr. Moertel had to leave. The rest of us didn't move a muscle.

"There is the decision of making Zac DNR/ DNI (Do Not Resuscitate/ Do Not Intubate) or not that you two need to make rather soon," Tammie warned.

I just kept thinking – *This can't be real, This can't be real! They were telling us in so many words that without a miracle – our son was dying!!*

The nurse in me came out and I was able to be rational for a few minutes. "I know Zac wouldn't want to just lie there and never be able to speak or do anything. Right, Nathan?"

"No. He would hate that. It wouldn't be how he would want to live."

"It wouldn't be Zac," Tammie said trying to help ease our decision.

"As much as I would want to keep him alive, if Zac had no hope of regaining consciousness or any quality of life, I couldn't put him through that. It wouldn't be fair to him," I said, grabbing for another kleenex.

The room was silent.

"But what if the bleed was small? Would it be safer to go in and stop it, without risk of damage?" I questioned.

Dr. Jess Barnum explained that Dr. Guillaume could go into Zac's brain and see how severe the bleed was and if it was major, he would just close, if it was more contained, surgery would be possible, but the uncertainty of damage would not be known until he got in there. We would talk to him more about that.

"What do you think, Nathan?"

"I think if the bleed is determined small then we go ahead with surgery, but if it is a large bleed –" Nathan's voice quivered "we leave him alone."

Nathan and I came to the decision if the bleed was big, we would do what we could to keep Zac comfortable. We couldn't bear it if we put Zac in a severely compromised mental or vegetative state.

Through my tears and what had progressed to "ugly-crying", I asked "THE" question I never thought I would have to really consider. "How...mu–ch...t–ime...?"

Both Tammie and Dr. Jess Barnum said they didn't know because of the unpredictablness of another bleed. "Right now you need to focus on Zac's happiness," Tammie stressed.

Even in the face of death, I could not be given an estimate. It usually seemed to be "six weeks" or "six months to a year." I was too devastated to be angry about not getting a prediction to help my family and I prepare.

Without a definitive timeline or absolutely no further possibility of treatment, I wasn't about to admit defeat. We had always been able to do something else. The Mekinist drug, to me, was "something else." Zac had always defied the odds and surprised the doctors. *Why not this time as well?*

I had been in and out of Zac's room a lot that day and Zac was questioning what was going on. Although still weak and tired, he was alert and feeling much better than he did a couple of days ago. He was still on several kinds of drugs, around the clock. I knew he suspected something was up. I'm sure he saw my red and swollen eyes and grew paranoid with the whispers out in the hall on the other side of the glass sliding door.

We were told to be honest with Zac, but not to take away his hope. *How could I, as his mother and biggest cheerleader of faith and 'never give up,' be the one to tell him he was dying? I couldn't!*

Tammie came back to talk with him. I felt she more than likely has had to be the bearer of bad news before and she willingly agreed to spare me the unthinkable pain.

Barb, Nathan and I gathered around Zac's bed as Tammie stood at the foot holding firmly onto his feet and ankles. "Zac, remember how your mom told you earlier that you wouldn't be getting anymore chemo?" Tammie carefully started out.

"Yah?" Zac looked concerned.

"Well, that's because it is too hard on your brain. I know you want to be healed, but it might not be down here on earth – but up in heaven."

I didn't know exactly what Zac was thinking. A tear streamed down his cheek. Without speaking those permanent awful words, Zac seemed to understand what Tammie meant. His only fear that he verbalized was, "Am I going to bleed to death?"

I didn't want Zac to admit defeat, so I reminded him after Tammie left, that there was always hope and that God could over-rule at any time what the doctors think to be true. I couldn't handle sitting there and allow Zac to process the news on his own. I tried to get him to talk and ask questions, but he remained silent.

"Zac, do you have any questions about what Tammie said?" I asked wanting for him to open up so badly and let me know what he was thinking.

"No," Zac quietly spoke.

"Do you understand what Tammie was saying?" I questioned hoping to be able to "read" him.

"Yes," Zac said showing no emotion.

Zac didn't want to talk. I didn't want to push and Nathan and Barb were at a loss for words.

I couldn't let it sit this way. "Zac, even though we can't use chemo anymore, there still is hope in the new trial drug – the Mekinist! I really think it's gonna work!"

Nathan perked up and said, "Zac, we aren't giving up. I think you came to this point, to use the Mekinist, and because of you, the doctors will know that it works and it will then be used on other kids."

"Yah, and they will call it the "Zac Attack," I chimed in.

Hope was not lost – not yet.

Nic, Jess, Zac, Lexie and Hazel at the pumpkin patch days before the brain bleed 10-13-13

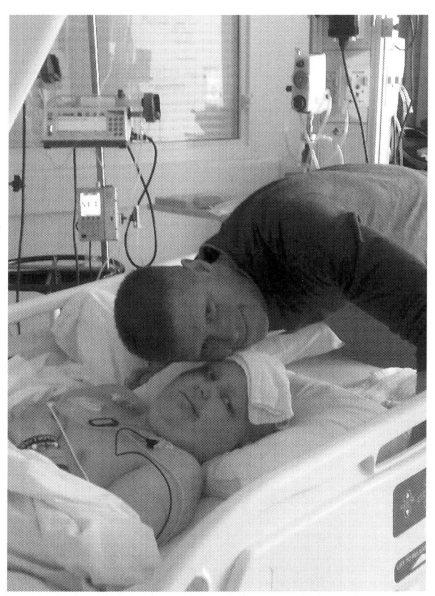

Zac and dad in PICU because of brain bleed. 10-19-13

CHAPTER 33

no more chemo

When you are told that almost half of your son's brain is full of cancer and they will be sending you home without any further treatment, it is not a very hopeful feeling. I was numb. I was afraid and my heart was breaking in a way like I have never felt before. It was hard to remain optimistic without the guarantee that Zac would be granted the trial drug and it would work.

I struggled as I watched a boy who looked to be about fourteen years old lying attached to life support in the room next to us. He came sometime in the early hours of the morning. I wondered what his story was as I lay motionless on my chair-bed waiting for sleep to come, pleading to God for my child's life. Little by little family came once the sun started to rise. People were standing and sitting along the hallway talking quietly among themselves while others were crying.

My heart broke for his mother who I was certain I had picked out. After life-support was disconnected and the family little by little faded away, I couldn't help but cling to the light of hope I still had. This boy's mother's had just been distinguished. As horrible as I felt for that mother, I was glad it wasn't me. I still had my sweet angel boy. *Please God, spare my son.*

After several days in the PICU, when Nathan and Barb would come, I felt comfortable enough to go for long runs alongside the Mississippi River to destress. Although Zac continued to require blood pressure medication, steroids, blood and platelets, he was stable and talking.

As I stared at the beautiful houses on the East and West Parkway, I wondered what more could we do that we hadn't done? I had nothing. It was incredibly hard to hold my head up and it only was because Zac was still the same sweet loving child that he always was. I could never let him down, so my attitude needed to remain positive and bright to keep Zac happy and feeling safe.

Finding the appropriate time to talk with Nic and Jessica was one conversation I kept putting off. I knew it would shake them up. Nic qualified for state in cross country, but I didn't think it would be wise to wait an entire week to tell him when Zac's situation was so critical. I wanted Nic and Jessica to have every opportunity to resolve any regrets they had with Zac. Every day was a gift at this point and I didn't know how many more we would be given.

Since Zac was unable to go to the Minnesota Vikings vs. Green Bay Packers football game that he had been given tickets to go to over a month ago from Child Family Life, Nathan decided to take Nic and Jessica to see if they could get any player signatures for Zac with the special player pass that was included. Zac was extremely upset that he couldn't go to the game he had been planning on going to for weeks. I tried everything to get him to be able to make the game – even bringing a nurse with to manage his IV drip, but it was too risky. Lexie decided to hang out with Zac and I while we watched the game on tv.

Aside from Jessica getting hit in the head by a football thrown by Adrianne Peterson during their warm-up, the Vikings did not approach them to give any autographs.

Zac quickly pushed his disappointment aside and watched anxiously, hoping for a win. "They've gotta win so Bryan has to wear Halle's Viking t-shirt to work tomorrow!" Zac panicked.

The bet was still on - whoever's team lost the game would have to wear the other teams t-shirt all day, the following day! For both guys it would be sheer torture and it wasn't looking good for Zac.

"It's not looking so good for the Vikings, Zac. I think you might be in trouble," I teased.

"I know!" Zac shrilled in disappointment.

"I know - we could just tell Bryan that you wore the t-shirt and he would ne—v-e-r K-n-o-w," I said in a mysterious voice.

"Na, mom. I can't do that. A deals, a deal," Zac adamantly said. "Or – could I?" He joked shifting his eyes back and forth.

I nervously waited for Nathan's text that they were on their way to the hospital. We had decided we would talk to the kids tonight. No more procrastinating. Father Al was on his way and agreed to sit with us when we told the kids. I felt having him there would alert Nic and Jessica to the graveness of Zac's health. In the past I had warned the kids many times of Zac's serious diagnosis, but he continued to rise above and plow through. They never took it seriously. This time I needed them to understand.

Barb was on her way too. She was going to sit with Zac and Lexie to keep them company. She was always able to give that special comfort to Zac. He asked everyday if "Aunt Barb was going to come" to the hospital.

It was 9 pm by the time Nathan, Nic and Jessica got to the hospital. There was casual talk and a little joking around until I had to force the inevitable. I told Nic and Jessica that we needed to have a talk and Father Al was sitting in.

The air became heavy. Nic looked as if he and Jessica were in trouble for something. Jessica had no clue what was going on. We headed down the hall to that same green conference room, for privacy, and closed the door. There was no turning back.

"Do you guys have any idea what this talk is about?" I asked wondering how I should begin.

"No," Nic plainly said glancing at Father Al for a clue.

Jessica remained silent sitting across from me in a chair, next to Nic.

"I will try my best not to cry, but things are REALLY serious with Zac," I said trying to keep my composure as I felt my insides crumbling.

"What do you mean?" Jessica questioned. "He's coming home soon, right?"

I had a hard time trying to speak as I felt my throat tighten and the tears burning behind my eyes. I didn't want to scare Nic and Jessica, so I waited as I tried to regroup.

"You both know that Zac's brain bleed is serious that's why he is in the intensive care unit and he is on a lot of medicine to help keep him stable," Nathan started until I was ready to resume my words.

"But the brain bleed stopped, right?" Nic cautiously asked looking from Nathan to me to Father Al.

"The brain bleed seems to have slowed way down, but Zac still needs blood and platelet transfusions once or twice a day because it has still not completely stopped," I explained as I got ready to shift gears. "I asked Father Al to be in on our family meeting, ONE – because he is family and TWO – because I wanted you both to know how serious this talk really is." I drew in a quick breathe like I was resurfacing from heavy water, preparing to go back in. "Dr. Moertel told Dad and me in a meeting a few days ago that Zac can't have any more chemo because it is too dangerous and it could cause a massive brain bleed."

Nic immediately hung his head and started to cry. He understood what I was saying. Jessica sat in the chair with her knees drawn up under her chin. She stared blankly at me.

I wasn't sure she comprehended what I meant without spelling it out, so I dove in – head first. "There is no more surgery and without further chemotherapy, Zac will – die."

I didn't have to wait for a reaction. Nic freely showed his anguish and continued crying. "No, no, no," he said rocking back and forth on the small loveseat.

I was glad that Nic could express himself, but Jessica I was concerned with because in spite of the look that she just had the wind knocked out of her, she was silent. Maybe she was trying to catch her breath.

Father Al was there for emotional support as well as offering the comfort that he possessed as being a man of God, a dear friend and one who understood from his past experience with his own daughter who had a brain tumor, before he decided to become a priest.

Questions were asked, explanations were given in terms that were easy to understand. Nic and Jessica handled it the best they could for such mature content. The pain and panic in their faces and voices were of complete agony. I hated darkening their world with such devastating information. I was not sure how we were going to handle trying to live normally with these words now spoken. We couldn't run away from it. This was the most helpless feeling in all the world.

Zac knew that Nathan and I were going to have "the talk" with Nic and Jessica. He didn't have an opinion or comment about it. He just knew they needed to know.

The night grew late and the kids had school in the morning, so around 11 pm they reluctantly headed for home, deciding they better not skip school for fear of the amount of homework they would have to catch up on.

My days grew more and more challenging trying to remain hopeful. My mind was constantly flooded with the nightmarish thought of Zac in a casket with his light blue dress shirt and tie on. Other times I envisioned his funeral or the gravesite. Again, my only temporary relief was whispering "Help me Jesus, help me Jesus!"

At nighttime when I would finally try to sleep, I lay on the pull-out chair-bed which was positioned behind Zac's, against the wall, and held my rosary tightly in my hand saying the rosary over and over until my body and mind were given permission to rest. Each time I was awakened by Zac, a nurse or a sudden jolt of fear, I would clutch the rosary that was still cradled in my hand and recite it all over again, trying once again to escape the strong hold of fear the devil continued to strangle me with.

On October 30, 2013, Zac was transferred out of the Ped's ICU back to the fifth floor where we first started fifteen days ago.

Zac was still having blood pressure issues and continued to require platelet's, but the need for them was spacing out.

It was comforting to be back in familiar territory - a place that was so full of hope for healing. I only wished I could turn back the clock to when we were able to do something to combat the cancer. It was different now. We wouldn't be coming back up here anymore, unless it was for an unstable platelets or an infection. I felt hollow inside.

I actually watched the rest of a movie after Zac drifted off to sleep. As a person who cries when I see someone else cry, I didn't shed one tear during a very sad part. I was numb as I continued to stare at the television. Nothing was as sad to me as what I was living.

I wouldn't walk around and not talk to people, but I was finding myself wanting to avoid people. At times I couldn't look at a passerby and smile at them like I usually did. I had to look the other way – as if I'm looking at something or I just hung my head. I was different. My world had been turned upside down. I prayed that I could dig deep to keep the hope alive like I had always done before. I prayed that in the next couple of days Zac would be granted the trial drug.

Zac took everything in stride. He continued to charm the nurses, joke around, and tried to beat his high score in Candy Crush and Temple Run. He appeared unchanged. He never let on that he was depressed. He grew quiet at times, which concerned me. He must have been thinking, but never offered up any information.

The only time I was able to get anything out of him was when Father Wehmann, our former priest came for a visit and I asked Zac if he wanted to talk about anything. He said, "No." I asked him if he was worried about anything.

Zac said, "No."

I wanted him to talk so badly. More for me, I suppose. I wanted to know how he was processing all the overwhelming news. I wanted to know if he was alright, but I didn't know how I should talk to him. I didn't want to scare him by bringing up the scary subject. He usually shut that stuff out until it was time to "walk through it." It wasn't time to do that and we still had hope in the trial drug.

"Zac, you have to be worried about something," I protested. I broke his stoic silence. Tears streamed down his checks. "I'm just afraid of when it's going to happen," Zac confessed timidly.

I couldn't contain my tears and I cried with him. Father Wehmann sat quietly with his hands folded and his chin resting on them.

The only other thing he said he was worried about was the way he looked. The steroids puffed him up immensely and I knew he felt trapped in a body he was losing control of.

Setting his worries aside, Zac was making the most out of his days and offering his friendship to those he came in contact - always with a kind word, concern for how their day was going and a sweet smile that didn't fully turn up on his right side because of all the recent brain trauma.

When Zac was transferred out of the PICU to his room on the fifth floor, it was just in time for four of the Minnesota Vikings to come personally to visit him. Zac was so excited! It was even a bigger deal that they came to see him since he was unable to go to their game, three days earlier.

Once the Vikings left Zac's room to go downstairs to the Amplatz lobby, I quickly persuaded Zac to go down as well. Not long after we were in the lobby, Zac was collecting Viking signatures all over his head and giggling in happiness.

CHAPTER 34

that cold november day

We arrived home late the next night after sixteen excruciating day in the hospital. We were welcomed home to signs taped up all over the house that Zac's classmates at Lakeside Elementary had made for him. In addition, my friends Shelley and Lynne came over and washed all of the sheets and made the beds, plus vacuumed and picked up the house!

Between Nathan trying to go into work, working on our kitchen addition that he had started months ago when we thought Zac was stable, driving kids to and from activities and spending time at the hospital, it was difficult to keep the house in order. As for Nic and Jessica, they were busy with school, homework, sports and hospital visits that consumed their days. I was ecstatic to be blessed with such loving friends. The last thing I wanted to do was clean the house.

Zac had made it home for Halloween. He had been so worried he would still be in the hospital. Frankly, I was too because his platelets were still low on Wednesday, the day before we left, but they felt comfortable enough to send him home. I think they made an exception because of how bad Zac wanted to go trick-or-treating and because we were told to "focus on Zac's happiness."

I drew Zac's labs Halloween morning and brought Zac to school because he wanted to go. I was shocked that he would even entertain the idea of going after having a brain bleed and spending sixteen days in the hospital. *Who does that?! Well, Zac did!*

The reception at school was so welcoming. Everyone was excited to see him, including the girls in the office.

I waited all day to hear about Zac's blood work results. I assumed we were in the clear when I got the phone call to bring Zac to Amplatz for more platelets. It would be too dangerous to wait until tomorrow.

In a few hours Zac was supposed to be going trick-or-treating! He was upset when I picked him up from school to bring him back to the hospital where he had only been away from for eighteen hours.

Once situated in the Journey clinic, Zac and I made Tammie, as well as the nurse know how we needed to move things along because of Zac's upcoming Halloween plans. They sensed Zac's urgency and felt bad that we weren't called hours sooner to come down. The platelets were run in as fast as they safely could and we were out of there.

Everything felt routine. It was almost like all the appointments that Zac had in the past nine-and-a half-years. It was almost like Zac hadn't even been in the hospital the last sixteen days or that we were hanging on the last threads of hope for Zac's life. Our main concern was getting back home and getting Zac dressed and ready to go trick-or-treating. That was the present moment and Zac was going to live in it.

"Don't talk to anyone," Zac instructed firmly.

He knew I was a "talker" and once I got going it would be awhile before I would be able to leave. "Don't worry, I won't," I reassured him. I wasn't about to disappoint a child who had one thing after another taken away from him.

We got home at 6:15 pm, hurried in the house and while Zac sat at the kitchen table eating a peanut butter and jelly sandwich, I took over for Jessica to finish getting Lexie dressed in her witchy costume so she could finalize the last details of her Bat-woman super hero costume.

Zac waited patiently for me to help him with his make-up. He wanted to go as a bloody hockey player. With fake blood and eye make-up to give him a black and blue eye – he looked pretty beaten up.

"Oh, yah! I look pretty SICK!" Zac said in approval of my artistic talents.

Zac made his way outside to where his chariot awaited. Well, it was a flatbed trailer that our good friends Lisa and Craig offered to bring over to pull the kids down our mile road – making it easier and more fun for Zac to be with a group. Lizzy, who was a junior, held a soft spot for Zac and recruited a few varsity football players to join Zac. Six guys came out in the cold drizzly rain to support a boy who they had come to care so much about.

Three of Lisa and Craig's kids, plus Nathan, Lexie, Lizzy and Thomas ignored the cold rain and set off with Zac and the football players to collect their treats.

Without even a complaint about his frozen fingers and toes or the fact that he didn't get to carve out the perfect pumpkin he picked out at the pumpkin patch a few weeks ago, Zac came home exclaiming – "This was the BEST HALLOWEEN EVER!!"

Knowing there were no more chemo appointments to bring Zac to really started messing with my head. I was constantly fighting thoughts of – *This will be Zac's last this… and this will be Zac's last time doing that…I hated it!* The way Nathan and I were talked to and the decisions we were told to make really tore me down. I struggled trying to hang on to any form of hope, but reality was not looking as bright as it used to be.

The only hope I had left was in the trial drug. Dr. Moertel soon informed me that we were denied the use of the drug because the company said that it was an "experimental" drug. Nathan and I were instructed to write letters stressing that it was for "compassionate use."

As the clock continued to tick, we waited for the answer to our appeal.

The first week of November, Zac was doing well. He didn't require any platelets all week. He attended school every day and was getting "A's" on almost all of his math and spelling tests. He was so proud of himself!

"I didn't even get to study for them! Ms. Cvar told me I could wait to take the test, but I said I would give it a try!" Zac could hardly contain himself.

"Way to go, buddy! High-five!" I said holding my hand up in front of his left hand.

"Yah, Ms. Cvar was really impressed," Zac said with a smug look on his face.

He WAS Zacstrong! He was so full of life, not letting any moment slip by without acknowledgment or praise. He amazed me in his outlook, excitement and love for people and God – even in the face of death. If he felt sorry for himself, it was only for ten seconds – just enough time to validate his pent up frustrations - and then he moved on.

Zac went to the nurse's office only one day that week to take a nap because he was so tired. Mrs. Johnson, the principal worried that maybe taking him to China Buffet the day before along with her son, Ben, Ms. Cvar, Mr. Maahs, Shelly (one of the speech teachers) her son, Max and Thomas was too much for him. I reassured her that they didn't cause him to be tired. Even Zac stuffing himself wasn't the culprit – it was just the way it was.

"He had a blast! He even came home saying 'That was the best day EVER!'" I told her. "I really appreciate all of you taking him to his favorite restaurant," I said as I wriggled up my nose at his choice of a favorite restaurant. "I can't thank you enough for everything you have done to keep his spirits up. Even when you and Principal Brenda came to visit him in the intensive care and brought him lunch and a kitty cocktail was so much appreciated."

My main goal was to continue to focus on Zac's happiness. It made all the difference in the world to see him smile. For the most part he seemed happy. Big things or little, it didn't matter.

On Friday, November 8, 2013, Zac decided to stay home from school. When he verbalized he was tired and didn't want to go to school, I knew he was not feeling well. I tried to turn my worry into making it a fun day, so once he woke up from a long nap we decided to make Christmas cookies.

Secretly, I was worried that if Zac didn't make it to Christmas he would never get the chance to taste his favorite Christmas cookies one last time. I didn't want to waste this opportunity. This was the same fear I had when Zac said he wanted to go to the Minnesota State Fair and because he was in the hospital for chemotherapy, it didn't look very promising. I worried that this might be his last "State Fair." The last day of the Fair, in a split second decision, I decided I would take Zac and Lexie, even if Nathan didn't want to go. I couldn't deny Zac something that he looked forward to every year. It bothered me that I had to explain to Nathan before he realized why it was so important that he came along. He didn't think like me.

It was difficult to live basing your plans on - if you should go somewhere or do something because it might be the last time. I struggled going to work thinking I needed to make money to help with our finances and at the same time not wanting to be separated from Zac in case something should happen while I was away.

I still didn't feel this was real, but I knew we weren't dealing with the flu. I believed there was still the chance that once we started the Mekinist drug, Zac would be healed or in the least, the cancer would shrink until Dr. Largaespada and his research team would find a way to stop the tumors for good.

Zac and I talked about how he would survive this to go onto do motivational speaking and strengthen the doubtful and empower the unbeliever's to believe in what could be accomplished when you lived in faith and with the courage to rely on God's mercy.

The weekend was pretty low-key, making Zac's favorite Christmas cookies - Cornflake Christmas wreath cookies with the red hot candies and frosting fifteen dozen sugar cookies after church on Saturday, while watching a Christmas movie.

Our routine remained much the same in respect to how we were living. Nathan was working and I was able to put in two shifts at the hospital. Zac was still doing his biomat therapy, oils and now swallowing twenty-nine pills a day. He took them like a champ using only a sip of water. He continued doing everything he knew he needed to do without complaining.

Zac wanted to go to school all the next week and Nathan even took him deer hunting with Shawn, one of his friends on Thursday November 14. Even with Zac's arm not functioning and being on crutches, he was excited to go. He loved being out in nature and hiking in the woods. To him being involved and part of the action was what made him happy. There was always a way to work around Zac's limitations. I suppose that's why we always said, "NEVER GIVE UP!" because if you want something bad enough, you'll figure out a way to make it happen. Zac did.

Friday November 15, 2013. I got up after a night of work, tired as usual and forced myself into the day. I got Lexie up and off to school as Zac finished eating his daily cheese omelet sprinkled with turmeric. Zac mentioned how he was feeling dizzy when he got up and made a few comments wondering about when his weight would start to drop. I was a little concerned his blood pressure medication needed to be lowered now that his body seemed to be adjusting back to his normal. As for his weight, I felt so bad for him! With the amount of steroids he was on, he looked incredibly uncomfortable. I hoped that maybe if I brought him in to the Journey clinic they could give him a diuretic to help take off some of the puffiness.

I drove Zac to school and went back an hour and a half later to drive Zac down to the cities for an appointment with Tammie. I was a bit relieved to have Zac checked over since he hadn't been seen by anyone for ten days - a record for Zac. I thought his visit was just going to be routine, but Tammie for some reason wanted Zac to have another brain MRI. I was put on alert that something could be very wrong. I heard what was said, but I still didn't comprehend what was meant by the words spoken. Tammie brought up planning "fun things." She made it sound more urgent than when she suggested it on October 24th.

I stared at her searching for clarity. I asked if we would have until January 5th, when we were planning a family vacation (first time in seven years) – compliments of the comedy actor, Kevin James. (Mall Cop, Here Comes the Boom, Grown Ups, Zookeeper and Hitch were some of his movies) I was met again with a similar stare and a long pause.

Tammie wasn't sure if Zac would have that long. Nothing more was said. Zac and I left to go home with a decrease in his blood pressure medicine and no diuretic because it wouldn't help in the way I had hoped.

On Friday, sun gave way to the heavy thick clouds that lingered into Saturday the 16th. The November day had a chill in the air that could be felt to the bone if you didn't keep moving. I was glad I had put up most of the Christmas lights and decorations two weeks earlier. It was always brutal trying to hang lights when your fingers froze because of the cold, and I had my work cut out for me. I also wanted to be sure Zac would have the chance to see the light-up figurines - Joseph and Mary with baby Jesus, Frosty, Santa and Rudolph and all the beautiful colored lights strung around the house and trees, like I always put up...just in case.

After making the kids a pancake breakfast, Zac busied himself trying to write his Christmas list. When writing with his left hand proved to be too slow and difficult, he asked if Nic would help him downstairs on the computer. Since Nic was spending time with Zac, I headed outside to continue the long process of raking a big yard with lots of trees. I waited and waited for Nic to come help me, wondering what could be taking him so long. I was getting frustrated that I was doing this huge job all by myself. I peeked in through the walkout sliding glass door and saw Nic and Zac still working on Zac's list. I couldn't help but let my rising hostility give way to a smile. It must be some list! I prayed Zac would live to see another Christmas and Santa would bring him everything he desired.

Nic's time spent with Zac was more valuable to me than having him help me in the yard, so I turned and walked back over to the swing set and resumed raking madly as the cold rain started falling. It took me hours to rake, but I was determined to finish as Nathan and Craig worked on the roof to our kitchen addition. We both felt the urgency to finish knowing winter was just around the corner.

Cold and wet, I was glad to be done raking. I anticipated the warmth of the house and thoughts of food before we would be heading to 5 pm mass when Zac told me he was having balance issues and had fallen four times since I had been outside.

Zac was standing in the living room when I approached him. "Are you feeling alright?"

"Yah. Just my balance and my right hand is numb again," Zac hesitated, "and I'm sorta having a hard time with talking."

"Do you have a headache?" I asked trying not to sound alarmed as my heart shifted into third gear.

"No, just my - my – h-a-...," Zac stumbled on his words.

"Your hand?" I said helping him find the right word.

"Yah. Now I can't use my crutches."

This was extremely different behavior for Zac. I knew I needed to take him into the hospital. At first I thought I should quick eat something because I hadn't eaten for six hours, but then I didn't know if I should call the hospital or take a shower. I was panicking! I needed to get my act together.

I drove Zac down to Amplatz in the dark night as the rain reflected off the cars tail-lights. I would update Nathan as soon as I knew something. Zac was quiet in the front seat next to me. I wished he would talk. I wanted so badly to know what he was thinking.

"Are you nervous?" I asked trying to stay calm myself.

"Yah, kind of."

"What scares you?"

"I'm not sure? Having to go back to the hospital again. I don't want to stay there like last time," Zac confided.

We ended up in the Emergency Room. He had a CT scan, another MRI and lab work up. The brain swelling increased a little more from what Friday's MRI showed and a small brain bleed was detected. I was relieved that it was a small bleed, but I didn't understand the ER resident doctor's demeanor, if it was just "a small brain bleed."

I ended up calling Barb while I waited in Zac's room to let her know what was going on. I needed someone to talk to who "got me." I called Carla as well. Just by talking to them I felt an immediate sense of support…like I didn't have to do this on my own. I was forming my support chain again. It had been one dark scary pit after another that Zac and I were falling in and lately, I needed more than one person to help pull me out – or at least to get to the edge of the pit to where I could rest my chin on until I could steal some fresh air.

I was a little perturbed at Nathan that he didn't drop everything to come with us. I hated when he asked "Do you want me to come with?" For the life of me I didn't understand his way of thinking sometimes. *Didn't he hear about the sudden changes in Zac that I was telling him about? He was standing right there in the kitchen when I was talking to him.* I knew Nic and Jessica could hold down the fort at home. Because I was already so nervous, frustrated at having to go back to the hospital and scared to death of what the doctors would find, I didn't have anything left to coddle and guide Nathan. He was a big boy. He would have to figure this out on his own. I needed to check my anger at the door. I didn't have any room for that and I knew Zac hated fighting. I didn't want him to sense that too.

I never wanted to be a burden to anyone. Barb and Carla almost always found a way to work around whatever they were doing to come to my rescue. I loved how I could tell them what was going on and they would show up. It was such a welcomed relief.

It was late and Carla was busy with her four kids so I told her I would be okay without her. Barb said she and her husband, Quinn, had just finished their dinner and were on their way. I totally spaced it out that they were celebrating his birthday. Lately birthday's, musicals, sporting events had escaped my mind. Life was too serious to have fun. If it wasn't hospital related, we were busy trying to finish up what had to be done with the addition and yard before winter.

Shortly after Barb and Quinn arrived, the resident doctor wanted to speak with me. *"Oh, no! Not again,"* I panicked. Quinn stayed with Zac and helped keep him distracted by playing Temple Run on his Ipod. Barb took my hand and we walked around the corner where the resident reaffirmed that the bleed was small, but it didn't look good. He said surgery wasn't indicated and there really wasn't anything left that they could do other than transfer Zac to the Pediatric Intensive Care and give him high doses of IV steroids to help with the pressure on his brain.

I tried to act tough. I had heard plenty of bad news that I thought I could remain composed. I thought wrong. I was weak - so much weaker than Zac. Zac carried himself with such dignity and grace. He was so mature for an eleven year old.

If I was in Zac's place, I think I would have taken my anger and frustration out on someone a long time ago.

Driving to the hospital that night, Zac did say, "I am so mad I want to swear!"

"Go ahead. Get your anger off your chest. It's okay," I said giving him permission.

Zac thought for just a second and then reconsidered, "Nooo, I shouldn't. It would be a sin."

"Only if you take the name of God in vain – and maybe a few of the really bad words – then – it's a sin."

"Nooo – I shouldn't."

"Zac, you are such a good boy. God won't be mad at you. You need to get rid of some of that stress. Go ahead – say it! Scream it! It's okay – DO IT!" I encouraged wanting him to purge himself of built up anger, I thought he had.

"Okay! - Okay!" Zac's voice rose – "THIS STINKS!"

I smiled. *That's it? This son of mine was way too good and pure. He definitely was a real live angel on earth.* My eyes were open. "Do you feel better?" I asked turning to see his soft pudgy face glowing in the headlights of the cars passing by.

"Yah, I think I do," Zac said with a smirk on his face.

"Can I tell you something?"

"Yah."

"That's not really considered swearing." He knew I didn't like that word, along with "shut-up" so we didn't use them in our house.

"Oh," Zac said and we continued our drive towards the hospital with me holding on to his hand.

Back in the PICU. Barb insisted on staying the night with me and Zac. It was comforting having her there for Zac as well as myself. Without trying, Barb and I could get extremely goofy to the point we would be laughing so hard we'd cry. We would get Zac in on it too. Laughter was the best medicine and even if it was for only a few minutes – we all felt the stress dissipate enough to allow us to breathe easier.

Just as the intensity of the last several hours lessened, Dr. Guillaume came in at 6 am. He said he could do surgery and remove about half of one of the brain tumors, but it wouldn't be a fix – which I already knew. It was his hope that he could relieve a great amount of pressure, but it came with the risk of right-sided paralysis and further brain bleeding. I wasn't sure if I was willing to take that risk

When I asked about draining fluid off of the brain from the new drain that was recently placed, Dr. Guillaume said it wasn't possible because now where the drain sat a septum formed in the pocket where fluid collected. By removing any fluid, it would collapse the pocket and creating an increase in pressure and more than likely a brain bleed.

I couldn't believe this! It was like Zac went through the last brain surgery for

NOTHING! Everything was incurable or in the wrong place or could cause more damage! I felt like I was sitting on a ticking time bomb once again knowing that it didn't matter if I cut the red or blue wire because either one or cutting none – would result I the same deadly outcome.

I continued to pray that the steroids would relieve the pressure and prevent any increase in the bleed. I thanked God for a stable night for Zac and prayed that although our appeal for the trial drug was denied by our insurance company, they would still allow Zac to use it under a "compassionate use" need. I was angered that the insurance company's big-wigs felt that because it was not approved for use for neurofibromatosis (Zac's underlying condition) that they did not want to waste their precious dollars on my son, but were willing to use it on a seventy-year-old man with melanoma.

Dr. Guillaume spoke with other oncologists who felt that surgery would not be in Zac's best interest.

Zac was as stable as he could be with his critical health. He was given the okay to go home since there wasn't much they could do other than continue on the oral steroids to control the brain swelling.

Dr. Moertel and Dr. Guillaume came into Zac's room late afternoon. I was told that although Zac was not given the Mekinist Drug under compassionate care, he was granted the use of it if we agreed to pay out of our pocket. I didn't even have to consider the price. No cost was too high to pay for the chance that I could save my son. Nathan and I agreed to pay the lowest negotiated price of $9,000 a month. I wasn't sure where the money would come from, but I knew we could drain our savings. We would figure it out.

Zac would be the first pediatric patient to use Mekinist. I believed this drug would work and Zac was going to be a major part of a breakthrough. I was eager to get the drug in my hands. It was going to be delivered from across the river, from the east campus. I would give Zac his first dose tomorrow.

Dr. Moertel and Dr. Guillaume explained that the second part to Zac's treatment plan would be another surgery, next week. Dr. Guillaume would remove about half of one of the brain tumors to allow for more room in his brain. Then they would send off a section of the tumor to Dr. Largaespada's lab where they would study it and already be able to determine if the Mekinist drug was working.

I was unprepared for that part of the plan. Thanksgiving was only ten days away. I knew that would mean Zac would be spending it in the hospital. I knew Zac knew that as well. I could see the look of utter disappointment on his face.

Quickly I asked if there would be any harm in pushing the surgery out to the first week of December because Zac had really been looking forward to having Thanksgiving dinner with family and the following day, he had been asked by the Minnesota Wild hockey player, Dany Heatley, to attend their home hockey game watching it in his suite. Dany had visited Zac when he was in the PICU a few weeks earlier and Zac casually asked him for his cell phone number so he could text him. Without a second thought, Dany obliged and they started texting.

Dr. Moertel and Dr. Guillaume looked at each other and agreed it would be okay to postpone the surgery for a week. The plan was set, but the vibe I got from Zac was unsettling. He didn't say anything. He stared straight ahead with a stone-face.

"Zac, what's wrong?" I asked figuring he was upset about another brain surgery. "Don't you want to do the surgery?"

Very quietly with a tear rolling down his cheek, he whispered, "No."

I was shocked. He had never spoken against any treatment plan. He was always agreeable. "But – if it will help get rid of the swelling in your brain and you can get off the steroids – would you do it?"

Just as quietly as he whispered "no," continuing to stare straight ahead, he said, "Yah."

"Okay," I verified. I was relieved he agreed to the surgery. I couldn't bear it if he told me he wouldn't and what that would mean. "Can I ask what you are afraid of?"

"I'm afraid the medicine might not work," Zac confessed.

I sat with him after giving him a hug and a kiss. He continued to not say much. His tears spoke many words. I knew he just wanted to live among his family and friends, doing all the things he used to be able to do. I knew he was incredibly tired of the life of medicines, surgeries and hospital stays. It had been so long since he was able to even have the freedom of running and using both of his arms with strength and ease. Living with his limitations was wearing on him.

Finally after waiting for the drug for several hours, I was told that we could go home and it would be delivered to our home the next morning. Zac was more than ready to get out of the glassed-in room. It was dusk and the sun was setting as we left Amplatz Hospital. Even sitting in the car was relief from the ICU room. It meant we were one step closer to home. Ahh...freedom.

Zac was quiet most of the drive home, so I began asking him questions – like – 'what's your favorite candy - your favorite sport - your favorite movie - your favorite thing to do?' I hoped he thought I was just making conversation, but secretly I wanted to make sure I knew my child. I was afraid with what we were up against that I might not know him as well as I thought I did. I wanted to know EVERYTHING about him because I was afraid I might not have much time with him.

I feared the future even though I had tremendous hope in the Mekinist drug. I didn't want him to be afraid. I wanted to do everything to keep him happy and keep his hope alive.

Much of the ride home, Zac was quiet. I knew he was thinking. I could see it on his face as we drove down a Highway 8 towards home as the headlights flickered off his sweet, angelic face. I wanted so badly for him to open up to me and tell me what he was thinking – what he was feeling – He was smart and he heard plenty of the conversations he had listened in on while playing with his kindle and Ipod. I just wanted to know. I didn't want him to battle with his thoughts, fears and questions or concerns alone.

As nervous as I was to find out the answerer to my question, I took the plunge and calmly asked, "So – what are you thinking?"

Zac continued to stare out the windshield. "Umm...nothing –"

I knew he was thinking of something. "There has to be something going on inside that head of yours," I commented hoping he would feel it was okay to talk.

"Hmm...no." Zac turned his head to look at me and flashed me a sweet grin. Oh, how I loved him!

"Okay," I said feeling a little disappointed that he didn't feel he could open up to me. Although his grin was sweet, I could see something behind his eyes that told me he was holding back from me. I didn't want to push him if he didn't want to talk about it. "If you want to talk, just remember, you can tell me anything."

"I know," Zac simply replied.

I had one more question to ask. I felt like Zac had a certain wisdom that he possessed and I needed to change the subject. "So – if you could change anything about me, what would it be?"

I actually was hoping he would say – "nothing, Mom," but he began speaking. *Oh, boy...*

"Well – you do too much," Zac carefully started. "You need to relax more."

"What do you mean?" I asked thankful that he didn't say I yelled too much or something like that. I listened intently, ready to take everything to heart that he said. I wanted to be a better person and I knew he had answers.

"Well, like you clean too much or you always have to be doing something. You should just sit down and relax and watch a movie with us," Zac honestly spoke.

"Okay. I promise I will try harder. I just want to be the best mom for you guys," I said explaining my reason for asking such a question. Secretly, I was asking because I didn't know how much time we had left if the Mekinist drug didn't work... weeks? Months? A year? I wanted to start my transformation now.

We pulled in our driveway at 6 pm.

Nathan came out of the house. "Hey, buddy, how are you feeling?" Nathan asked as he opened the passenger door to help Zac out. The he turned to me and asked. "Do you still want to take Lexie to gymnastics or do you want to stay home and make dinner?"

Even though Zac chose to have his favorite meal of tacos and it was easy enough to make, I didn't feel like making dinner. I was exhausted. "No, I should take Lexie since I've been gone since Saturday. She probably could use some of my attention."

Nathan slowly helped Zac move towards the base of the garage steps that led into the house. As I shouted out instructions in regards to Zac, Lexie came running out of the house in her leotard, flip-flops and a sweater.

"Lexie, it's cold outside!"

"Jessie told me to hurry!" Lexie explained.

"Hurry, get in! You'll be fine. You'll just have to run fast inside the school," I said as I buckled her in her car seat.

"And – Nathan -," I added approaching him giving him one last instruction, "don't push Zac into eating or doing something he doesn't want to do. He's a bit down."

I knew Nathan always meant well, in his militant ways, but I also knew when Zac didn't need to be pushed. Today he needed more compassion and sensitivity.

"Don't worry, I won't. You better go or you'll be really late." I could tell he was already getting perturbed by my continued instructions. I was just uncomfortable leaving Zac immediately after getting home from the ICU.

By the time I got home with Lexie, Zac was downstairs watching television, relaxing on the reclining loveseat. Even though it was a school night, I let Lexie stay up a little longer than usual and sit downstairs with Zac. Zac cherished his time spent with others and I knew Lexie had spent plenty of time alone when we were gone and enjoyed her brother's company.

Once Lexie was tucked in bed, the rest of us sacked out downstairs and watched a Hallmark Christmas movie. I loved Christmas movies. For the most part they involved some sort of crisis that always ended up working out in the end. There was such hope and magic – something I craved. In my life I dealt with too much sadness, pain and terror that I didn't like engaging myself with those types of realities when I was trying to escape mine.

One by one, Jessica went to bed, then Nathan and reluctantly, Nic. "Morning comes way too fast when you have to get up for school. I'd better get to bed," Nic said as he bent down to give me a kiss on the cheek. I wasn't about to move off the couch where I was comfy and warm under a fleece blanket.

Zac and I continued to watch 'Switching Christmas,' making small talk as we both fought to stay awake. Zac was planning on sleeping in the next morning and would decide if he felt like going to school.

"I think I'm going to go to bed," Zac finally decided as he wiggled his way to the edge of the loveseat.

"Yah, I'm getting pretty tired myself," I said as I got up to grab his crutches and help him down the hallway into the bathroom. "Do you need help in the bathroom?" I asked setting up his toothbrush, still wanting to provide for his independence as much as possible.

"No, I think I can do it."

"Okay. Call me when you're done and I'll help you into your room and we'll say prayers."

As always, we started our prayer to St. Michael the Arc Angel – *"defend us in battle. Be our protection against the wickedness and snares of the devil. May God rebuke him, we humbly pray and do thou, oh Prince, oh Heavenly Host, by the power of God, cast into hell, Satan and all the evil spirits who prowl about the world seeking the ruin of souls."*

"Most sacred heart of Jesus –"

"Have mercy on us."

"Most sacred heart of Jesus –"

"Have mercy on us!"

"Most sacred heart of Jesus –"

"Have mercy on us!!"

The remaining prayers would follow as I blessed Zac with holy water from Lourdes…on his head, his eyes, his heart and right leg. We waited in hope and faith for his complete healing to come, yet one more day.

I kissed him on his soft lips. "The phone is right by your bed. Call me on my cell phone if you need me. Love you, sweet angel."

"Love ya too."

I closed the door and plopped back down on the couch into my spot I had previously nestled into. *I should just go up to bed. It's going to be hard getting up in the morning to get Lexie off to school.* Too late…I was already cozied in and pressing play to resume the previously pre-recorded movie. There was only forty-five minutes left and I could get into bed shortly after midnight.

There was something about the quiet of the night with the fireplace flickering and not having to answer to anyone that was so enticing that I had a hard time giving up to much needed sleep.

12:45 am – and I crawled into bed. It felt so good to be home.

Zac and Chisago Lakes high school football team ready to go trick-or-treating. 10-31-13

CHAPTER 35

wake up call

I jerked awake a little before 5 am by my cellphone ringing to the tune of Transcyberian Orchestra's - 'Carol of the Bells.' It was never too early to get in the Christmas Spirit.

"Zac?" I groggily answered.

"No, Mom, it's Nic. Zac says he has a really bad headache."

"Okay, I'll be right down."

I jumped out of bed, threw on my pajama pants and robe. Nathan stirred. Without him asking, I told him Zac had a bad headache.

I knelt down by the side of Zac's bed. "How bad of a headache is it – on a scale of one to ten?"

Zac hesitated – "F - I - V – E," he said beginning his labored breathing he had done the last time he had a brain bleed. *Great, his five meant an eight or a nine, I worried.*

"Mom, I woke up to Zac trying to call you. He was having a hard time dialing the phone and he could barely talk so I took the phone from him to call you," Nic explained a bit stressed.

"Thanks, Nic. You're a good big brother to Zac."

I was so glad they shared a room and that Nic was there to look out for Zac. I was pleased as to how they got along, for the most part. I was actually surprised when I asked Nic if we ever got our addition done and put on another bedroom – if he would want his own room or share it with Zac. He said, "I like sharing a room with Zac. It would be weird not to."

I ran upstairs to grab the stash of narcotics. Zac was beyond Tylenol. As I held the cup for Zac to take a sip of water with his Hydrocodone, I remembered what Dr. Guillaume had said in reference to the pressure on Zac's brain – "It would probably be more comfortable for Zac with his head elevated. That way the pressure is more easily dispersed."

Oh no. I had him lying flat on his back with only one pillow to prop his head all night! I grabbed another pillow and place it under his head. "Is your head any better?" I hoped, with adjusting the elevation of his head.

"Yah, maybe a little."

"Or do you want to go on the couch where you can be reclined? I'll lie on the couch next to you."

"Yah. The – c-c-o- u- c- h," Zac stammered looking for the right word.

Something was wrong and I was at loss for what to do. We hadn't been home from the hospital for even eleven hours! What could the doctors do differently aside from loading Zac up with more steroids? We needed the Mekinist - AND –NOW! It should be delivered in a couple of hours.

Very slowly, I got Zac up to the side of the bed. He had such difficulty moving and his balance seemed off. If he couldn't make it to the couch, I decided I would carry him, baby-step by baby-step, Zac made his way where I had covered it with a thin black fleece blanket covered with little white ghosts. I tucked him in and sat by him for a moment, stroking his arm as I watched him. He seemed a little more comfortable. I prayed that the headache was attributed to the increasing pressure of lying flat the past five-and-a-half hours.

I crawled under the blanket I had wrapped myself in only a few hours earlier. I was afraid to close my eyes, but my exhaustion from the past three days won and I drifted off to sleep.

After fifteen minutes, maybe twenty, I awoke to Zac's breathing, which was becoming more heavy. The pain was increasing. In between each deep contraction-like breathing, he was quiet and appeared to be sleeping. I lay there and listened minute after minute, dozing momentarily.

"Zac, is it getting worse again?" I asked after one headache contraction that seemed worse than the previous.

"Maybe ah – ah – a – l – I –t – t- l – e." Zac searched for the right word.

The minutes passed so slowly without much change in comfort for Zac.

Nic was now awake and getting ready for school. When he saw me reposition myself on the couch, he walked closer and leaned over the big over-stuffed chair. "Is he okay?" Nic whispered, tilting his head towards Zac.

"I'm not sure what's going on, but I think after I get Lexie off to school, I'll be calling Dr. Moertel."

I continued to lay on the couch motionless after Nic and Jessica shut the door from the house to the garage. Nathan had left for work fifteen minutes earlier. I knew that meant it was 6:45 am. I thought I had thirty-five more minutes to lie on the couch and maybe catch a couple minutes of sleep. I even entertained the idea of having Lexie skip school if I fell asleep and didn't wake up in time to get her on the bus.

Ten minutes passed and Zac's breathing became more labored and he started to moan occasionally.

"Zac, where's your pain now on the scale of one to ten?"

In a quiet whisper, he said, "Seven."

I couldn't wait around to give him more pain medicine. I couldn't stand to see him in such pain again. I feared it would escalate and be a replay of October 19th all over again.

Even though Zac wasn't crying or complaining, his labored breathing was enough for me to slip into my white doctor's coat. I wasn't about to sit back and allow for his pain to get out of control this time!

As scared as I was, I was becoming angrier. *How could God allow such a pure innocent boy to suffer so greatly?! He had nothing but love for God - above all else. He was a young eleven-year-old boy so full of faith. Where was God in all of this?!*

I grabbed the bottle of oxycodone. It had been only about two hours since I had given him 5mg. I wished I would have given him the full 10mg then. I brought his cup that he used for brushing his teeth to his lips for a sip of water and popped the tablet in his mouth. I prayed for relief from his pain.

I sat with him for a bit before I went upstairs to wake Lexie up and get her off to school. I figured I might as well since I planned that I would be taking Zac back to the hospital. My hands began to shake as I brushed Lexie's hair. I tried to wait as long as I could before calling Dr. Moertel, but as soon as Lexie was on the bus, I ran inside and called his cell phone.

"Chris Moertel."

"Dr. Moertel, its Carol Ann. Zac's not doing so well. He has a horrible headache that he woke up from a little before 5 am." I continued to explain how everything came about and what I had done to try and make him comfortable, which hadn't resolved anything. "Do you think its pressure or a brain-bleed?" I finished in a panic as I started to cry.

Dr. Moertel asked when I last gave Zac his steroid. With all of the commotion, I was late in giving it to him! My hope returned thinking that would help.

"Give him the Decadrone and call me back in an hour and let me know if you see an improvement," Dr. Moertel instructed. "If not, I want you to come in to the hospital."

I took the small white pill out of the medicine cup I had prepared and set it on the coffee table by where he laid on his biomat. He would be skipping the other ten pills. I popped one more pill in to Zac's mouth.

"Zac, I'm going to take a quick shower," I said in anticipation that I would be taking him to Amplatz. I wasn't sure how long we'd have to stay this time.

Nervous to leave him, I frantically – but in a calm-sort of way made sure he would have everything he might need in arms-reach.

"Zac, I called dad. He's on his way home, but here's the phone in case you need to call my cell phone – but I'll hurry and shower and come right back down. Here's the remote in case you feel better and can watch tv. Bear-bear is right here," I said as I tucked him I next to Zac. "Okay, I'll be right back."

"M – a - a – o – m – m…" Zac struggled to speak.

I knew he needed something. *What did I forget?* I quickly scanned the area around where Zac listlessly reclined.

"P – p - p – p – l – e – e – z – z…"

That's all he had to say and I thought I knew what he needed. "Do you need the urinal?"

He nodded his head half a nod.

"Sure." I ran into his bedroom where I set it overnight, just in case he would have needed it. It was such an ordeal if he needed to go to the bathroom in the middle of the night – especially now that he couldn't use his right arm. This was just easier.

I helped Zac go to the bathroom and set it by him on the loveseat in case he would need it later.

I don't think I took a faster shower than I did that morning. I jumped out of the shower, brushed my hair and threw on my clothes. I stopped. *Was Zac calling me?*

Nothing.

There it was again.

I ran to the banister and leaned over the railing as I called down. "Zac? Do you need me?"

Silence for a moment.

"M – a – a – o – mm..."

He needed me!!! I ran down the stairs, two at a time and I saw Zac slumped over with vomit down the side of his face, on his blanket and the urinal in his left hand with a small amount of vomit that made it in there.

Oh, my God! I moved quickly towards Zac, then realizing I needed a towel to clean him up, I ran into the laundry room and raced back to him.

"Oh, Zac! I'm sorry! I'm sorry!!" I felt horrible that I left him to shower. I hated the idea that he was all alone to fend for himself. I hoped he wasn't moving much because his pain was so bad, not because he couldn't.

I knew his pain was horrendous and he couldn't move. I quickly called Dr. Moertel. I was slightly out of breath. I explained that Zac was worse and what just happened.

"Bring him in to Amplatz, but don't go to the ER. They will want to admit him to the ICU. Instead, bring him up to the Journey Clinic. I'll call them to alert them that you are coming and what is going on," Dr. Moertel's voice did not waver.

"So just go straight up to the Journey Clinic?" My mind was fried.

"Yes."

"Okay," I whispered. I could feel myself ready to cry. "He's in so much pain –"

"I know. We'll give him some morphine when you get here."

I wiped the tears from my eyes. *Time to hold it together.* "Nathan's on his way home. He should be here any minute – so we should be there in about an hour or so."

As I resumed cleaning Zac up, I could hear Nathan walking in the house. "Nathan?"

He came down the stairs and stared at the scene before his eyes, not quite sure of what to do. He waited for my instructions.

"He's not doing so good?"

"We're heading to the hospital," I informed.

"What do you want me to do?"

"Help me change his clothes. Then you change out of your uniform and stay with him while I pack and finish getting ready." In my fear I lost my brave-front and started to cry. I worried Zac was having a massive brain bleed and Nathan and I decided not to do anything except keep him comfortable. *Was this the end?*

Together Nathan and I carried Zac up the flight of stairs, out into the garage and into the van. I sat closely next to him, supporting him in my arms.

The drive to the hospital was the longest ever. "Drive faster," I commanded

Nathan as I held Zac close. I could see how intense the pain was. I felt helpless as I watched him lie there silently – not a word of complaint.

Nathan pulled the car around to the front of Amplatz. As soon as we stopped, Zac threw up again. This time I was prepared and had one of the blue emesis bags on hand. Nathan got out of the car just as a guy from the valet parking approached.

"We need patient escort! Tell them we need a cart! Not a wheelchair!" I ordered. I started crying out of fear for what lay ahead. I was so afraid of the pain that Zac was experiencing and what it meant. I felt so guilty that he was going through all of this excruciating pain all over again, for one too many hours without the appropriate pain meds. *I shouldn't have worried about taking a shower and washing my hair! We could have been here sooner.*

"Hurry!" I sobbed out of desperation.

Not quite running, but more of a hurried jog, we passed through Amplatz lobby, down the corridor through the electronic double doors and to the elevator. Without looking directly at the people we passed, I could feel them staring at me falling apart as I raced my precious child for help. I stared straight ahead, only turning my head momentarily as I whispered soothingly, but firmly to Zac to "Hang on, we'll be upstairs in a minute and get you some medicine to take away your pain. Hang in there, baby."

We were quickly directed to an all too familiar room where I had taken Zac so many times before for a clinic visit, blood or platelet transfusion. He was always so bright and chipper – talking with Simon and Nika at the front desk – to joking around with the nurses or sharing what he had recently hunted or hockey games he attended or thrilling events such as trick or treating or his excursion to China Panda. But, not this time. No one had ever seen him in this state of being.

Deanna, a nurse Zac frequently had, helped position the cart against the wall.

"Can you get him something for pain – like morphine?" I anxiously pleaded, praying I wouldn't meet any resistance.

"Of course. I know Dr. Moertel called ahead of your arrival and said he was putting orders into the computer. They should be in. I'll go check," Deanna calmly spoke.

Zac laid there motionless except for the slight rise and fall of his chest as he resumed his rhythmic breathing.

I leaned over the bedrail and kissed his sweet soft face again, reassuring him relief from his pain was moments away. "Deanna just went out to get your medicine. She'll be right back."

I stared at Nathan, terrified. I knew Nathan was feeling the same terror as I watched him raise his arms and run his hands slowly through his military cut hair. He usually did that when he was stressed. He forcefully exhaled.

The only relief I felt was when Deanna came back and injected Zac with morphine and a few minutes later, Zac's breathing became relaxed.

Somewhere between the drive to the hospital and from the first moments we got into the room in the Journey clinic, I called my sister Barb, Carla and Father Al.

Barb showed up first. There was no joking around to get Zac to laugh and forget his troubles. Not this time. There was little talk. Mostly silence as we waited for Dr. Moertel to come in.

Barb and I stared at one another in dismay as Dr. Moertel came in with a loud booming voice. "It doesn't look like you're feeling so good there, Zac."

"Does he not know how bad off Zac is?" I telepathically asked Barb with widened eyes in shock. I figured he knew how serious it was from our phone call a few hours earlier.

Dr. Moertel continued to speak loudly, so hoping he would get the hint without me being rude, I whispered, "He's in a lot of pain. The morphine seems to be kicking in, but he did throw up a second time from the pain once we pulled up front."

Not much was known without having a CAT scan. Dr. Moertel said he had already talked with Dr. Guillaume and they both agreed that surgery could be a possibility to reduce the swelling. My dying hope flickered and grew into something brighter. I had thought surgery would no longer be an option.

It was close to noon when Dr. Guillaume stopped in briefly before we were headed down to CT. I was grateful for his presence and the time he took to answer my frantic questions. Having Father Al cancel his entire schedule to be with us was so appreciated.

"I'm going to check the surgery schedule while we wait for the results." Dr. Guillaume had a look of determination on his face. "We'll discuss the results and our options back up in the Journey Clinic very soon."

There was no real increase in bleeding, but the swelling was significant.

Dr. Moertel and Dr. Guillaume met up with Nathan and me where we nervously waited with Zac who appeared to be resting comfortably with the morphine and Decadron on board. Barb and Father Al were gathered around Zac in prayer.

Surgery was an option. Dr. Guillaume felt surgery would be risky, but he thought he could safely remove half of the swelling. I was elated! I was grateful there was still something we could do.

"Now keep in mind," Dr. Guillaume cautioned, "surgery is not a cure."

"Yes, we understand," I spoke for Nathan, as well as myself.

"By doing surgery, how much time would it buy?" Nathan asked.

"Three, maybe four months – if he doesn't develop a brain bleed before that. But eventually we will be facing the same problems with swelling," Dr. Guillaume honestly predicted.

"But, by doing the surgery, then we will have the chance to use the Mekinist!" Without barely taking a breath, Nathan eagerly said, "I say we do the surgery. Zac didn't come this close to getting the chance to use the Mekinist, not to even use it!"

I wanted to take any chances – if it meant the possibility of saving Zac's life. Nathan and I believed that he didn't come all this way for nothing. We had such hopes in what was going to "be" as a result of Zac using the Mekinist.

But something inside me was unsettled. I lowered the bedrail and leaned over Zac and whispered, "Zac, they can do surgery!" I thought Zac would be relieved to hear something could be done, but there was that heavy feeling in the pit of my stomach again. *Maybe it was fear?*

Zac's eyes remained closed. He had been sleeping, not moving the slightest bit for the last couple of hours. *This poor child! He had suffered so much.* I knew he had to be exhausted from the six hours of unrelenting pain. I was relieved the medicine was working and he was able to sleep.

CHAPTER 36

the ultimate decision

Surgery was on and we waited with Zac in his pre-op room while questions were answered, check lists were completed and the consent for surgery was signed. Zac hadn't spoken a word since before we left for home. He lay there motionless, sleeping for the past several hours.

As nervous as I was, my hope was back and gave me new strength. The support of Barb, Father Al and knowing my parents were on their way kept me standing. Dr. Guillaume came in to the small white room to go over the surgical procedure, what he expected and to answer any further questions.

I did have a question, but I hesitated to ask it because I felt it was a dumb question and I knew what Dr. Guillaume's answer would be. *I'll just let it be* - and Dr. Guillaume was out the door.

We all gathered around Zac as Father Al led us in prayer. Our trust was in God.

While we waited for Zac to be taken into surgery, I thought of all his suffering up to this point. It was more than anyone should ever have to endure and Zac did it without complaining. Yes, he hated it, but he knew complaining wouldn't make it any better. I couldn't understand how he did it.

It brought to mind the screen-saver that Zac, a few months earlier, had changed his Ipod to. It was a passage from the Old Testament of the Bible, written in black and white –

'Come to me you who are weary and heavily laden, and I will give you rest'
- Jesus

One day while Zac was in the hospital for one of his chemo weeks and I was handing him his Ipod back after charging it, I felt it was a perfect time to ask my burning question – "How come you decided to put that scripture verse as your screen saver?" I wasn't sure if he actually knew what it meant. I knew he was spiritual, but he was only eleven years old. *Did he understand more deeply than I gave him credit for?* I wanted to hear his reason. I casually looked at him so he wouldn't think I was making a big deal out of it.

He looked briefly at me, then looked down, shrugged his shoulders and said, "Emm – eh –ohh" as if saying – "I don't know."

I wasn't sure if he was embarrassed or afraid he was disappointing me by having that for a screensaver. I felt it best to leave it alone. I didn't want to force him if he didn't feel like talking.

With the hum of light conversation in the pe-op room, I suddenly reflected on several of my in-depth conversations with Zac. I thought more about his suffering and I suddenly began to think and worry whether surgery would cause him more harm than good.

Surgery was minutes, maybe seconds away. We had already agreed to go forward with surgery. That was that. Then Dr. Guillaume came back in Zac's room.

"Sorry, I just forgot to sign one last paper."

Something in my head told me to ask my silly question. *"Just ask!"* I got up the nerve and asked – "Dr. Guillaume, I have a question for you," I light-heartedly began. "I pretty much think I know your answer to my question – but- if Zac was your child, would you go ahead with the surgery?"

He was silent and stared blankly at me.

I had a sudden stab of fear piercing my heart. *Oh, no! He's not answering my question as quickly as I assumed he would.*

"Ahh, umm…well –" Dr. Guillaume uncomfortably stammered.

The room fell silent.

Feeling bad for Dr. Guillaume, I swallowed hard and answered for him with another question. "You wouldn't do the surgery?"

"No, I don't think I would."

Part of me hated myself for asking the question. I didn't know what to think now. I completely trusted him and by not proceeding with surgery, it meant death was imminent. My heart sank into my gut. I suddenly felt like I was going to throw up. "But you said you thought you would be able to safely do the surgery?"

"Yes, but I don't know for sure." Dr. Guillaume paused. "Could we go somewhere else to talk?"

I knew even though Zac was sleeping quietly, he could hear. I was pleased Dr. Guillaume respected Zac enough to put this unpleasant conversation on hold to spare him any further stress.

Father Al, Barb, Nathan and I followed Dr. Guillaume around the nurse's station to a vacant room tucked in the corner and closed the door. He looked squarely at Nathan and me and said, "The tumor is growing rapidly and because of the countless chemo treatments and radiation, Zac's brain is friable. The last time I did surgery, his brain tissue in certain areas, when manipulated, easily bled. The tissue is very easily shredded. I'm not saying we can't do surgery, I'm just not sure how it will turn out."

I was very uncomfortable with the conversation. I wasn't about to let Zac's life end without exploring all aspects of surgery. "Have you done this type of surgery on another child in a similar scenario?"

"Yes, back in Washington. The parents decided to go ahead with the surgery. It was messy – with a lot of bleeding. I couldn't help but wonder if I did him more harm than good."

Nathan and I asked a few questions and without asking point-blank, we got the feeling the boy never made it out of the ICU alive.

Dr. Guillaume could see our despair. "No decision you make is the wrong decision. Whatever you choose, you don't want to be left with regret."

The tension had grown incredibly from only moments earlier when our hope had been restored.

"I think we should go ahead with surgery," Nathan spoke, breaking the silence.

Just then, Carla tip-toed into the room and walked behind me and put her arm around me with a look of confusion and deep concern on her face. She knew something was really wrong. I turned to her and sobbed.

"It's okay, it's okay," Carla comforted, trying to find the impossible right words.

"I don't know what to do. I don't know – what – to – do!!" I started shaking with fear as everyone stood in silence with the ultimate question hanging over our heads – waiting for an answer.

I didn't know how a father or a mother could ever make such a decision – especially when Nathan and I fought with everything that we had to keep Zac going...to give him the best life possible. I didn't want to be responsible for making the decision, so I asked everyone's opinion.

Barb and Carla were at a loss for words. Father Al spoke honestly when I turned the question on him. He answered with yet another question – "How much more suffering does he have to go through?"

I didn't like what I heard. Where was the hope in all of this? How was I supposed to know how this would all play out?

"I think you and Nate should spend some time talking alone," Father Al suggested in a parental tone.

As obedient children, everyone turned to exit the room one after the other leaving Nathan and I alone in the room. We stared silently at each other not wanting to speak. I stepped forward and he met me halfway and we embraced, holding each other tightly as we cried.

"How are we going to decide? I don't want to hurt him," I spoke first.

"I still think we should do it. The Mekinist is right here! What if we decided NOT to do surgery and we find out months later that it would have worked?!" Nathan confidently said.

"But what if he doesn't make it through the surgery? What about Nic, Jessica and Lexie not being able to say goodbye?" I continued to cry as I spoke of such finality.

"Well, then God makes that decision. I still think Zac is the "ONE" who is supposed to use the Mekinist – to show the world what it will do," Nathan added.

"- And call it the ZacAttack?" I found myself smile slightly in hope that Nathan was right.

We both stood there, staring at on another, still afraid to make a final decision. Something continued to gnaw at me about proceeding with surgery, the same way it did with asking Dr. Guillaume my "dumb" question. "I still don't know, Nathan. What if he never gets to leave the ICU?"

"Just think of it this way – Dr. Guillaume said Zac could have three or four more months if surgery works out. By then he'll have had the chance to use the Mekinist and - what if it works?! I really think we have to try." Nathan's reasoning was convincing.

Nathan felt so strongly about trying. I, on the other-hand continued to struggle with that unsettling gnawing that continued to eat away at my core. I didn't know what it was really trying to tell me. I just knew by saying "No" to surgery, I felt like I was giving up on Zac – something we said we would never do. I felt like I was handing my son over. I couldn't do it! I didn't want to make the ultimate decision either – to just stop everything and wait for death or try for a possible chance at life – but at what expense to Zac?

"Okay, we'll go ahead with surgery if that's what you feel strongly about. We'll let God decide," I concluded.

After what seemed like an hour, we stepped out of the room and walked part-way down towards Zac's room where Father Al, Barb, Carla and now Emily, our social worker were gathered, talking quietly among themselves when Dr. Moertel briskly approached them saying, "What's going on? I heard that surgery might be called off."

Emily moved towards me. I was happy to see her. Something about her brought me comfort. I talked with her a little before Dr. Moertel made his way towards Nathan and I, as I faintly heard Father Al telling Dr. Moertel to go and talk privately with us.

Inside the corner room where we stood only moments ago, Dr. Moertel came clean with Nathan and me. "I have to apologize. I started thinking of Zac as an experiment to see how the Mekinist, together with surgery, would work on the cancer cells and I stopped thinking about him as a person."

I was a bit taken-aback, but none of that mattered in this moment with what was staring us in the face. The three of us rehashed the proceeding conversations until Nathan sternly looked at Dr. Moertel and point-blank asked him, "Do you honestly think the Mekinist will work? What percentage of a chance would you give it?"

"Honestly? I don't think it's going to work. I'd give it maybe a twenty percent chance. I really think the cancer is too far gone for the Mekinist to catch up with it."

The look on Nathan's face was complete devastation. We had just decided to move forward with surgery. We still had a glimmer of hope and now, to be told our only reason that Zac suffered so long – to reach the *possibility* of a cure that the Mekinist held for him – was only a twenty percent chance!

I felt beaten down. I had picked myself up so many times and I was just finding my strength to get to my knees and now I was flat on my face. My hope was gone.

"Nathan, we can't do it. I can't put Zac through another surgery only to cause him more pain. I don't think he'll make it through surgery and if he survives surgery, I know he wouldn't want to stay in the ICU only to be in pain, completely paralyzed or unable to speak – only to die there. He wouldn't want that. He'd want to go home." As brave as I was speaking, I could start to feel myself die inside.

Tears rolled down my face. I was surprised I had any left.

Nathan was solemn. He hung his head and quietly spoke trying not to let his voice crack in his grief. "I was so sure the Mekinist was going to work. We were so close – but hearing what you just said, Doc, I don't think it's worth it." Nathan broke down and put his hand to his forehead as he pressed his fingers into his temples.

Momentarily, I became the strong one and wrapped my arms around him.

"I'm really sorry guys. I'm so sorry." Dr. Moertel stood there for a moment before asking, "Do you want me to go out there and tell them surgery is off?"

"Yes," I whispered, as I hung onto Nathan.

When Nathan and I were ready to leave the corner room, I walked out and right into Zac's room where he continued to rest. I held his hand and kissed him gently as my tears dripped on his face. "Hey, Zac, you don't have to have surgery. Is that okay with you?"

Zac heard me. He didn't speak, but gave me a slight nod of approval. I remember him clearly saying only twenty-four hours earlier when we were waiting to be discharged from the PICU that he didn't want to have another brain surgery. It took a lot to finally get the message, but I did.

I was freeing him. No more surgeries – no more. I had to let him go. He was dying. I was not ready. I didn't want him to leave me, but by staying – it would only involve inflicting him with more pain. I couldn't do that to him for my benefit in trying this one last thing – the trial drug.

I knew Zac hated sitting on the sidelines although he NEVER ONCE complained. He only wished. He found excitement and glory when the hockey players skated up to him standing on the bleachers – raising their sticks to him or waving at him. He soaked up the energy the football players extended to him as they reached out to him to give him "knuckles" and he relished in the attention poured on him by his sister, Jessica's soccer team when they surrounded him for good luck and words of encouragement pre and post games.

I realized I had to let his wishes be heard and let him pass to a place I could not go with him. I had been with Zac every step of the way up to this moment, but now, I knew he would have to lead me. Up to this point, I thought I knew what pain was. I knew heartbreak from a broken engagement, three miscarriages and the separation from Nathan when he was serving in the military overseas, but I had never felt this type of pain where it felt like your heart was being pulled from your chest – half of it removed and the remaining shoved back into a hole now much too big for what was now barely beating.

Carla volunteered to go pick up Nic from hockey practice and then to drive to our house to get Jessica and Lexie who were there making dinner with Debbie Krenz.

Nic was confused as to why Carla had the coach call him off the ice. He kept asking questions and all Carla dared to say was, "I'm not sure, but your mom wanted me to come get you." She knew the news would be devastating for the kids and should come from Nathan and me.

Back home, Carla felt the challenge of trying to hurry Jessica, Lexie and Debbie to finish preparing their dinner and quickly eat so they could get on the road. The urgency to leave was great.

Without alarm, Nic, Jessica and Lexie were off to a place that would change their lives forever. I don't know how Carla was able to maintain her composure and keep the kids from not having to suffer one second more with the agony and devastation that was only miles ahead. That was Carla. She had such a sense of what others needed and always put herself out there to help in any way possible. I was so glad she was thinking for me and went to pick up Nic, Jessica and Lexie. My mind shut down and I had a hard time focusing on what was going on around me. I wanted to make sure Zac suffered no more pain. As his mother, that was my last wish for him.

I also now had the job to inform my other children that their brother was dying. I had warned Nic and Jessica three, maybe four other times that Zac was extremely sick and his life was in danger, but this time it wasn't a warning. *How would I utter those words? How was I to help Lexie who was only five-years-old, understand?*

When Carla got to the hospital, Nathan and I met Nic, Jessica and Lexie outside of Zac's room. With the assistance of the Child Life Specialist, which was more for Lexie, we told them the news in that same small green room that we sat in only a month ago to tell them of Zac's medically predicted outcome. Back then I still had a small sense of hope because of the Mekinist, but now, for the first time, all of my hope had vanished.

Slowly Zac's room filled up with close family, including his "adoptive big brother," Jake Parenteau, his grandparents, close aunts, uncles and cousins. Father Wehmann came by and Father Al had remained by his bedside since 11 am that morning. It was now after 7 pm.

The room was lightly dimmed. I put my phone on to play all of the comforting Christian songs that Zac loved, from – Chris Tomlin, Sidewalk Prophets, to Jeremy Camp and Mercy Me. Everyone talked quietly among the rears. It all felt so final now.

I now came to accept the opportunity of making the final memories that the Child Life Specialist talked to me about a month ago when Zac was in the ICU for his first brain bleed. I wasn't ready then to accept that fate for Zac. I was actually angry that she suggested that Zac and our family do a hand mold or read the books on preparing your child or siblings for death. He was still living and breathing. We still had hope and I didn't want to scare Zac when he didn't want to talk about the possibility of dying.

Everything changed so quickly. Our time with Zac was now limited to hours or possibly up to a week, no one knew for sure.

Zac's breathing started to become labored again and his blood pressure became high which told me he was in pain again. I was told he couldn't be with the amount of morphine he had been given, but his breathing repeated the same contraction-like wave pattern as earlier that morning. I wasn't about to allow my child to suffer any further, so when I thought he needed the morphine, he was given the morphine.

"It's okay, Zac," I tried to comfort through tears, "if you want to go now – you can."

Our plan was to get hospice care into place for the next day in our home. We had the choice of staying in the hospital in hospice care or be at home. I knew Zac loved home more than anything. As scary as it seemed, it would be more comfortable for us all to be in the coziness of our own surroundings.

I continued to remind Zac that we were taking him home tomorrow. I wanted him to know before he was to depart this earth that he would have one last chance to go home to where he liked to play Xbox with his brother or his friends, or where we had family night and ate dinner downstairs and watched a movie.

I wasn't so sure we were going to make it home. I had continued to post entries on Caringbridge throughout the day to keep everyone informed as to where Zac was at. I knew there were many people who loved and adored Zac. I felt they deserved to know what was going on. I knew many of them wanted to be able to say their "goodbyes," but not at the hospital.

Barb was in the process of setting up a sign-up for friends to come over for about fifteen minute increments. The plan would be put into place once we got Zac home and settled.

Once everyone left and it was just Nathan, Zac and me, we began reading, one by one, the texts and Caringbridge guestbook messages to Zac. I wanted to make sure he knew how much he was loved and how much he touched countless numbers of people's lives.

I kept telling him over and over, "You did a good job. You are such a GOOD boy. I am so proud of you!"

Zac struggled more with his breathing to the point it scared me. I had a difficult time believing the hospice nurse when she said "It sounds bad, but it is not painful for him." I was told that his death would be quiet and peaceful and he would just fall asleep. This was anything but peaceful! A few times his breathing changed and I thought he would be leaving us in a moment or two, but then he started up with his gurgly breathing.

It was 1:33 am.

Nathan was tired and so was I. I had just finished posting another Caringbridge entry and Nathan curled up to sleep on the fold-down couch that I had slept on a hundred times. I slipped my pajama pants and long underwear top on to be a little more comfortable until the sun came up in a couple of hours. I put the bedrail down and I pulled the recliner chair up as close to the side of Zac's bed as I could. I wanted him to know I wasn't going to leave his side. As tired as I was, I wasn't about to miss out on any of the time I had left with him. How tired I was, was nothing compared to the suffering he was going through.

After adjusting myself and the chair several times, I ended up dozing off with my feet now planted on the floor, my body bent over my lap and my head lying on a pillow by Zac's shoulder. I slept twenty minutes! I was afraid I slept hours. I was still holding on to Zac's hand which still felt warm, but after checking his nailbeds,

I noticed they were slightly bluer. His breathing was still gurgly, but quieter than what it had been. I scanned the monitor for his blood pressure. It was relatively lower than what it was from when he was struggling with his breathing when I suspected he was in pain.

I resumed caressing my fingers up and down his arm as I reassured him, "It's okay, baby. I'm right here with you. I'm right here."

I wanted to be strong for him. I wanted him to feel safe, but in my sorrow I began to weep again. I didn't want to let my son go. I knew now that I needed him more than he needed me.

"Zac?" I whispered, picking my head up off the pillow that was positioned next to Zac. "It's okay with me if you want to go to Jesus now." I rested my chin on the back of my other hand as I watched him continue to breath.

CHAPTER 37

going home

November 20th, 2013

Before the sun came up, I washed my face and got myself dressed. I wanted to be ready to take Zac home when everything was all arranged. I didn't want to stay in the hospital when it could no longer offer me any hope.

Jim was our nurse. Zac and I always liked Jim. He was a happy, quirky kind of guy about five foot-five-inches tall and balding on top. He was a man of compassion and did a great job in making sure Zac was well taken care of before we were ready to go home.

Dr. Moertel, Tammie, Dr. Jess Barnum, Dr. Sadak, Dr. Sidel and several other doctors, nurses and other hospital staff stopped by to say their final goodbyes to Zac. I was becoming numb to the finalities of the goodbyes. I was slowly feeling myself die alongside Zac. *So – this is what it feels like when there is no hope?* I still couldn't believe this nightmare was my reality. I continued to walk through it because I had to be functioning for Zac. I didn't want to let him down.

Papers were signed and instructions were given to me if I needed to give Zac meds on our drive home. We left the fifth floor of Amplatz for the very last time. We went down the back way to be as discrete as possible to avoid the onlookers. I almost wanted them to see. I wanted to shout *"Can't you see! My son is dying!"* I wanted them to take some of my pain away. I didn't want to do this. I didn't want to face what was ahead of me, but I knew I had to. I was terrified!

It gave me courage to know my sisters, Carla, dad, mom and brother-in-law, Dan were at the house waiting for us and getting things set up. The hospital bed was to be delivered along with the oxygen, medication and other supplies. I wanted the family room in the basement to look comforting and peaceful for Zac – the way Zac felt it to be.

I cradled Zac in my arms as Nathan drove. My brain was racing. I had flashes of Zac's life and I thought of all the things he wouldn't get to do. I was disappointed knowing we wouldn't be able to take our family vacation to Florida like we had planned for January 5th. Zac wouldn't get the chance to meet Kevin James, like I had been arranging with Kevin's manager, Robert. The kids were so excited to finally be going on a family vacation.

Bryan, our friend wanted so much to do something nice and lift Zac's spirits up, so after he asked me who Zac's favorite actor was, I told him – Kevin James.

"I've got an idea," Bryan thought out loud, "but don't say anything to Zac until I know where this is going."

Bryan only had to make one phone call to Kevin James's managers, Robert, Scott and Jeff to leave a message. The following day, Bryan received a returned phone call. He was shocked at the quick response that he at first thought it was a joke. He was elated for Zac when Jeff said, "Yah, Kevin loves doing things like this! What were you thinking?"

When Bryan explained Zac's grave situation, Kevin was more than willing to comply. I took over on trying to arrange the details with Robert, but told him maybe Kevin could come visit us because we didn't know how our financial situation would be if we had to pay for the $9000 a month trial drug.

"Aside from that, what would you like to do?" Jeff asked.

Not quite understanding what he was getting at, I told him our previous intention of a family vacation and Zac's wish to visit Disney World, Sea World, Universal Studio's and to meet Kevin James. It was perfect when we found out that Kevin lived in Florida. Our next phone conversation, Scott informed me that Kevin volunteered to pay for our entire Florida trip! I was so excited for the kids.

I was nervous even thinking of taking Zac away from the hospital and doctors, but Tammie had sternly encouraged me to "Keep Zac happy – take a family vacation where Zac wanted to go." I felt her urgency, but I still was in denial. *We'll go on a vacation, just in case, but Zac is going to beat this.*

I don't know why, but for some reason as I held Zac in my arms on our drive home I felt compelled to call Kevin James's managers. I don't know what I expected, but I wanted Zac to know I tried to make his wish come true. I guess I just wanted to know I did everything in my power to bring him happiness.

"Zac's not going to be able to make the trip," I bravely told Robert. "We are on our way home from the hospital and I felt I needed to call you for some reason. Zac is...dying."

"Oh, I am so sorry," Robert genuinely consoled. "What can we do?"

"I'm not sure –"

"Do you want Kevin to call and talk to Zac?" Robert quickly suggested.

A visit would be a moot point, but I was grateful for the offer. "Yes. That would be nice. Zac can't talk, but he can hear. We'll be home in another forty minutes."

That was the last thing I could do for Zac. He would at least get to hear personally from the man who made him laugh so many times because of his movies. We watched Kevin's movies over and over at home and in the hospital. It brought a joyful escape into a world of silliness and entertainment that was otherwise difficult to come by.

Nathan pulled in the driveway and drove all the way around the house to the north side where our walkout sliding glass door was. Very carefully, Zac was carried into the house and laid onto the centrally placed hospital bed with the fireplace to the left of his feet.

It was 12.41 pm.

I was pleased at the warmth that Barb, Marie and Carla created with the candles on the fireplace mantle where our one and only family portrait sat among the decorative fall leafy vine. The fireplace warmed the cold November day and the refection off the ceiling and on to the foot of Zac's bed gave a sense of calm. The family room, freshly vacuumed, with the furniture newly rearranged, looked inviting.

As I adjusted Zac in bed, the phone rang. I almost forgot I was expecting Kevin James to call. I grabbed the phone.

"Hello?"

"Carol Ann, it's Robert – is now a good time?"

"We just got in the house and are getting Zac settled," I said a little out of breath.

"Oh, we can call back once you are ready."

I didn't for once put someone ahead of my own needs – well, Zac's needs, and I was okay with that – even if I had to keep Kevin James waiting. I was impressed that Robert would even politely suggest that "he" call back.

I placed the soft fleece blanket back under Zac's head and shoulders as I had it in the hospital. I covered his cold feet and legs with his blue prayer afghan that someone from St. Bridget's Church had knitted for him prior to his craniotomy, when he was five-years-old.

I was relieved that Zac wasn't struggling to breathe like he had in the hospital and on our drive home. It scared me and I knew it would scare Nic, Jessica and Lexie.

It was close to 2 pm.

We were all gathered around Zac when the phone rang again. Jessica answered the phone this time. I knew it was Kevin James and I was so proud of her maturity as she spoke briefly with him before handing me the phone.

I explained to Kevin how badly Zac wanted to meet him, but his health had quickly taken a turn for the worse. I reminded Kevin that he couldn't speak, but I would put him on speaker-phone so he could hear him.

For a phone call, it was almost as if Kevin was right there sitting next to Zac's bed. He didn't hurry in his one-sided conversation. He offered comfort and recognition of Zac's bravery and courage. He told him he had read his Caringbridge and "hoped to aspire to be more like" him.

I was pleased.

Not long after Kevin hung up, Zac's breathing returned to the gurgly-like struggle. It seemed worse than it had been the night before. I felt Zac's struggle and I didn't want him to suffer any longer. When asked, the hospice nurse didn't feel like it would be that long before Zac would pass.

"It's okay, Zac - you can take Jesus's hand. You can go," I gave my permission, once again. I didn't want him to think he had to keep hanging on for me – as much as I didn't want him to leave me.

After a little more time passed, I remembered what a palliative care specialist shared with me – "Sometimes the child will not want to leave if his parents are both in the room because he doesn't want to disappoint them."

I didn't want to leave Zac for a second, but I didn't want to prolong his agony. "Nathan, Zac might be hanging on because he doesn't want to hurt us. We need to go upstairs."

I didn't feel right walking away. It felt cruel, but I waited with Nathan briefly before going back downstairs. I figured if he hadn't left then, he wasn't going to leave when Nathan and I were away from him.

Zac's breathing grew louder and intensified. There were longer pauses in his breathing. Zac was getting closer to making the transition into Heaven.

2:03 pm

Zac stopped breathing. The room was silent except for the weeping and sniffling, but I wasn't convinced he was gone. I remembered being told that sometimes the breathing can stop for up to ten minutes and the person can suddenly resume breathing. I mentioned this to everyone, especially to Nic and Jessica so they could prepare themselves. They were already in shock as they watched their brother dying. Lexie was too afraid to be downstairs. As soon as she was called to see Zac, to say "goodbye," frightened at seeing him, she turned and ran back up the stairs. I hadn't seen her in over an hour.

I had my stethoscope by Zac's bed and I listened carefully. I waited and waited. I didn't hear a heartbeat. I sat back on my heels as tears streamed down my face, and suddenly – Zac gasped for a big breath of air as if he had just resurfaced after being under water for too long and began breathing again. Nic sobbed in agony. I cried out loud.

"Marie!" I panicked. "Call Father Al! Zac's waiting for Father Al!" I concluded.

Everything wasn't as it should be. Zac made it home to his favorite place on earth. Everyone said their "goodbyes" either in person, by message or phone, but one extremely important person to Zac was being waited for…"Papa" (Father) Al.

"Father Al said he is actually only fifteen minutes away," Marie reported. "He said he decided to head up here early for a meeting and that he would call and cancel."

I was relieved, because the night before he didn't know if he would be able to stop by today. I was a bit surprised that he couldn't drop everything to be with us, but then again, we were told Zac may live for a week. I forgot I had to share Father Al.

It was 2:40 pm

Father Al was at Zac's bedside. More prayers were said and Father Al blessed Zac one last time. I held on to Zac's hand as I continued to give him permission to go be with Jesus and his buddy, Mike Lizotte, who he had looked up to ever since he started coaching Nic's hockey team.

"Zac, you are such a good boy. I am so proud of you! You've done everything God has asked of you to do. It's okay for you to go. You're NOT giving up! You've won the battle! I love you my sweet angel. I love you…"

My bravery didn't last much longer than my first "I love you" – then I buried my face in Zac's shoulder and sobbed. I missed my sweet baby already.

3:05 pm

Zachary took his last agonizing breath and was fully escorted into Heaven by his angel's (more than likely his "two Jesuses"). My precious son was now at peace. No more needles, no more headaches, no more chemo or physical limitations…

CHAPTER 38

one last goodbye

As happy as I was for Zac, knowing he was free from everything that no child should ever have to endure – I was devastated. We didn't get the chance to really talk about dying and going to Heaven to wait for us. I never got the chance to make sure he wasn't afraid or find out how he felt about dying. We didn't "really" get to say "goodbye." A part of me died on November 20, 2013.

The house was somber. I was thankful that Barb spent the night. She would walk with Nathan and me as we now had the duty of planning Zac's funeral. I didn't want to do it, but I knew he deserved to be honored and I wanted to make sure it was done the best way possible.

I pulled myself out of bed by 11 am, showered and tried to make myself look like I had eyes, but the puffiness was undeniably there. We went to Grandstrand Funeral home to make most of the arrangements. It was comforting to know Nathan was friends and played hockey with Tom, the funeral director. He was warm, kind, compassionate, patient and giving in many ways.

I couldn't believe I had to pick out my son's casket. My visions came to pass. I chose a casket with two ivory angels on each end and a silky lining that had a rosary imprinted on it – something Zac usually had in his hand that brought him so much comfort. I would have to decide which clothes I would have Zac wear and bring them to Tom. I didn't know how I would be able to. I didn't want Zac or any of his clothes to go anywhere. It was difficult to find the right clothes since most of them didn't fit any longer after all the steroids that he was pumped full of. How unfair! We ended up choosing the Chisago Lakes hockey jersey that was signed by all of Nic's hockey team and given to him the year before. He always wore it with pride.

We then drove a couple of miles to St. Bridget's where we chose the scripture readings and songs and discussed how the funeral would go. I continued to cry on and off at the realization of what I was actually doing. This wasn't supposed to be Zac's ending. I didn't want to bury my son, and now, I had to choose the cemetery and the right spot on this unseasonably cold, windy November day.

Which cemetery to choose wasn't difficult. I went with Green Lake Cemetery. It was a large lot on a hill that overlooked a big lake. The spot wasn't difficult either to find. It was closest to the lake and underneath a small maple tree. Zac and I would always point out the most brilliant colored maple trees in awe. It would be a nice spot to visit and have a picnic or just sit quietly. Nathan gave up our burial plots at Fort Snelling and paid for the next two spots next to where Zac would be laid to rest. I didn't want him to be alone. Even in death, I felt relief that I would one day take my final resting place next to Zac and Nathan.

It wasn't much longer and the sun began to set. We headed home in preparation to support Nic in his first varsity home game of the season.

I didn't know how I could put myself out there in the public eye. It had only been twenty-seven hours ago that Zac passed away. I was a mess. But as with Zac – I gave myself no other choice than to support him every step of the way through his journey. The night before, I quickly made up my mind that I would do the same for Nic.

Just the previous night, a few hours after Zac passed Nic briefly questioned what he should do about his first game of the season after suffering such a traumatic loss.

"Nic, you don't have to go. Your coaches and team would understand," I assured him.

"Yah, I know, but I think I should play. I think Zac would want me to play," Nic intensely thought. "I can't believe he's not going to be there for my first game. He talked about how excited he was for the season to start. He was *so* close." Nic hung his head as his eyes teared up again.

"If that's what you think you should do, then we'll be there to support you." *Great. That means I have to go.* I wasn't ready for something that was supposed to be fun or involved so many people, but I wouldn't let my other son do this without his mother's support.

The ice arena was packed. The bleachers were filled and people were standing all along the railing at the top. I nervously weaved my way through the crowd with my mom on one side of me and Barb on the other, our arms hooked together. With my head tilted down, I felt as if I was trying to avoid the paparazzi, but there were no cameras, only people turning their heads and staring as I squeezed through. A few were bold enough to approach me, giving me a hug and offering their sympathies.

With the best intentions, Barb tried to shield me from the many people who wanted to talk to me. A few times I had to give her the *'It's okay,'* and I put myself "out there" to accept their sincere apologize. I knew they cared and I didn't want to be rude. I just wasn't myself. I didn't feel like socializing. I had just lost my son.

That night a tribute was paid to Zac. A brief speech was given about Zac's passing after a long fight with brain cancer – then a moment of silence which was followed by a ten-minute clip that a man from a local cable company had shot a few years earlier was played on the white painted wall.

Zac grew up "coaching" most of the boys from the hockey bench and locker room. Zac took it seriously. He wanted the boys to play hard, give it all they had and to win. So - with X's and O's, he drew a line with a marker demonstrating the path the players should follow on the ice.

"You have to go A –R –O –U –N –D them. No penalties, only hat tricks – Whoooh!!" Zac was so enthusiastic about the sport.

Even though he was only an eight-year-old then, he knew exactly what it meant to be a team player. He patted each player on the back as they exited the locker room out on to the ice.

"Remember – NO penalties – only hat tricks!" Zac reminded them.

Overhead the speakers sang out two of Zac's favorite songs – 'I want to Live Like That,' by Sidewalk Prophets and 'I Can Only Imagine' – by Mercy Me. I could hear sniffling all around. I wasn't the only one crying. These songs spoke exactly about who Zac was. They were perfectly chosen and I hoped the people would forever associate them with Zac.

Prior to the game, the Rosemount hockey team gave our coaches an envelope to give to Nathan and me. It was a sympathy card with money collected from their team. The compassion was incredible.

For a moment I worried that out of sympathy, the Rosemount team might throw the hockey game, but they didn't. Both teams played hard, but Chisago had a little more invested in the win. Chisago won their first home game 3 -2.

Sunday, November 24, 2013 – four days before Thanksgiving was the visitation. It was held at St. Bridget's Church in Lindstrom because the funeral home wouldn't accommodate the large number of people expected to attend.

Nathan and I stood in line for hours as people came to offer their condolences and share in our sorrow. The receiving line had to be rerouted up the stairs into the social hall from outside, down another set of stairs and around the church. People told us they waited two hours to see us.

I was humbled by the incredible outpouring of love and support by all of the people who braved the bitter cold and waited outside until the line would allow them to come into the warmth of the church – to wait some more.

I quickly began to learn that I had to let the insensitivities go along with the misspoken words that were meant to be comforting. Had I not, the anger I was feeling toward God would escalate towards the people around me. I didn't want to turn into a cold-hearted witch.

People came to the visitation and again the following day on November 25th to the funeral from the surrounding communities. People came from out of state who knew Zac well, people who met him once or had only heard of him or read about him on Caringbridge – to say their final "goodbyes."

The church was overflowing. People were parked blocks away. We were blessed to have four priests concelebrate Zac's funeral. Everything was done beautifully – from the flowers, to the music to the heartfelt homily spoken by Father Al. I couldn't believe I was there - about to bury my son. I couldn't believe it was my family and me sitting in the front pew looking at the casket where Zac's body laid. I felt so numb and so heavy with grief that part of me felt like I was in an out-of-body experience.

When the mass concluded, the casket was carried out of the church and through a bridge of hockey sticks so proudly erected by the Chisago Lakes Wild Cat varsity hockey boys for their inspiring "teammate." As stated by our friend Dean – "The funeral procession was something you'd see with celebrities, dignitaries and heros. Zac was them all. The procession headed down the road at dusk. I looked as far as I could see to the front and saw nothing but tail lights and four-way flashers and to the rear – more headlights and four-way flashers. The procession was well over several miles long. There was an Honor Guard, police cars and fire trucks. They all wanted to be a part of Zac's final goodbye. The on-coming traffic pulled to the side to pay tribute to the local little boy. They all knew Zac or knew of him." I was touched beyond words at what I was seeing as a result of the lives Zac had touched.

People were there in support of an eleven-year-old boy who showed his love for others as well as for God. He wore his body of armor so bravely. I wouldn't doubt if St. Michael himself, picked it out and handed it to Zac. We all prayed constantly to him for strength and courage.

Zac's armor was easily seen as one of courage, strength, bravery, love, faith and hope. He radiated it. It defended him in his battles and protected him many times from the evil that was cast his way through the cancer. He NEVER once said, "I can't" or gave up. Even when the devil of cancer took over his body, God remained strongly implanted on his lips and in his heart. In his most agonizing moments, Zac would ALWAYS call out to God for help. He was what several people told me that Zac was "the closest they had ever come to knowing Jesus."

CHAPTER 39

in proud victory

Everything felt different now, even hockey. I always looked forward to seeing Zachary's number thirteen jersey (for the year 2013) hanging up behind the players during their games. It was a good reminder for the boys, as well as the people in the stands, that Zac's spirit was still present.

The hockey boys practiced hard and even played harder. They ended up undefeated in their home arena where Zac had coached and cheered them on all his life. It was the greatest season in the history of the town. They were onto their last play-off game of the season. They had to beat Princeton to be able to go to the State tournament. It would be the first time in nineteen years, since 1995, that Chisago High School would make it to State, if they could come out with a win.

I have to admit, it was the first time since Zac's passing that I was somewhat excited about something. I could hear Zac chanting - "They have to win, they just HAVE to!"

The Cambridge-Isanti arena was packed shoulder to shoulder. The anticipation for the start of the game was incredible, but not as incredible as the intensity of the stress that radiated out of everyone there. You could almost taste it! After the warm up and before the start of the game, the Chisago hockey players encircled the goalie who was securely standing in front of our net, ready to defend.

Silence fell upon them as Louis spoke, "There's a little boy in heaven who wants us in the State tournament."

They all shouted in approval and knuckled each other with their hockey gloves on. The game was on!

I have never been to a more intense game! There wasn't a moment of silence as the two teams battled back and forth as the fans cheered. Crushing hits were made, as goal after goal was scored. With exactly one minute left in the second period, Chisago lead 2-1. Louder and louder, the noise level grew. Princeton tied it up in the third with Chisago Wild Cats answering back with only seven minutes left in the game. Back and forth they went. Short-handed open goal net, Chisago scored again to take the lead. It was 5-3 when Princeton, Tigers knocked one in on the power play to make it 5-4, with 40 seconds left. For the first time, I was sweating in an ice arena! I knew both teams wanted the win. No on liked to lose. I prayed under my breath and in short outbursts with my friend Linda at my side – "Zac! Mike! Zac! Mike!" we screamed at the top of our lungs trying to channel them to intercede for a win for our boys.

We came so far in a very difficult hockey season in suffering the loss of Zac. It wasn't just felt by Nic, as he played for his brother, but by the whole team. Zac's spirit was at work in these boys.

The seconds felt like minutes when Princeton pulled their goalie and it was six players on five. The clock ticked down and Chisago Lakes held on to a 5-4 final.

"Chisago Lakes wins 5-4! They are the Section 5A Champions. Chisago is headed for the state tournament – for the first time in nineteen years! What an incredible game!" shouted the radio announcer, Cory McKinnon.

The hockey players were ecstatic! They threw their hockey gloves high in the air and skated over to Jake, their goalie. One by one they jumped onto him in a hog pile. Their excitement and pride in their hard fought win was celebrated for a few minutes before the team skated towards their cheering fans on the other side of the glass – with Louis close behind. Raised over his head, Louis held high Zac's number thirteen jersey in proud victory.

In Zachary's short life on earth, he quickly learned what many of us may never come to really understand. He knew what it meant to live with dignity. He showed us through his suffering and through his joy. He laid down the groundwork for us to follow by his example.

Although when I started writing Zac's story, Zac and I planned for a different ending. It was supposed to be an ending with his healing here on earth – because he fought with faith and hope. My hope was not God's Will. Something I now know I have absolutely no control over. So, I am left with no understanding as to why it had to be this way, but the knowledge that Zac was sent here and did accomplish his mission. I think he was the one who helped heal many broken hearts and mend undesirable ways of others.

As I will continue to journey in my grief through this life, I will do so graciously and with faith, knowing we were given a rare gift, one to be passed on – an incredible gift – shared by the BELIEVER.

In Proud Victory! Off to MN State hockey tournament in honor of Zac!

AFTERWORD

I know Zac isn't here on earth any longer, but at times, I feel I could easily open an invisible curtain and there would be Zac. I feel him so close at times. Then other times, he seems so far away.

I know he "shows up" at times when I (or my family) need him the most. I want to share just a few…

* It was maybe a week after the funeral and I drove to the cemetery. Right before I was about to get out of the car, I noticed a red hot candy on the floor of the passenger side. I knew it fell off of Zac's Cornflake Christmas cookie wreath we had made only two weeks earlier. It must have fallen off when we were eating them on the way to a doctor's appointment. I reached down and picked it up. My first instinct was to throw it out on to the driveway, but then knowing it was Zac's, I didn't want to waste it, so I decided I would eat it. I didn't care about the "five-second rule" anyway. Something held me back from putting it in my mouth and I carefully cradled it in my mitten as I walked along the packed down snow-path I had created from my daily trips to visit Zac's "spot." I decided to place the red hot at the head of where Zachary was laid to rest. It seemed right.

The following day when I returned, I noticed a small pinkish-red color from a distance as I approached the grave. (I hated that word – "grave," it sounded too morbid). I was pleased to assume that someone came to pay Zac a visit and left a flower.

I knelt down on the snow and reached for the flower. I almost picked it up, but instead withdrew my hand after lightly touching it. It wasn't a real flower. Not even an artificial one! It was a crystalized looking flower that blossomed up from the red hot where I had placed it on top of the snow. Immediately I knew - it was a gift from Zac letting me know he loved me.

The red-hot flower, close up. 12-18-13

* A few days later, extremely heavy with grief, I noticed my lighted plant in the corner of my dining room began to blink on and off. At first I thought, *Oh, great, the lights are going to go out.* There were random lights on the string that had been burnt out for quite some time, but they never completely burned out. It was always a pain restringing lights around and through the leaves and I wasn't in the mood to do it. Day after day, at random times, the lighted plant would start to blink on and off, almost in Morse code. I knew Zac knew how much I loved lights, so I began to question if this was actually a way Zac was trying to let me know he was close by or if I was just crazy I my desirable notion.

The more I tried to dismiss my thoughts, the more the lights blinked. Jessica even noticed one January day the unusual blinking. Up to this point, I never mentioned it to anyone for fear I would get "that look." At times, even at night, I would be awaken by the flickering lights reflecting off of my bedroom wall. I would get up and stand before the plant where a statue of our Lady of Fatima stood in prayer. I started talking to the plant and became convinced that it was Zac's way of communicating with me. Depending on the conversation and tears, the lights would blink in faster bursts or blink a few times, pause, and blink faster.

I know it may sound far-fetched, but the lights continued to do this throughout the day from the end of November until they occasionally would blink come February ninth when I stood by the plant, talking to Zac, waiting for my blinking response. Sometimes I had to wait a few minutes. That day, I waited twenty minutes when I was given one last blink. I believed through lights, Zac wanted me to know he was still around. The lights stopped blinking six months later when Jessica, Nathan and I were struggling in life. It was then, after Nathan and I prayed to Zac for guidance and support that Jessica noticed the next morning the lighted plant blinking again. Zac was back. The visit lasted about ten days before it stopped. The plant continues to remain steadily lit. I believed Zac came to lift up our spirits and let us know that he could only help so much and the rest we needed to figure out on our own.

*On February 7, 2014, Nic turned sixteen years old. I could tell Nic was struggling with the sadness of Zac not being there to share his birthday. We were struggling with a lot of "those firsts" so soon after his passing.

I felt the absence of Zac's presence greatly as I was lining up Nic, Jessica and Lexie for a photo shot of Nic blowing out his candles on his double decker Boston Cream Pie-cake, he requested. As I was about to snap the picture, I noticed Zac's memorial card with the picture of his beautiful face and gentle smile, somewhat in the picture I was about to take. I paused for a moment and lined up the camera to where I got all of them in the picture just right. *Now I have all of my kids in the picture.*

Nic blew out his candles - all of them. I set my camera down and turned on the kitchen lights as Lexie continued to blow on the candles, over and over, trying to disperse the rising smoke that was coming off of the candles.

"Lexie! That's enough. You're spitting on the cake," Nic said trying to get her to stop.

"Uhh, M – o – m – m – m..." Nic strangely called with a hint of worry in his voice.

"What's wrong?" I asked turning around.

"This candle just relit – all by itself – even after Lexie was blowing on them about ten times!"

We all stood there in shock. I had the lighter by me at the counter and I didn't use or own "trick" candles.

"Zac's here," I verified. "He didn't want to miss your birthday, Nic."

These are just a few of many, "TOO coincidental to be – "Incidences." Many may think I'm reaching, but then again, who *really* knows?

THE GIFTS THAT ZAC GAVE...

(The following are the original letter's, but have been shortened)

Dear Carol Ann & Nate –

I am writing this note to you to let you know how Zac continues to impact me and my faith on a regular basis. I can let you know what a special person Zac was to many of us.

Meeting Zac, you knew he was special!!! His ability to instantly and charismatically draw you in was immediate and positive! Prior to him coming to Lakeside, I knew of him, his story and battle, but I didn't know the rarity of the love he could share.

Zac was Christ-like in so many ways.

He would permeate the room with his smile, joy and love! He loved people and we in turn LOVED him! He gave each of us hope. What other student has impacted over seventy-plus staff members and made each of us feel special at Lakeside? Zac was God's gift to those of us who met him.

Zac's impact on each of us can be compared to how Jesus had that significant impact on his followers. Shouldn't we strive to be like Jesus? Zac showed us how to do that with a JOYFUL heart. God is good. He wants each of us to change our hearts and be like Him. Zac helped me see that.

He will continue to be that influence. His story will continue to live on and ripple through lives.

I will be one of Zac's followers because "I am ZACSTRONG!"

Krista Lakeside 5th grade teacher

Carol Ann & Nate

...I am truly one that is completely blessed by your son. I have never met a child in my twenty years of teaching that has had more of an effect on me and every single person he has ever come I contact with. I also have never met any adult I my lifetime who has more courage, faith, hope and strength than Zac.

I have two stories I'd like to share with you –

The fifth grade choir was putting on a concert and everyone was in the gym watching and listening to them. I had this strong overwhelming feeling to look towards the door to the gym. I looked down and I saw Zac sitting there watching the concert in his wheelchair. It was as if all sound and people disappeared and I could clearly see this bright glow of angel wings surrounding Zac. It was that moment I knew Zac imprinted my heart in a God way.

The second time he made a huge impact on my life, I was going to have heart surgery. A HUGE amount of fear hit me and overwhelmed me to the point I was going to call it off. One of my friends was trying to get me to rationalize everything and then pointed to my ZacStrong bracelet and said, "If that kid can go through all he has gone through, you can do this." From that moment on, I was still afraid, but thinking about Zac and his faith, strength, hope and courage allowed me to see and feel different. I thought about Zac and every time I did, I got a sense of calmness. The day of surgery, the last item I took off was my ZacStrong bracelet.

I am one person that Zac has made an outstanding difference in their life. I can't even begin to imagine ALL of the other people, lives, moments – that he has impacted, changed and touched. He truly is a gift from God and he will forever continue to change other's lives.

Brenda Lakeside 5th grade teacher

Dear Carol Ann

I need you to know that Zac has become a part of who I am as a person today. It is because of his being that I have become a better person. He has inspired me to look at the positive all of the time.

I continuously ask myself "How would Zac react?" "What would Zac do?" As life challenges present themselves, I will continue to do my best to be ZacStrong. Zac's life was way too short for us, but I know that what he was able to accomplish in his eleven years will far exceed the positive influence I can have on others for my remaining years. This was Zac's gift to us. I will do my best to follow his lead.

Forever ZacStrong
With Love, Greg

Carol Ann and Nathan,

...It is truly amazing how many people Zac touched, but also how many hearts he changed. I will always remember Zac and the memory is uniquely beautiful and angelic.

With peace & Love in Christ Jessie Barnum

I think the best memory I have ever shared with Zac is the night we broke your guy's nice picture frame. Zac, Nic and I were all downstairs, home alone, playing nerf. We had bases set up and the entire downstairs was a disaster! While the lights were off, I threw a pillow down the hallway. The pillow knocked the picture off of the wall and broke the frame. Nic and I were so scared we were going to get in deep trouble, so we figured since Zac was the youngest he would be in the least amount of trouble. We all agreed to tell Nate and Carol Ann that Zac threw the pillow and Zac took the blame for it.

I am going to miss Zac, but I know he is in a much better place. Every time I go into your bathroom, I read the picture – 'Life is not measured by the amount of breaths we take, but by the moments that take our breath away." Zac truly took my breath away in almost everything he did. He was the sweetest and most optimistic person I have ever met. God gained an angel in heaven, that's for sure.

Zac, I am truly blessed to have had you in my life and it is my honor to call you my friend.

Love, Kyle

Hi Carol

...When I entered the church (for Zac's funeral) I felt an overwhelming "Presence"- it seemed to fill every inch of the church. I thought I must be in the presence of a saint. Even though it was very sorrowful, I felt a feeling of peace and joy. I have been to many funerals in the 80+ years I've roamed the earth and I've NEVER felt anything close to the feeling I felt that day! As soon I got outside, it was gone. I am expecting him to be a saint (declared that is – he's already one).

Love, Percy

Dear Nate, Carol Ann and Family,

...Part of Zac's legacy will always be the lessons he taught his friends and classmates...lessons that many people never have the chance to learn, even as adults.

Zac taught all of his classmates to be strong and brave in the face of adversity. Through Zac, the children learned how to be compassionate and how to show compassion to others. I think all the children in their classroom were just nicer to each other because they realized it was the right thing to do.

Zac taught his classmates to fight to stay in the game.

Zac taught Erik perspective on what is important in life and reminded him that it was not material things, but our love for friends and family that really matter. I remember one day when Erik came downstairs and stated it was "the worst day ever," because a friend was not able to play. When I reminded him to compare his worst day to Zac's, his whole demeanor changed. In that one instant, Zac helped Erik put things into perspective and prioritize what was truly important in his life.

Zac taught Erik to honestly pray from the heart and not just recite a prayer. It was your son, Zac that lead Erik to that special place of really deep faith.

These lessons of strength, compassion and faith were special gifts from a special child with a special purpose and they will live on in all of Zac's friends.

Love,
Colleen, Rich, Erik & Shane

DEDICATION

* I want to dedicate this book to Zachary who changed my life forever. Because of him and what he taught me, I will continue to strive to 'Live like Zac.' Until I see my sweet angel again…I will love you forever.

* I also want to dedicate this book to my children Nicholas, Jessica and Alexandra (Lexie). I am so grateful for your support and patience in the months that it took me to write your brother's story. Many nights you waited, without complaining until I would quickly get a meal on the table. Know how much I love each of you for the beautiful individuals that you are. Thanks for your understanding as to why I was driven to share your brother with the rest of the world. I love each of you more than you will ever be able to comprehend. If it wasn't for you – I may not be here today.

* To Nathan – I dedicate Zac's story to you…I couldn't have done it without your support and trying to understand where I was coming from with my moods, depending on where I was in Zac's story and where I just happened to "be" in that day. I know it hasn't been an easy journey for either one of us. Thank you for your patience, your strength, for being "there" and for loving me. I love you.

* And to the rest of you (who are too many to name) who supported, prayed for and loved Zac, as well as the rest of us – we wouldn't be where we are today if it wasn't for you. You know who you are…This book is dedicated to you.

ACKNOWLEDGEMENTS

* To my sister Barb, thank you for coming to the hospital at a moments notice to offer your support to Zac and I. For all the meals you brought me so I could have something other than Zac's leftovers, for sharing in the playful and obnoxious stories we came up with that brought Zac so much laughter and allowed me to forget for a moment, for being with me through so many of the hard-parts so I wouldn't have to feel so alone. I love you.

* To Carla, we may not be of the same blood, but I think of you as a sister...thank you for always making it work to come help out – one way or another, for the visits, the food, your shoulder to cry on...you always seemed to know what I needed. I am so glad I have you in my life. I love you.

* To Stephanie, your loving heart showered Zac with acceptance, love and most of all the ability to be blessed with the life and friendship of your child, Thomas. Whether it came from you or up above, Thomas never treated Zac as different. He gave freely of himself to play day after day and when Zac wasn't able to run any longer, he sat by his side and was just there for him. You willingly had Zac sleepover, several times, without worry as to having to give him all of his medications. You always said "We'll figure it out. Everything will be fine!" You were like a second mom to Zac and a very special friend to me. I love you.

* To Father Al...you came into our lives at the right time – from the moment Zachary's condition became much more serious – until his last breath – and beyond. You gave us comfort, love, and a special friendship that will remain forever, and you strengthened my faith at times when I felt abandoned by God. You truly are a blessing and I will love you forever. Thank you for always being there.

* To Dr. Moertel, I am so thankful that we found you when Zac was 2-years-old and that you were with us on this unbelievable journey the entire way. Thank you for your knowledge and expertise in your fight right along side us in trying to save Zac's life. Not only were you Zac's oncologist, but our friend. Thank you for never giving up on him.

* To Tammie and Dr. Guillaume who worked beside Dr. Moertel, thank you for your continual care, compassion and honesty, for both Zac and me. Your job was not just a "job", but an opportunity to give hope. Thank you for keeping that alive in Zac and us. Without both of you, I couldn't have done what we had to do.

* To Emily, you were my rock while I had to face many nerve racking appointments and conversations alone. Thank you for your calming strength when you helped me process information or just sat with me in silence. Thank you for your friendship you freely gave Zac and your gentle way of just putting both of us at ease.

* To all of the nurses and Health Unit Coordinators in the Journey Clinc and in Amplatz Children's Hospital for cared for and took extra time for Zac to put a smile on his face in a place where no child should have to make a part of their life. You make a big difference! Thank you!

* To Kirsten, a special thank you for capturing (in what became the cover photo) all that Zachary exemplified – COURAGE,STRENGTH, BRAVERY, HUMILITY, FAITH and so much LOVE! Your photograpy and your friendship are priceless.

* To Jake and Shannon, the newest of Zac's friends, you came into his life at a critical point and you went out of your way to visit and play games with him. You made Zac feel special and loved. But by knowing him – you became loved and felt special because that's what radiated from him.

* To the people at Lakeside Elementary School, St. Bridget of Sweden Church, Chisago Lakes Hockey Association and teams, our families, neighbors, friends at USSA, my coworkers at University of Minnesota Health Hospital, Nathan's coworkers at the State of Minnesota and anyone I may have forgotten to mention - thank you for your compassion, prayers, meals, gas cards, financial support – the list goes on and on...Your friendship and love for all of us is forever invaluable.

* To my mom and dad, thank you for your constant love and instilling in me a strong faith at such a young age. The devil tried to break me, but my faith continues to save me!